D1526175

Discipline and Power

*The University, History, and the Making
of an English Elite, 1870–1930*

Discipline and Power

The University, History, and the Making of an English Elite, 1870–1930

REBA N. SOFFER

Stanford University Press
Stanford, California

Stanford University Press, Stanford, California
© 1994 by the Board of Trustees of the Leland Stanford Junior University
Printed in the United States of America

CIP data appear at the end of the book

Stanford University Press publications are distributed exclusively by Stanford
University Press within the United States, Canada, Mexico, and Central America;
they are distributed exclusively by Cambridge University Press throughout the rest
of the world.

Original printing 1994
Last figure below indicates year of this printing:
05 04 03 02 01 00 99 98 97 96

To Robert K. Webb,
gentleman and scholar

Preface

This book owes a great deal to the unfailing generosity and kindness of many people. The National Endowment for the Humanities, which supported me twice, made it possible to think through this project initially and to complete it finally. In London, Brenda Weeden and Helen Young of the University Library, the University of London and J. N. McCarthy, Executive Secretary of the Royal Historical Society, were consistently helpful, and Michael Thompson's assistance was indispensable. I am also most grateful to Dorothy and Arthur Owen and Elisabeth Leedham-Green of the Cambridge University Library; to Reginald Stokes, Charles Wynn and Philip Johnson of the Seeley Library; to Richard Gutteridge, Librarian at Selwyn College; to Michael Halls, King's College Library and the Librarians and Archivists of Emmanuel, St. John's, and Trinity Colleges; to Glenise Mathesen of the John Rylands University Library, Manchester; to Donald Porter of the Bodleian Library; to the Librarian of Exeter College; and to John Simmons of the Codrington Library, All Souls College. Quotations from the G. W. Prothero Papers are given by permission of the Royal Historical Society and those from the Oscar Browning, J. H. Clapham, and Political Society Papers and the Whitney Manuscripts, by permission of the Provost and Fellows of King's College. And last, but far from least, to Penelope Bulloch, John Jones, Jane Smith, and Alan Tadiello, who made working in the Balliol College Library such a great pleasure.

For their amiable good fellowship in Oxford, I want to thank Patrick Nairne, then Master, and the Fellows of St. Catherine's College, who made me a Christensen Visiting Fellow, and the Principal and Fellows of Mansfield College. In Cambridge, Owen Chadwick, then Master, and the Fellows of Selwyn College, and especially John Morrill, were gracious in their hospitality, as was Barry Supple, Master of St. Catharine's College. For stimulating and provocative conversation, I am indebted to Michael Brock, Owen Chadwick, Geoffrey Elton, Michael Freeden, Jose Harris, Colin Matthew, Harold Perkin, John Prest, John Roach, Marjorie Reeves, Sheldon Rothblatt, Harold Silver, and Robert K. Webb. I am also greatly obliged to Barbara Dover for her help with the figures. Sheldon Rothblatt, with Talmudic skill, and John Roach, with unparalleled knowledge of the field, both read an earlier version of this book. Bob Webb read two versions and provided the kind of incisive, valuable criticism that few authors are fortunate enough to receive. Last of all, I am obliged to Kenneth Walker, an intelligent and professional editor, and to Ellen Smith and Norris Pope of Stanford University Press, for their interest in making books.

The title, *Discipline and Power,* is not intended to imply a Foucauldian itinerary. As understood in the period from the 1850s to the late 1920s, "discipline" was the order necessary to the building of character and nation and it was also the organization of knowledge within a specialized field of study. "Power" also had a dual connotation. On the one hand, it meant the ability to control self and situation so as to accomplish particular ends and, on the other, it meant the traditional exercise of authority that governed and led. The English generations studied in this book were the first to recognize that influence would depend increasingly upon organized knowledge and its application. That recognition led them to attempt the mastery of both kinds of discipline and both kinds of power.

R.N.S.

Contents

Introduction   1

1. Consensus and Tradition   10

2. Truth and Objectivity   31

3. National History Established   53

4. The Professors Interpret History   78

5. The Professorial Tradition Continued   99

6. Tutors and Teaching   128

7. Students and Learning   157

8. Life After the University   178

   Epilogue: The Sin of Omission   205

   Notes   213

   Sources   275

   Index   301

Figures

1. Degree courses taken by graduates of King's College, Cambridge, 1882–1929   182

2. Number of careers of history honours graduates from Balliol College, Oxford, 1873–1913   186

3. Number of careers of history honours graduates from Balliol College, 1914–27   186

4. Number of careers of history honours graduates from King's College, 1876–1913   187

5. Number of careers of history honours graduates from King's College, 1914–29   187

6. Number of careers of history honours graduates from King's College and Balliol College, 1873–1929   188

7. Careers followed by history honours graduates from Balliol College, 1873–1913   189

8. Careers followed by history honours graduates from Balliol College, 1914–26   190

9. Careers followed by history honours graduates from King's College, 1876–1913   190

10. Careers followed by history honours graduates from King's College, 1914–29   191

11. Careers followed by history honours graduates from King's College and Balliol College, 1873–1929   201

12. Careers followed by history honours graduates from King's College and Balliol College, 1873–1929 (firsts and seconds combined)   202

Discipline and Power

*The University, History, and the Making
of an English Elite, 1870–1930*

Introduction

From the 1860s Oxford and Cambridge universities became increasingly effective, dynamic forces in British national life. Different interests, multiplying as the century proceeded, clamored for agendas that they wanted the ancient universities to adopt. Governing bodies, professors, tutors, public school teachers, coaches, examiners, Parliamentary Commissioners, graduates, and the public held a variety of views, often conflicting, about the ends higher education should serve. But they all agreed that university teachers must prepare young men for the leadership of church, state, and empire. With a clear sense of their mission, Oxford and Cambridge were remarkably successful in turning out graduates who monopolized the dominant positions in public and private life in Britain and throughout its empire. One explanation for that success is that the universities conferred a new authority on ideas. The newly modern universities took competing concepts from within the university and from the outside world, subjected them to prevailing standards of acceptance, and dispatched them to the various agencies of influence. But there are few systematic explanations of why certain concepts triumphed over others, often independently of merit or utility. This book attempts to explain how a dominant ideology was cultivated and then certified and why it persisted as part of the structure of the old universities and of the new civic universities that imitated them.

The consensus that moved these universities to shape the opinions of a select governing group, and the decisive impact of this group upon national life, were relatively neglected by historians until the mid-1950s.

In 1955 Noel Annan sketched the ubiquitous influence of a small, inter-related, and self-perpetuating caste that he described as the Victorian in-tellectual aristocracy. Four years later, John Roach reasoned that an un-derstanding of that powerful national elite depended upon an analysis of the universities that produced them.[1] Within a decade, the first penetrat-ing inquiry into the Victorian university appeared in Sheldon Rothblatt's *The Revolution of the Dons*, an anatomy of the intellectual, spiritual, and emotional life that animated Cambridge teachers and their students in the late nineteenth century.[2]

During the past generation, the historiography of the university and its component parts has taken several distinct directions. The most com-mon, often inspired by filial loyalty and produced with love, are the his-tories of various colleges and of the dominant figures who established a unique character for their college.[3] A second genre has concentrated on identifiable communities within the universities, such as the Oxford Union or the Cambridge Apostles, which provided models for the roles graduates would fill in the real world.[4] Still other historians have focused closely on precise questions such as the relation between university de-velopment and university finances or the reluctance to accept postgradu-ate studies, while others have turned to wider, occasionally comparative, research into the university's elusive historical essence.[5] Several have at-tempted to demonstrate the influence of the universities on particular national and imperial ends.[6]

Most recently, there has been a growing interest in the creation of university disciplines. The continuing proliferation of this subject has led to both narrow institutional chronologies of different areas of study and to broader efforts to place disciplines within an intellectual and socio-logical milieu.[7] Among the disciplines, the subject of history has been especially attractive to historians, probably because it is the one they know least badly. Thoughtful and original scholars, writing persuasively about different individuals and domains, have discussed various aspects of the study of history as a liberal art in schools and universities. But they all tend to be concerned with the relationship between history and a political culture that became increasingly problematic after the Reform Act of 1867 created an urban democracy that could have been indifferent or hostile to the values that the intellectual aristocracy extracted from English history.[8]

I am indebted to the historians who have investigated major issues in the intellectual and institutional history of the universities and in the historiography of the nineteenth and twentieth centuries. But *Discipline and Power* departs from other work both in its general subject and in the kinds of evidence upon which it is based. Beyond politics, I rely on intellectual, institutional, biographical, sociological, comparative, and prosopographical analysis to explain both contested and received ideas in their complex national context. There are compelling reasons for approaching the elusive origin and development of ideas through a systematic study of professions. The new disciplines organized knowledge, they organized the people who decided what was worth knowing, and they organized the processes of thinking. With intellectual and economic authority to include and exclude, professional groups sustained concepts and their methods of verification beyond the lifetimes of individuals and groups. And perhaps the most important aspect of the new disciplines for the historian of ideas is that they reflected important social and cultural shifts in the late nineteenth century. Traditionally, the assignment of the most important positions within society and politics depended upon family connections. But during the last quarter of the nineteenth century, the ancient universities established two even more important factors of selection: friendships, developed often in public schools, but made lasting in the Oxford and Cambridge colleges, and probably most critically, the study of liberal arts disciplines.

The acceptance or rejection of new disciplines was part of a larger debate about the relative merits of continuity and change within an expanding society. Areas of study that reflected and reinforced a pervasive agreement about the essential importance of a liberal education to national development survived and prospered. As college and university bodies evolved, they each attempted to regulate the new subjects and those who taught them. Among these contending fields, history provided the most consistent moral panorama able to satisfy a variety of intellectual, emotional, and aesthetic needs. Victorian Gothic design, so prominent a part of the English landscape, has been described aptly as symbolizing "at the same time High Tory paternalism, Christian ... morality, bourgeois earnestness, class deference, socialist idealism, rural virtue, truth, honesty, and chivalry, a 'national' heritage."[9] Far more pervasively than artistic style, history was the familiar center of a broad Victorian consensus about God, country, and good.

A wide reading of manuscript and printed materials, not consulted before, allows me to show how the writing and teaching of history actually shaped the ethos of graduates who guided domestic and imperial government, secondary and higher education, the professions, religion, letters, and even business and industry. The contents and conclusions of each chapter rest on the written testimonies, private and public, left by the makers of the modern British university about their fundamental beliefs and purposes. These testimonies reveal how both immediate and long-term activities were affected by assumptions, motives, interests, doubts, and certainties that persisted far more than they changed over time. Some records, surprisingly complete, provide detailed accounts of what people thought and did in response to identifiable provocations and events. I have also found less complete documents, relatively mute in themselves, and have combined them with other fragments to resurrect a continuing dialogue that clarifies both constant and fluctuating patterns of behavior. University and faculty papers, the minutes and memoranda issued by tutors, professors, faculties, governing bodies, colleges, and students contribute a wealth of virgin material. Boards of faculties kept minutes of meetings; records of examination questions; written examiner's reports; correspondence about grading, standards, curriculum, teaching, and examinations; and minutes of discussions about the awarding of degrees to particular candidates. Any one set of university chronicles, such as a faculty's minutes, tend to hide more than they display. Together, these various accounts retrieve the impelling forces that affected universities and their students.

College tutors and university professors formed a small community. Nearly everyone knew each other, and they talked constantly about issues that concerned them. I have tried to place these people within the contexts they would recognize as their own. The evolution and extension of their thinking and conduct appear in their letters to other historians, colleagues, students, family, friends, and people in public life. What they discussed most of all (aside from personal scandal) was teaching, curriculum, and the kind of training that history ought to provide. Private correspondence, read within the larger connection of the author's life, times, and other writings, demonstrates how the subject of a scholarly monograph or textbook, the sources upon which it was based, and the structure of the narrative, and the interpretation, reflected shared convictions about the meaning and uses of history. Some teachers of history, in both the secondary schools and the universities, published textbooks and, less frequently, monographs based upon research. Most teachers, including those with scholarly interests, wrote extensively about instruction and curriculum. They contributed occasionally to scholarly, popular, and pedagogical journals, and frequently to faculty and institutional discussions about programs and policies. The treatment of their subject, whether in casual correspondence, university committees, parliamentary testimony, or systematic public writing was almost always consistent with their understanding of the greater, public uses of history.

The development of history as a discipline was hardly transparent while it was occurring, and it has become even more opaque with the enigmatic effect of retrospection. Without the reports of student history clubs, other remaining evidence such as examination papers implies that the subject was decided entirely by what could be readily tested in the final examinations. But student society records deny this conclusion by demonstrating a breadth and depth of interest, on the part of teachers and students, that went far beyond examination requirements. If there were no accounts of the lectures given by influential history tutors, then a reading of syllabus descriptions and set topics in tutorials might lead, mistakenly, to the impression that teaching was dull, pedestrian, and geared solely to producing first- and second-class graduates. These student papers and lecture materials, which I was fortunate enough to discover, have been used for the first time in this book. Far more elusive are the choices and policies made orally and never recorded. These are not recoverable because they pass into oblivion, together with personal memories, and their effects upon the institution may be invisible at worst and ambiguous at best. But the remaining mass of public and private documents is sufficient to reveal clearly how crucial the study of history was to the university's expansion into a national institution committed to nurturing an elite meritocracy.

These papers show that reformed, but still conservative, universities successfully transformed a set of values, encoded in the concept of "liberal education," into a licensing system for a national elite. Chronic controversy from the 1850s onward about whether universities should provide a liberal rather than a professional or expert education often concealed other reinterpretations of a liberal tradition that went back to the eighteenth century.[10] Historians believed that in their teaching and writing they were continuing a tradition which, by cultivating character and mental abilities, led to a discovery of truth proven by historical events. Within universities, newly professional college teachers exercised unprecedented influence over teaching and students. When the authority conferred by teaching was challenged by demands that university offices depend on special knowledge, the "specialists" tended to lose. A national debate about whether the university should train a more expert elite provoked energetic discussion in the new civic universities of the twentieth century, because they owed their existence and continued support to local communities dependent upon expert knowledge. But in the new universities, as in Oxford and Cambridge, "professionalism" was repudiated in favor of a liberal or nonspecialist education. Among the historians, especially in Oxford and Cambridge but mostly at the other universities too, the professors emphasized the scholarly or professional enterprise, but they constrained scholarship within national ideals. History was taught, studied, and tested by a set of assumptions deduced far more from a national consensus about patriotic duty than from historical methods or from the pressing weight of evidence in time.

Chapter 1 examines the emergence of the modern university, where traditions persisted more than they changed. A dominant liberal arts tradition was invigorated by the adoption of new honours degree subjects that ordered teaching and learning and, with important structural changes, made careers possible for college teachers. The result was an independent university with unrivaled influence upon its students and through them upon Victorian thought and conduct in every sphere. The nature of that influence depended both on the university teacher's authoritative construction of knowledge and the acceptance of that construction by students, colleagues, and the greater educated public who wanted proficient learning to prevail over the obscure. Chapter 2 considers the English identification of history with truth, objectivity, and the celebration of valuable continuities. Those harmonies were closely associated with the definition of national character. American dedication to nation was as strong or stronger than English patriotism, even among historians who insisted that public problems cannot be resolved by admiring historical processes. But in England only the rare patriot, such as James Bryce, pointed out that love of country was not diminished by national criticism. It was generally outside England that historians emphasized the intractability of social, economic, and political problems by finding their roots and development in conflict and upheaval. As the Western powers expanded their nations into empires, they had to address the multiplication of unprecedented difficulties within a context of tension between communitarian and individualistic values. The satisfaction of national pride and culture, and the rendezvous with destiny that it often implied, whether in England, Germany, or America, reflected the distinctive meaning of government, education, and history in each country. When these conflicting values confronted each other, first on the battlefields of the Great War and then at the peace table, the English historians responded by further entrenching a eulogistic interpretation of their own history.

When history was established as an honours degree course at Oxford in 1872 and at Cambridge a year later, a debate began, continuing still today, about the form and contents of the field. During the 1860s and early 1870s, the study of history could have developed as a rigorous training in the historian's craft that might have initiated a different role for liberal arts disciplines and perhaps even altered the definition of a university. Instead, history became an extension of the classical teaching of character and conduct. Chapter 3 is about the substance of that debate and the reasoning of its participants. Economic history might have challenged the essentially political content of the curriculum and attracted students to contemporary events. But it was overshadowed by concentration on the constitution. In Oxford, Cambridge, and the new universities, the study of the distant past, and especially of the origins of political institutions, inspired communal ideals of service in a nation of individuals.

The next two chapters deal with the definition of history by the professors within conventions that informed teaching and learning in the schools and universities for at least half a century. Chapter 4 describes the coherence and unanimity of purposes among historians, the differences between the role of professors at Oxford and at Cambridge, the reconciliation of religion and history, and the schemes of exegesis enshrined in Oxford by William Stubbs and in Cambridge by J. R. Seeley. Chapter 5 follows the professorial tradition into the 1920s through Stubbs's and Seeley's successors. At Oxford, E. A. Freeman, J. A. Froude, and F. Y. Powell in the Regius Chair of History, established by George I in 1724 and first filled by a historian in 1866, and Charles Oman in the Chichele Chair of Modern History, created by All Souls College in 1862, were willingly subservient to Stubbs's tenacious prestige. C. H. Firth, who succeeded Powell, never questioned the prevailing view of history but he did try, unsuccessfully, to give the School a new direction. H. W. C. Davis, briefly Regius Professor from 1925 to 1928, continued the constancy of teaching and interpretation, but his successor, F. M. Powicke, was unprecedented in confronting the values and methods of the Oxford School. In Cambridge, although Lord Acton, J. B. Bury, and G. M. Trevelyan never agreed about the fundamental structure of history or about the ways in which it should be studied, their tenures were characterized by persistent analysis of curriculum and examinations. The Historical Tripos (the final examination for undergraduates reading history), because it was so diverse and included political thought as well as historical narrative, reflected the wider range of interests characteristic of Cambridge historians. But the study of history in Cambridge remained generally true, as in Oxford, to the creed that history must train morally responsible leaders.

The tutors, who taught the history honours candidates and supplied them with substitute fathers and brothers and powerful, familial college attachments, are the focus of Chapter 6. Their intellectual, institutional, and social life was centered on undergraduates and they taught, and occasionally wrote, within well-established colleges in chronic conflict with an amorphous university. This chapter also discusses the philosophy of examinations and the role they played within the university and society. Chapter 7 concentrates on the students, what they were expected to learn, and the effective organization of their university experience in extracurricular societies that went beyond traditional studies to establish independent and enduring conventions. In Chapter 8, I compare the subsequent careers of all first- and second-class history honours graduates at Balliol College at Oxford and King's College at Cambridge from the mid-1870s until the rise of totalitarianism and the Great Depression challenged prevailing habits of mind and conduct. Balliol and King's produced the greatest numbers of history students in each university, and a majority of them apparently heard what was said to them in lectures and tutorials because they chose careers that fulfilled lessons in high-minded obligation. The Epilogue raises questions about whether the universities encouraged and rewarded merit and reflects on the various interpretations of a liberal education.

The Sources at the end of this book are meant to enable readers to find unpublished and published materials about the nature and institutional shapes of English intellectual life from 1850 to 1930. They begin with archival materials on the ancient universities and their colleges, and continue with the published works of the Regius and Chichele Professors of Modern History at Oxford, the Regius Professors of Modern History at Cambridge, and other university historians. The next sections concentrate on writing about history in British universities before 1930, biographies and biographical essays, recent work on the relationship between developing universities and intellectual life and on historians and the study of history. The Sources conclude with books dealing with history, education and universities in Germany, the United States, France and other European countries, economic history, and the history of the professions.

A national faith in the evolution of England may have provided considerable personal and communal satisfactions, but it did not necessarily prepare anyone to cope with the unprecedented development of democratic government, or the extension of increasing public and social services, or the threat of mass irrationality, or an economy increasingly tied to the greater world, or the growth of virulent nationalism outside of England, or colonial movements for independence. But the nineteenth- and twentieth-century belief in history as evidence of national rectitude was in many ways a surrogate religion. Unlike the sciences, which competed with religion by revealing an essentially rational and self-explanatory world, history provided an accommodating bridge between secular and religious convictions. By the 1870s, historians had left behind an arbitrary Calvinist God, punitively intervening in human life, to assume instead that God was a reasonable Englishman who encouraged individuals to make themselves and their society conform more to His benevolent and meliorist will. Encouraged by their belief that the study of English history was uniquely successful in developing character and institutions, and sustained by the conviction that God was on their side, idealistic university graduates set out to recreate the greater world in their own image.

Chapter 1

Consensus and Tradition

Intellectual life in England during the late nineteenth and early twentieth centuries was shaped more by idealizations of the past than by accommodations to the present. It was not World War I, but rather the unprecedented worldwide depression of the 1930s and the concomitant rise of fascism that led the English to reconsider fundamentally those political, social, and economic priorities that had guided conduct for the preceding half-century. For the first three quarters of the nineteenth century, university students had read Greek and Roman classics as demonstrations of the interdependence of civic virtues and individual responsibilities. But they had limited occasion to apply these texts in their daily lives. Then, from the 1880s, widespread opportunities for graduates expanded rapidly in local and national government, in imperial service abroad, in the burgeoning professions, and even in business, commerce, and industry. Those graduates with first- or second-class degrees moved from the university directly into positions of considerable influence. Graduates of Oxford filled the greatest number of eminent positions, followed closely by Cambridge graduates. By the late 1920s, men and women from civic universities, taught there by Oxford and Cambridge graduates, were also competing actively for prestigious posts.[1] Until at least the interwar years, the last entirely elite generations wrote honours examinations as rites of passage from cloistered colleges to corridors of power. An admittedly amateur class, taught to believe that they were equipped to dispatch complicated and escalating problems at home and abroad, approached unforeseen crises with an assurance that perplexed experts on the continent and in America, where public service was tied increasingly to newly professional and specialized standards of competence.[2]

What the English graduates had in common was a unique educational experience determined by the special institutions and traditions of their universities. Scottish higher learning, from the eighteenth to the last decades of the nineteenth century, differed markedly from the English in educational traditions, curricula, and student bodies. But, when it became apparent in the late nineteenth century that Scottish students would be excluded from high levels of the civil and imperial service, determined by examinations geared to Oxford and Cambridge teaching, they too adopted the degree courses of the reformed English universities.[3] Higher education in England, directly and indirectly, provided a complete and enveloping educational environment which created durable patterns of behavior and permanent habits of thought. The graduates' faith in themselves, which in retrospect appears naive, even arrogant, rested on an ethos which reflected and reenforced the values that permeated English society. From the middle of the nineteenth century, higher education became an earnest training in character and civic duty.

After midcentury, the conversion of universities into secular institutions with enlarged public responsibilities depended upon changes so closely connected and historically interdependent that it is difficult to say which of the changes were the most important, or even which was cause and which effect. During the next 70 years, there was interminable discussion about the objects of the university, but there was little genuine conflict. Instead, a broad, deep-seated agreement about the urgent demand for national and imperial leaders came to prevail. Commitment to that agreement often sacrificed introspection and critical reflection. The perceptions, emotions and traditions which created the modern English university and its new disciplines were not rooted in skepticism or doubt. What they mirrored was rather a broader national confidence in coherent intellectual and moral values and their patriotic uses. In contrast to the Oxford and Cambridge models, the German universities, and especially the University of Berlin, were divided by a war between the antithetical principles of academic freedom and national power.[4] What is so extraordinary about the English universities is that freedom, in every sense of the word, was rooted in an ideal of an evolving nation which used power to create a greater moral good.

The changes occurring after the 1850s introduced new directions for the universities. It is less obvious that the apparently new coexisted with and largely depended on much older attitudes and practices. Until after World War II the university remained a conservative institution which drew its students and teachers from the upper classes and, increasingly, from the upwardly mobile middle classes. In spite of reforms in the 1870s, which allowed college Fellows to marry, lead a secular life, and retain their posts, the universities continued to be almost exclusively male, quasi-monastic communities.[5] In almost every subject, the teaching emphasized masculine strengths, manly virtues, and an active life in the world of affairs. When the women's colleges developed from the mid-1870s, they too tended to adopt the same concept of virtue and responsible activity, even though women had very few opportunities to enter careers where such ideals could be applied.[6] But for both men and women, the university provided a temporary and sheltered retreat from the responsibilities of the external world. Inside that retreat, the continuities were often less conspicuous but more permanent than the reforms. The curriculum and examinations adopted by the 1870s and 1880s were to remain substantially the same for the following five decades.

*

The remarkably consistent purposes originating in the old universities and adopted in the new, were propagated and protected by at least three crucial innovations. First, Oxford and Cambridge established an autonomy that allowed them to influence society far more than any social agency influenced them. Then, in the second half of the nineteenth century, when progress came to be measured more precisely by the application of particular skills, the English universities protected their liberal arts traditions and their autonomy from outside interference by introducing new disciplines in the form of precisely defined honours degree courses that organized the newly recognized knowledge for teaching and examinations. And finally, when teachers were given the opportunity for full-time careers in the university, they developed a special kind of authority over their students.

The distinctive independence of the modern or reformed university is evident from a consecutive reading of the reports, memorials, minutes, papers, and memoranda in Oxford and Cambridge college and university archives from the 1840s. Freedom from external intrusion was maintained by such internal mechanisms as degree courses, curriculum, appointments, teaching, and examinations. The way in which traditions persisted or changed was affected by a complex variety of factors. The original purposes of the university and the new ends adopted over time were difficult but not impossible to reconcile. Personnel responsible for administration or for policy decisions were often unaware of their own myopia or, when they saw clearly into the future, were proven helpless before the inertial weight of the system. Even when long-range plans were thought out carefully, they could be confounded by unpredictable circumstances, such as the agricultural depression of the 1870s, which cut deeply into college and university revenues, or by growing competition among incompatible interests exercising new political and economic powers at the polls and in the growing marketplace. These various interests approached the universities as clients with specific suits. But the conflicting demands of the new constituents, especially in the growing industrial centers, were rebuffed by a reformed Oxford and Cambridge. Instead, they continued to be defined around conventions, some more structured than others, that furthered older, wider, still prevailing interests and values. At the same time that the old universities achieved considerable independence from the outside world, they also adopted and entrenched the aspirations and beliefs of the traditional society in which they lived.

In a review of the activities of eighteenth-century Oxford, Roy Porter has asked perceptively whether that history should be seen "as nothing other than the posturings of a crew of footling academic politicians, Swiftian pygmies mistaking themselves for giants, lacking the diplomatic knowledge to defend what they held dear, bent on turning their causes into lost ones?"[7] But for the nineteenth century and first two decades of the twentieth, far more appropriate questions to ask of both Oxford and Cambridge might be: Was the persistence of attitudes and traditions a matter of inertial drift or was it a conscious decision taken by powerful officers of the university? If it was deliberately chosen, as the testimony suggests, was it forward-looking or last-ditch conservatism? Every institution, and none more than the university, has its confusing layers of secret history and the interior depths are often concealed behind the public facade. Those scrutinising the university from outside, as well as those attempting to direct it from inside, were often stymied by the incongruence between planned policies and their consequences. Within the university, the bureaucratic structure implemented policies so ponderously that when they were finally set in motion their effects occasionally turned out to be entirely different from what their planners had expected. Those responsible for crucial decisions often kept their own counsel, or they ignored and perhaps even disguised motives serving either selfish ambitions or institutional interests that clashed with other public goods.

In defence against external intrusion, the universities argued that they were serving national ends through the continuing traditions of a liberal arts education meant to form mind and character. That tradition was reasserted by the universities in every crisis, real or potential. In 1877, when the universities were debating the designs of their new degree courses, a German professor, with unseemly pride in his long list of publications, criticized the English university for its lack of serious scholarship. Dr. Edward Pusey, the formidable Regius Professor of Hebrew at Oxford, replied: "We make not books but men." Henry Latham, a Fellow of Trinity Hall, Cambridge and tutor in mathematics who became Master of Trinity College, rushed to support Pusey. A liberal education, he explained, "concerns itself with the good and the cultivation of the pupil; valuing any accomplishment it may give him, for the new perceptions it opens out, for the new powers it confers, or for any other good it may do the man, and not regarding the work produced. . . ." Latham boasted that the "credit of an English university depends on the character of the students it turns out."[8]

"Character" meant the successful assertion of rational will against every kind of vicissitude. As Stefan Collini argues, the idea of Victorian "character" was "an expression of a very deeply ingrained perception of the qualities needed to cope with life."[9] Increasingly, public life became the playing field on which the qualities of character, learned at school and fortified at university, were tested. A generation after Latham the same emphasis on character was asserted even more vigorously and was associated even further with national obligations. The Oxford historian J. A. R. Marriott praised his university in 1907 for, "above all," setting "forth a high ideal of personal conduct and civic responsibility."[10] Latham in the mid-1870s and Marriott thirty years later were hardly suggesting new goals for higher education. On the contrary, they were each describing the values which consistently marked the ideal of a liberal education. Self-reliant and self-propelled, the graduate who translated his education into specific public service would continue to give the university its principle of justification until at least World War II.

Despite criticism from parliament, the press, and various public groups, the university changed only when change served either vested or upwardly mobile interests to do so. From midcentury Dissenters from the established church and many other national, civic, and business groups demanded greater proficiency in government and industry, and from the 1850s the fledgling professions began to develop as organizations of expert practice. In an atmosphere which admired activity—the more bustling the better—ancient universities, with their well-deserved reputations for sloth and isolation, became conspicuous targets. Major legislation, from outside and from within the English universities wrenched them out of the Middle Ages and put them into the modern world. But when university agencies appeared to be changing most, as in their acceptance of new degree courses, they were really bolstering traditions antagonistic to novelty. When prolonged controversies occurred, like the one between tutors and professors about the appropriate training of undergraduates, the traditionalists generally prevailed. William Whewell, the logician and Master of Trinity College, Cambridge, predicted correctly at midcentury that legislative prescriptions directed to the universities would be "evaded by some merely nominal conformity to them."[11]

Five years after Whewell's prescient observation, the Northcote-Trevelyan Report envisioned a civil service independent of patronage because it would be driven by ambition and encouraged by a rewarding rise through the ranks. The authors of the Report also thought a desirable effect of these reforms would be the modernization of the universities. Success in the new civil service examinations was intended as a sufficient inducement "to quicken the progress of our Universities" more "than any legislative measures that could be adopted." The three key provisions of the Report were intended to "provide by a proper system of examination, for the supply of the public service with a thoroughly efficient class of men; to encourage industry and foster merit, by teaching all public servants to look forward to promotion according to their deserts, and to expect the highest prizes in the service if they can qualify themselves for them." Through examination, the "first appointments" would be placed "upon a uniform footing, opening the way to the promotion of public officers to staff appointments in other departments than their own." The only existing agency able to equip these candidates for examination was the university. The Report argued that "we need hardly allude to the important effect which would be produced upon the general education of the country, if proficiency in history, jurisprudence, political economy, modern languages, political and physical geography, and other matters, besides the staple of classics and mathematics, were made directly conducive to the success of young men desirous of entering into the public service."[12] But attempts to persuade the universities to teach a wider curriculum, more directly applicable to the competitive civil service examinations, failed. Those graduates taking the examinations for the highest level appointments had to spend additional time on their own or with a coach in preparing for subjects such as modern languages and geography.

The old universities quietly rejected what they felt was irrelevant to their essential interests. From their point of view, competence was proven by a high class in honours examinations that they devised and administered within the universities. As late as 1917, the Leathes Committee on the Civil Service tried to use civil service examinations to encourage modern studies. But the universities ignored the new topics. Civil service candidates, after they took their degrees, were forced still to cram in those subjects required by the examination but not taught in the normal university curriculum. The Civil Service Commissioners were defeated by the universities again, as they had been consistently since 1855. Sir Stanley Leathes, First Civil Service Commissioner from 1910 to 1927 and Chairman of the Committee, should have known better, as he spent most of his adult life as a history tutor at Cambridge. Two years later, the university's autonomy was challenged again. In 1919, three separate agencies attempted to place the universities under a measure of external control. A Committee of Vice-Chancellors and Principals was set up to anticipate necessary funding for the universities. They then provided that information to the second new body, the University Grants Committee, which had been created to advise the Treasury and Ministry of Education on university finances. The third agency, the Association of University Teachers, represented academics on matters of careers and salaries.[13] But these groups were hardly neutral or even independent, since they were made up essentially of university men sympathetic to university traditions.

*

In 1908 the young Cambridge classicist, F. M. Cornford, slyly recognized that a heroic stand for independence could mean the right to be passive in practice. He saw that the various academic factions, no matter what their differences, all agreed that it was crucial to prevent change. Cornford's factions included the Conservative-Liberal, "a broad-minded man, who thinks that something ought to be done, only not anything that anyone now desires, but something which was not done in 1881–82"; the Liberal-Conservative, also "a broad-minded man," who thinks that "something ought to be done, only not anything that anyone now desires; and that most things which were done in 1881–82 ought to be undone"; and the Non-placet, who refused to do anything because he was a man of principle. To avoid confusion, Cornford defined a principle as "a rule of inaction, which states a valid general reason for not doing in any particular case what, to the unprincipled instinct, would appear to be right." And, finally, the "Young Man in a Hurry," was "a narrow-minded and ridiculously youthful prig, who is inexperienced enough to imagine that something might be done before very long, and even to suggest definite things." Was Cornford correct to see the universities as successful strongholds of stubborn resistance to the modern world and its ideas? Did the great majority of Fellows and university officers agree, as Cornford claimed, that there is "only one argument for doing something: the rest are arguments for doing nothing?" The argument for "doing something is that it is the right thing to do," but that was compounded by "the difficulty of making sure that it is right."[14] Was Cornford right? Yes and no.

Most contemporaries, and successive historians, saw the series of university reforms which began in the 1850s as reluctant responses to public criticism. But outside interference was resisted continuously and successfully in spite of formidable and recurring attacks.[15] Throughout the century that began in the 1850s innovations in curriculum, finances, staff, and teaching were rarely the result of irresistible pressures from either parliament or the public. Only those changes were accepted which the university's officers and teachers believed would protect and extend traditional educational aspirations. The medieval and early modern university had deliberately created a closed community purposefully segregated from the outside world so that a "higher" life could be assimilated and practiced. Both the isolation and the emphasis upon a superior set of values persisted when the university became a secular, increasingly national, institution.

What made Oxford and Cambridge "modern" after the 1850s was their willingness to become a transitional, rather than a recalcitrant, retreat in which undergraduates would learn to govern themselves so that they could lead others. In 1874 the undergraduate Arnold Toynbee wrote to a friend to explain that at Oxford "one's ideal of happy life is nearer being realized than anywhere else—I mean the ideal of gentle, equable, intellectual intercourse, with something of a prophetic glow about it, glancing brightly into the future, yet always embalming itself in the memory as a resting-place for the soul in a future that may be dark and troubled after all, with little in it but disastrous failure."[16] The sense of the university as a place of refuge and a source of the strength needed for acting upon the real world, was certainly not unique to Toynbee. His contemporaries, too, recognized that they were in transition from irresponsible immaturity to a maturity which bore, from their point of view,

serious and unprecedented responsibilities. Instead of the secure legacy
of family place and fortune, they came into the precarious inheritance of
a world they perceived to be in crisis.

Although university men were hardly insensitive to consistent external criticism about their privileged isolation, national irresponsibility,
and intellectual anachronism, they moved according to selective decisions taken by their own self-governing and self-determining bodies.
Those decisions were informed consistently by an overwhelming agreement about the need to preserve traditions. Even before the Royal Commissions visited either Oxford or Cambridge to investigate them, both
universities had instituted new degree courses. Although the universities
undertook reform for a number of reasons, an impelling motive was to
preempt and control changes that might otherwise have been forced
upon them. In 1848 Cambridge introduced two new tripos or degree subjects: one in the Moral Sciences, which included history and law, and
another in the Natural Sciences. At Oxford the Examination Statute of
1850 created Schools of Natural Science, Law and Modern History, and
Mathematics and Physics. But until 1866 the new Oxford Schools could
not be taken as examined degree subjects unless the candidate completed
the traditional liberal arts course of Litterae Humaniores or Classics,
known as "Greats."

When John Henry Newman defended university traditions in the
1850s, by arguing that they prepared individuals to "fill any post with
credit, and to master any subject with felicity," he was emphasizing one
among many interpretations of the ideal of liberal education. An understanding of knowledge as an end in itself and "of the objects of the university" as the production of a "gentleman" with "a cultivated intellect,
a delicate taste, a candid, equitable, dispassionate mind, a noble and
courteous bearing in the conduct of life"; was bound to be questioned
in an industrial society where power was held increasingly by skilled professional groups who were not necessarily gentlemen.[17] Within the universities, especially after the 1860s, Newman's ideal was altered by subjecting knowledge and the gentlemanly ideal to patriotic goals. The
concept of a gentleman came to depend more on national performance
than on class or family origins. College tutors, professors, and the other
university officers quarreled about how best to select those graduates
who would "fill any post with credit" and "master any subject with felicity," but they agreed that higher education must promote a national
elite.[18] Although loath to bring the lower classes into Oxford and Cambridge, the universities reached out through extension teaching to those

among the less privileged who wanted to improve themselves so that they, too, could contribute productively to national life.[19]

How any definition of liberal studies fitted students for public life was questioned by members of parliament, disappointed graduates, businessmen, industrialists, and other critics. These skeptics were countered in the offices of the Home and the Indian Civil Services where, from the 1850s, the highest officers were recruited by examinations based largely upon liberal disciplines, especially classics. Success in the Civil and Indian Service examinations, as in university examinations, depended upon meeting internal standards of achievement dictated entirely by teachers in the Oxford and Cambridge colleges. When these teachers certified an undergraduate's success by means of honours examinations, which the teachers set and read, the new graduate went on to public examinations, modeled upon those within the university. In turn, these examinations gave the successful graduate access to careers which offered opportunities for promoting the public good. By the end of the 1870s, the universities had secular, career teachers supported by fellowships, and a small group of professors who were rarely or intermittently part of the teaching structure. The university's commitment to liberal education was defined newly by civic rhetoric. English society was altered far more by the extension of the university into the community than were the universities by society's attempts to regulate them.

Parliamentary regulation succeeded only when a significant community of university interests found reform desirable. Complaint within the country against inadequate teaching in the Oxford and Cambridge colleges resulted in the recommendations of the Royal Commission of 1852 and their implementation in the Oxford Act of 1854 and the Cambridge Act of 1856 which addressed the quality of the fellows. Then the Test Act of 1871 permitted Dissenters to be elected to fellowships at both universities. But the major spur to widespread improvement in teaching was that fellows were no longer required to enter religious orders and live within a college. Instead they became professional college teachers with a secular career that could include marriage and a domestic life outside the colleges. Six years later, following the suggestions of the Cleveland Commission of 1873, appointed to inquire into the property and income of the Universities of Oxford and Cambridge, the Oxford and Cambridge Acts of 1877 reformed the Statutes of the universities and their colleges to increase the effectiveness of the colleges as teaching bodies. These changes mattered to the youngest, most aggressive members of the university who welcomed the reforms enthusiastically by converting them into traditions.

Self-government of the universities was a tradition of long standing and not merely the result of a struggle between government and the universities. Once the reforms of the 1850s to the 1880s were carried through, Oxford and Cambridge remained entirely free of government controls. Even when the University Grants Committee was created and consistent government funding introduced after World War I, the freedom of the universities was scrupulously preserved. That meant that the future leaders of England's political, economic, and intellectual life were educated in institutions, beginning with public (actually private) schools, that were independent from government interference. Such independence may well have affected their later attitudes to education, government and society generally. Unlike continental students, whose history of confrontation with government often led to hostility towards authority and suspicion of the abuses of political power, English undergraduates, and especially those who studied history, tended to view the state as a series of evolving institutions that promoted civic and individual freedoms.

The university itself was perceived by its members as that institution best able to continue and deepen the concept of English freedoms taught in the public schools from the 1860s. A university education which began with the classics, supplemented for many by history, was expected to train the judgment to recognize the appropriate balance between change and continuity in national life. But governing bodies, heads of colleges, and fellows often believed they were preventing or promoting change when, in effect, they were caught in a larger inertial drift. Individuals and groups were frequently divided by issues that were more rhetorical than real. Conventions of university debate often obscured what was really happening from contemporaries. Persistent, chronic debate within the university rarely moved it to change because the English university was governed less by open discussion than by entrenchments along the paths of greatest resistance.

Reformist rhetoric often disguised conservative intentions. As Francis Cornford observed so acutely, such arguments as "Give the system a Fair Trial," deliberately forestalled any possibility of change. A "Fair Trial" was given only to "systems which already exist, not to proposed alternatives." Existing university institutions, he wryly argued, were always justified on moral as well as academic grounds: "Even a little knowledge of ethical theory will convince you that all important questions are so complicated, and the results of any course of action so difficult to foresee, that certainty, or even probability, is seldom, if ever attainable." How, then, did one discover the morally imperative course of conduct? "It follows at once," Cornford concluded, "that the only justifiable attitude of mind is suspense of judgment, and this attitude besides being peculiarly congenial to the academic temperament, has the advantage of being comparatively easy to attain."[20] The qualities which defined the "academic temperament," however, were taken far more seriously by college teachers than Cornford's pastiche admitted.

*

If the first factor that made the university modern was its successful achievement of independence from outside interference, the second was the establishment of autonomous disciplines that organized knowledge within specialized areas of study. Academics accepted those changes that benefited them and their vocation while rejecting others they saw as a threat. The creation of disciplines, more than any other innovation, was necessary for the transformation of the university. But it was not sufficient. Assumptions about the form of the discipline, the choice of a specific curriculum, and the kind of examinations that best tested the student's competence, were inseparable from the institutional arrangements of colleges within the universities, and from the external pressures of a greater society increasingly informed and led by university graduates. Disciplines were shaped by external and internal criticism, conceptual challenge, economic pressures, political principles, institutional lethargy, personalities, tensions among conflicting interests, individual preferences, aesthetic inclinations and the actual content of each discipline. All these factors played a crucial part in the growth of the universities.

The development of disciplines is a complex story that involves the recovery and integration of intellectual, institutional, and social dimensions. Within the liberal arts disciplines, History and English, at both universities; the Economics Tripos at Cambridge; and the Philosophy, Politics and Economics course, created at Oxford in 1920 and known as Modern Greats, were able to establish themselves to the exclusion of potentially more radical, more critical, and less reverential systems of learning, such as sociology.[21] What the successful new arts disciplines had in common in their formative years was at least the tacit assumption that England's just and evolving institutions produced an equitable society that encouraged individual opportunities. The acceptance of new disciplines depended upon their compatibility with those existing social and intellectual traditions embodied within the university and the larger national culture it represented. The study of England's past, of her literature, her thought, or her politics, was taught by vicarious example and exemplary thinking. On the playing fields of the public schools, the next generation of leaders were taught reliability and fair play. But it was in the university liberal arts courses that they mastered the intellectual requirements for a life at the top.

Each of the new arts disciplines concentrated upon the traditions and institutions which conserved the best qualities of English society and provided dramatic object lessons about the imperatives of political, social, and personal obligation. Before the reforms of the 1850s and 1860s, gentlemen either collected a pass degree or simply left the university without any degree. The university was irrelevant to a future decided by family estates and inherited fortunes. A career in the Church, army or government, or the enjoyment of patronage, had not depended upon intellectual performance at Oxford or Cambridge. But the new emphasis upon honours degrees in the reformed university meant that future place came increasingly to depend upon an individual's earning a high class in honours examinations. Family and fortune remained important arbiters of future careers. But during the last three decades of the nineteenth and into the twentieth century, a well-placed honours graduate, in any discipline, had a passport to the highest public and private offices, even without the advantages of good connections or money.[22] By the end of the century, higher education became synonymous with the demonstration of merit revealed in a final honours examination that tested a student's mastery of conventional traditions of learning, based upon a selective reading of set and limited texts. While some honours candidates certainly revealed originality of mind or critical judgment, their course of study was not structured to encourage those attributes. The new disciplines, which perpetuated states of mind far more than organizations of knowledge, transformed the modern English university into a forward-looking agency of conservative influence.

*

The third essential development that shaped the modern university was the opportunity for the brightest graduates to become professional career teachers. Election to many scholarships and exhibitions, after the 1850s, was freed from statutory connections to particular cities or public schools. While family precedents continued to be a factor in a college's acceptance of undergraduates and fellows, demonstrated merit in competitive examinations became an increasingly more important measure for selecting both prospective students and their teachers.

Until the early 1870s, Oxford and Cambridge universities had been little more than limited holding institutions through which the college teachers, or fellows (dons), passed briefly and inconsequentially. Changes occurred very slowly because the young college fellows, who were most likely to be reformers, treated their university posts as a kind of social welfare until suitable clerical livings became available. From the 1870s, however, a newly secular faculty, in search of satisfying vocations, found them in teaching the new honours degree courses. Energetic young men became professional teachers with a wide variety of quasi-familial and intellectual responsibilities. They assumed the role of elder brothers in the domestic life of the college and they learned new subjects so that they could teach them. J. R. Green, who wrote pioneering if too-picturesque social history, observed in 1870 that the "modern reforms" had gotten rid of the "old Don of port and prejudice." What he saw were new teachers "hardly older than the boys they teach" and although the "young Don is a little priggish, as young people are apt to be, . . . he is for the most part eminently genial and good-humored."

What Green did not foresee was that from the 1880s, the age of dons would rise and their long and settled tenures would help to maintain the coherence which gave each college its distinguishing character. But the colleges, their students and the larger society were not always well served by the longevity of teachers often without any experience of the outside world. The result was an increasingly closed society preserved and perpetuated by one generation after another. Students learned what their teachers had been taught and those students who became tutors repeated almost identical lessons to the undergraduates who came after them. There was little opportunity for new blood or new ideas to enter and possibly challenge thinking and teaching because conventions were strengthened with repeated use. At Balliol between 1882 and 1920, less than 4 percent of the teachers came from another university. At Trinity College, Cambridge, 97 percent of the Fellows were Trinity men and at King's College 85 percent were produced by their own college.[23] But Green was right to admire the familial affection of those "who have been rending one another in pamphlets and on platforms," but were "in common room the best friends in the world."[24] That friendship continued to rest on the secure familiarity of shared experiences.

The relationship between a student and his college rested essentially on the tutorial system of individual teaching, or the "supervision" as it was called in Cambridge. That kind of personal scrutiny of a student by a college teacher meant that individuals could be personally fostered and encouraged. But for those unfortunate enough to have a tutor they found incompetent or uncongenial, there were few, if any, alternatives and they might have to remain under his direction for the entire three years of their college life. In spite of these potential problems, English undergraduates, although few in number when compared to the larger population, were especially privileged. American and German universities may have employed much larger and more heterogeneous faculties to provide greater numbers of students with extensive specialized training within every discipline, but students in those countries attended large lectures and rarely received the attention lavished upon the English undergraduate. By 1906 the University of Berlin had 468 teachers; Harvard had 554; while Oxford had only 262. The number at Cambridge was even smaller. As late as 1930, well after the creation of the civic universities, there was still only one university student for every 1,150 young people of university age in England in comparison to one for 690 in Germany and one for 125 in the United States.[25] But those English undergraduates fortunate enough to be in a university had one obvious advantage over their American and German contemporaries; they enjoyed the highest proportion of teachers to students.

Before entering the university, most of these privileged undergraduates had already been to a public school where they boarded during their adolescence. Especially after Thomas Arnold's midcentury reforms at Rugby, widely imitated by the other public schools, the essence of the private, secondary schools' curricula was the deliberate training of character and public duty. The heart of the curriculum was the study of Greek and Roman civic virtues that were tested by the playing of athletic games intended to foster both team spirit and individual heroism. The residential houses in these public schools were governed by a hierarchical system of older boys grappling with an environment where hormones may have been more compelling than the larger ethos of the school.

Then, in the last quarter of the nineteenth century, the college teacher transformed Oxford and Cambridge colleges into substitute households dominated by adults who molded their members to a degree never attained by the earlier universities, by the home, or by conventional religion. The universities were able to create a homogeneous governing class because they organized liberal education, in all its social, intellectual and moral aspects, within the intimacy of college life and loyalties. There undergraduates and the dons who taught and guided them were protected against intrusion from the outside world. College life was comfortably predictable in its routines. Servants relieved undergraduates and those dons living in college of the inconvenience of domestic chores. External distractions rarely got further than the porter's lodge. Within the college, undergraduates were given a certainty of identity and of place free from the tensions endemic to family life. Religion, especially at the time of the Oxford movement before midcentury, had traumatically affected young men. But from the 1870s, in both Oxford and Cambridge, the expression of faith gradually became a peripheral and intermittent practice of ritual conformities or a matter of justification by good works in the secular world. Ordinary youthful experiences and religion may not have had as profound an effect as college life.

The amorphous, ill-defined functions of the university can be explained, largely, by the college's continuing educational and administrative independence from both the university and from those outside its concealing walls. The colleges also set a social and intellectual tone and perpetuated standards of conduct that indelibly colored their teachers' and students' subsequent lives. As full-time teachers, within a close-knit collegiate life, dons perpetuated models for the thought and conduct of their junior colleagues as well as for their students. It was the vitality and diversity of its colleges more than the curriculum that gave Oxford and Cambridge their singular place in the history of undergraduate instruction.

The development of the colleges provided a milieu in which teachers achieved concentrated authority over their students. In the calculated process of forming character, teachers attempted to replicate themselves in their students insofar as they required that they, too, be dedicated to a life of higher ends. Students were encouraged to heighten their intellects, imaginations, and emotions into an inner life which would remain a perpetual source of fulfilment. This emphasis upon personal goods was entirely compatible, they assumed, with a wider social altruism. When an individual's latent capacities for thought and feeling were enriched, he was expected to recognize the necessity for carrying out social obligations. A university graduate, because he had enjoyed special privileges, was responsible for enhancing the quality of life for those who had not been so fortunate. His ability to do that depended upon the values he learned in college. The teacher's authority was not derived from offices or ideologies as much as from uniformly binding values, perpetuated by the stable institution of the college.

*

The authority of the professions that emerged at the end of the nineteenth century was based upon a command of esoteric knowledge, expert practice and demonstrated competence. In eighteenth-century professions, the production and consumption of professional products tended to be "market-dominated."[26] But by the latter part of the nineteenth century, the new professions were setting the terms by which they would provide services. Professional communities assured their status and security of tenure essentially by finding a clientele prepared to believe that the professional possessed special authority. Medicine was recognized as authoritative because sick people, government agencies, and industrial managers became convinced that doctors would solve multiplying problems of private and public health.[27] In contrast to the popular demand for professional groups such as doctors or lawyers, however, the clients of university teachers in the second half of the nineteenth century were restricted almost entirely to the small number of students attending Oxford and Cambridge.

It was only at the end of the century that a discipline became an organized body of knowledge within a closed society of shared wisdom. An esoteric body of learning called "history" or "literature," that involved judgments beyond the grasp of other educated people, developed very slowly. But the possession of particular knowledge, even when passed on through teaching, was a property of the working lifetime of particular people. When that knowledge was written down systematically and published, it assumed more of a life of its own and remained current for a longer period of time until challenged or replaced by newer organizations of knowledge.

Although the college teachers of the new liberal arts subjects such as history tended largely to be teachers more than scholars, they were able to combine both the authority of office and the authority of knowledge. On the one hand, they were an integral part of the college tradition. But, on the other, they taught an organized body of learning, essentially to ensure their students' success in honours examinations. Most college teachers did little original research, but some wrote textbooks and they encoded what they knew in the examination questions, repeated from year to year. Very few university teachers attempted to discover or master a special, unexplored subject. Specialized inquiry continued to play a very limited role because college teachers generally were too overburdened with personal supervision of students, teaching, and examining to attempt original research.[28] Instead, their select organization of knowledge in examinations, lectures, tutorials, and textbooks became in itself a venerable tradition transmitted from one generation to another. Moreover, research, writing, and teaching depended upon the narrowest in-

stitutional acceptance within a small academic world generally indifferent to external standards of approval or disapproval. When tutors
appointed new fellows, their self-perpetuating college elections usually
chose men as like themselves as they could find in temperament and in
ability, and especially in commitment to college rather than to their
discipline. It is hardly surprising that the college teacher should have
thought himself more a professional teacher than a professional historian, or classicist, or mathematician.

The unique relationship between don and student gave the university pervasive influence in English life. On the continent, university
teachers distanced themselves from their students by enforcing both
their authority and their political preferences. As a result, universities
there were often ideological and intellectual battlegrounds for competing
political, sociological, and economic beliefs. But in England dons and
students were united by a common acceptance of appropriate purpose
and conduct. A college teacher indirectly influenced the real world of
affairs through his students' subsequent careers, which were determined
by college associations and by the patronage of their teachers which extended those associations through generations. Well before he became
Master of Balliol in 1870 and until his death in 1893, Benjamin Jowett's
close connections with the foreign and diplomatic services allowed a
stream of Balliol graduates to dominate them.[29] Jowett established the
tradition at Balliol, crucial to the college's success, that the don's real calling was tested by his ability to unify intellectual and moral instruction.[30]

That sense of calling was not limited to Balliol or to Oxford, and it
was recognized nationally that the college teacher performed an indispensable duty to the greater community outside the university. In the
second year of the Great War, H. A. L. Fisher, who had been a history
tutor at New College and was then President of the Board of Education,
asked Lloyd George to save college teachers from going to the front and
dying there. David Davies responded from the office of the Secretary of
State for War that Fisher should confer privately with the heads of colleges and universities, avoid publicity, and "select a certain number of
the brainiest and most efficient . . . men upon whom the future of their
colleges and universities depends." Davies thought that the Secretary of
State "might easily get them transferred from a fighting unit to a labour
reserve, A.S.C. or Garrison unit, where they would run far less risk of
being 'outed' than they do at present." If Fisher found time to compile
such a list of the "crème de la crème," Davies wrote, he "would be ren-
dering a great service to the country."[31]

At Cambridge, although teachers drawn from many colleges collectively controlled the teaching of degree courses from 1859, the colleges remained centrally important into the twentieth century. When the Asquith Commission of 1918 divided the Universities into "faculties," some older tutors, like the classical historian T. R. Glover, a Fellow of St. John's since 1892, saw the reforms as moving the center of "academic life" from the "College (and a very good centre, too, with its diversities of types)" to the "'faculty' (a group of people of one interest.)" His colleague G. G. Coulton, who only came to St. John's in 1919, saw the college in the decade succeeding the reforms as a place where there was still loyalty "to one's College and antagonism to an impersonal tyrant called the University." As late as the 1940s, Glover, although disgusted at the adoption of "American" standards of efficiency and the triumph of a scientific and theoretical mentality, was relieved that the "Cambridge College, in spite of imports and Ph. D's, research and practical people, is still a nursery of culture and character." [32]

*

Questions about appropriate teaching, curriculum, examinations, and personnel for new degree courses were debated fiercely outside the older universities as well as within, and by the late 1870s, there were attempts to alter the traditional structure of higher education. A Subcommittee, reporting to the Annual Committee of London University's Convocation in 1877 to 1878, recognized the importance "of the advancement of knowledge as an object of national interest." The Subcommittee adopted the rhetoric of "national interest" and extended its meaning to include a new research emphasis for the universities. But the Senate, the governing body of the university which represented the examiners, preferred the older liberal arts emphasis and the debate ended there.

Nearly a generation later, Edward Sonnenschein, a graduate of University College, Oxford, a famous classical scholar, and the Professor of Greek and Latin at Mason College in Birmingham, returned to the earlier debate to argue that universities should be founded for research. In 1896, Sonnenschein proposed a University of the Midlands to be composed of professors from the university colleges of Bristol, Nottingham and Birmingham, who would do research and prepare students for exams. A year later, Joseph Chamberlain campaigned for a university that would incorporate postgraduate education, the advancement of learning, autonomous and powerful faculties, and professorships with security of tenure. These varied voices were united in wanting universities to go beyond traditional teaching and examining to the advancement of knowledge and research at the highest levels. Their ideal was faculties or departments within unitary rather than federal institutions, run by academic senates that embodied the views of researchers and professors, as well as teachers.[33]

The civic universities went beyond Oxford and Cambridge to recognize scholarship in every field of knowledge, both theoretical and practical, as part of the university's appropriate curriculum. Outside Oxford and Cambridge, higher education in England displayed extraordinary institutional diversity by the beginning of the twentieth century. The new universities endorsed technical, vocational and professional, as well as liberal, forms of education. But even in the most esoteric sciences, teachers and students were expected to approach their study with the thoroughness and methodological rigor that they associated, ideally, with a liberal arts academic training. T. F. Tout, the founder of Manchester's school of administrative history, predicted in 1902 that the civic university would "impress itself upon the life of the community" by making "all knowledge its province," and by studying "useful" subjects with "academic thoroughness and method."[34]

Before the end of the century, Hastings Rashdall, the Oxford classicist and historian of medieval universities, had demonstrated that the original purpose of university education had been to train the professions.[35] In 1902, however, he reminded audiences at the new universities of Birmingham and Liverpool that a liberal arts education was "the best that is now available" as preparation for any career. He pointed to the public services, and especially the Indian Civil Service, which were chiefly recruited from men of high university distinction who turned out to be "practically abler and more competent than their predecessors" because they were first- and second-class honours degree graduates. Rashdall proposed to strengthen English commerce by introducing men of similar "caliber and similar education" into the higher posts of great commercial houses where practical skills could be learned in the offices before they moved on to work which required "brains and education." What Rashdall wanted every student to have, including those intended for business and industry, was a "general training of mind and character of the type which it is the especial business of the universities to afford."[36]

Rashdall was preaching to an audience that hardly needed conversion. Liverpool and Birmingham, like Manchester and London, never questioned the fundamental value of traditional liberal education, but unlike Oxford and Cambridge, they insisted that it must be secular and even specialized when the occasion demanded. The middle classes, the major boosters and beneficiaries of the civic universities, were committed to the values associated with the ancient universities. As David Jones indicates, "the financial and social rewards of liberal education and white collar and professional employments were their primary goal."[37] The civic universities created their own traditions within a broad mandate to inform and guide the cities that supported them.[38] In so doing they attempted to demonstrate that prescriptive remedies could be extracted from every kind of learning. But the kind of learning most valued by the founders and civic groups who created and extended their universities was a nonspecialized liberal education. The new traditions, like the old ones they thought they were imitating, rested on a confirmation of higher education as essentially the study of broad subjects which not only continued the knowledge of the past but anticipated and guided the knowledge of the future. And, by the turn of the century, they viewed liberal education as a means for fostering interdependent social and individual goods rather than as an essentially disinterested study of knowledge or, primarily, as a means to personal cultivation.[39] As Oxford and Cambridge abandoned their narrow religious and caste character in encouraging the new, often Dissenting, middle classes to justify themselves through merit, the concept of liberal education also shed its exclusive aristocratic qualities.

Chapter 2

Truth and Objectivity

In the unreformed university education rested upon the transmission of assured knowledge. But in the reformed university "one of the new elements in assured knowledge was the proposition that less knowledge was assured than had hitherto been supposed."[1] This proposition troubled university teachers because it challenged their choice of a vocation. Their reliability as teachers rested on the discrimination of true from false knowledge. It became very important, consequently, to agree upon the criteria for recognizing truth. The new understanding of liberal studies as a critical search for contingent truth came to play a determining part in the new sciences. But it was not the interpretation taught to Oxford and Cambridge history students. In the historical past, late nineteenth- and early twentieth-century teachers of history found testimony they believed was true. The new teachers questioned earlier oversimplifications, but they continued to believe with their predecessors that the past contained authentic and authoritative lessons.

Discussion about the nature of history was endemic in Cambridge, but Oxford historians tended to reject theoretical and methodological debates. In particular, they wanted to divorce their subject from both art and science because each of these forms of knowledge had serious limitations. Art was associated with intuition, imagination, subjectivity, and creative license that often altered or ignored the truth. Science was no more appealing. Although the sciences also searched for truth, they arranged their discoveries within repeatable, predictable, deductive patterns of cause and effect that denied the force of individual will. Stubbs's fear, typical of the Oxford school, was that reductionist attempts to make history scientific would create self-fulfilling prophecies in which history would be used as "a mere political weapon." History was not a science, because "probability" was the "very guide of History, and its conclusions are moral and not mathematical inferences."[2] C. H. Firth was willing to use science as the "discovery of truth" and art to "represent" conclusions so long as history remained "a branch of learning to be studied for its own sake and because it was useful to people in daily life." But Firth knew from his own experience as a researcher that the truth was not easily discovered or represented. A generation before Collingwood, Firth saw that the relative importance of facts and their meaning changed as each age wrote history "over again to suit itself."[3] James Bryce, too, weighed the relative claims of "critical" and "imaginative" approaches to history. While the critical historian concentrated on constitutional and diplomatic history, where "positive conclusions are (from the comparative abundance of records) most easily reached," the imaginative scholar was drawn to dramatic and personal elements in "private life or features of social and religious custom." But the qualities of both had to be combined and supplemented further by a desire for truth. Bryce, from his perspective as a historian who had become the Professor of Jurisprudence at Oxford, wanted the historian to be a keen observer and a "sound and calm judge" able "to feel as those of other ages felt and to recreate that world."[4]

By the late nineteenth century academic historians in both Oxford and Cambridge reached a consensus about appropriate methods. But that tacit and unexamined consensus was not arrived at by serious discussion of varying, distinct, or opposing positions. Every sound student was expected to yield to the force of evidence which would lead him to the truth. Once lessons were extracted, they had to be presented in a coherent literary form that made them attractive and significant to undergraduates. Intellectuals in the late nineteenth and early twentieth centuries wanted the methods of disciplines to be "scientific," in the sense of rigorous, and they wanted the results of methodical inquiries to be presented with imaginative art.[5] R. B. Haldane argued in 1914, as most intellectuals and historians then would have, that truth in history requires "that the mind of the reader should find itself satisfied by that harmony and sense of inevitableness which only a work of art can give."[6] A widespread appreciation of the aesthetics of history did not mean that history had to conform to a pleasing picture, but more fundamentally that history, like any other truth, was recognizable by its internal coherence and its "sense of inevitableness." History properly done revealed a fit between a narrative and the familiar, moral proportions of the good life.

Only the most extraordinary undergraduates studied history with a developed aesthetic sense and, as they studied narrative surveys, or "outlines," in selected books, it was even more unusual for them to think of themselves as apprentice scholars. It is hardly surprising that undergraduates were not contemplative. Very few ever are. It is more puzzling, however, that their teachers rarely reflected on the nature of the study and teaching to which they devoted their lives. Students who read history for an honours degree usually came from public schools where they had been introduced to the subject by an enthusiastic teacher. In the many diaries, letters, and memoirs in which individuals explained why they chose history, the personal effect of schoolmasters and dons far outweighs other factors such as inclinations, random circumstances, or discriminating choices.[7] But the writers of these accounts, including many who became university historians themselves, accepted their teachers' historical narratives uncritically. Doubts about the meaning of history were rare possibly because of the general, tacit assumption that the meaning of history was unequivocal.

*

The subject, modern history, came to be identified almost entirely with the study of England's political and constitutional development. National history integrated traditional standards of thought and behavior, the problems of the present, and expectations about the future to fulfil antiquarian and romantic idealizations of a past in which individuals acted heroically, but rarely tragically. And simultaneously, evolutionary apologetics transformed apparent losses into national gains. At Oxford, all the Regius Professors, beginning with Goldwin Smith (1858–65), and continuing with W. Stubbs (1867–83), E. A. Freeman (1884–92), J. A. Froude (1892–94), F. Y. Powell (1894–1904), C. H. Firth (1904–25), and W. H. C. Davis (1925–28) described the study of history as an essential civic education that groomed individuals for leadership. In Cambridge, too, all the holders of the Regius Chair—J. R. Seeley (1869–95), Lord Acton (1895–1902), J. B. Bury (1902–27), and G. M. Trevelyan (1927–54)—associated the study of history with preparation for the noblest kind of citizenship.[8]

At both universities the patriotic confidence of the Regius Professors was endorsed and repeated by the tutors who tended to remain disciples of Stubbs in "tracing the Divine Purpose in the long evolutionary process which had ended in making England top nation."⁹ At Oxford from 1877 to 1916, the most popular history tutor was A. L. Smith at Balliol who produced more history graduates than anyone else at any contemporary British university. In a characteristic lecture, Smith explained to secondary school teachers that history had to provide a "general idea of the past on which the present is built up; . . . of the continuity of national life; . . . of the great inheritance transmitted from past generations to be handed down by us unimpaired to the generations to come, . . . a necessary part . . . of the moral equipment of a civilized man."¹⁰ In Cambridge, especially from 1908 until the 1930s, almost every student in the Historical Tripos went to J. H. Clapham for lectures that prepared them for the compulsory economics paper in Part I of the Historical Tripos honours examinations. From him, they learned lessons about character and progress very much like those taught by A. L. Smith at Oxford, even though Smith was a liberal and Clapham a conservative. When Clapham published a new edition in 1939 of the first volume of his *An Economic History of Modern Britain* (1926), he responded to the criticism that his reading of industrial development was too optimistic by writing that there were certainly "hardships, injustices, and undeserved humiliations" which working people had endured but that "excessive concentration on these and other shadows of the historical landscape has led historians to ignore the patches of sunlight."¹¹

Smith, Clapham, and their peers at Oxford and Cambridge, while recognizing the shadows, concentrated on the sunlight. They found that the political behavior of historic individuals illustrated heroism, villainy, altruism, nobility, cupidity, error, and their consequences; the study of the constitution revealed the growth of legal and social institutions—and for Clapham, economic institutions—based upon reason, consent, and liberty. English history, first in the universities and then in the public schools, became the living study of those traditions responsible for individual distinction and national greatness, by supplying models to emulate, mistakes to avoid, and even procedures for discerning the truth.¹² In the historical development of English institutions, and especially the constitution, undergraduates admired the virtues of the great and good and despised the vices of lesser, unacceptable men. The way in which they studied history encouraged the idealization of those who had served country and God. Teachers and writers of history believed themselves to be objective because they rigorously tested evidence. But the effect of their teaching and writing was a coherent narrative sequence or a completed series of documents that provided evidence for their national faith.¹³

Historical periods which were likely to provoke passions instead of reasonable impartiality tended to be avoided as subjects unsuitable for immature undergraduates. William Whewell in 1837, the year before he became Knightbridge Professor of Philosophy at Cambridge, had argued that the universities must teach "a spirit of respect" rather than a "spirit of criticism" and "select subjects which consist of undoubted truths." The University of Sydney, Australia, founded in 1850 as an offspring of Oxford with teachers who were graduates of Oxford or Cambridge, established a curriculum that excluded modern history because it was considered an inflammatory subject. Stubbs never lectured on subjects like the Thirty Years War because it recalled the "very same influences which are at work this moment."[14] T. F. Tout, James Tait, and A. F. Pollard were all Oxford-trained historians who were critical of the ways in which history had been taught at Oxford. But when Tout and Tait created a flourishing school of history at the University of Manchester, they concentrated on medieval administration while Pollard, the seminal figure in establishing history at the University of London, focused on the Tudor development of liberty rather than the religious conflicts of the Reformation. Each of the three, although an independent and prolific scholar, chose to study events characterized more by consensus than controversy. Historians like J. H. Round, for whom the sixteenth century provoked intense emotions, were not university teachers. Academic historians worried consistently that the events of the past would be enlisted, selectively, to abet the political and religious emotions of the present. Some Cambridge historians attempted to introduce more recent history, but students, until the 1920s, consistently chose the earlier periods.

The university study of history was not intended to test contemporary debates among various groups or to introduce new or alternative values. If there was one common assumption held by the tutors, professors, examiners, and writers of history, it was that historical events had tried and proven England's social, economic, and political institutions. Historians did not misunderstand the past in the naive sense of thinking either that the same causes always produce the same effects or that every effect has an identifiable cause. They recognized that both constraints and opportunities had shaped issues and their outcome. But university historians believed, as an article of faith, that the opportunities were always greater than the constraints. On the basis of that creed, they selected those conditions that were essentially important and ignored those that appeared fortuitous or peripheral. Moreover, they were convinced that the past, which was essentially knowable, continued to exercise a benevolent dominion over the present.

The fields of jurisprudence and literature, in common with history, concentrated on "texts"; anthropology studied fixed "societies"; and geography was shaped by existing land patterns. Each liberal discipline treated its own subject as if it were nearly complete rather than an evolving, changing, and arbitrary organization of knowledge. But the historians, far more than their colleagues in law, literature, anthropology, or geography, first approached their subject as if events, institutions and behavior were frozen in time. As increasingly original and specialized research produced new textbooks, monographs, biographies, and collections of documents, history became less an observation of a fixed past and more an interpretation of cumulative change. These apparently inconsistent perspectives succumbed to the overriding conviction that history, whether a study of unchanging phenomena or of evolving causes and effects, taught enduring truths about people and policies more important than any apparently fortuitous circumstances. While experiment explained the present for scientists, historians regarded the present as foreign and dangerous territory. But they did not realize that they actually began with their own time and read it backwards into the past. If the sciences used a methodology of classification, organization, and interpretation to predict the future, history used these methods to predict the past.

History received an important position in the universities because a historical habit of thinking had already led Victorians to imagine individual and national development as a process extending from primitive origins to a civilized present and a still better future. Some history was also taught in moral philosophy, classics, law, and later in languages, literature and anthropology. Beyond the effect of theories of progress and a romantic interest in origins and colorful individuals, historical explanations were consistent with general observations of constant advance in standards of living, economic opportunities, political institutions, education, social order, and a legitimate imperial dominium. Although academic historians took great pride in the evidence of national development, they treated the past as a recital of cautionary lessons. During the first three decades of the twentieth century, just as in the greater part of the nineteenth, the study of history guarded, transmitted, and promoted fundamental conceptions which resisted radical revision. The inheritance was preserved and perpetuated scrupulously, with only minor additions and corrections. Although there was the odd "radical" such as Goldwin Smith, the university reformer and Regius Professor of History at Oxford from 1858 to 1865, the study of history remained deeply conservative and independent, generally, of the political preferences of its writers. Admiration of English history tended to transcend party in the university and in the wider educated public.

The pervasiveness of an ethos that saw the university's principal function as the preparation of students for that highest ethical obligation, citizenship, crossed the entire political spectrum. In Oxford this was evident in the careers of the liberal A. L. Smith and the conservative J. A. R. Marriott. Marriott, a Fellow at Worcester College, was also a university extension lecturer from 1887 to 1939 and Secretary of the Oxford University Extension Delegacy from 1895 to 1920. The Summer Schools, which brought extension students to Oxford as summer residents, were attended predominantly by women. Marriott later defended their presence at Oxford by arguing that since women were admitted to the electorate in 1918 and became a majority in 1928, was "it not supremely fortunate that a whole generation of women should, before the fortunes of Britain were committed to their hands, have enjoyed the advantage of that liberal training in citizenship which, by providing teaching both within and beyond the limits of the university, Oxford and Cambridge showed themselves willing to give?" Marriott took considerable pride in playing "a part, however modest, in preparing the women of England for the discharge of such a responsible duty." [15] At Cambridge, too, as the careers of the conservatives G. W. Prothero and Clapham, the radical Oscar Browning, and the liberal G. M. Trevelyan reveal, political preferences had little to do with a common, national reading of the values vested in history. [16]

*

History accommodated simultaneously the transient subjectivity of time, place, thought, and institutions and the permanent objectivity of measurable impetus towards a just society. Most historians, for three generations, accepted some variety of teleological history, whether providential or secular, in which development, restoration, and reconstruction were complementary. History, more than any other liberal arts study, made it reputable to indulge an antiquarian passion, a romantic yearning for a comprehensible, valiant, and decisive past. At the same time, a student could admire and accept selected changes as improvements. Nostalgia was mitigated by some species of progressivist apologetics. Ambiguities, ironies, subtleties, losses, and regrets were submerged in the larger meaning of history as national maturation. The historical spectacle displayed reasonable and equitable criteria that were extracted as standards for appropriate activity. History gave the governing community, no matter what the politics of its individual members, confidence in itself. Even more crucially, history appeared to document the elasticity of British society able to accommodate change while maintaining its character and institutions.

History teachers drew freely upon a huge cast of historical actors as worthies and blackguards in complex morality plays that dramatized the disappointments of pursuing power, authority, or wealth without a principled dedication to law, justice, and equity. A certified curriculum in history was intended to equip individuals to recognize what was reasonable and, still more important, what was right. Biased and self-serving distortions were screened out, it was assumed, not only by the lessons evident in historical behavior, events, and institutions, but even more by the rigorously objective methods which were supposed to govern the study of history. Peter Novick has argued that in late nineteenth- and early twentieth-century America, the professional historian's ideological commitments and social optimism "both reflected and reinforced their belief in objectivity. . . . Their confident evolutionism gave an explicit moral meaning to history which made explicit moralizing superfluous." [17] English historians responded to the objectivity they recognized in history very differently. Even though the meaning of historical events was clear, the university historians, as teachers, felt that they must emphasize explicit moral lessons as a necessary consequence of their obligation to teach the truth.

It was largely moral commitments that prompted university historians in England to separate history from propaganda. By the end of the nineteenth century, there was a broad agreement about what historians ought to do. They were expected to recognize the objective evidence that was there for every student who sought it out. If scrupulous methods were followed, then the historian could reveal the true nature of historical figures, events, and institutions. In both Oxford and Cambridge, historians rejected nonacademic or popular history because it did not meet their standards of scrutiny. At midcentury, the question of Homer's accuracy as an historian of his own age was decided easily by W. E. Gladstone on the basis of the "self-consistency" of the text and, "in the last resort," by his own "inward tastes and feelings." Gladstone trusted intuitive certainties about human nature and political institutions to expose the higher meaning of a historical time and he was personally satisfied by his own test of the text. The main issue for Gladstone was not whether Homer correctly recorded a series of events but whether he truly and faithfully represented manners and character, feelings and tastes, races and countries, principles and institutions: "Here lie the pith and soul of history, which has fact for its body."[18] Gladstone was often more comfortable in judging the ancient past than modern politics. Unlike Gladstone and other Sunday-afternoon historical writers, Oxford and Cambridge historians wanted historical evidence to be verifiable by objective procedures that revealed the truth. Even J. A. Froude, in spite of his recognition that the historian subjectively selects the facts which interest him, argued that the past could only be studied by the rigorous comparison of documents.[19] With the aid of technical tools and systematic scholarship, the past could be resurrected and better understood. On the basis of that understanding, individuals and groups could learn to control the present and anticipate the future.

The broad reading public had been the audience for the history written by Gibbon and continued by Macaulay and others in the first six decades of the nineteenth century. What the university historians did was to narrow their focus to a smaller, more select group who were to be the new managers of power. Unlike their predecessors, the university historians seldom recognized, as Edward Gibbon had done, that "it was indeed the historian who made history."[20] From the 1870s, the undergraduate interested in politics, economics, and society no longer formed his views by occasional exposure to popular historians or to journals such as *The Nineteenth Century, The Saturday Review,* or the *Fortnightly,* which had earlier molded opinion. As the university came to replace more informal sources of knowledge by systematically educating young people within its own walls, a degree course in history increasingly organized what they read and thought.

*

Outside the universities, few historians survived and those only marginally. Hardly any flourished.[21] University historians competed with nonacademic writers mainly in the genre of biography. Biographers, such as John Morley in the late nineteenth century and John Grigg and Roy Jenkins in recent years, usually relied on sources of income distinct from their historical work. But they attracted an intelligent and appreciative readership, including academic historians, because of the literary as well as historical quality of their work.[22] In the United States, until at least World War II, everyone agreed that serious historical work must be separated from amateur interests. Some historians, intent upon maintaining a rigorous professionalism, wanted to take measures to prevent dilettante membership in the American Historical Association.[23] But the separation between academic historians and independent scholars was less clearly drawn.[24] Writers for the *American Historical Review*, into the interwar years, included such respected private historians as the Pulitzer Prize winner James Truslow Adams. There were other celebrated historians, such as H. O. Taylor, Henry C. Lea, and George Louis Beer, fortunate enough to be independently wealthy amateurs.

Increasingly, and especially after World War II, American historians restricted the profession to Ph. D.'s produced largely in American history departments. But until the doctorate became the professional license to practice, it was difficult to control the profession in a country as large as the United States and especially at a time when new universities were growing so rapidly. The early founders of the American historical profession, searching for principles by which they could establish their standing, borrowed the research emphasis of the Germans which allowed them to judge historical work by a set of standards which appeared to be objective. American historians initially needed some overriding definition of the profession that would unite people from different regions and different kinds of universities and colleges. An insistence upon technical skills permitted them to define methods of research and writing which they argued were unique to their craft.

In Germany, historians differed markedly from both their English and American colleagues in that they were the beneficiaries of state largesse and elevated social, economic, and intellectual status. But the Herr Doktor Professor established his authority independently of the office the state conferred upon him. He did this by creating the ideal of an apolitical discipline above persons, offices, and ideologies. The German academic historians made their case for intellectual autonomy, academic freedom, and place within the academic community by concentrating either on a cultural and philosophical synthesis or on methods and procedures for recovering the past accurately. Although their work was as inherently political as that of English or American historians, the German historians explicitly disavowed any attempt to draw historical conclusions immediately applicable to the present and future.[25] German university historians, with considerably more political and academic power than their colleagues in other countries, claimed that their position depended upon their knowledge. In 1932, an international group of scholars met to consider the nature of universities in a changing world. The German spokesman, director of studies and head of the theological seminary of the state church of Saxony in Luckendorf, argued that the German universities were in crisis because the new students, introduced by the reforms begun in 1918, were "practical and professional-minded."

If this type "gains the upper hand among the students," he warned, the Humboldtian ideal of disinterested scholarship for its own sake would be threatened for the first time and the "existence of the university" would be "seriously menaced."[26]

German universities and the disciplines within them were established and fostered as departments of the state. The development of history as a discipline in England depended rather on the expansion and secularization of independent universities. The adoption of honours degrees at both Oxford and Cambridge occurred within a traditional system of private college employment which provided the only source of income and social identity for the great majority of historians. Charles Firth's independent wealth, derived from a Sheffield steel family, was a notable exception among historians and the house he built in Northmoor Road, conspicuously larger than his other North Oxford neighbors, led to great resentment. Perhaps some English historians, following the example of G. M. Trevelyan, would have chosen to do their research and writing outside the university if they could have afforded it. But even Trevelyan, who came from a family of historians and statesmen with financial security, taught in universities occasionally, although without any permanent position, until his appointment as Regius Professor in Cambridge. Although English academic historians wanted to reach as wide a public as possible, they largely rejected the independent scholar who represented more a threat to their own security of place than to any concept of the historical "profession." Apart from the scholar with private means, there were some who took good degrees in history, needed a salary, and wanted to be practicing historians. But they were unable or unwilling to find work within the professional community of university teachers. Few alternative sources of employment were available to them. There were a limited number of organized enterprises such as the *Dictionary of National Biography*, The Royal Historical Society, the *Cambridge Modern History*, and the *English Historical Review* which provided desultory income and occasional status. These opportunities were transitory. It was only within the growing universities that historians found a reliable, secure career.

Although American academic historians accepted the work of scholars from outside the universities, they subjected that work to the standards imposed upon "professional" historians. Unlike the English academic historians, their American and continental colleagues emphasized the reproduction of specialists who would carry on the historical profession for which they had been trained.[27] In America, influential and vigorous founding fathers, such as Herbert Baxter Adams at Johns Hopkins, argued that explanation had to rest on critical scholarship. In 1885, for the next generation of undergraduate and graduate students, Adams saw the "main principle of historical training" at his university as the encouragement of "independent thought and research." He pointed out that American universities had already begun to develop "a generation of specialists." Adams's interpretation of America's past was hardly disinterested in that he saw the "essential idea of history" as the "growing self-knowledge of a living, progressive age." But at the same time, he believed that such "self-knowledge" was best encouraged by applying Droysen's definition of historical method as "merely *to understand by means of research.*" Even in secondary schools, he argued, students "should learn to judge for themselves by comparing evidence." Adams assumed that even the most independent thinker would be guided by historical reality to find that late nineteenth-century America was, indeed, a "progressive age." [28]

By the end of World War I, David Levine has argued recently, American institutions of higher learning had modified the *Gelehrten* ideals that Adams had promoted. No "longer content to educate" they set out instead "to train, accredit, and impart social status to their students." [29] But upwardly ascendent career goals were compatible with a broad, introspective, and occasionally populist tradition of historiography. Arthur S. Link, the distinguished biographer of Woodrow Wilson, found in the American Historical Association's annual reports and in the *American Historical Review* since 1884 a "range and diversity" arising from the training of many early leaders of the association by German professors who "stressed the universality of history" and from the strength of that tradition in the United States. In the annual reports of the first 25 years, the emphasis was upon "social, cultural, and economic history and on the experiences of so-called ordinary folk." Link stressed "the degree to which young historians heeded the call of their mentors to write this kind of history." [30]

In contrast to the American understanding of their nation as an amalgam of disparate social, economic and cultural groups, English historians thought of England as a country created and maintained essentially by compatible political institutions. Their almost exclusive concentration on the study of politics lent itself to a pious patriotism which admired the steady historical growth of liberty and the limitation of power. The English study of history remained a national narrative about high politics and the constitution, in which social, economic, cultural, scientific, or popular phenomena were important largely as illustrations of the endurance of political communities, institutional developments, and moral imperatives. Evolutionary, and still more, progressive interpretations of national development were more difficult to sustain when historians turned their attention to the effects of industrialization, population growth, urban blight, and the growing evidence of irrationality as a factor in behavior and thought.

A comparison of contemporary English and American historians reveals that both groups selected their subjects and evidence on the basis of deeply held preconceptions. The focus of American historians extended beyond political and constitutional studies because of their individualistic ideals and suspicions about government. Edward Eggleston's presidential address of 1900 to the American Historical Association rejected E. A. Freeman's equation of history with politics. James Harvey Robinson worked on social and cultural history for years before he published his famous *The New History* in 1912.[31] Robinson was both a "New" and a "Progressive" historian, as were Frederick Jackson Turner, Carl Becker, and the Columbia school around Robinson and Charles Beard. Although hardly social revolutionaries in their emphasis upon the value of nationalism, these historians were impressed by the discontinuities and anachronisms in American history. In England no important historian wrote a book as controversial as Beard's *An Economic Interpretation of the Constitution of the United States* (1913). A minority among American historians, these men were, as Peter Novick points out, "hardly marginal to the profession" in that Robinson and Becker were on the *American Historical Review*'s editorial board by 1914 and all of them attracted a new generation of graduate students, such as Arthur Schlesinger, who became the leaders of the profession.[32]

Even those American historians who found a great deal to celebrate in their nation's history were often critical of its political development. In 1931, James Truslow Adams, outside the university but very much part of mainstream American historiography, traced the development of the "American dream" which promised the "fullest development as man and woman, unhampered by the barriers which had been erected in older civilizations, unrepressed by social orders which had developed for the benefit of classes rather than for the simple human beings of any and every class." Repudiating the ascendancy of materialistic values, he argued that the "communal spiritual and intellectual life" of Americans "must be distinctly higher than elsewhere, where classes and groups" are separated. Adams had "little trust in the wise paternalism of politicians or the infinite wisdom of business leaders."[33] While Adams was challenging established authority in America, the teaching of history at Oxford and Cambridge still attempted to equip selfless, paternal, and wise leaders in every influential profession.

The juxtaposition of English and American historians, in spite of certain common traditions, is not entirely fair because both their systems of higher education and their forms of government differed so greatly. English higher education, even after the founding of civic universities that responded to local needs, continued to be part of a larger establishment that served both church and state. The London School of Economics and Political Science had a deliberately secular and occasionally radical curriculum, but it was staffed largely by Oxford and Cambridge graduates who attempted to train national leaders. Although its founders and teachers deliberately repudiated the curricula at Oxford and Cambridge by offering degree courses systematically organized around pragmatic social, economic, and political knowledge, only a few conspicuous teachers, such as Graham Wallas, leaned towards the left. Historians at Oxford and Cambridge, and their students teaching in the civic universities, usually avoided any exploration of conflicts between liberty and equality, private and public goods, economic groups, or social classes.

Higher education also included, although at a level that everyone recognized as lower, teaching colleges, seminaries, technical institutes, workingmen's colleges, and university extension programs where Oxford and Cambridge teachers were conspicuous. These alternatives to the traditional university degree may have provided their participants with greater economic and social opportunities than they would otherwise have had, but they were not avenues into the establishment itself, which was recruited essentially from the relatively few graduates of Oxford and Cambridge. Although national in their larger purposes, the English universities did not become truly public until after World War II. Only then did the government provide working-class students with the financial support that allowed them to matriculate and to complete university degrees. In the United States higher education was both private and public but the most prestigious universities, those closest to Oxford and Cambridge in the quality and social class of their students, were mostly private. Another factor in American higher education was that each institution competed with others at the same level for students and for funds. That competition led to greater experiment with curriculum and teaching to make the institution more attractive in an academic marketplace where students and parents often shopped before buying. Harvard, under Samuel Eliot, had introduced an elective system which allowed undergraduates a wide choice in the courses they attended; Columbia provided a broad "general education" program which had to be completed before a student could specialize; and Swarthmore provided seminars for its pupils. A final distinction was that English secondary students who attended the largely private grammar or "public" schools learned intellectual skills and a body of material in their final two years that was not available to most American students until their first two years at a university.

Diversity in American education reflected the experimental and evolving character of American public culture. The heterogeneity of the American system of government, bounded by a federal constitution but directed mainly by the variations of legislation and practices within states, is not comparable to the British government's reliance upon both homogeneous national and local institutions and the endurance of tradition. An essential expression of tradition was the dominant role of the Anglican Church in the establishment and governance of public institutions. Many private American universities have historic and continuing ties to various churches, but the national Church of England, part of the government of the state, controlled public higher education. After the 1850s when Dissenters were allowed to become students and, after the 1870s, hold fellowships, the Anglican Church still defined the religious life of the national universities.

The relationship between the traditional universities, the Anglican Church, and the state was based upon a shared high culture. Oxford and Cambridge became the guardians of that culture and attempted to preserve its values in the innovations they accepted. The honours degree course in history, designed to develop a sense of national pride and citizenship, was entirely consistent with those values. In the United States where both individualism and regional interests were often stronger than a sense of community or an allegiance to the concept of nation, patriotism and the obligations of citizenship were defined in a multiplicity of ways. Unlike their British colleagues, American historians wrote and taught history in American schools and universities with a wide divergence of views about individual and public roles in national life.

*

Perhaps the most critical difference between English historians on one hand and their American, German and French colleagues on the other, was that the English had not suffered the traumas of civil wars or revolutions since the seventeenth century. There was no national legacy of internal divisions and irreconcilable hatreds within England. The Great War, and especially its cost in promising young lives, could have weakened the historian's traditional testimonial to England's unique historical successes. Remarkably, the war, in which the victors lost so much, confirmed and even strengthened a nationalistic, Whiggish interpretation of both the past and the future.

Another of the many ironies of the war was that in a country where the universities were more closely tied to the production of the governing class than anywhere else, that class excluded university teachers when they attempted to influence events. During World War I, for the first time, university historians tried to demonstrate that their historical knowledge gave them a special competence in foreign affairs. Until then, historians-as-teachers, unlike doctors and lawyers, rarely claimed an ability to dispatch problems, immediate or long-term. Instead, they emphasized repeatedly that their teaching was general rather than specialized. They consistently identified themselves as teachers of a broadly humanistic liberal subject. When they came forward after 1914 as specialists in German, or Balkan, or other continental histories, their new position was not as credible as it might have been. It is especially ironic that the impulse which moved them to offer their services was not so much a claim to special knowledge as the patriotism which they had always taught as part of a liberal education.

When the Great War began, most university historians devoted their energies to anti-German propaganda. In Oxford, a new optional subject was added for examination on the "Development of the Theory and Practice of International War," an oblique recognition in the history curriculum that Britain was engaged in a massive, unprecedented war.[34] Although teaching for the Modern History school was largely unaffected by the war, within one month after hostilities began, Oxford history teachers published *Why We Are at War* to make clear the case for German guilt. The authors, Ernest Barker, H. W. C. Davis, C. R. L. Fletcher, Arthur Hassall, L. G. Wickham Legg, and Frank Morgan, relied on the German and British White Books to argue that Britain was fighting a just war to protect the independence of small states and the rectitude of law. In common with historians in other universities, the Oxford school blamed the war on those elements in German culture that had provided an idealization of *Staatsrecht* in opposition to England's historical emphasis on local institutions and liberty.[35] When the war was over, C. R. L. Fletcher and other Oxford tutors wrote *The Great War, 1914–1918: A Brief Sketch* (1920) to demonstrate the contrasts between Britain and

Germany in which Britain emerges not only as top nation, but as a model for the rest of the world.

The causes for Britain's entry into the Great War were clear to historians, but many ordinary Britons were confused about why they should go and fight. To explain the historical imperatives, the historians became missionaries who, in popular lectures, pamphlets, and articles in the press, contrasted Britain's moral, rational, and free evolution with Germany's immoral, irrational, and subservient development. J. Holland Rose, and twenty other Cambridge graduates, received more requests to speak than they could meet.[36] In London and all over the country, A. F. Pollard, whose field of research and writing was Tudor England, lectured repeatedly on "The War: its History and its Moral." Pollard attempted to provide accurate public lectures in University College, London, on "The War Week by Week," by using special information from the War Office.[37] In a letter to *The Times* on August 20, 1914, entitled "A Fight to the Finish," G. W. Prothero, a founder of history teaching at Cambridge, the first Professor of History at Edinburgh from 1895 to 1898 and then editor of the *Quarterly Review*, urged qualified speakers to tell the working classes "the truth" about Germany. "We have to cope," he wrote, "with an unscrupulous aristocracy, with an aggressive military caste, and with the principle that Might makes Right carried to an extreme that civilization cannot endure."[38] Prothero wrote manuals, pamphlets, essays in popular papers and journals, and handbooks for the Historical Section of the Foreign Office, which he headed, besides lecturing throughout the country. He also appealed successfully to the Oxford Delegacy for the Extension of Teaching to provide lecturers on the historical causes of the war. Unlike most of the other anti-German lecturers, Prothero actually had studied German history.

Among the first to respond to Prothero's call was the Rector of Exeter College, who lectured in Wales. Then, C. Grant Robertson, the history tutor at Magdalen College, Oxford, to Edward, Prince of Wales, from 1912 to 1914, came forward as a specialist who had studied the evolution of modern Germany, both in Germany and "from all the sources available," and wanted to put the results of his study at the public's disposal. But Robertson, a Fellow at All Souls since 1893, was a student and teacher of eighteenth- and early nineteenth-century English political and constitutional history. It was only the year after the Great War began that he wrote, together with J. A. R. Marriott, *The Evolution of Prussia.*[39] In 1914, he agreed with Prothero, that the extension lectures should be a "serious and dispassionate discussion" not only of the causes of the war, but of the "tremendous issues at stake for Western civilization, of the principles and ideals for which the British State stands. . . ." A defeat in the war would not only affect Britain, but the "rights of small and weak nationalities" and "the cause of free and democratic government throughout Europe and the whole world." The format Robertson recommended was for lectures followed by questions and a full and open discussion. "Is it wrong," he asked, "to wish to cooperate in this plain duty of citizenship?"[40] It was consistent with Robertson's most cherished values that when he gave the Creighton lecture in 1928, his topic was "History and Citizenship." History was understood as a warrant for national obligations by almost every academic historian in Britain. For the great majority of historians who wrote from 1914 to 1939, the origins of the war and later the consequences of the peace at Versailles were questions to be answered more by moral standards than by dispassionate and objective inquiry.[41]

Very few historians questioned the absolute condemnation of Germany. H. H. Henson and James Bryce were two Oxford graduates worlds apart politically in that Bryce was a lifelong liberal and Henson a lifelong conservative. But both men admired certain German traditions. Neither taught history at Oxford and neither identified himself with the Oxford School's traditions of interpretation. Bryce and Henson each accepted the culpability of German leaders while finding mitigating circumstances for the acceptance of that leadership by the German people. Unlike the authors of _Why We Are at War_, Bryce and Henson were unwilling to see English history as a progressive development of individual and institutional freedoms in contrast to Germany's regressive and authoritarian constraints. Bryce, a historian with a cosmopolitan rather than anglocentric view of history, had great difficulty persuading himself that anti-German propaganda was his national duty. In a pamphlet written in the early fall of 1914, Bryce argued that German intellectuals supported the war only because of false information given them by their government. The "Gelehrten have not committed themselves to the monstrous doctrines" of Bernhard. "They could not, they dare not, even if they believed them, which I trust they don't."[42] When Prothero was troubled by what he read as Bryce's pro-German pamphlet, Bryce reminded him that the British knew from their own sad experience how patriotism "leads men to acquiesce in or defend aggression and injustice." The doctrine "'Our Country right or wrong' . . . seems to have now so seized the German soul that even good men will close their eyes to facts." Bryce was suggesting that a similarly uncritical patriotism in England could have effects that were equally disastrous. As early as 1914, Bryce was already thinking about an international organization to prevent future wars and in 1917, he sent the government a memorandum proposing the organization that was to become the League of Nations.[43]

Henson, who had turned down the Regius Chair of Ecclesiastical History at Oxford in 1908, published his *Wartime Sermons* for Macmillan in September 1915. Although it was not Henson's intention, the preface turned out to be a good example of the dangers of historical prophecy. He described the German people as "completely hoodwinked as to the causes and conduct of the war into which their Government has plunged them. The hope of the future lies, less in the conquest, than in the disillusionment, of the enemy. Once the network of the lying and sophistry, in which the Germans have been living for some years past, has been broken through, and the fearful moral isolation into which they have been brought has been realized, there will be an immense revolution in the public mind of Germany, and securities for European peace will have been created far superior to any which could be gained by victorious entry of the Allies into Berlin."[44]

In addition to extended teaching and writing, some historians were coopted into government work during World War I. H. A. L. Fisher became the President of the Board of Education, not because he was a historian but because Lloyd George thought of him as an "educationalist." Those few who did develop highly specialized contemporary fields of study were unable to get their competence taken seriously by government policy makers. R. W. Seton-Watson, a pupil of H. A. L. Fisher's at New College with first class honours in Modern History in 1902, became a specialist on Austria-Hungary and the Balkans as a result of nine years of systematic study, travel, and personal friendship with the leading political figures in those countries. There was no other Englishman with Seton-Watson's detailed knowledge of these countries. In August 1914, he offered his services, without pay, to the Foreign Office for the duration of the war. His offer was refused. Instead, Seton-Watson joined other historians to make up an informal group who met frequently to discuss the problems of the war. This group included Z. N. Brooke, W. Allison Phillips, J. Holland Rose, Harold Temperley, G. M. Trevelyan, Basil Williams, and A. E. Zimmern. Seton-Watson and Trevelyan made an unofficial visit to the Balkans in January 1915. In a memorandum written in February they urged the unification of the Balkan peoples. The memo-

randum was rejected.[45] Prothero became head of the Foreign Office's
Historical Section in 1915. But when he tried to bring his knowledge
of German history to the Versailles peace negotiations, he was told,
brusquely, that he was not needed.[46] Arnold Toynbee, at the Foreign Office's Political Intelligence Department from 1917, tried to persuade Lloyd
George to forestall a threatened conflict between Islamic peoples and the
British Empire. But Toynbee was ignored even though he was the specialist in political intelligence about the Islamic world.[47]

*

One of the most devastating effects of World War I was the reduc-
tion of every kind of experience, public and personal, to confusing fragments. After the war was over, university historians tried to resume a
prewar standard of normalcy. They responded to the fear of incoherence
by looking steadfastly backwards to more coherent times. The Great War
was not a turning point in the life of the university. What was taught and
what was learned continued as if the war had never occurred. In Oxford,
except for the expanded number of women students and the introduction of new, short diploma courses for those whose education had been
interrupted or started late, the Honours School of History, in common
with the other Schools, remained largely unchanged. Every college was
decimated by the death and maiming of undergraduates and their young
teachers, as the long memorial lists on their walls so sadly testify. But the
curriculum did not attempt to address the issues raised by the war years.
A Special Subject on International Relations, introduced in 1919 as one
among ten optional papers, was replaced in the Examination Statutes of
1922 by "the Concert of Europe, 1813–1822." Neither paper dealt with
recent history, let alone with the war or the League of Nations then being
created. Even where changes were introduced, there was a considerable
discrepancy between requirements on paper and what was actually studied. It was not until the Trinity Term of 1915 that the paper on the continuous political history of England was extended to the year 1885 and in
1924 questions were set for the first time on the history of America.[48] But
A. J. P. Taylor, who came to Oriel College as an undergraduate in 1924
and received a first class in his history honours examinations, was
"hardly aware that any history existed beyond" the middle of the nineteenth century.[49] The year after Taylor took his examinations in 1928, a
third alternative was added to the prescribed English History periods in
Group B, which allowed a student to offer the years 1760 to 1901.[50]

After the war Cambridge historians were pleased to find that history
was attracting the greatest number of students in the " Humane studies"

and that among the 300 candidates for the two parts of the Historical Tripos in 1921, there was an "increasing tendency" to concentrate on "modern periods, although the influence of Maitland is very great in the study of Constitutional History."[51] That tendency was fostered energetically by H. W. V. Temperley, who became Reader in Modern History in 1919, the editor of a six-volume account of the Paris Peace Conference the following year, and the author of a study of the League of Nations, two years after it was established in 1922. As part of their effort to provide a wider perspective for history students, the History Board tried from 1919 to invite foreign historians to lecture at the University, but it was not until 1923 that they were able to find funding.[52] Temperley summarized the general feelings of most of his colleagues when, as the first Professor of Modern History in 1930, he said that it "is the duty of a University like Cambridge to see that its outlook goes beyond need or race or content. . . . It might be said that the history school here will only be of national importance when it has something of an international outlook."[53] But the syllabus during and succeeding the war did not contain any historical topics after the middle of the nineteenth century. The only subjects to include the recent past or to touch on contemporary issues were Political Science B and Political Economy.[54]

In his autobiography, the historian Goronwy Rees remembered the force of E. M. Forster's plea to "only connect." Those "two words, so seductive in their simplicity, so misleading in their ambiguity, had more influence in shaping the emotional attitudes of the English governing class between the two world wars than any other single phrase in the English language."[55] The university emerged from the war as an intellectually and ethically solvent agency of "connection." Students returned in great numbers, but many had been shattered in the war. Oxford and Cambridge mourned the 20 percent of their men who would never come back. Once again, but with more restorative meaning, the university became a place of retreat and *Bildung*.

Among all the degree courses, the study of history appeared most capable of explaining apparently inexplicable events. Criteria of belief and conduct formulated by historians two generations earlier were passed on to a new generation. After the war, teachers and their students largely agreed that, with the sufficient understanding history taught, an enduring public good could be realized. The university graduates from the late 1870s through the 1920s thought of themselves as generations without precedent. Chosen for a unique destiny, they would overcome the errors of the past. Throughout Europe the tragic realities of the Great

War provoked disillusionment with the prewar world and those who had led it into disaster. But in Britain, an inspirational faith in national history was reaffirmed and those who fought and survived, as well as those who died, became heroic emblems of dedication to a cause greater than themselves.

Chapter 3

National History Established

At the beginning of the twentieth century, an Oxford man defined the distinct traits of Cambridge scholarship as "meticulous accuracy," a "dislike of large views," and a "rather supercilious attitude towards other culture than its own."[1] This description may better fit Oxford, but it is far too simple for either university. Although the historians of the two ancient universities were unanimous in purpose, at least three major differences separated them. First, the college tutors controlled and organized teaching at Oxford, while intercollegiate faculties presided at Cambridge. In the early 1850s, the Executive Commissioners created universitywide Boards of Studies at Cambridge which defined the contents and structure of particular disciplines independently of the colleges or their special interests. At Oxford, however, the colleges remained supreme and the college tutors settled all issues about their disciplines among themselves. Historians at Cambridge also taught within their colleges, but they simultaneously participated in a universitywide faculty, which planned comprehensive lectures and appointed the teachers to carry them out. Congenial institutional and pedagogical relations between professors and college teachers reflected compromises about teaching, curriculum, and syllabuses that were considered and then settled in the Boards of Studies.[2] These contrasts in organization affected the other two distinctions: debate about history was conspicuously absent in Oxford and chronic in Cambridge; and finally, while both Oxford and Cambridge history teachers concentrated their lives on their colleges and the students within them, Cambridge teachers thought of themselves additionally as belonging to an international community of historians. Some Oxford professors, excluded from teaching, maintained connections with continental and American historians, but those contacts rarely affected the study and teaching of history in their university. Cambridge professors and tutors alike were involved actively in the greater historical profession, and they brought these wider concerns to the Historical Honours Tripos.

At Oxford, the study of Modern History began modestly in 1853 as part of the School of Law and Modern History. Created by the Examination Statutes of 1850 as one of three new degree-granting courses, the new School could be taken only after completing the classical School of Litterae Humaniores or "Greats." After 1866, when students were permitted to specialize solely in Law and Modern History, the School concentrated increasingly on country gentlemen and notoriously idle pass men who needed "a valuable educating influence upon their minds."[3] Between 1853 and 1872, 797 men graduated in Law and Modern History under that influence. Then, in 1871, the uneasy alliance between the two disciplines was dissolved and separate Schools emerged. Modern History, established as an independent honours degree by 1872, began with the fall of Rome and concluded in the eighteenth century. Within a generation, the Honours School of Modern History had transcended its limited origins and, by the turn of the century, held great expectations for its students, who, in numbers, rapidly overtook and then surpassed those in Greats. In response to the growth in opportunities for public careers in the civil and imperial services, local government, teaching, and business in the late nineteenth and early twentieth centuries, the School prepared graduates to fill these positions at home and abroad.[4] The School retained an emphasis upon character and conduct as its essential purpose, but it promised additionally that a study of the past would explain "modern civilization" and "political and wider ethical problems."[5]

At Cambridge it was regarded as necessary but not sufficient to dedicate the university to the training of individual character in preparation for the exercise of national obligations. Beyond that, an appeal to the highest intellectual standards was essential for the success of any academic venture. At least from the second half of the nineteenth century, Cambridge teachers and students rose above the remarkably flat terrain around them by elevating their university to "the glacial altitudes of the higher brow."[6] Systematic attempts to found a school of history, first by Henry Richard Luard in 1866 and then by A. W. Ward in 1872, envisioned a subject that would teach independent thinking based upon its intrinsic intellectual worth.

When Cambridge began to think of a degree in history, Luard, a Fellow of Trinity and Registrary of the University, was one of the examiners in the Moral Sciences Tripos. But he rejected the example of Moral Philosophy, because it meant "little more than the mastery of certain stated books."[7] Instead, Luard proposed a Historical Tripos which would rely essentially upon "original documents." And he expected the examiners "to prevent the possibility of cram, by themselves avoiding the stock historical compendiums that may be found for the period." The advantages of such a course of study would be that a student would "be led to think and to examine for himself—to weigh authorities against each other, to sift contemporaneous statements." Finally, he urged that the curriculum concentrate on limited periods which could be studied and understood in some depth.[8] Luard's expectations for the potential of history at Cambridge were not widely shared. Henry Sidgwick, a consistent Cambridge reformer, complained to James Bryce in 1867 that few Cambridge dons had "any strong opinions on the subject of history."[9] In March 1867, instead of the creation of a new history tripos without Moral Philosophy, as Luard had suggested, the Moral Sciences Tripos ejected both history and law while retaining moral, political, and mental philosophy, logic, and political economy. Beginning in 1870, the two discarded subjects were combined awkwardly and unsatisfactorily in a Law and History Tripos.

A. W. Ward quickly saw that the new Tripos would not serve the interests of either law or history. Ward had been a Fellow of Peterhouse from 1861 until his marriage in 1879, and from 1871 to 1872, when Professor of History and Literature at Owens College, Manchester, he was also a nonresident member of the Board of Legal and Historical Studies at Cambridge and an examiner in law and history. Ward submitted *Suggestions towards the Establishment of a History Tripos* (1872) to the Senate, where a Syndicate was considering how best to separate law and history.[10] He began a wide-ranging discussion of examinations and curriculum, teaching, and university encouragement for students reading history by urging Cambridge to go beyond its traditional concern with character formation and also teach historical methods, procedures, and critical standards. Perfunctory study of obvious works of reference, required for Honours candidates in Modern History within the Law and History Tripos, did not, Ward pointed out, test "*Historical power.*" What students of history should learn was "knowledge which has been accumulated by reading, which has been sifted by criticism, . . . illustrated by comparison, and . . . invested with a literary form of composition." Historical judgment required Historical Geography, Politics, Economics, Constitutional Law, and a more advanced knowledge of English History than outlines could provide.[11] An admirer of German historical teaching for its rigor and depth, Ward advocated the German prerequisite of general history for secondary students taking their university entrance exams. With such preparation, university study could concentrate on both specialized and broad history in lectures and in seminars, where technical as well as literary skills would be taught by "practice and precept."[12] Ward deliberately rejected the Oxford requirement of set books and authorities for a more individualistic, supervised guidance which would conclude in a student's production of an original piece of research.

The Syndicate which created the Cambridge Historical Tripos in 1873 passed over both Luard's and Ward's recommendations. Instead, J. R. Seeley, Regius Professor of Modern History, persuaded the syndicate to accept his interpretation of history as a discipline that must teach applicable political lessons.[13] J. P. Whitney, one of the first students to take the Historical Tripos, was troubled by the conflict between Ward's "Thought without Fact" and Seeley's "Fact without Thought." But, in retrospect, when Whitney had himself become a don at King's, he recognized that Seeley's political emphasis was compatible with research while Ward's historical interpretation, best represented by G. W. Prothero, admitted that the study of the past benefited present politics.[14] The new Cambridge degree enshrined Seeley's view of history as past politics, but it also included ancient history and those theoretical subjects "which find their illustration in history" such as political economy, international and constitutional law, and "The Principles of Political Philosophy and General Jurisprudence."[15] In these singularly Cambridge subjects, a wider, more contemporary syllabus was introduced and continued.

*

Oxford and Cambridge historians alike saw their curricula, whether focusing on early English constitutional history or upon more recent events and other nations, as meant essentially to empower a generous conception of intelligent citizenship rather than to further a professional discipline. But as the newer liberal arts subjects grew at both ancient universities, what was actually taught tended to become increasingly narrow rather than broader.[16] A more specialized curriculum, with a concentrated focus, meant that national values could be taught more methodically. While Cambridge and Oxford historians tended to agree that the lessons carried by history fitted students for an adult life devoted to higher goods, they differed about how best to teach those lessons. Cambridge historians concentrated on mastering the tools and contents of history as a professional organization of knowledge, clearly separate from other disciplines. At Oxford, it was assumed instead that history shared the same body of knowledge as the other liberal arts disciplines except that its subject was the past.

The Honours School of History at Oxford created and maintained a remarkably cohesive discipline with substantial effect throughout Britain and the entire English-speaking world. Even those graduates such as W. J. Ashley, Ramsay Muir, A. F. Pollard, James Tait, and T. F. Tout, who criticized the way in which examinations dominated history teaching at Oxford, agreed with the Oxford School that history documented national character, free institutions, and moral obligations. Tout and Tait created the important Manchester School of administrative history, where George Unwin, A. G. Little, H. W. C. Davis, and F. M. Powicke taught. Ashley introduced the first Commerce degree in Britain at Birmingham, whose history faculty included C. R. Beazley. Muir went to Liverpool to shape its History School and to win a charter for the University in 1903. At the University of London, Pollard launched a School of History and the Institute of Historical Research as a center for post-graduate study. R. S. Rait, a proselytizing history graduate and the first Professor of Scottish History and Literature at Glasgow, became vice-chancellor and principal of that university. Oxford graduates also dominated the Historical Association, the Archives, the Public Record Office, the *Dictionary of National Biography*, the *English Historical Review*, the Victoria County Histories, and the Historical Manuscript Commission. Within the public schools, where the future governing elite were first exposed to the assumptions which affected their adult decisions, some of the most effective teachers, such as John O'Regan of Marlborough and C. K. Marten, Provost of Eton, were proselytizing believers from the Oxford School. From the time of Thomas Arnold, as Gary McCulloch demonstrates, public school boys learned the ethos of leadership and public service through the classics.[17] By the late 1870s, first in the university, and then in the public schools where university graduates taught, history reenforced and deepened those earlier lessons.

The Cambridge historians' interest in a variety of historical interpretations allowed both dons and professors to approach their subject from either specialized or general perspectives. In part the Cambridge syllabus reflected a compromise between the earliest Historical Tripos and the changing interests of the professors and tutors. From 1885, required subjects for examination were intended to test thoroughly a knowledge of "original authorities and of the Constitutional History of England." But, while Oxford concentrated almost entirely on England's national traditions and institutions, Cambridge attempted to supplement national history with foreign topics and thematic approaches. Seeley's legacy of history as scientific lessons in national politics remained within the curriculum even after Lord Acton introduced his cosmopolitan reading of cultural and intellectual history through a new select subject in the History of Thought, Literature, and Art, that was adopted together with a provision that the Modern General European History Paper could include American history. The Special Subject was extended to 1848 and questions on the History of Political Theory were included in the Paper on Analytic and Deductive Politics. But the "point of view" of the Tripos, as Prothero told history undergraduates in 1893, was "throughout historical rather than theoretical." [18] This curriculum ran until 1909 when J. B. Bury, Regius Professor since 1902, attempted to limit history to a rigorously scientific discovery and classification of facts. But Bury was overridden by the Board which adopted instead the principle of "a correct general knowledge . . . rather than minute acquaintance with details" and instructed the Examiners to give credit for excellence in "style and method." [19] When G. M. Trevelyan succeeded to the Regius Chair in 1927, his inaugural address repeated his 1903 repudiation of Bury's emphasis upon the scientific nature of history. For the rest of his long working life, Trevelyan continued to demonstrate that history was an art.

*

Although there were marked differences between the Oxford and Cambridge history curricula, constitutional history, defined by William Stubbs as the "unravelling" of the "string which forms the clue to the history of human progress" was the heart of both schools.[20] The study of the economic past, which might have challenged politics as a subject even more applicable to contemporary needs, was unable to assert itself. At both universities, the late nineteenth-century discovery of economic history fell awkwardly between the old political economy, the emerging discipline of economics, and the concentration of history on politics. T. W. Hutchinson argued in 1978 that when the integration of economic analysis, theory, and history characteristic of classical political economy was shattered, economic history was left "largely to rebels and outsiders."

Recently, D. C. Coleman amended Hutchinson's view to find that from the 1880s to 1910 "the first major steps were taken by which economic history came to be recognized as a subject suitable for study in British universities."[21] In Oxford Arnold Toynbee's lectures for the academic year 1881–82, his only intercollegiate course, were reconstituted and published posthumously as *Lectures on the Industrial Revolution* in 1884 and W. J. Ashley's first volume of his *Introduction to English Economic History and Theory* appeared the following year. Coleman notices that J. E. Thorold Rogers, in his second tenure as Drummond Professor of Political Economy at Oxford from 1888 to his death in 1890 and as a lecturer at Worcester College, taught the subject for the Modern History School's paper on political economy, while completing his eight-volume *History of Agriculture and Prices* (1866–1900). But as Alon Kadish observes, Thorold Rogers had no followers because his "abrasive personality and his dislike of the rising college teaching system isolated him from the mainstream of historical and economic studies at Oxford." As a professor, Rogers was effectively cut off from teaching and his work as a tutor within the History School was very limited because his college, Worcester, did not belong to the intercollegiate system of lectures.[22] Toynbee, when alive and after his death, made a greater impression upon a university graduate's sense of obligations to society than upon the Modern History School. Ashley, Toynbee's student who obtained a First Class Honours in Modern History in 1881 and was eventually elected to a Fellowship at Lincoln College in 1885 and then appointed at Corpus Christi College, was the first product of the History School to concentrate on economic history, even though he was required to teach the large variety of subjects required by the School.

Ashley believed that a study of economic history would enable the leaders trained at Oxford and other universities to deal with the modern industrial world more skillfully. In 1886, two years after Stubbs had resigned the Regius Professorship and while Ashley was still an insecure tutor at Lincoln College, a group of some twenty graduates, teachers, and undergraduates formed the Oxford Economic Society. With Ashley as Secretary, they met twice a term to discuss original research in economic history and contemporary economic issues, and once a term to discuss economic theory. A decade later, Ashley went to Toronto as Professor of Political Economy and Constitutional History and then to Harvard to become the first Professor of Economic History in the English-speaking community. In the new world he concentrated increasingly on contemporary history. He returned to England in 1901 as the first professor in the School of Commerce which he founded at the University of Birmingham, and developed an introductory course on the "modern development and the present structure of industry and trade in the British Empire" to educate "the officers of the industrial and commercial army" who would "ultimately guide the business activity of the Empire." [23] Ashley became a tariff reformer and a polemicist for Tory policies in his first decade at Birmingham, but he always counted Stubbs, together with Arnold Toynbee and Gustav Schmoller, as the three greatest influences upon him. [24]

Ashley admired Stubbs most for emphasizing the central importance of institutions. He regretted, however, that even the three "majestic volumes" of Stubbs's *Constitutional History* were reduced, in preparation for the honours examinations, to a "comparatively simple set of facts and formulae." It was one of the persisting ironies of the History School that Stubbs, who wanted a contextual study of original documents, should have provided the *Constitutional History* (1874–78) and the *Select Charters* (1870) from which extracts could be selected entirely out of context as examination questions. Stubbs would have preferred to have the student read a single book and explore its "mechanism and materials" or use the special subject as a first step in the study of original sources that would lead to a further and deeper investigation. [25] Although it was not his intention, Stubbs's major bequest to the History School at Oxford was a set of "authorities" which encouraged opinions to conform to his for more than two generations.

An "authority" in history was understood either as a compilation of primary sources, usually interpreted by the compiler, or as a secondary synthesis, generally of constitutional and political narrative. In Oxford, primary sources, including even a few current ones such as J. S. Mill's *Political Economy*, were recommended to students. When history teachers wrote their own authoritative texts for students, as they did in the *Essays Introductory to the Study of Constitutional History* (1886; 1901) they relied almost wholly on Stubbs for their "foundation." [26] In the new historical teaching "the interleaved and underlined 'Charters' found a congenial place by the side of the interleaved and underlined 'Ethics.'" [27] But while Aristotle's *Ethics* was closely read from cover to cover, Stubbs's *Charters* was assigned in bits and pieces. From the date of publication, the *Charters* became, as Charles Oman recalled, a "sort of bible, from which a candidate was expected to identify any paragraph without its context being given." A. L. Smith's lectures on the "Steps to Stubbs" taught Oman which parts were of primary importance since the book itself "gave no help towards the sifting out of the crucial passages from the mass of strange Latin and Norman-French in which they were imbedded. And the mere translation was hard enough, for the book lacked a sufficient explanatory vocabulary of technical terms." [28]

Ashley's own experience as a college tutor in the late 1880s made him recognize, with some sympathy, why predigested "authorities" were so central a part of Oxford history teaching. The force of collegiate competition for distinction in the honours examination drove tutors to push their own students towards first- and second-class honours degrees. In preparing for examinations, it was a "great convenience" to have a "neatly rounded body of doctrine, respectable for the authorities it relied upon." When Ashley reviewed D. J. Medley's *A Student's Manual of Constitutional History* (1894), intended to provide a foundation for someone "driven by the thirst for a 'first,' " he described it as a "Dictionary of Institutions—each taken separately and traced chronologically" without any understanding of the relation between institutions and "contemporary conditions." [29] As part of his *Manual*, Medley presented the opposing arguments of recent historians, an innovation in the Oxford tradition which Ashley welcomed. But it was not enough. What historians needed, he thought, beyond a compilation of authorities was a "Reconstruction" in writing and teaching, based upon evidence taken from social and economic, as well as political life. [30] To achieve that Ashley had to leave Oxford. There was no chair of economic history in Oxford until 1931 although L. L. Price, far more interested in theory than in history, was appointed Oxford's first Lecturer in Economic History in 1907 and the first Reader from 1919 to 1921. [31]

Simultaneously in Cambridge William Cunningham, whose *Growth of English Industry and Commerce* appeared in 1882, was appointed a university lecturer in history in 1884 and lectured on economic history, which became a separate paper for the Historical Tripos in 1885. Alfred Marshall, as the Professor of Political Economy, had emphasized an analytical and theoretical discipline of economics which remained part of the Moral Sciences Tripos until his creation of a new Economics Tripos in 1902. Cunningham had received first class honours in the Moral Sciences in 1873, but his explicitly historical view conflicted with Marshall's emphasis. By the end of the century, Cunningham's views were no longer taken seriously at Cambridge, even though in common with Seeley he concentrated on the development of the English state and saw economic change as a product of national policy. [32] It was not until 1908 that the teaching of economic history was undertaken by a man trained in history, J. H. Clapham, who made the division between economic history and economic theory complete. [33] In 1909, English economic history became a compulsory special period in Part I of the Historical Tripos, rather than an optional special subject, and political economy was reduced to an optional paper in Part II.[34] But there was no Cambridge chair in economic history until 1929 and when it was created, Clapham was appointed to fill it.

*

Although constitutional history continued its dominance over both universities' curricula, critics of the Oxford School, such as Ashley, wanted the constitution to be taught as the *meaning* of related institutions which grow and decay. But the critics, including Ashley, readily accepted Stubbs's premise that the whole of history had meaning—a purposeful movement "to some goal."[35] Frederick Pollock, a lawyer with historical interests, was alone among them in charging that any study of institutions as entities that are "growing" concludes inevitably in a "speculative optimism which tries to see that whatever is becoming or is continuously in a way to be, is best."[36] When applied to the English constitution, this evolutionary optimism confounded an understanding of its actual historical development.

A generation after Pollock's criticism of the Oxford School's Whiggish history, J. R. Tanner, at St. John's College, Cambridge, continued Stubbs's treatment of the constitution as "a long historical evolution" which permitted the student to acquire "some knowledge of the way in which history was made." But Tanner also based the subject on charters and original documents in order to teach both methodology and historical skepticism. Moreover, the "perception of the difficulty of arriving at certainty, as between different views," he told his Cambridge colleagues in 1909, corrected the "natural tendency of young men to rest content with dogmatic certainty." Constitutional studies were attractive because they were still unsettled by scholarly controversy and that compelled students "to think for themselves and learn the difficulty of finding the truth."[37] But in spite of viewing constitutional history as a cautionary study in skepticism, Tanner found in 1928, after nearly forty years of teaching for the Tripos, that the "ultimate victory of the Whig view" of "the Revolution is a striking instance of the value of public debate in Parliament. As soon as the other views were subjected to criticism, their inadequacy stood clearly revealed and it became evident that common sense was destined to triumph over sentiment."[38]

On the historical stage the constitution was the constant backdrop for throwing into relief the growth of legal and social institutions based upon liberty and consent. Ironically, the relatively unchanging curriculum in the Oxford History School remained at odds with the evolutionary reading of history which it sanctified for so many decades. In the twelve-volume *Political History of England* by prewar Oxford historians, the volume on 1760 to 1801, published in 1924, and the one on 1801 to 1848, published in 1906, find that the heroes were Burke and Pitt rather than Price and Fox; that the Reform Act of 1832 was a remarkably peaceful "completion of the earlier English revolution provoked by the Stuarts"; and that the Poor Law Amendment Act of 1834 "permanently" improved "the condition of England."[39] In Cambridge, too, the history of England was read largely through progressive eyes. When H. M. Gwatkin was Dixie Professor of Ecclesiastical History and a teacher of English history at Cambridge, he asked his pupils to write essays illustrating "the progress of England in seventy years by comparing the statesmanship of Pitt with that of Walpole," and tracing "from 1757 to 1832 the chief steps by which the House of Commons became directly responsible to the nation."[40] A constant subject for debate in the three prewar revisions of the Cambridge Historical Tripos in 1885, 1896, and 1909 was whether or not English History should be the standard against which all other nations were measured. When E. A. Benians urged the Board in 1909 to study American and Colonial history as independent fields rather than as parts of English Constitutional History, he failed to persuade them, as F. W. Maitland had failed in 1896.

One explanation for the flourishing state of English political and constitutional history at Oxford and Cambridge is that it appealed to a wide spectrum of both liberal and conservative historians as a conclusive demonstration of the values that they all thought most important. Constitutional debate changed after the Reform Acts of 1867 and 1888 intensified fears in the existing political parties about the coming of democracy. But Whig, liberal, and conservative historians could still believe that the constitution had demonstrated a historical ability to accommodate competing social groups, political conflict, and institutional variety.[41] An idealized view of a stable constitution continued to provide the context for understanding Britain's past and its future. Nearly all university historians writing from the 1870s, no matter what their political sympathies, agreed that continuity was more valuable than change; that survival indicated genuine merit; that even the most intractable problems could be dispatched effectively by an educated mind; that self-sacrifice was rewarded; and that the English constitution and national character worked together to promote material and moral melioration.

By 1900, liberals expected reform to occur within constitutional traditions, while conservatives "saw themselves as the party of the constitution and as the guardian of those classes whose interests and influences were embodied in it."[42] The study of history brought together a liberal, elitist code of civic responsibility and a conservative reliance upon a managed constitution in a broader agreement about the intrinsic worth of traditional conventions, existing social structure, and national institutions. For Tories who saw themselves as the national party of patriotism, the inherited constitution was to be protected from unwise changes advocated especially at the century's end by Irish nationalists, radicals, and every species of socialist.[43] Liberals, welcoming extensions of individual opportunities within a stable society, read the constitution as an historical record of political, economic, and social progress. Charles Oman, who considered himself the rare political conservative in liberal Oxford from the early 1880s into the twentieth century, learned from Hereford George, a history tutor of New College, to concentrate on "the constitutional side of English history." Until then Oman had read history either as illustrating archaeology or else as "romance—the story of the heroes and villains of all the ages. To consider it as a process of constitutional evolution was rather a new idea to me."[44] That idea, which he shared with liberals such as A. L. Smith, remained with him for the rest of his life as a tutor, historical writer, and finally as Chichele Professor of Modern History.

More constant than political ideologies and preferences, the constitution was especially useful for teaching purposes because it could be approached by those skills which historians defined as special to the study of history. Research historians and teachers proceeded by cumulative and comparative analysis, a method which differentiated them from the other new Arts disciplines such as literature or anthropology. Explicit historical tools, such as paleography and diplomatic, were introduced to establish the authenticity of the political and constitutional documents upon which the teachers relied.[45] But these techniques did not encourage a larger discussion among historians about what constituted verifiable evidence in history.

*

Until the early 1870s history and law was a combined course in both universities. When history became an independent subject for examination, it inherited a methodological legacy from law that submitted historical materials to quasi-judicial tests of evidence. Historical facts were placed within a set of precedents and consequences that together constituted a discernible tradition. Historians proceeded in their research, writing, and teaching by a juridical method of challenge, testing, and comparison which validated particular historical testimony as part of a greater lineage. The legalistic methods accepted by historians had two effects on the study of history. First, they led to the convention that a judicious, trained observer, studying the evidence, must come to the truth. Second, since truth was ascertainable, a self-denying devotion to its pursuit followed, intellectually and morally. An attempt to attain truth, because of its intrinsic value, was a higher, more serious end than personal ambition, wealth, power, or even happiness. And there was a moral seductiveness about the austerity required by a search for truth. That kind of personal test appealed to the lingering asceticism which gave the secular university its anomalous, cloistered character.

A school of history, the first Chichele Professor of Modern History in Oxford told his inaugural audience in 1862, must form "the judicial mind for the purpose of dealing in the best manner with all the problems of thought and practical life."[46] Juridical metaphors were used commonly by the Oxford school to connect the study of history with the training of sound judgment. Stubbs saw history as an "endless series of courts of appeals" ever "ready to reopen closed cases." Study of the past accustomed "us to trace events to their causes, . . . origins to their roots, . . . narratives to their authorities, institutions to their germ; it trains us to the pursuit of origins." The student of history should learn to balance evidence in order to challenge testimony, and to piece together the truth. Since many historical questions could not be answered decisively, we "learn to suspend as well as to use our own judgment for decision. . . ." But Stubbs's own search for origins revealed Divine Providence which guaranteed moral development. The effect of suspended judgment for Stubbs was not the lawyer's skepticism but the historian's toleration, hope, patience, and capacity to endure contradiction.[47]

More practically, the study of law taught that legislation was embedded in historical circumstances. But some Oxford-trained historians, especially those who advocated a more professional discipline, such as J. H. Round, T. F. Tout, and A. F. Pollard, protested that the lawyer's reverential approach to the past violated a proper understanding of history as the study of development. Law, like classics, was a static subject and the lawyers, like the classicists, treated the texts they studied with veneration. "The lawyer's vision is bounded by his 'books,'" Round wrote, but "the historian goes behind his books and studies the facts for himself." Even more seriously, law distinguished between private and public morality, a distinction which the historians found fundamentally immoral.[48]

The lawyer with the greatest effect on the study of history was F. W.

Maitland. He was also a legal historian and a creator of the Historical Tripos in Cambridge, but his influence was delayed until a generation after his death in 1906. That remarkable tabling of Maitland was due in part to the division of disciplines which began in the 1870s: Maitland was appointed as a teacher of law and not of history. But a more formidable obstacle was his originality of mind. The lessons which Maitland drew from law and from history were so different from those of his contemporaries that few were then prepared to follow him.[49] Concentrating on legal concepts, Maitland was interested in the ways in which those concepts revealed the underlying society. He accumulated testimonies from a wide variety of sources and rejected constitutional history, as Stubbs had studied it, because it was a "history of just the showy side of the constitution, the great disputes and catastrophes." What the historian must produce was not "merely the facts but the atmosphere of the past, an atmosphere charged with law."[50] Maitland understood the study of law as a means of deliverance "from superstitions" because it demonstrated that people "have free hands." Stubbs and most of his colleagues trusted some form of divine intervention in history, but Maitland trusted the evidence of human will which he believed could be found in the structure and contents of the law. The "only direct utility of legal history" lay "in its lesson that each generation has an enormous power in shaping its own law."[51]

Repudiating the Whig tradition's emphasis on the progressive achievement of personal and public freedom, Maitland, a political liberal, stressed the crucial role of central government in creating the English nation. Paradoxically, Maitland saw that legal entities very often had consequences that were neither intended nor anticipated. Trial by jury had a royal origin; the writ of habeas corpus was a royal prerogative; Parliament had started as an extension of royal power; and representation was originally resented as a burden. Instead of finding evidence that the government of boroughs became increasingly democratic, Maitland found that the "general rule is that it strongly becomes more aristocratic."[52] Maitland hailed Henry II's centralization of royal justice and he attributed the changes in English law from 1154 to 1273 not to legislation but to the incessant decisions of a powerful central court.[53] Among his contemporaries, the only ones interested in an analysis of the interior parts of government were the isolated conservative, J. H. Round; the Professor of Jurisprudence at Oxford from 1883, Sir Frederick Pollock; and, in the early twentieth century, T. F. Tout.[54] Maitland warned historians not to draw general conclusions from particular instances of uncorroborated or limited evidence. The historian's temptation to predict the past could be avoided by adopting the meticulous methods of the lawyer who searched for and verified his evidence piece by piece. To Maitland, law was a window into a social, economic, and political time.[55]

The model of law, as perceived by either Stubbs or Maitland, was meant to provide history with a modus operandi. But British history was less about method and more about the revelation of morality. At Oxford the source for ethical studies was classics and at Cambridge, classics and the moral sciences. These traditional subjects illustrated desirable qualities of character, philosophical ideals, standards of behavior, and analytical thinking. While classics (known as "Greats") continued into the twentieth century to be thought of as teaching "extreme mental acuteness" by developing the "power of 'seeing round' a question," and fastening "at once upon main issues," the course of study was criticized increasingly as too literary, ahistorical, and "unduly narrowed by traditional canons of style." H. W. C. Davis, when a tutor at Balliol, worried because his student V. H. Galbraith was "still very much in the Greats stage of thought." Davis wanted him to concentrate instead on "the discovery and verification of hard facts."[56]

The older universities had stressed classics as the core of liberal training in character and mathematics as the model for mental rigor. Mathematics exemplified logical reason, but it was based on abstract principles, not easily translated into practical policy. Classics, as taught in the Litterae Humaniores School at Oxford or the Moral Sciences Tripos at Cambridge, demonstrated ideal precepts of conduct and thought. Classical scholars quarrelled about whether Homeric or classical Greece was the more Victorian, but they all found in the ancient Greeks moral and spiritual qualities and institutions which, they believed, still informed Victorian life.[57] By the end of the nineteenth century, university teaching of the classics was directed essentially towards forming an ethos of personal responsibility for collective good. Benjamin Jowett, first a classics tutor and then Regius Professor of Greek and Master of Balliol College, provided the central text and its meaning by translating and interpreting Plato as a moral and political reformer seeking the good life for the whole community.[58] Jowett's ethically idealist reading was carried further in A. E. Zimmern's *The Greek Commonwealth* (1911), which idealized the good civic society and those who worked to achieve it, and in Ernest Barker's studies of Greek political thought, which eulogized philosopher-statesmen.[59] The study of classics provided persuasive arguments and examples for a rational and controlled state dominated by virtuous men. The aspirations of the noblest Greeks and the intellectual and moral qualities they represented, provided incentive for undergraduates to enter a career of public service. A clearly marked road ran from Jowett's Balliol directly to the Indian Civil Service and to the highest offices of English government. But good intentions, no matter how truly good, are rarely a sufficient guarantee of effective action.

There is no question about the crucial part of classics in forming tenacious attitudes about contemporary ethics and politics. The most telling complaint against classics, however, was that it was set in a dead and alien world that was irretrievably finished. First William Stubbs, and increasingly other historians, such as J. R. Seeley at Cambridge, revealed the historical incompatibilities between ancient and modern times in politics, economics, society, class structure, religion, and ethics.[60] Stubbs elevated modern history over classics because a study of the ancient world was the study of "death" and of the "skeleton" while modern history studied "life" and the "living body."[61] For him, the "living, working, thinking, growing world of today" was especially suited to call forth the "powers" of a "practical generation."[62] Classical scholars, whether concentrating upon Homer or fourth-century Athens, found spiritual qualities and institutions among the ancient Greeks which they believed also influenced their own lives. But historians like James Bryce protested that arguments drawn from classical experience were inapplicable to modern life because each country had its own national character. In 1867, during the debate on the Second Reform Act, Bryce attempted to show that the experience of the small Greek republics could not be used to discredit "a (moderate) Democratic reform in this country," because "ancient institutions were not analogous to modern ones."[63]

*

In the last decades of the nineteenth century, history challenged classics and became an honours degree course, first at Oxford in 1872, at Cambridge a year later, and at London and the civic universities by the twentieth century. From the turn of the century until the 1920s at Oxford and from the 1920s at Cambridge, history attracted the greatest number of students in the arts disciplines. There were at least two reasons for history's growth in popularity at the expense of other disciplines. First, and especially at Oxford, history was taught as classics had been by a reliance upon set texts. For those who had already studied the given books of the classics in public school or even in the university, the transition to another discipline that studied texts in a similar way was an easy one. More importantly, the study of history confirmed the conventional Victorian sense of the historic structure of free English institutions, developed from precedent to precedent. Stubbs's view of the evolving organic constitution, taught at both universities, emphasized the continuity of institutions. In the late nineteenth century the dominant history teachers in Cambridge, all active advocates of imperial federation, assimilated the empire and its administration into the historical continuum of English historical institutions. No other discipline offered an explanation that so readily became a justification of the origins and existing nature of both English society and its extension into the empire.

After history was introduced as a degree course, some colleges pushed their students into reading for a fourth class honours in history, originally considered easier than a pass degree. Within a decade, however, the new subject was drawing "large numbers of really able men, especially among those who look forward to a political career." Within one more decade, students were taking an honours degree in history because it implied ability and the "acquisition of a solid body of definite knowledge."[64] An understanding of historical facts, as T. F. Tout maintained in 1920, kept the politician from "gross error" and taught the "plain citizen" to "discharge his civic duty."[65] Unlike classics, the study of modern history was explicitly didactic in its provision of object lessons drawn from successful, consistently evolving experience. National history offered a more precise blueprint for public policies according to Britain's constitutional development of individual liberties, balanced and diffused powers, political morality, and most important, of opportunities. The Greeks, for all their virtues, perished. The English and their institutions not only survived, they prospered.

If the new administrators first learned the lessons of character in the organization of public school life and a classical curriculum, that lesson was strengthened by the study of great Englishmen and their effect upon events. Even more critically, history revealed how institutions restricted and guided what might otherwise have been aberrations of character or well-meaning but impulsive and insufficiently rational conduct. As models for Victorian and Edwardian local government, education, social reform, and colonial policy, the classics were too static. Greek and Roman texts were studied essentially for their demonstration of the immutable qualities in human nature and society. But history provided a dynamic explanation of the conditions under which institutions and traditions developed. In Victorian England, the most obvious and compelling verities were not perceived as fixed but rather as complex elements in process. Modern history, in contrast to the alien setting of the classics, was immediate.

In the unreformed university, classics was meant to stamp mental and moral qualities upon leisured gentlemen. The eighteenth-century impression of a gentleman was closely linked to the idealization of aristocratic service. Governance was the obligation of those whose leisure gave them the breadth of view and independence to rise above mere self-interest. Although the aristocracy promoted an altruistic ideal of public benevolence that was frequently self-serving, that ideal survived because it was often true, especially when accompanied by evangelical imperatives. But, by the first half of the nineteenth century, men such as Robert Peel and W. E. Gladstone moved upwards from the middle classes to assume broad public obligations. The formal study of history, in the late nineteenth and early twentieth centuries, tried to make aristocratic values less aristocratic by providing social, ethical, intellectual, and civil lessons that could be appropriated by dedicated people, independently of their social background.

At Oxford, ancient history belonged to the honours degree in Classics. But at Cambridge, the Historical Tripos began with the study of the Greek and Roman world. When that Tripos was reformed in 1909, the value of ancient history was questioned. R. G. Glover, a historian of Rome, argued that the classical period was pedagogically preferable to the medieval because the former contained ideas which were "particularly free, and . . . powerfully expressed," as they were "again in the modern period."[66] What he meant was that the ancients were more like early twentieth-century English people than the unchanging and religiously preoccupied people of the Middle Ages. J. B. Bury, Regius Professor of Modern History from 1902 and a classical scholar, agreed with Glover about the superior "educational value" of ancient history, but not because it was an exemplary model for English life. Instead, Bury joined Maitland in a minority view that the past could only be understood as a genuinely foreign time whose study overcame the "very unfortunate . . . boom in English History" which gave a "deplorable note of insularity" to the Tripos.[67]

Unlike classics, modern history was intended to be more than a source of ethical and psychological inspiration. Classics demonstrated that the important qualities in human nature and society were the timeless, unchanging truths that had moved the ancients. History, which also tried to reveal truth, concentrated instead upon the dynamic, evolutionary process by teaching object lessons drawn from continuous, developing, and successful traditions. History was taught first by Oxford and Cambridge tutors and finally by public school teachers, preparing their students for the Oxford and Cambridge examinations, as part of ordinary and familiar experience. The student's own past was recorded vividly in local records, agricultural patterns, and architectural remains still evident in every village and town. But history teaching, at every level, came to mean the grand vista of national political history.

Even if classics had dealt with a world genuinely analogous to late nineteenth- and twentieth-century England, history could only have grown at the expense of classics. The differences between history and classics may have been more important to the historians than the similarities, especially since they were attempting to establish an independent degree course, but in retrospect the common assumptions and purposes shared by both disciplines are striking. The historians, like the classicists, studied societies with fixed and laudable values. Greek and Roman society resembled British society in an essential permanence of structure and form. Even though historians believed in the progress of their society, they expected changes to occur in accordance with well-delineated traditions established as the constitution had been perfected. Historical authorities were consulted in the same way as classical authors had been—to reveal the processes by which stable development and enduring qualities of character and mind had developed.

*

The new historians, until the twentieth century, were mostly young men fresh from their own degrees in Litterae Humaniores at Oxford or in Classics and the Moral Sciences at Cambridge.[68] Almost all of them had received their training in these courses and it was natural for them to rely upon the pedagogical strategies used by their teachers. The result was that history teaching established itself in dependence upon a catechetical reading of a limited number of set texts that were considered authoritative. A tradition of learning as textual commentary and disputation, prevalent within the university since the twelfth century, was adopted by the early history teachers because it was the only model of teaching they knew. Their inexperience in history was confounded by the fact that when they first began teaching in the 1850s and 1860s, there were no generally accepted books and no agreement about the methods most appropriate for training in the new subject. Asked to teach unfamiliar subjects, tutors tended to adopt published works that were readily available as required books. What was initially an expedient resort to familiar practice and convenient texts became, as a result of repeated use and self-interest, an entrenched institutional tradition. The tutor's initial ignorance of the field, the diffuseness of the new degree in history, its lack of system, and precious little time, compelled them to concentrate on what they knew best. As their teaching was extended to greater numbers of students and longer hours of supervision, there was no time left to explore and analyze new, unorganized materials.

It was not until the early twentieth century that some of the traditional authorities were undermined. F. M. Powicke, who received a first-class honours in modern history and went on to become Regius Professor at Oxford in 1929, watched with approval. But then to his dismay he saw that one finality was "swept aside" only "to put another in its place." When the belief in authorities was finally shattered in the 1930s, he argued, the confidence of the historian in his ability to train national leaders disappeared too.[69] Powicke looked back from the middle of World War II to the late nineteenth and early twentieth centuries with a distinct sense of loss. A search for moral certainties in history became increasingly untenable after the Nazi horrors, even in so hermetically sealed a community as Oxford. But in his inaugural address fifteen years earlier, Powicke had still discerned among his colleagues a "constructive idealism" which gave new meaning to history by searching for those forces which confirm "fair dealing and mutual understanding." In his inaugural address in 1929, Powicke had welcomed equity as "the criterion" of historical judgments which would be "fundamental and ethical indeed—wanton cruelty and destructiveness . . . will be condemned." He was not assuming that morality was inherent in historical development, but was rather, in the tradition of his predecessors in the Regius chair, urging historians to make discriminations based upon a clear knowledge of right and wrong.[70]

Oxford tutors inherited the School's "deposit of faith" and then handed it on to the undergraduates they taught.[71] But Cambridge tutors like H. M. Gwatkin, who as an undergraduate had taken four Triposes at Cambridge (excluding history which was not yet offered) and received first class honours in each, challenged any unquestioning acceptance of historical literature. From 1868 to 1874, he was a Fellow, and from 1874 to 1891, a Theological Fellow at St. John's. Then until his death in 1916 he was Dixie Professor of Ecclesiastical History. As a tutor in both theology and English history for more than a generation and as the Dixie Professor for another fifteen years, Gwatkin sided with "truth against tradition." He told his students that "authority" was "nothing more than the presumption of evidence." No matter "whose was the authority, he had the habit of going to the evidence himself and he taught his pupils to do the same." [72] But at Cambridge, as at Oxford, the study of received authorities persisted as the core of honours examinations in history.

*

Within the Cambridge understanding of history as a school for statesman, Seeley's much advertised teaching of history as practical politics prevailed. When Lord Acton became the new Regius Professor of History in 1896, he disagreed with Seeley's interpretative scheme, but quickly disclaimed any intention of reorganizing the Tripos. Instead, Acton's refusal to chair the History Board inaugurated a tenure marked consistently by the absence of forceful leadership that might have created a school of history at Cambridge that could compete with the Oxford school. Had Acton been more committed to shaping a Tripos that reflected his own interests, he would have found a powerful ally in F. W. Maitland, who criticized the contents of the new program as still "too English, much too unhistorical, and much too miscellaneous." Concessions were made to Acton and those who wanted more diversified, less Anglocentric studies, but the Tripos remained a monument to the memory of Seeley. [73] It is ironic that Maitland who, among Cambridge historians of his time, was to have the most enduring influence on the study of history, deferred to the History Board because he was not himself a teacher of history. But privately and in his writing, Maitland was contemptuous of what remained at the heart of Seeley's views: a Whig interpretation of history and the attempt to make history or politics "scientific." [74]

Seeley's protracted legacy was gradually diminished in the two politics papers, renamed "Political Science A" and "Political Science B" in the Tripos reforms of 1909. "A" was a comparative survey of political institutions leavened by the history of political theory and the definition of political terms, while "B" emphasized the history of political thought. Both papers rejected Seeley's insistence upon an exclusively empirical study of political institutions. Instead, they expected students to think critically and abstractly about controversial problems not readily resolved. [75] More than any other requirement in the curriculum, the Political Science papers brought reflective and analytical issues into the study of history. There was no comparative subject in Oxford until the acceptance of the new degree course of Philosophy, Politics, and Economics (known as "PPE" or "Modern Greats") in 1920.

*

Although the interests of the Cambridge history faculty were broader than those of the Oxford historians, their Tripos also concentrated on the distant past. When Alfred Marshall, who was to shape and dominate the Cambridge School of Economics for 25 years, lobbied for a new Tripos in Economics and Political Science in 1902, he was opposed by some of the history faculty on the grounds that economics was already adequately covered in the Historical Tripos. Marshall's response was that the unity of the western world required a constant study of recent and contemporary history, entirely lacking in the Historical Tripos.[76] But from its inception, the Cambridge Tripos required "theoretical subjects" and emphasized the importance of research. After 1899, when there were two parts to the Tripos, an introductory Part I and a more "specialized" Part II, the history teachers argued only about where the theoretical and methodological subjects would be studied most profitably.

As late as the mid 1920s A. J. P. Taylor found indifference to historical method and meaning at Oxford. Taylor had no fond memories of his university. Even taking into account a view colored by personal distaste, his complaints echo those of many contemporaries and predecessors. Looking back after sixty years and an extraordinary career as a historian, Taylor recalled: "I did not receive the slightest tincture of training in historical research. I never asked the question—How do historians know?"[77] The Oxford School accepted tacitly that they knew what history taught them. An enduring Whiggish reading of a supposedly objective historical record affirmed that welcome change occurred continuously in England, although that change might be slow, sometimes imperceptible and, rarely, retrograde.[78]

It is significant that prewar historians trained at Oxford who deviated from this tradition, such as R. H. Tawney, J. L. and Barbara Hammond, and L. B. Namier, were not asked to remain. Inclusion and exclusion were not governed by objective "truth," but rather by whether or not historians accepted the views of Britain's past that prevailed at Oxford. J. L. Hammond, who had taken second class honours in Litterae Humaniores in 1895, earned his living largely as a liberal journalist and civil servant. But in 1903, two years after marrying his Oxford contemporary, Barbara Bradby, he wrote *Charles James Fox*. Then beginning in 1911, together with his wife, he published a series of social histories, attacking a progressive interpretation of the social and economic condition of ordinary people and emphasizing suffering and injustice instead. It took a generation until the work of the Hammonds was recognized at their university. Both of them were awarded a D. Litt. by Oxford in 1933 and four years later, J. L. Hammond was made an Honorary Fellow of St. John's, his old college.[79] Namier, who always felt close ties with Balliol in particular, and Oxford generally, was turned down for a Fellowship at All Souls in 1911 and was never offered a position at any other Oxford college.[80] The history that Namier wrote upset orthodox Oxford interpretations.

In sharp contrast to the anglocentric introversion of the Oxford School's immersion in England's distant past, the Cambridge historical school, from its foundation, took an international, often contemporary, bent. Although the center of Cambridge history teaching was the English constitution, that concentration did not preclude wider historical interests. Prothero, the manager of the Historical Tripos in Cambridge until the end of the nineteenth century, had been a member of von Sybel's seminar at the University of Bonn during 1873 and he remained a student of German history. His subsequent career after 1899, when he became editor of *The Quarterly Review*, was devoted to enhancing England's international reputation. In 1901 he launched a successful campaign to found a British Academy that would fulfil the Cambridge ideal of broad scholarship. Together with Seeley and many other Cambridge historians, Prothero wanted more "professional" studies displayed in prestigious national institutions that would present England as an intellectual as well as a political power.

A. W. Ward was another Cambridge historian who benefited from foreign schooling. Ward's early education was in Saxony and for the rest of his long and productive life, he kept in close touch with continental and American developments in modern history. At Cambridge, where he directed research students, he was an energetic advocate of a more cosmopolitan training for all students, including undergraduates.[81]

Seeley never studied abroad, but he publicized German historiography as well as German politics. His successor, Acton, was often accused of being more European than British. F. W. Maitland knew German scholarship well enough to model himself on Savigny and to undertake a translation of the German legal scholar's *Geschichte des römischen Rechts*. G. G. Coulton taught for a while at a private school in Heidelberg before returning to Cambridge. H. W. V. Temperley, who received first class honours in history in Parts I and II in 1900 and 1901, became interested in studying central Europe and the Balkans in 1905.[82] By 1910 he had translated the Hungarian historian Henry Marczali and within the next decade published *Frederic the Great and Kaiser Joseph* (1915) and *History of Serbia* (1917). John Fair has argued that post–World War I British policy towards the Balkans was considerably influenced by "Temperley's authoritative advice."[83] It could not have been lost on Cambridge undergraduates that Temperley, the new Reader in Modern History from 1919, was also the man who edited the six-volume *History of the Peace Conference of Paris* (1920) and wrote *The Second Year of the League: A Study of the Second Assembly of the League of Nations* (1922). Z. N. Brooke, influenced by late nineteenth- and early twentieth-century German historical literature, also had a sense of an international community of historians. At Cambridge he taught and lectured in history for 34 years, as well as serving as an editor of the *Cambridge Medieval History* and as Professor of Medieval History, following C. W. Previté-Orton.[84] At Oxford there was continuous resistance, largely by the tutors, to any national organization for the study of history, but Cambridge teachers believed that membership in such groups gave them a deeper and more accurate understanding of current scholarship and teaching.

Oxford students studied mostly English constitutional history as an "ideal bridge between speculation and government," which equipped them "for the direction of affairs."[85] History was an exhaustive encyclopedia for leaders and a basic primer for the new democracy. As A. L. Smith put it, history taught the "continuity of national life . . . the great inheritance transmitted from past generations to be handed down by us unimpaired to the generations to come."[86] Cambridge historians attempted to extend and diversify their curriculum so that it would serve a wider conception of intelligent citizenship. Alfred Marshall urged in 1896 that the Historical Tripos, like any other university course, must be sufficiently wide ranging to foster those "faculties" which had to develop fully in later life.[87] A decade later, G. G. Coulton surveyed the embryonic stage of medieval social history and concluded that "what the world most needs is a series of honest and plainspoken pleas from different points of view." At the same time, however, he confessed that he was "convinced that the world has made real inward progress, and that the historian's most definite duty is to measure this progress as accurately as we can."[88] Thirty-six years later, after he had created a school of medieval studies at Cambridge and was witnessing a second world war, Coulton confessed that common sense "suggested to me from the first that *homo sapiens* is, on the whole, an improving animal, and History has seemed to confirm this probability more and more. There is no horror even in 1942, so I believe, which cannot be outmatched from the records of distant centuries. Man is not a fallen angel; the facts concordant with sane faith tell us that we have struggled painfully upwards, and exhort us to struggle still. In that faith I have continued half a century, practically unchanged."[89] Coulton might well have been speaking for the teaching and study of history as they were established and perpetuated at both Oxford and Cambridge. The differences between the two universities in their organization of the new subject were less important than their shared belief in moral progress, guided by men trained in history.

Chapter 4

The Professors Interpret History

As an expanding society responded to the emerging claims of professionalization and specialization, these problematic and changing concepts were shaped by debates within disciplines as well as by questions
of social status and economic position. New opportunities for genuine
university careers in the second half of the nineteenth century left both
professors and college tutors scrambling to achieve a satisfying role.
There was considerable uncertainty about the degree and kinds of specialization that should be taught within disciplines, and the positions
taken by various tutors and professors were not always clearly drawn.
Although nearly all English professors of history advocated a "professional" education for historians, they derived the concept more from
their understanding of the purposes of the university than from considered reflection about the organization and maintenance of a historical
discipline. To these professors, professionalism meant that an honours
degree in history would best train men for public office, where they
might, for example, decide about Indian agriculture or British policy
towards Germany, by requiring them to study Indian or German languages, history, politics, society, economics, and culture. At the same
time, to protect the autonomy of history as a university discipline, they
argued that an honours degree in history should equip students with
those specialized, or professional, techniques of original research that on
the continent and in the United States distinguished the academically
trained historian from the amateur writer outside the university. But in
spite of the professorial ideal of powerful, self-sufficient disciplines, the

strongest traditions within both Oxford and Cambridge valued the production of nonprofessional graduates. The true amateur, White's Professor of Moral Philosophy reminded Oxford after World War I, was a serious student attempting to "converse with wisdom" rather than to advance knowledge of a subject.[1] The universities attempted to remain a common enterprise of senior and junior students pursuing a learning that was higher precisely because it was not directed towards an application. Although disagreement developed about the meaning of a liberal education, the agreement which persisted was that specialized training, because it was essentially narrow, interfered with the development of the broadest, and therefore most widely applicable, intellectual and ethical competence.[2]

What the professors of history said and did owed as much to university traditions, essentially beyond their control, as to the evolving subject of history. The well-intentioned but indecisive university reforms of the 1850s had described professors as both scholars and teachers, but chairs were awarded by electors who were not necessarily at the university and who often acted from political and religious motives. At Cambridge, as we have seen, professors were able to take a leading part in appointing teachers and in setting curricula, reading lists, and examinations. Seeley, Acton, and Bury endorsed a more "professional" education for historians, with the support of influential tutors such as Prothero in the late nineteenth century and Clapham, Previté-Orton, Brooke, and Temperley in the early twentieth. But at Oxford, professors had no part in selecting or managing history tutors, who were appointed independently by their colleges. And when compulsory attendance at professorial lectures was abolished in 1861, professors were cut off from any real influence. They gave public lectures but students reading for an honours degree rarely attended them; history professors at Oxford had less influence upon undergraduates than novice tutors.

From the 1860s the Regius and Chichele Professors of Modern History at Oxford found themselves isolated. To justify some role commensurate with their nominal status, these professors argued that the study of history, guided by the professoriate, must be based upon the original and comparative investigation of documents. The college tutors, who prevailed over the professors, argued instead that the teaching of standards of thought and behavior was more imperative than the development of any subject. Oxford tutors adamantly resisted the creation of a professional discipline of history, in the sense proposed by the professors, as both inappropriate to a liberal arts education and as an infringement on the autonomy of the college. Of course, none of the professors ever questioned the value of a liberal education; rather, they argued that teaching undergraduates to do historical research effectively strengthened traditional values. If there had been a program of postgraduate studies in history, an option reluctantly and half-heartedly adopted after World War I, the professors might have been able to fulfil their ambitions. But from the beginnings of the History School, the examinations, and the teaching and curriculum upon which they were based, were granite monuments both to the tutors' successful perpetuation of the generalist traditions of college teaching and to the professors' impotence.

Professors at both universities were expected to do original and pioneering work of some distinction and so might have provided the aggressive leadership in research that was characteristic of both American and German historians. But the maintenance of handed-down canons of collegiate teaching at both traditional universities allowed few conceptual or methodological experiments. The professors failed to establish "schools" in which students and younger dons could become innovative disciples.[3] In contrast, Tout and Pollard, Oxford graduates at Manchester and London, used their professorships to create institutional guarantees that allowed them to control the subject, the students, and the curriculum. Further, each of them founded distinct schools of history by making their own particular research and writing the basis for organizing and closely supervising teaching and examinations.[4]

Oxford professors of history were separated from their Cambridge colleagues by at least six divergent practices. First, the Oxford School was restricted largely to the study of English political history, while the Cambridge historians ranged widely over British, European, and Imperial topics that included intellectual, cultural, and economic analyses. Second, while Oxford expected honours students to flourish in the real world because they had been steeped in the development of England's ancient institutions, Seeley launched the teaching of *Realpolitik* in the contemporary world. A third attribute unique to the Cambridge Tripos was that when the history faculty imposed its authority over the colleges, the professors were expected to guide the Boards of Studies.[5] Fourth, the Cambridge professors' concern with scholarship in Cambridge was shared by the most influential of the tutors.

A fifth distinction was that the Oxford professor usually lectured to empty halls, while his colleagues in Cambridge, beginning with Seeley, attracted "very large" classes "recruited from many other departments" as well as his own.[6] By statute, every Cambridge professor and reader was to devote himself either to research and the advancement of knowledge in his department, or he could confine himself to the preparation of important public lectures. From the 1880s, the professors of history, although required to meet only one of the statutory requirements, managed to fulfil both. Unlike the lonely Oxford professors, Seeley actively taught undergraduates reading for the Honours Tripos. Not only did he supervise the recently revived teaching of modern languages, but he gave public lectures for one hour every week during two terms, on history, historical method, and authorities, and he held a conversation class one hour a week during three terms. The average attendance at Seeley's lectures was about 90 men and 60 women. And the prolific Dixie Professor of Ecclesiastical History, Mandell Creighton, gave three undergraduate lectures a week during term, which were attended by 40 to 60 students. In addition he was expected to be "at all times at the disposal of the students of his subjects" whom he advised and directed.[7]

Finally, unlike the Oxford professors of history who held common opinions about both the inner sense of history and the way in which it should be studied, each of the Cambridge professors developed his own heterogeneous and influential writings. The effect of that writing upon the Cambridge study of history was very different from the tradition which characterized the Oxford School for more than three generations. Those differences emerge in an analysis of the views of Stubbs and Seeley.

The tenures of both men coincided with the unsettling of traditional views about God and the world. As mid-Victorian graduates entered public life, they confronted a society in which the future appeared to be ominously different from the past. While social, economic, and political issues became less volatile and there was evidence of growing stability, a rise in the standard of living, diffused prosperity, expanding commerce, and scientific innovation, these trends were accompanied by problems of urban blight, public ill-health, and the increasing numbers of an underclass of unemployed. Fears about an uncontrollable future were partially allayed by an idealistic reading of these unprecedented tendencies as inherently improving and as amenable to planned improvement. To demonstrate the validity of their idealism, intellectuals called upon the long perspective of history to document the constancy that was not immediately apparent in the short view. Evangelical religion and the High Church leanings of the Oxford movement gave way to a greater diversity of religious and intellectual interests, nourished by a confidence in historical evolution. In 1859, *Essays and Reviews* (by Frederick Temple and others) questioned religious dogmatism and Charles Darwin's *Origin of*

Species challenged biblical accounts of creation. The credibility of both books rested on an appeal to the historical sense of their readers. Within the next three decades, English historians adopted both German higher criticism and evolutionary science to make pluralistic and diverse religious interpretations compatible with a secular eschatology deducible from history. Perhaps even more importantly, a consensus developed among historians that incorporated these new evolutionary interpretations into the narrative of English history to reconcile informed, responsible free will with beneficent, divine purpose.

Their interpretation of national history also allowed Victorian intellectuals to face the increasing proliferation of social and economic interests with equanimity, if not always with optimism. Changing patterns of family life, work, and recreation could be viewed as modern adaptations consistent with standards going back to the free, village life that was thought to be especially English. By the 1870s, national history, encouraging national harmony, was taught as part of the new provision of education for ordinary people from elementary levels to adult extension movements. And, as independent cultural traditions arose within regions and classes, the potentially divisive effect of local loyalties was superseded by the new understanding of English history developed in the universities and taught everywhere. Seeley and Stubbs, while approaching these centrifugal forces differently, made them seem less intractable by placing them within cohesive narratives in which individual free will supplemented and sustained divine will.

Both professors were members of the Church of England, with opposing ideas about the purposes of religion in general and of the Church in particular. But both found moral values, ethical behavior, and God's beneficent purposes revealed in English history. Both discounted God's retributive characteristics and emphasized instead His reliance upon individual conscience and human institutions that together served the same essentially meliorist, divine ends. Relying upon free individuals who chose generally to behave responsibly, God sustained the life of the community while simultaneously promoting effective individual activity. Stubbs and Seeley, despite their other differences, understood English political and religious institutions as God's check upon possible individual aberrations or moral lapses. Although recognizing that those institutions were imperfect, they believed them to be the means by which higher values were maintained and transmitted. In the late nineteenth century, both men accommodated shifting intellectual, religious, economic, and political forces and a precarious social balance, by presenting their national history as a demonstration of a benevolent providential dispensation. The achievement of public good was not considered a necessary product of the historical process. On the contrary, professors and teachers in both Oxford and Cambridge treated history as a succession of lessons on the origins of private and public obligations. At both universities—paradoxically so at Oxford where tutors resisted the professors' attempted intrusion into their pastoral influence over students—the professors' interpretation of the central meaning of history was accepted. There is no reliable way to measure what students actually learned in the history honours degree courses, but there is considerable evidence in examination questions, lecture notes, and personal and published writings, of a growing unanimity among tutors and professors about what was important in history. What the professors affirmed and the tutors accepted, was that England, more than any other country, had gained a merited stability, marked by expanding liberties and opportunities in every sphere of public and private life, a rising standard of living, and a widespread deference to moral and spiritual values. That agreement began in the 1860s and persisted through World War II.

Inaugural addresses in Cambridge set the tone for a new tenure and were then supplemented by published lectures, articles, and books intended to develop the specialized fields in which the professors actually worked. Oxford professors, segregated from ordinary teaching, used their inauguration to make an impression, for only in an inaugural lecture were they likely to have so wide, attentive, influential, and captive an audience. Hardly insensitive to the occasion, each of the incoming Oxford professors of history said very deliberately what he thought history was, what the professor's obligations and opportunities were, and what the History Honours School ought to teach. These addresses, while consistent with the professor's published works and private papers, were also "political" and, like all political activity in any arena, were undertaken to serve certain interests. History, as a living pageant, displaying the complex writing of moral law, became the professor's central subject in the Oxford Honours School in history. Interpretations of that law rested on a faith in the individual's capacity to triumph over evil.

*

The Oxford history professor's moralistic mission began in 1841 with the appointment of Thomas Arnold as Regius Professor of Modern History.[8] For his inaugural address, Arnold chose a theme that echoed not only in every subsequent inaugural until the 1930s, but in the tutorial lectures attended by undergraduates reading for the honours degree. The essential character of modern history, Arnold maintained, was "that it treats of national life still in existence" and the character of that life revealed essential moral truths.[9] Following Arnold, Goldwin Smith was appointed in 1858, the first holder of the chair who claimed to be a historian. Smith's credentials for such a claim were dubious. Sidney Lee's article on Smith for the *Dictionary of National Biography* describes him more accurately as a "controversialist."[10] However, in 1861 Smith published his five *Lectures on Modern History, Delivered in Oxford, 1859–61.* Six years later, he published a eulogy on the characters of John Pym, Oliver Cromwell, and William Pitt in *Three English Statesmen,* his only historical work during a professorship devoted largely to liberal journalism and university reform.[11]

Goldwin Smith's inaugural lecture launched his tenure by describing the noble historical ends initiated by individuals deliberately moving history forward. Within the continuity of historical processes, he unveiled the "law" of "effort," a "series of struggles to elevate the character of humanity in all its aspects" and applauded history as "the march of human progress." Although he was a Manchester liberal convinced that reform depended upon personal commitment, his lecture emphasized the progress of the "race" rather than of the individual. It was obvious to him that the increasing knowledge and wealth of the race, or the "Christian nations," improved the moral state of mankind rather than of particular men. Each of the three great elements in human progress, "moral, intellectual, and productive," was necessary and interdependent, he argued, but history proved that the moral was the most essential.[12] Smith was clear about the purposes of the new school of Law and Modern History that he headed: it was meant to teach the "rich to do their duty."[13]

*

While Smith was still Regius Professor, Montagu Burrows was appointed the first Chichele Professor of Modern History over ten other candidates, including William Stubbs, J. E. Thorold Rogers, E. A. Freeman, and J. A. Froude.[14] Burrows's earlier career and his appointment were both extraordinary. After a career in the navy, he came to Magdalen Hall as a married undergraduate in his mid-thirties. Although without the preparatory benefits of a public school education, he took a first class honours in Litterae Humaniores (1856) and another in Law and Modern History (1857). Then he became a popular history coach and wrote *Pass and Class* (1860), a best-selling guide for undergraduates. Burrows won the Chichele Chair because the electors approved of his opposition to both tractarianism and the "Higher Criticism." As he was to say later, his *Pass and Class* apparently more than "compensated" with the Chichele electors for his "absence of historical reputation." A few years after his appointment, his "inferiority" to the historians among the candidates he had defeated, "whose reputations were growing, was no doubt remarked upon by hostile critics." But "it was notorious that neither Stubbs nor Freeman, who successively became Regius Professors, could ever keep a class together, so they could not have personally helped forward the School; Froude had turned such wonderful somersaults in religious professions that he would at that time have done more harm than good. . . . I at least kept up an average attendance of 20 men during many years, and published books or articles in leading reviews every year." [15] His most distinguished student was James Bryce, in law. Burrows wrote on a variety of topics, including university reform and education for women, and he had a strong commitment to professional standards for the study of history. After his appointment he edited historical documents and wrote not only articles but fourteen books including *The Worthies of All Souls* (1874); *The Cinque Ports* (1888), which drew upon his knowledge of early naval history; and *The History of the Brocas Family of Beaurepaire and Roche Court* (1886), based upon an original study of the unpublished Gascon Rolls.

Burrows recognized that the professors would never be an effective part of the teaching body and resigned himself to reaching the university community through an annual public lecture. But he took great pride in the developing History School, which in one generation became the most flourishing school in the university, and he pressed for more specialized undergraduate classes, such as medieval orthography, to increase the employment possibilities of young graduates. He was careful to distinguish antiquarianism, "a reverence for naked, unadorned facts," from history "which searches for motives, comparisons, and consequences." [16] Whether Burrows did the School of History any good is a moot point. He does not seem to have done it any harm.

*

Although Burrows's recognition of the marginal role of the history professor at Oxford was proven right by the experience of Chichele and Regius Professors well into the second half of the twentieth century, the one conspicuous exception was William Stubbs, Smith's successor from 1866 to 1884, who shaped the History School for the next three generations. The first recognized scholar in the chair, he wanted to found a historical school in England and brought to the Historical School at Oxford three attributes essential to its success. First, unlike his predecessors, his scholarly reputation and future promise as a publishing historian were welcomed by other historians as a "confession that such a subject as history exists." During his seventeen years as professor, he published a major work every year except 1877 and 1881.[17] His prominence gave the new School credit throughout Britain and abroad, and it drew the most interested students to him. Second, he insisted that historians practice a disinterested neutrality that distanced the School from the political controversy characteristic of Goldwin Smith's tenure. Stubbs was chosen by the Derby-Disraeli government over Freeman and Froude because he was a "moderate Conservative" whose "teaching on religious questions would be thoroughly trustworthy" and whose "ability and knowledge would make the appointment unobjectionable."[18] The interpretation of history that Stubbs pursued was sufficiently "moderate" to satisfy the liberals, tories, and Anglicans who were his colleagues and students. And finally, his optimistic and gratifying narrative of organic constitutional growth became the center of Oxford's history curriculum. Around Stubbs's work, a consistent scheme of teaching and examining was organized and taught in Oxford, Cambridge and the new universities. In his *Select Charters* (1870), Stubbs gave college teachers a set of documentary "authorities" and in his *Constitutional History* (1874–78), he explained English history as a moral theodicy.

Solely by his own reputation as a scholar, Stubbs maintained the status of history within the university and the fame of Oxford as a "nursery of historic study among the Academies of Europe."[19] But he seriously underestimated his own influence within Oxford. He felt, wrongly, that he had failed to reach tutors or large numbers of students. In 1876 he complained publicly that he had "sometimes felt a little hurt that, after preparing and advertising a good course of lectures . . . I have had to deliver them to two or three listless men" because the most junior assistant tutor was offering a course on the same subject at the same time. Stubbs had no objection to college tutors preparing students for the honours examination, but he had hoped that the best of those students might come to him as well. After eight years as Regius Professor, Stubbs said that he was "quite willing that my character as a professor should stand or fall by my other work."[20] But his willing was hardly free. Privately, he wrote to his successor Freeman to warn him against the "tutorial bias" which, since 1874, had prevented him from getting any of the better men.[21]

Of all the Professors of Modern History, Stubbs had the least cause for bitterness or disappointment. A year before his death in 1901, when Bishop of Oxford, Stubbs generously acknowledged the role of his successors Freeman and Froude whose "successful pupils" expanded the History School "through the length and breadth of Britain."[22] But it was

Stubbs who trained most of the teachers, writers, and administrators responsible for original research, editing, and the comparative collections of documents. It was Stubbs's students who founded history schools all over Britain. These pupils, all Brackenbury Scholars, came to Stubbs by the accident of his responsibilities as Chaplain and Honorary Fellow at Balliol. They included Ashley, Tout, Round, Poole, Richard Lodge, and Charles Firth. Stubbs's unique achievement was to produce "scholars," not "statesmen."[23] But his influence upon the Oxford School went considerably beyond the production of future historians.

Stubbs gave the School an ordering, unifying principle of study in the systematic and organic narrative of constitutional history. Although he tried to be an objective and dispassionate historian, that narrative reflected his larger view of English life as consistent, optimistic, without troubling ironies or ambiguities, and above all, satisfying as a majestic panorama. Stubbs's interpretation was reassuring, but it was also limited. Acting, as he readily conceded, upon "clerical and conservative principles," he thought that he could write history without ecclesiastical or political bias.[24] Stubbs wanted to be judicious, fair-minded, and objective. But dedication to truth and justice was often mediated by his unexamined theological, psychological, ethical, and political commitments.

The grand historical scheme that Stubbs laid before Oxford was didactic and complacent because it was justified by his religious convictions. History was a theodicy in which moral forces always triumphed over the immoral. Stubbs's Christian conservatism avoided the problem of evil by minimizing human capacities for understanding. But some historical lessons were transparently clear to him: next to theology, the study of Modern History was the "most thoroughly religious training that the mind can receive."[25] It followed that the greatest reward for the student of history was the discovery that the "eternal wisdom . . . rules among the kingdoms of men as certainly as in the Kingdom of Christ."[26]

Stubbs was a true believer who concealed his biases, even from himself, behind the facade of a dispassionate historian translating original documents into magisterial prose. His rhetorical gifts often obscured his combination of High Church Anglicanism, Whig history, and civic responsibility.[27] In the Church of England, Stubbs saw the original model for the development and maintenance of English liberties and the institutional guarantor of the values he identified uniquely with England. The "unity of the Church in England was the pattern for the unity of the state."[28] History was a justification of "the workings of the Almighty Ruler of the world"; and the best historian, which Stubbs genuinely tried to be, bore witness by scrupulously marshalling evidence of the divine designer's "hand of justice and mercy . . . ever leading the world on to the better, but never forcing, and out of the evil of men's working bringing continually that which is good." [29]

Stubbs's psychological and ethical premises were derived from his understanding of original sin as mitigated by divine dispensation. With God's help, the moral person could transcend his own worst nature. That transcendence allowed him to act in history but he was not empowered to decide moral issues either as an individual or as a student of history. Only God judged. The role of the historian, far more modest, was to display God's moral canvas and the way in which He had drawn upon it. When students learned to see that canvas they would learn, above all, that success is "certain to the pure and true; success to falsehood and corruption, tyranny and aggression, is only the prelude to a greater and irremediable fall." [30] But his view of the historian as a teacher of morality, who was expected to act morally but was constrained from dispensing moral judgment, led him into difficulties. Stubbs admitted, at the end of his tenure, that he had "more dread of making enemies, than is at all consistent with a properly constituted moral courage." [31]

As titular head of the dominant history school in England, he remained publicly neutral within the university and without. Although only a few friends knew about them, Stubbs had strong feelings about contemporary issues and people, and especially about those who embarrassed the Church or hesitated about acknowledging the higher meaning of history. Stubbs was especially bitter about Froude, who was to reach the Regius Chair as an elderly man in 1892. Froude's youthful apostasy, including his attraction to the Oxford movement, made Stubbs suspect both his orthodoxy as an Anglican and his competence as a historian. Stubbs was equally dubious about Charles Kingsley, Froude's brother-in-law, for promoting a Christian Socialism that appeared heretical. Froude gave a lecture in Edinburgh that moved Stubbs to write privately:

> Now Froude instructs the Scottish youth,
> That Parsons do not care for truth.
> The Revd. Canon Kingsley cries,
> That History is a pack of lies.
> Whence come these judgments so malign?
> A single word explains the mystery,
> For Froude thinks Kingsley a Divine,
> And Kingsley goes to Froude for History.[32]

A practical result of the conflict between Stubbs's strong sense of right and wrong and his reluctance to judge so that he could act on that sense was that he never reviewed books and "abstained from controversy, religious, political, or historical."[33] The insistence that contemporary history, because it was controversial, had to be avoided was among his most permanent legacies to the History School. As Regius Professor, Stubbs never lectured beyond the early seventeenth century because he had "often questioned whether it was desirable to exercise the minds of young men, old enough to have political feelings, not old enough to exert a calm historical judgment, on periods of history teeming with the very same influences which are at work this moment."[34] When Stubbs died in 1901, F. W. Maitland speculated that he might have been "a very great judge."[35] But if Stubbs had sat on the bench, he would have had to struggle to reconcile his psychological preference for neutrality and his moralistic inclination to be a hanging judge.

Stubbs's values led him to a historical doctrine of personal obligation to Church and State. He urged that the teaching of history begin in elementary schools, so that it would "raise up a generation who will not only know how to vote, but will bring a judgment, prepared, trained, and in its own sphere exercised and developed, to help them in all the great affairs of life." History was a qualifying study for any level of public participation because it formed judicial habits, a knowledge of national institutions, and an intelligent perception of the ideas that lay behind those changes responsible for the present. The study of national history in the schools and universities would prepare the new voters, along with the old, to understand the relations of Church and State, of the legislative to the executive powers, of the Crown to parliament, of the several courts of justice, and of the estates of the realm to one another.[36]

He viewed the stock of accumulated information as secondary in importance to the habits necessary for moral citizenship. But to Stubbs, research in primary sources revealed a series of connections that completes what has been imperfectly understood, or a series of developments, or a delineation of characters, or "the rehabilitation and analysis of traditions."[37] In his *Constitutional History* (1874–78), Stubbs integrated the Church, parliamentary government, local communities, political liberties, progressive order, circumstances, and institutions to reveal a vital, unitary organism. But when Stubbs warned that "all generalizations, however sound in logic," are false, that "there is no room for sweeping denunciations, or trenchant criticisms in the dealings of a world where falsehoods and veracities are separated by so very thin a barrier; . . . that such bywords as reaction and progress are but the political slang which each side uses to express their aversions and propensions," he was not calling either for historical skepticism or suspended judgment but rather for an acceptance of contradictions.[38]

Some Oxford historians believed that the understanding of contradictions depended upon a study of the present as well as of the past. In keeping with Stubbs's dictum, however, the present never intruded on the formal curriculum. Those who wanted history to address current problems tended, as A. L. Smith did, to lecture occasionally on subjects such as trade unions, that were only marginally useful for the examinations, or to organize present-minded historical lectures for the university extension movement, the Worker's Educational Association, and other extracurricular audiences outside the university. Another choice, rarely taken, for those who wanted history to be concerned with contemporary matters was to leave Oxford and traditional historical teaching as Stubbs's student Ashley did.[39] But within the academic study of history, long after the death of both Stubbs in 1901 and Ashley in 1927, Stubbs's views continued to govern the curriculum in history for thousands of undergraduates. In his *Select Charters* and his *Constitutional History*, Stubbs provided both an explanation of the secular and religious meaning of history and the authoritative materials upon which college teachers depended.

*

The founder of the Oxford School had an influence upon the study of history that was unmatched in any country where English was spoken. Trying to create a Historical Tripos that could compete with the Oxford School, Seeley was not as successful as Stubbs, but he nevertheless gave the study of history at Cambridge a distinctive and continuous structure. Appointed Regius Professor of Modern History in 1869 by Gladstone, Seeley had been Professor of Latin at University College, London for six years. He was also the author of *Ecce Homo* (1865), a controversial, liberal, and humanistic discussion of Christ's life and purposes. Once in the Regius Chair, he became a strenuous advocate of history as the most important subject in the university. Two years before his appointment he had argued that the ablest, most learned men must be induced to remain at the university as professors to give "reading men," upon whom further learning depended, erudite lectures and to give the "dilettanti" of the "lecture room" upon whom "the general cultivation of a country depends," those general views that they needed to become efficient citizens.[40] Five years later he helped form the Society for the Organization of Academical Study and, together with Henry Sidgwick, was among the 70 petitioners who asked the Cleveland Commission to redistribute university revenues in support of advanced scholarship.[41] Seeley's advocacy of the position that money must be found to encourage mature study, scientific research, and a genuinely higher education continued throughout his tenure at Cambridge. Seeley, preceded as Regius Professor of Modern History at Cambridge by Sir James Stephen and Charles Kingsley, was the first occupant of the chair to be recognized as a historian within his university and throughout the country.

In his inaugural address Seeley described history as "the school of public feeling and patriotism . . . the school of statesmanship," a conception of history that dominated the discipline at Cambridge well into the twentieth century.[42] Seeley portrayed the historian, as he may have thought of himself, as a kind of secular priest, reading the auguries of the times.[43] History grasped the unity of development and revealed the tendencies by which countries progressed. He hedged his interpretation of progress by making it simultaneously inevitable and dependent on an elitist leadership; it was not "generally the spirit of progress . . . which brings about great reforms in a country, but the pressure of need." But reforms could not occur "in a community in which the spirit of progress is not active" in well-educated, intelligent leaders. In order to equip those leaders properly, university history teachers had to be contemporary men whose historical understanding of the preceding 300 years allowed them to address current concerns. Seeley admired Humboldt's foundation of the University of Berlin in early nineteenth-century Germany because there the "higher life" became "one of the bulwarks of the State . . . a kind of spiritual weapon."[44] In England Seeley wanted Cambridge, too, to be a training ground for knowledgeable politicians who would govern the state wisely and well.[45]

Cambridge was to be a "seminary" preparing the "young men from whom the legislator and the statesman of the next age must be taken."[46] There they would learn the ethical and political laws which could be extracted from historical studies to provide a "theory of human affairs . . . which is applicable to the phenomena with which life has to deal." Seeley saw history as a practical blueprint for steady progress, which taught "public feeling and patriotism" as a prerequisite for rational political judgment and activity.[47] History could teach everyone who wanted to learn because it was a "political science," composed of political economy and history together, that demonstrated the place of government in human affairs.

Seeley defined "political science" as a normative, empirical, political philosophy, a set of principles upon which politics should be based. Seeley's "science of history," as Richard Shannon argues, beyond providing the power of knowledge, relieved "people of perplexity about what had happened in the past, and why."[48] History was described by Seeley as a reliable "compass," necessarily "reassuring," because it showed the student that his life was not aimless but rather a voyage "to a definite port." Even if the student failed occasionally, he could go on "supported by faith in a law of Good, of which he has traced the workings" in history.[49] Changes no longer appeared "capricious" because he learned "to refer them to laws" and to derive strength from their essentially progressive operation so that he could fill his appropriate station in life. All Seeley's lectures and writing tried to provide current historical lessons, especially for politicians. He lectured not only to those ready to be converted, like the Cambridge undergraduates attempting a good honours degree in the Tripos, but to the Council of Church Reform Union and to popular audiences such as the Christian Socialist Working Men's College.

A political science was possible by the late nineteenth century, Seeley believed, because there was finally a sufficient inductive accumulation of sound historical knowledge. That knowledge equipped university graduates "to take a side" in the controversies besetting Britain.[50] History, significant only in proportion to its pragmatic bearing upon the present, made people "wise before the event."[51] The importance of events was not measured by how they appeared to contemporaries at the time because "it is not the business of the historian . . . to put his reader back in the past time, or to make him regard events as they were regarded by contemporaries." This would be useless because great events are "commonly judged by contemporaries quite wrongly." The true test of events was their "pregnancy," the "greatness of the consequences to follow from them."[52] Contemporary history led "to knowledge by suggestive interrogations."[53]

Although Seeley argued that the study of history should go beyond a "vulgar view of politics which sinks them into a mere struggle of interests and parties," he rejected H. T. Buckle's emphasis, in his best-selling *History of Civilization in England* (1858–61), on physical and material environment. Seeley was equally dismissive of "scientific discoveries or artistic masterpieces" and completely alienated the young G. M. Trevelyan by describing history which attempted to be literature as "a foppish kind of history . . . which produces delightful books hovering between poetry and prose." These "perversions," Seeley thought, occur when history is separated from "practical politics." While not denying other influences upon history, Seeley saw the historian's province as uniquely that of the "politicist" whose study was the "political group or organism—the state."[54] When he interpreted, collected, and organized facts or compared existing states by their resemblances and differences, his goal was to reach explanatory generalizations.[55] Historical details were important only as "a basis for generalization"; for the "solution of some problem; the establishment of some principle, which would arrest the attention of the student, and might be of use to the statesman. History pure and simple, that is narrative without generalisation . . . appeared trivial, unworthy of serious attention."[56]

Instead of explaining either parliament, popular politics, or the constitution, Seeley lectured and wrote about the state as the heroic agent in English and European history, to be studied by an inductive, observational method similar to that of astronomy or the natural sciences. Seeley's colleagues throughout Britain concentrated on the thirteenth to the seventeenth centuries, but he was far more interested in the nineteenth century as a new, energetic age with an unprecedented revolution in government, the economy, and culture. As a liberal who believed that the individual should be free from the interference of coercive power, Seeley was impressed with the abolition of monopolies in religion, politics, and the economy. But he was more excited by novel habits and ways of thinking which encouraged "perpetual change and unintermitted improvement" in political movement and he shrank "from stationary politics as from stagnation and death." The most unique element of the age was the "absolute sovereignty" of organized public opinion.[57] Although the regime of public opinion was more equitable than its aristocratic predecessors, it was also more uncultivated: "to deal with the whole department of culture, it is evident that you must have a Government of the wisest, and no one has ever supposed that the government of public opinion, at least such as we see it in this age, answered that description."

If the schools taught politics—and Seeley urged, without success, that the schools and universities should include the political developments of the nineteenth century in their curriculum—they could correct the ignorance of public opinion which had great power but an inadequate education. Optimistically, Seeley believed that "statesmen" who have "taken courage to assume once more their natural position of leaders" were "devoted to forming and educating public opinion." The result would be an "age of constructive policy . . . when the difficult reforms will be possible, when the highest statesmanship will be able to count upon support in attempting the highest tasks."[58] Seeley intended the universities to override the influence of the press, political leagues, and public meetings, by putting the "wisest" into government where they could properly educate public opinion in its own and the state's best interest. The kind of education he admired occurred when the "mind was roused and stimulated by questions, not by answers." But Seeley had no intention of allowing ordinary people to come to their own conclusions about appropriate public conduct. On the contrary, the historian would offer them solutions which necessarily rose above subjectivity and arbitrariness because the historical testament, when read by a trained student, was explicitly objective.[59]

When Seeley wrote about the historical testament of nineteenth-century Germany, especially in his three-volume *Life and Times of Stein, or Germany and Prussia in the Napoleonic Age* (1878), he was actually preparing a contemporary lesson for Britain. In recent German history, Seeley recognized, as Disraeli had, a new kind of efficiently expanding state. *Stein*, an essay based upon printed sources, was considered Seeley's major work by late nineteenth-century historians. It is about the social and political resuscitation of a defeated and demoralized Prussia by an austere, deliberate, nationalistic policy of discipline and education. Seeley considered Stein a great statesman because he saw "so clearly and habitually" the importance of a unified Germany. One of the things that made Stein extraordinary to Seeley was that he "considered himself to belong to the English school of statesmen" and it was to "English history" that he seemed to have "owed the whole awakening and development of his intellect." To Seeley, Stein was more than a statesman; he was the agent for God's providential achievement of German unity. As a result of his own experience, Stein believed that there was "no calamity so dark and universal, no prospect so impenetrable . . . but that Providence might be trusted speedily and splendidly to restore the daylight." Seeley found in the German patriot a mirror of his own public ambition and private faith. Both men trusted providence and sought a higher purpose in national growth which each tried, in very different ways, to aid and abet. Stein had the power to act imperatively; Seeley tried to explain the imperatives of power. The Prussian wars of 1813, 1866, and 1870, made possible by Stein's military reforms, were such imperatives because they "reconciled the modern world to war," by revealing war to be "a civilising agent and a kind of teacher of morals."[60]

An acceptance of expansionist war as morally necessary enabled many late-nineteenth century liberals, such as Seeley, to become liberal imperialists. Confusing military force with moral force, they were able to accept power politics as a good thing when judged by its ends rather

than its means. Seeley understood imperial destiny as the state's cooperation with the intent of Providence. England had no choice, when faced
by the developing power of nineteenth-century Germany, except to ex-
pand her empire. Seeley insisted that England's international possessions
were essential to the moral development of both England and those living within the Empire. He opposed Home Rule for Ireland and, in the
1890s, led a group of the Imperial Federation League, who lectured all
over England on "National Unity." Seeley reinterpreted both English history and politics in the framework of aggressive national states.[61] His
Expansion of England (1883), a course of lectures at Cambridge, suggested
how an English Stein could forge England's future growth as a world
power. When, on Lord Rosebery's instigation, Seeley was made Knight
Commander of the Order of St. Michael and St. George, it was for his
services to the Empire.

In the incomplete *Growth of British Policy*, published posthumously
in 1895 and intended originally as a historical background for the *Expansion*, Seeley defined the period between the settlement of Utrecht and the
fall of Napoleon as "English ascendancy on the sea and in the New
World," which launched the expansion of England.[62] The historian could
explain English history until 1688 as the development of constitutional
liberty. But after that date, the history of England was not the history of
parliament but the history of expansion.[63] The *Expansion* predicted an
organic imperial federation like the American state. "Development" or
"progress" in English history was measured by the growth of Greater
Britain throughout the Empire. Expansion was "profound, persistent,
necessary to the national life."[64] "Modern British history" was divided
by Seeley into "two grand problems . . . the colonies and India."[65] Solution of those problems, beyond common sense and common morality,
depended upon history.

What history taught Seeley about India was that, of all countries, it
was the least capable of evolving a stable government. In a circular and
self-serving argument, Seeley conceded that English rule may have diminished whatever political capacities India originally possessed by un-
dermining "all fixed moral and religious ideas in the intellectual classes,"
but he concluded that it would be the "most inexcusable of all conceiv-
able crimes" to withdraw English government from a country so dependent on it.[66] Since he could not find traditions of liberty or popular institutions in Indian history, there was no question in Seeley's mind that
the British rulers had a superior, more vigorous civilization than the native races.[67] The liberal side of Seeley's imperialism was that he never

justified the Indian empire in terms of the advantages, commercial, military, or any other kind, which India could bring England, but solely for the good England could confer on India. Unlike India, Greater Britain, that is the expansion of Englishmen by emigration into the colonies, was to be understood as a remedy for poverty and as a system of defense in case of war. England and her colonies together were not an Empire "but only a very large state" whose population and institutions were English throughout.[68]

In Cambridge, the emphasis upon contemporary history inaugurated by Seeley was reenforced by George Prothero until 1894 and continued into the 1930s by H. W. V. Temperley's diplomatic studies and J. H. Clapham's economic history. Seeley's ideas also found their way into other influential historical writing. The *Cambridge History of the British Empire*, published in the 1920s under the direction of A. P. Newton, the first Imperial History Professor at London University, was a "classic historiographical monument" to Seeley's view of empire. The contributors to the *History* "fixed their gaze on imperial policy, constitution-making, and administration, and on the projected activities of British Government, as if the organic imperial state had already come into being to do everything of significance in these countries while their indigenous inhabitants slept." Like Seeley, their "standpoint was anglocentric and their values Anglo-Saxon."[69] Newton, in rhetoric similar to Seeley's, carefully told young students that Britain was the greatest of all colonizing powers and that "the study of colonial history must always be preponderantly concerned with her activities."[70] At Cambridge during the last quarter of the nineteenth century Seeley, the most indefatigable Regius Professor, abetted by the most influential of college history teachers, George Prothero, and by J. R. Tanner, the constitutional historian at St. John's College, lectured undergraduates and intelligent opinion outside the university about the imminence of imperial federation as a corollary of English history.[71]

*

The Cambridge school of history created by Seeley shared with Stubbs's school at Oxford an admiration of England's progressive evolution, a discovery of divine intervention in times of crisis, and an understanding of history as a schooling in citizenship. Unlike their colleagues in France and Germany, and even some in England like Max Müller, the first Professor of Comparative Philology in Oxford from 1868, both Stubbs and Seeley repudiated a philosophy of history and attempted instead to construct a self-explanatory narrative based upon an empirical collection and comparison of facts. Both historians believed that the historical record compelled the assent of any unprejudiced reader. But within these common assumptions, there were considerable differences.

For Stubbs, the main work of the historian was the painstaking affirmation of the continuities and stabilities responsible for England's constitutional success. He shunned contemporary issues and studied the past as the gradual evolution of limited institutions towards increasing national harmony and a balance of powers. For Seeley, the present determined the past. Historians were not interested in reconstructing or even understanding what was essentially a foreign time and place. Instead, only those aspects of history were worth studying which could explain and solve contemporary problems. Sides had to be taken as a moral obligation once history presented the historian with the right side. Historical details were useful only for establishing the generalizations or laws of history, on which a political or prescriptive science would be based. Seeley's central subject was the English state, expanding by war when necessary, because the ends justified the means. A unified empire, serving those it governed, was morally right. While the tory Stubbs venerated the past for creating free and just institutions, the liberal Seeley saw the past as a burden that had to be discarded so that a better future could be fashioned.[72] Stubbs discovered in history a stable society based upon the limitation of power and the protection of the individual, while Seeley saw instead a scheme, progressively grander, that culminated in an organic imperial federation. But even at Cambridge, Stubbs's emphasis on England's constitutional past defeated Seeley's concern with the present and the future. While Seeley left a legacy that encouraged studies wider and more international than England's political history alone, the subject that remained of greatest interest, especially to students, was the development of the constitution.

Stubbs, Seeley, and the other professors rarely saw history with ironic detachment. Instead, they constructed a narrative in which accomplished solutions were always more important than obstinate problems, and they taught moral lessons as if they were deduced from an unequivocal historical record. Although differing about the importance of particular historical individuals or events, they found moral truths ordering the behavior of powerful people and anonymous groups, the development of law and institutions, and the character of time and place. If they had found a discrepancy between ideals of justice, equity, freedom, opportunity and actual historical tendencies and events, then a moralistic reading of history could have fueled a radical, prophetic discontent. Instead, until the 1930s, their largely conservative, priestly temperament prevailed. Not only in England, but in the United States and Germany, too, history became a discipline which emphasized continuity and consensus more than change and conflict. Quarrels, and especially denominational issues, which inflamed emotions were avoided. Oxford historians who opposed Froude's appointment as Regius Professor blamed his inaccuracies upon his blindly passionate involvement in the Reformation.[73] But like Froude, historians in Oxford and Cambridge preferred to view history as a complex morality play. Leaders could have a wholesome effect upon public opinion and conduct only if they knew how to choose rationally and sympathetically among competing policies. That choice depended, above all else, on understanding right and wrong. Unlike the "professional" German historians who confused their privileged status within the state with genuine power and imagined that scholars could aggressively influence the course of history as well as describe it, or American historians, who offered to analyze and solve foreign policy problems, most English historians did not seek to play a central role themselves.[74] Instead they were content to follow Stubbs and Seeley in teaching a higher style of thought and behavior that would prepare their students to lead Britain into a future consistent with the proven historical values of her past.

Chapter 5

The Professorial Tradition Continued

The history professors who succeeded Stubbs and Seeley never had as much influence, but each one provoked questions about the intrinsic importance of the subjects he taught. Even those professors who were largely rejected had some effect because the consensus within the field was still new enough to require defence. When a professor's ideas were unpopular, their university colleagues were compelled to think through and present their own views with clarity sufficient to challenge and repudiate the unacceptable positions. Although the result was a larger debate about history, the outcome generally confirmed prevailing intellectual and institutional habits. In areas of greater agreement between the professors and the existing traditions, there was less debate and less introspection. The Oxford Regius Professors E. A. Freeman, J. A. Froude, and F. Y. Powell, never moved beyond Stubbs's shadow. When their successor C. H. Firth attempted to give the School a new direction, he failed. In spite of limitless energy and stubborn persistence, Firth was defeated by the institutional strength of the college teachers. The constancy of teaching and interpretation was continued by his successor, H. W. C. Davis in his brief tenure from 1925 to 1928. Maurice Powicke, appointed after Davis, was the first holder of the chair to be openly, if ambivalently, critical of the Oxford school's emphasis upon the evolution of character and institutions. At Cambridge, during the tenure of Lord Acton, J. B. Bury, and G. M. Trevelyan, there was more chronic discussion about the curriculum and examinations than at Oxford but the Historical Tripos was sufficiently broad to absorb changes without threatening the fundamental structure of history teaching.

*

At Oxford Stubbs was followed in 1884 by Freeman, who returned to a reformed Oxford after a hiatus of 30 years. Ill health, his own remote position as professor, and the unfamiliar curriculum, teaching, and examinations so alienated him that he essentially withdrew from the school's activities. Freeman's position was made even more untenable by the conspicuous discrepancy between his preaching and his practice. He wanted history to be a "science" based upon the "mastery of original texts," but he understood "science" as equivalent simply to "knowledge." Few reliable secondary syntheses existed in either medieval or more modern history during Freeman's tenure, and essential documents were just beginning to be investigated and sorted out in the archives. But he rarely left his own library and refused to do original research or to learn critical methods.[1]

As was the case with Freeman, Seeley's historical work tended increasingly to be dismissed, especially after his death, because he had relied exclusively on printed sources. In contrast, Stubbs, Maitland, and Firth continued to be widely recognized as proper historians because each man made strenuous efforts to collect, scrutinize, edit, and print charters, rolls, statutes, and other evidence. Freeman preferred to follow a "comparative" method which found analogies, parallels, similarities, and unities, especially in his insistence upon Aryan antecedents for British political institutions.[2] In architecture, archaeology, and comparative philology, he discovered evidence for the progress of peoples from subjection to self-government. In that progress, he admired heroic figures, such as William the Conqueror or the Emperor Frederick II, who used absolute power effectively.

Freeman's thinking was rooted in a romanticism that culminated in the liberal, nationalist climax of the European revolutions of 1848. He saw the past not only—in his famous phrase—as "past politics" but as a universal "great drama" dominated by "heroes and restorations" and the "interpenetrations of cultures."[3] Contemporaries saw him as an "epic poet," not a "calm and unprejudiced observer" but the "last of the historians" who wrote history "as romance."[4] His most characteristic book was the patriotic *History of the Norman Conquest: Its Causes and Results* (1867–79). Like Stubbs, who was perhaps his closest friend, he saw the origins of English independence and political wisdom in local

institutions. He celebrated the free communities, which he believed were
the historical backbone of England, because of their traditions of institutional diversity. And he believed that genuine freedom depended upon
the continuity of individualism and self-government.

Unlike Stubbs, however, Freeman delighted in controversy. His
public writing and private letters were passionate, polemical, and patho-
logically sensitive to criticism. He was obsessed by pedantic issues of
spelling and dates, and he attacked almost every contemporary historical
writer, often on the most trivial issues. It apparently never occurred to
him that they would respond in kind: "It certainly does seem to me that
I am constantly jeered at—for no reason that I can see—in a way that I
don't see other scholars are."[5] When Freeman died, T. F. Tout wrote that
since young Oxford historians had become more interested in research
during the past decade, it was "but reasonable to regard the Regius Professor as one of the incentives."[6] But Tout's close friend and colleague at
Manchester, James Tait, had found Freeman so unbearable that he kept
a special and full section in one of his undergraduate notebooks, headed
"Freeman's Pedantry."[7] Another section of the notebook might have
been equally full had Tait collected examples of Freeman's arrogance.
Freeman was convinced that anything he did not know was not worth
knowing. When James Bryce told Freeman that he knew too little about
Egypt to judge its effect upon other civilizations, Freeman replied: "I
confess my ignorance of Egyptian history: only is there anything to be
ignorant of? . . . I will not believe that Egypt had any effect upon Greece."
A. V. Dicey perceived Freeman's tragic flaw to have been "neither unfair-
ness, in the ordinary sense, nor personal rancor, but something like
absolute blindness to certain aspects of things which were of no interest
to him."

When Bryce reflected upon the character of Freeman's life and influence, he concluded that Freeman had been not only "conspicuously indifferent" to interests other than his own but, more seriously, unwilling
to "lay his intellect alongside of yours, apprehending your point of view
and setting himself to meet it." Freeman never understood why colleagues and students did not flock to him and he was deeply hurt by his
failure to attract young teachers to work under his supervision.[8] Without
any more "authority on the subject to which he had given his life than
some young man" appointed by his college, Freeman watched his audiences dwindle.[9] In his second year as Professor, although he had given a
first set of statutory lectures which attempted a "call and an introduction

to historical study in general," he was lecturing to three students and a middle-aged clergyman from North Oxford, who, when he was unable to attend, told Freeman that he would send his daughter, "a very intelligent girl of 14." [10]

*

The Regius Professor appointed in 1892 was a man Freeman had attacked violently. Stubbs, too, had little use for J. A. Froude.[11] Then 74, Froude returned enthusiastically to an Oxford that had repudiated him 43 years earlier as the apostate author of *The Nemesis of Faith* (1849).[12] Although his reception, especially by those interested in research, was less than enthusiastic,[13] Froude gave a vigorous inaugural defending his own relativistic, moralistic, and dramatic interpretation of history. To his colleagues' considerable surprise, he lectured to overflowing audiences of undergraduates and tutors, as well as North Oxford folk. But the three books based upon his lectures, and published in the two years before his death, *Erasmus* (1894), *English Seamen* (1895), and *The Council of Trent* (1896), further eroded his reputation as a sound scholar.

History was an art to Froude ultimately because science was subject to deterministic laws of cause and effect which were incompatible with the free will necessary for moral conduct. Froude was, like his Oxford critics, a moralist. Three decades before he returned to Oxford as Regius Professor, he wrote that opinions "alter, manners change, creeds rise and fall, but the moral law is written on the tablets of eternity. . . . Justice and truth alone endure and live." There was one repeated lesson in history: "the world is built somehow on moral foundations"; and in "the long run, it is well with the good and ill with the wicked." [14] That lesson was dramatically displayed in the theater of history. In Froude's history-as-moral-drama, the historian was playwright, actor, and director. The spectator's part was to "sympathize with what is great and good . . . , to hate what is base." [15] The drama provided inspiration, solace, and transcendence because eventually heroes were rewarded and villains were punished. If the historian wanted "truly" to represent people's actions in the past, he could do so only as a "dramatist who faithfully draws the characters and makes intelligible the circumstances that surround them." [16]

The ideal stage for Froude was set in early sixteenth-century rural England, and he mourned its loss. But he comforted himself by believing that its essential moral and spiritual qualities could be resurrected.[17] Unlike the other historians of the Oxford school, Froude viewed history as progressing convulsively. That meant that historical qualities of intrinsic worth were endangered periodically by wars or other historical paroxysms. But Froude's reading of English history as spasmodic was compatible with a continuously evolving national history because Froude would not allow anything of value to disappear.

In spite of the disdain in which many historians held Froude, his scouring of archives and his reflections on the meaning of history made him a much more contemplative and accurate historian than most of his critics. Froude's *History of England from the Fall of Wolsey to the Death of Elizabeth* (1858–70) was the result of a systematic reading of hundreds of uncatalogued documents in England, Spain, and France. "Whatever may be said in deprecation of Froude's historical work," H. A. L. Fisher wrote, he was "one of the very small band of English historians who have based a comprehensive and artistic presentation of history upon paleographic research." [18]

Although Froude found social or political progress for the mass of mankind a dubious concept, he believed in moral progress which he thought was perceived best by reading the original documents of any given time. He also insisted that the teaching of history should rely upon such original authorities as Statute Books from which the true history of the English nation could be extracted. Nevertheless he recognized the subjectivity of even the most apparently objective knowledge. What we call facts, he maintained, were filtered through the fallible, passionate, and prejudiced minds of those who recorded them and the historian could select those he found most suitable. History, passively ironic, would "make no objection." Froude reported that when Napoleon was asked "what is history?" he responded: "a fiction agreed upon." [19] While documents were "less submissive to manipulation" than "facts," Froude compared history to a child's box of letters, where we pick out the letters we want, "arrange them as we like, and say nothing about those which do not suit our purpose." [20] When Froude became Regius Professor, he held fast to his caveat that verification in history was "impossible." Evidence was derived from books, which could not be cross-examined in a witness box: "The writers on whose authority we depend, shared . . . in the illusions of their age. . . . The hero or sage to one party is a knave and an idiot to another." While we can know what events happened in general, we cannot know how or why they happened. All history was essentially "mythic," or conjectural. [21]

*

The least successful of all the Regius Professors was F. Y. Powell, Froude's successor in 1894, who had even less influence upon the History

School than Froude. Powell was appointed by Lord Rosebery, who had been a student at Christ Church College, where Powell had lectured on law. Two years after receiving a first class in the Honours School of Law and Modern History in 1872, Powell came to Christ Church under the sponsorship of Sidney Owen, his former tutor. After S. R. Gardiner refused the Regius Chair, there was no opposition to Powell as a second choice. In the 1880s, Powell had frequently led the Historical Seminar, begun under Stubbs to encourage an interest in history among students and tutors that was more specialized than the honours examinations required. Contemporaries thought of Powell as the "chief influence among the younger students and teachers of history at Oxford."[22] When H. A. L. Fisher was elected to a Classical Fellowship at New College, he went to Powell, who "was reported to be omniscient," and came away with an awakened interest in Modern History as a "salutary corrective to that view dominated by examination requirements."[23] But when appointed Regius Professor, Powell had written only a schoolbook on history. Except for a few articles and a rare review, he published no historical work in his eight-year tenure. His one effort for the History School was a plea for the training of archivists:[24] his only learned publication was an edition of the Icelandic sagas, *The Corpus Poeticum Boreale* (1881), done in collaboration with the Icelandic scholar Gudbrander Vigfusson. The *Origines Islandicae* (1905), written with Vigfusson, was published after Powell's death.

As professor, Powell notoriously neglected social and academic obligations. Firth, not himself the easiest man to get on with, found Powell unstable and conspicuously wanting in "business capacity."[25] Powell's inaugural lecture, a disorganized appeal for increasing the facilities for research in Oxford, broke every record for brevity by coming to an abrupt halt after twenty minutes.[26] Even his admiring biographer, Oliver Elton, admitted that Powell had no effect upon teaching or students. Charles Oman's harsher verdict was that as "far as the School of Modern History was concerned," Powell "might as well never have existed." Powell himself never expected to succeed. When Tout congratulated him on his appointment, Powell replied: "I hope I shall not disappoint my friends. I am quite aware of the unsuitability and of my own shortcomings."[27]

*

C. H. Firth, who succeeded Powell in 1904, was eminently suited for the chair because he was a recognized historian, the Ford Lecturer at Oxford in 1901 and 1902, and a former tutor. A Scholar at Balliol, President of the Historical Seminar, and the winner of the Stanhope Prize Essay of 1887 for *The Marquis Wellesley,* Firth became a tutor at Pembroke College and then the second Research Fellow at All Souls, succeeding S. R. Gardiner. But when Balfour appointed Firth as Regius Professor, the tutors suspected, rightly, that he would be the first holder of the office to campaign relentlessly, as he had done when a tutor, to make a professional study of history supplement existing teaching. His academic battles, mostly fought and lost in the arena of the Modern History Board, were on the side of university departments, new Schools for Modern Languages and for English, professional postgraduate study, and equal educational opportunities and rewards for women.[28]

Although defeated consistently, Firth remained unrealistically optimistic. In spite of his long years in Oxford, he always misread the position consistently taken by the tutors. Firth had written confidently to Tout in 1892 that "in a few years you and I (if we can get our great works published) will have more reputation and more power" than the "wicked four," Edward Armstrong, C. R. L. Fletcher, A. L. Smith, and Arthur Johnson, who led tutorial opposition against any attempt to make the study of history professional.[29] Smith appears in this academically conservative company because although an innovative, remarkably well-read, and wide-ranging teacher, he often opposed curriculum change when existing requirements already interested and stimulated students. Although in support of "substantial relief from the mere mass and bulk of memory work," he remained unwilling to "pull up the plant by the roots to see if it is growing."[30] Unlike Smith, Firth never understood that external fame, based on scholarship, had little to do with the reputation of history tutors, which was confirmed rather by the national careers of their former students.

Of all the Regius Professors until the 1930s, Firth was the most prolific both in the discovery of new documents and evidence and in the writing of original works of historical interpretation, concerned essentially with the seventeenth century.[31] The tutors recognized that the distinction of his scholarship qualified him for the Regius Professorship, especially since his historical work was largely consistent with the traditions of the school. Although the new Regius Professor certainly irritated the tutors by his pressure for a more professional school of history, his subsequent historical work, while in the chair, never disappointed them. *The Last Years of the Protectorate, 1656–1658* (1909) was an entirely political history which portrayed Cromwell as a heroic and selfless defender of civic and religious liberties for the good of nation and God.[32] Firth was attracted to the seventeenth-century historian Gilbert Burnet because Burnet transformed his autobiographical memoirs into the *History of my Own Time* (1723 and 1734). His "moral purpose," Firth wrote with approval, was to make the study of history a necessary training for the governing groups in church and state "in order to make them better qualified to take part in the government of their country and more attached to its constitution."[33]

In his famous lectures on Thomas Babington Macaulay's *History of England* (1849–61), delivered at Oxford before the Great War, Firth praised Macaulay's effort to make history include social as well as political life by describing "common people as well as kings and statesmen." That was not because Firth was an early advocate of social history, but rather because he saw Macaulay as giving history "some of the charm of historical romance by employing the materials" of the historical novelist. He was especially sympathetic to Macaulay's treatment of history as a "department of literature," and critical of those who saw history as a science that revealed underlying laws. When Firth described the discovery of historical truth as "scientific," he meant only that historians must have systematic methods. But the presentation had to be literary so that the ideas expressed "leave a lasting impression on the mind of the person to whom they are addressed."[34]

Although Firth was sympathetic to many elements in Macaulay's *History*, he disliked Macaulay's disparagement of the past in comparison to the present. Instead, Firth argued, the historian should show how "seventeenth-century England developed into nineteenth-century England." When Firth examined the legislation which Macaulay had neglected, such as the Agricultural Subsidy Act of 1689, he found that it was "part of a deliberate national policy for the development of the nation's resources, which both the landed interest and the commercial interest agreed in holding expedient. A similar desire to develop and protect the manufactures and trade of the country inspired the commercial policy of the government, and was generally accepted by all parties."[35] The role of the Glorious Revolution of 1688, for Firth and his colleagues alike, was to unify the nation and give it the common purposes which had marked its history so conspicuously ever since. Firth faulted Macaulay for not doing justice to social, economic, and intellectual history, but he endorsed the Whig historian's conviction that part "of the purpose of a history of England should be to bring out the unity of spirit which pervades the different manifestations of the national life."[36] While Firth often had original insights into the material he studied, he never broke with the Oxford celebration of a unified and meliorative national development. It never occurred to him or to his colleagues that a national history might more accurately explain the causes and consequences of events by also showing the disunities that arose from conflict of interests among groups, individuals, ideas, religions, and classes.

Firth thought, mistakenly, that the recognition of his scholarly achievements meant an acceptance of the changes he advocated. His inaugural address, *A Plea for the Historical Teaching of History* (1904), was a familiar critique of the Oxford school of history. Firth's description of the ineffectiveness of the professor and his call for advanced training continued the inaugural tradition established by his four predecessors. But unlike them, Firth, as a tutorial member of the History Board for a decade, had resolutely pressed those views. The *Plea* argued that an Oxford history student never acquired "the mental habits of a scholar" and instead "remained too long the passive recipient of other men's knowledge," learning "results instead of methods; not how to find out, but what to remember." Firth did not object to the School's emphasis upon a body of knowledge meant to guarantee success in the honours examinations, but he thought it was insufficient. After students completed the general historical background provided by the Modern History School, those who were interested in becoming future historians should have the opportunity to receive a more professional training from the professors and the university teachers of history. Firth never disputed the tutors' assertion that a liberal arts education was the essential purpose of a history degree, but he did not want that education mistaken for the specialized discipline that should be required for awarding fellowships and other teaching positions. What disturbed Firth was that "like all paper currencies," the teaching of history at Oxford drove "out better money."[37]

When Firth printed his *Plea*, he added a conciliatory preface explaining that he was attacking the Oxford system and not the individuals working within that system. Privately, Firth wrote to R. H. Hodgkin, history tutor at Queen's College, that "I have had no professional training myself except the School, and have found it a very inadequate training (that is exactly what they resent). I have every right to say so, and . . . they are not justified in taking it as a personal attack upon themselves."[38] Twenty-three tutors and lecturers, including Hodgkin, repudiated Firth's *Plea* in a rousing manifesto that defended the college teacher's position. Since everyone, including Firth, agreed that undergraduate instruction in history was part of a liberal education, the curriculum had to be based on a general and humanistic understanding of national development. With the generosity that comes most easily to those who know that their position is unassailable, the teachers conceded that teaching should be combined with research and original work, when possible. Moreover, they had no objection to the provision of more advanced courses for those few students who wanted professional careers as historians. But there was no doubt that their priorities lay "in that very intimate and personal form called the College system."[39]

J. A. R. Marriott looked back on this debate 40 years later to recall that he agreed with the tutors because the demand for professional historians was "strictly limited," and he also agreed with Firth that it was the professor's proper function to train professional historians, no matter how few they might be. But he argued still, as the tutors had in 1904, that the History School, while giving the budding historian a good preliminary training "had a further and wider purpose. My own view was and is that a better school for statesmanship it would be difficult to devise: that it afforded an admirable training for public service, for politics in the widest sense, and that it could confidently claim to be judged by results." Marriott was a product of that school. It was, he insisted, "because I so conceived the purpose of the school, that I was content to spend the best part of a lifetime in its service." The word "service" for Marriott, as for so many other Oxford historians, was an important term of approbation. Marriott won the New College Prize in history, but only a disappointing second class in the history honours examination in 1882, because he took it while ill with pneumonia. When he had to choose a career, he thought only about how he might best serve "the State." But he could not decide initially on whether that service should be in the Anglican Church, politics, public school teaching, or the Indian Civil Service. Instead of any of these options, he decided to spend most of his life as a tutor, but he also managed to serve in Parliament for the city of Oxford from 1917 to 1922 and for York from 1923 to 1929.[40]

While this controversy between Firth and the tutors was occurring, a young American named Frank Aydelotte was a Rhodes Scholar at Oxford.[41] In Aydelotte's personal copy of the tutors' printed letter to Firth, he wrote marginal comments which reveal not only his grasp of the substantive issues of the debate, but the considerable differences between American and Oxonian students. When the tutors argued against Firth that students already dealt with original sources in "special subjects consisting of wholly original authorities and offering a wide option as to periods and topics," Aydelotte observed: "Of course what these Dons fail to see here is the difference between going back to certain prescribed authorities, following someone else's track, and really *exploring* for one's self and forming new or unpublished opinions." To the tutors' argument that a trained researcher or archivist might not necessarily be a good teacher, Aydelotte wrote: "Right for undergraduate work but very wrong for training men who are past that stage." What Aydelotte did not recognize was there was no postgraduate training for those studying history, although some did stay an additional year to try out for essay and prize competitions in history or for college fellowships.

The tutors, in an attempt to reach an accommodation with Firth that would not undermine their college teaching, agreed that they wanted "to strengthen" the "existing machinery" in "accordance with your suggestions." Like Firth, they welcomed to Oxford the first Professor of English Literature, Walter Raleigh, and the Corpus Christi Professor of Jurisprudence, the Russian, Paul Vinogradoff, whom they commended for "his assistance to the History School in his lectures and seminars." Raleigh and Vinogradoff were, with Firth, the three members of the aggressive professorial interest who fought for research in the university. As professors, however, they were effectively prevented from implementing their program. Aydelotte saw that they were powerless. Raleigh was "treated as if he didn't exist," and Vinogradoff was "simply disgusted with Oxford" and a lack of pupils.

To implement Firth's recommendations for recruiting postgraduate students, the tutors suggested printing an explanatory pamphlet about the new postgraduate B. Litt. degree for circulation in the United States and the empire. But, as Aydelotte observed, no pamphlet would be effective in encouraging graduate students to come to Oxford without the "better training needed for the tutors & Prof's who are to give this Post grad *instruction*." Although the tutors urged the History Board to adopt theses or written work as requirements for Fellowships in history, Aydelotte pointed out how far that was "from the practice of at least some of the men whose names are signed to this."[42]

Firth replied to the tutors in a printed letter that denied he had intended to make the History School exclusively professional. What he wanted was both general education and an elastic curriculum which would provide more opportunities for the professional teaching of undergraduate and postgraduate students who wanted careers as practicing historians. But until after World War I, teaching and curriculum remained substantially unchanged. The few new classes offered in paleography and diplomatic, sources, bibliography, and historical methods, did not attract students because specialized training was not required for a career as a history teacher, archivist, tutor, or fellow. R. L. Poole, the first teacher of paleography and diplomatic at Oxford and the editor of the *English Historical Review*, defined paleography as dealing with the "external elements of a written text," while diplomatic explored "its internal organism." These skills, he admitted, were not really "history," which is "occupied with the matter of a text" but they were essential to the historian as "primary, critical sciences."[43] By 1930, these introductory skills were relegated almost entirely to postgraduate courses and had "no part in the Honours School of Modern History."[44] Firth introduced a thesis option for undergraduates in 1908, but it was in addition to the required work rather than a substitution for any part of it. The result was that few candidates for the honors examinations in modern history chose the thesis.[45] During the whole of Firth's tenure, only two postgraduate seminars were offered at Oxford: one on the seventeenth century by Firth himself, and the other on the social and legal history of the Middle Ages by his closest ally in the School, Vinogradoff.[46]

*

Firth was condemned to fail because professors had only marginal influence at best. He might have been less of a failure had he had the support of Charles Oman, the new Chichele Professor of Modern History from 1906. Twenty-one years as a tutor had persuaded Oman that his duty was to college teaching and liberal education. Oman was a leading member of the Non-Placet Society, founded in 1886 to resist the conversion of the university into an institution of research and higher scholarship. He actively fought the idea of a D. Phil. degree. When that degree was finally accepted in 1917, he was occasionally put "nominally" in charge of some of these "visitors" and "wondered how the University could consider it consistent with its dignity to confer degrees on subjects for which it failed to produce any teachers or lectures."[47] What Oman meant was that he did not really supervise the foreign students who came to take the D. Phil. and there was no real postgraduate program designed for them. In his inaugural he had tried to make it impossible for such teachers and lecturers to be produced by attacking Firth's *Plea* for representing the researcher rather than the "professional University teacher." With all its defects, Oman contended, the School of Modern History provided "a very sound knowledge of the general outlines of history," which was the essential foundation for original work, and a method for comparing facts through the study of textual authorities.[48] Idiosyncratically, especially for a teacher, Oman insisted that the "true historian was born and not made," with the traits of zeal, "insatiable curiosity, a ready mind to shape hypotheses, a sound judgment to test them, and above all, dogged determination to work at all times and in all places." Oman translated his own habits of thinking and working into the "real" requisites for a historian which were more important than "any array of technical training."[49]

Politically, too, Oman stood conspicuously apart from the liberal disposition of such popular history teachers as A. L. Smith and H. A. L. Fisher. He admitted, with pride, that "always, when writing history," he had "some thesis to develop." What his "political Conservative bias" meant to him was that he did not allow "the people of whom I disapprove" to "get off with impunity." He disapproved of J. R. Green for his democratic evolutionary theories in which great men and wars were unimportant. For Oman, very much in the Oxford school, "history has been mainly affected by the personalities of a limited number of outstanding men."[50] As late as 1939, Oman still suspected social history, especially from the bottom up.[51] He also rejected such conservative evolutionary interpretations of history as C. R. L. Fletcher's, dismissing a view of history as a "regular and logical process of events," in favor of a "cataclysmic narrative."[52] Among pupils at New College from 1885 to 1905 there was, he remembered with distaste, "a very clever fellow, given from his earliest years to the gentle art of 'debunking,' who could see nothing but sordid motives in every historical personage, and sneered at every movement of reform—naturally he became a journalist on the 'left wing.'" Although unsympathetic to the left, Oman was satisfied, as were his more liberal colleagues, that "the large majority" of undergraduates "were idealists and optimists more or less—as is usual for a talented young man with some ambition for a career, whatever may be his political bias at twenty-one or twenty-two years of age."[53]

Only after he had become Chichele Professor did Oman learn about the solitude of professorial office. Initially the only professor to defend the primacy of the tutorial tradition, he found as the years passed that his chair excluded him from teaching and influence, and he thought again about the relative merits of tutorial and professorial functions within Oxford. His authority over students ended, and he was never again asked to examine in the Honours School, because the "tutorial influence" completely controlled the schools. Compelled to "lecture to empty benches," Oman found it "a disheartening experience when spread over many years."[54] His solution was either that students be required, or at least encouraged, to attend professorial lectures or that professors be relieved entirely of teaching so that they could do research and write. Oman wrote extensively on many diverse subjects that he knew very little about. J. H. Round, painstaking and meticulous, was appalled at Oman's "turning out 'history' books like a sausage machine." [55] But Oman, whatever his idiosyncrasies, was committed to a Modern History School that firmly trained "the good citizen" through a study of political history. In his understanding of the meaning and uses of history, Oman remained, like his colleagues and predecessors in the professorial chairs, a quintessential Oxford historian.

*

Firth's successor in the Regius Chair in 1925 and Oman's contemporary was a Balliol colleague who had taken a first class honours in Greats in 1895. After Henry William Carless Davis was elected to a Balliol Fellowship, he grew interested in history, and before World War I established himself as a medieval scholar.[56] After delivering the Ford lectures in Oxford in 1924 and 1925, having spent three-and-a-half years as the Professor of Modern History at Manchester, Davis was elected Regius Professor. Although the greater part of his life was spent in Oxford, Davis had made a wartime reputation by organizing the Trade Clearing House, later absorbed into the Foreign Office and expanded into the War Trade Intelligence Department. He was part of the British delegation to the Peace Conference, a delegation conspicuous for the number of Balliol men. In 1919 he acted briefly as Director of the Department of Overseas Trade in London. When the war began, he collaborated on the Oxford pamphlets against Germany and published *The Political Thought of Heinrich von Treitschke* (1914). His active service on college and university bodies throughout his career included a curatorship at the Bodleian Library, and after returning to Oxford in 1919, he became editor of the *Dictionary of National Biography.*

A product of prewar Balliol, Davis continued to be generally content with the study of history in Oxford until his untimely death in 1928. His inaugural address stated that "our business in a modern University is not exclusively that of making efficient statesmen or efficient civil servants," but he accepted the priority of that mission and remained an Oxford tutor who was as unwilling in 1925, as he had been in 1904, to accept Firth's appeal for research or professional historical training for undergraduates.[57] But he had no objection to specialized training for advanced students, and he hoped to encourage their presence in Oxford. What he thought of as a major reform was the university's recognition of the importance of recent history, which he understood as the study of the nine-teenth century.

Davis's conversion from medieval to modern history was evident in his Ford lectures on *The Age of Grey and Peel* (1926). There, he went beyond traditional constitutional history to examine "the history of the idea of parliamentary reform," radical political societies, and the under-lying ideas of Whigs, Tories, radicals, and social reformers.[58] But his main emphases were on great men and on the progressive development of Victorian society. In his inaugural he granted that medieval studies "supply the finest discipline that can be offered to the Historical begin-ner" because the "patient study of texts trains the critical faculty" and the "historical imagination," and because medieval ethical, religious, and political ideas are still influential and constitute a "system which satisfied the mind and the conscience and the religious instincts of Europe for at least four hundred years." But there were also "many minds to whom modern history makes a more urgent appeal."

Modern history did not mean "scientific" history to Davis, and he followed Firth in rejecting explanations based on repeatable cause and effect. Instead, history was the study of our "common humanity" in "the most eminent examples that it has produced of every type of human excellence." But the social history of ordinary people was worthless to Davis who believed that whatever is valuable first appears "somewhere near the summit of the social fabric and percolate(s) downwards." Ox-ford and Cambridge graduates, such as Davis, considered their own privileged status and its concomitant demands as a legacy from earlier leaders who had answered higher calls often at the sacrifice of personal goals. It was up to them to create and perpetuate the values that would then trickle down. Everything in their university life reenforced that les-son. Progress was not a steady "perpetual ascent" because it depended upon those at the top acting on behalf of those below them. When Davis concluded that it was "reassuring that although human development has always been one sided and ill-balanced, human nature has constantly dis-played new aptitudes and won expected victories," he was inviting his-tory graduates to shoulder their larger social and intellectual burdens.[59]

*

Davis had turned away from medieval history to more modern sub-jects. Maurice Powicke, his replacement, persevered as a working medi-evalist whose view of history and of the greater world was considerably more modern.[60] When Powicke returned from Manchester to Oxford as

Regius Professor in 1929, he found "very little difference between the School as it is today and the School of 1900." Despite changes in the curriculum, the undergraduate in 1929 "has the same kind of work to do as he had then . . . and the traditions of A. L. Smith and Arthur Johnson are still the strongest force in the School." The one significant change was that whether "they like it or not, our teachers are now regarded as members of a large professional class."[61] But in the active life of a tutor into the 1960s, as Richard Southern noticed in his inaugural address as Chichele Professor in 1961, "almost no academic change" seemed "worth the sweat of bringing it about."[62] And a student could still complain in 1970 that the authorities to be "learnt" were "fixed and finished items to be classified, to be called upon to furnish illustrations, and above all to be known." The documents "were not so much evidence as information and illustration" which "'contained' the answers . . . it was enough to marshal them in the right order."[63]

Unlike many of his contemporaries, Powicke's perception of history was marked indelibly by the events and repercussions of World War I. After a pietistic overview of the thirty years of historical work done by historians trained at Oxford, but not necessarily teaching there, Powicke devoted his inaugural lecture to a brief for more "professional" teaching at Oxford, even for undergraduates. He accepted "the view that the main purpose of the Oxford School is to educate a man to understand modern civilization," and "that the study of history cannot be dissociated from concern with political and wider ethical problems." But just "as we have our traditions of public service, so we should have our traditions of scholarship." And he believed further that a scholar's habits were as valuable for a man or woman entering any occupation as for those who would become practicing historians. The study of national history, so central to the history curriculum, had been finished by the war which "shattered" all the conventional frameworks "of human life." In "a constantly narrowing world, the old constructive impulses, such as the sense of race, of nationalism, of class, or the organization of the State on the basis of force, have become so incompatible with each other that we cannot take them as our guide." Instead there would be a wider outlook dominated by the "need of mutual understanding and equitable behavior between man and man, nation and nation, race and race." While insisting that historical judgments must remain "ethical," Powicke wanted such judgments based upon "an appreciation of the facts and of the evidence for the facts." He rejected an antithesis between the subjective and the objective and revealed his modernity still more by arguing, as many scholars of the 1930s were to do, that just as "the prevailing interests of an age offer a way of approach to history and reveal some of its hidden shapes, so the true scholar finds strength and insight in reliance upon the things which mean most to him."[64] Independently, Powicke arrived at R. G. Collingwood's famous dictum that every age rewrites history to meet its own private and public needs.

*

Powicke was the first Regius Professor who attempted to understand the thinking and purposes that had led his predecessors to define historical studies. That may be because he had not succeeded in moving either the curriculum or the teachers of history at Oxford. In 1944 he confessed to his admiration of the Cambridge historical school for their "long and varied tradition of broad and liberal interests maintained by Seeley, Acton, Ward, Bury, Creighton . . . Gwatkin, and Whitney." While professorial contacts in Oxford were diffused through academic channels, in Cambridge the medium was personal, "powerful, impressive and sometimes almost incredibly learned."[65] Powicke's envy may have been misplaced. The Regius Professors who succeeded Seeley were recognized as scholars, but their relations with the Tripos were as diffused, through different academic channels, as their contemporaries at Oxford.

When Seeley died in 1894, Lord Acton was chosen from outside the universities to be the new Regius Professor. Sidgwick was troubled by the appointment because "Acton's reputation is not . . . sustained by solid books."[66] In Acton's obituary, seven years later, F. W. Maitland wrote that there was no question as to the immensity of Acton's learning, but he asked whether that "daily consumption of a German octavo" benefited him and the world "or was it only a stupendous feat of intellectual voracity?" For those who admired Acton, even more than for those who did not, there remained the vexing question, as Maitland put it, "Was ever such disproportion between intake and output?" Why did Acton's reading and note-taking conclude, disappointingly, in little more than a published inaugural lecture in 1895? Maitland's answer was that Acton never published because of an "acute, almost overwhelming sense of the gravity, the sanctity of history."[67] Acton's admirers believed that he was brilliant, but they also recognized that he was afflicted with a fundamental incapacity to translate a widely ranging collection of facts into the ordered precision of print. But, in spite of his lack of publications, Acton created "a very deep impression" on most people who knew him.[68] James Bryce, a close friend for many years, and the only person whose advice Acton sought when he was considering the Regius Chair or the publication of random pieces, acknowledged Acton's deficiencies as a professor, as a writer, and even as a lucid speaker.[69] But he attributed those faults to "the overfulness and subtlety" of his thought and the "character of his mind, with its striving after a flawless exactitude of statement."[70]

Acton's tenure as Regius Professor was not successful because he fled from university and faculty responsibilities and avoided contentious issues. Although he was made an honorary Fellow of All Souls College, Oxford in 1890, together with W. E. Gladstone, he had been educated abroad and his experience of English universities was marginal. After Rosebery appointed Acton to the Regius Chair, Trinity College elected him an honorary Fellow. In 1896, Acton founded the Trinity Historical Society and became its first president. But his lectures as professor, as Oscar Browning observed, although marking a "great epoch in the Cambridge teaching of History," could "only be understood by those well acquainted with the subject." Browning, who had tried, unsuccessfully, to succeed Seeley, lectured on the same topics as Acton because the Regius Professor's lectures were not sufficient to prepare students for their final examinations. Except "for his name and authority," Browning complained, Acton had no "great influence on the Cambridge School." Acton never presided over Historical Board meetings and he would "never give a decided opinion on a disputed question."[71]

Although Browning, especially in his *Memories* (1910), was usually the least reliable of witnesses, his description of Acton's minimal role on the Historical Board was echoed by Thomas Thorneley, who came as an undergraduate in 1874 and remained as a Fellow of Trinity Hall until 1910. A university lecturer in history, and the first secretary of the Board of Historical Studies, Thorneley recalled that the Regius Professor "could hardly be persuaded to open his lips, unless directly appealed to, and even then, if the question admitted of a monosyllabic answer, that was the form it took."[72] Although asked repeatedly to preside over the Historical Board meetings, Acton always declined. After he had undertaken the editorship of the *Cambridge Modern History* in the fall of 1896, his major effort to further historical knowledge, he consistently pleaded illness and overwork and in 1900 wrote to J. R. Tanner that the "burden which you are good enough to wish to lay upon my shoulders would weigh less heavily upon other men."[73] Acton did become seriously ill in the summer of 1901. He resigned his editorship of the *Modern History* and died before the first volume appeared in 1902.

Another reason for Acton's relative lack of influence on the Cambridge Tripos was that his ideas were not sufficiently clear. His views were, however, largely compatible with prevailing English historiography, which emphasized progress towards greater political liberties, stronger moral character, and a more just and stable society. Since Acton published so little during his lifetime, his working ideas about history have to be extracted from his fragmentary notes. If the processes of his thinking and the quality of his mind are to be inferred from his collected slips of paper now in the Cambridge University Library, the jury may never come in. They are distressingly ambiguous. While they expose a mind fragmentary in its observations and essentially unfocused in its thinking, they also document the eclectic and sweeping extent of Acton's interests. As a student who used Acton's library for nearly 40 years, Owen Chadwick records a sense of gratitude and affection for a man who "loved knowledge for its own sake and the instrument of learning for the sake of knowledge . . . the great library of a single mind . . . simply bought with the ideal of understanding the past, and through the past, the present."[74] When Charles Oman visited that library at Shropshire shortly after Acton's death, he saw vast quantities of notes, files, and unopened parcels of books from continental publishers.[75] Acton made clear his love both of bits and pieces of knowledge and of grand schemes, but he never integrated or questioned either the separate bits or the broad plan.[76]

The most novel aspect of Acton's thought for English historians was his conviction that history, properly interpreted as the history of ideas, transcended national boundaries. In the future, he predicted, historians would no longer study a chronology, or national history, but rather concepts such as "toleration, conscience, credit, sorcery, criticism, education." Intellectual history undermined narrow or national treatments because ideas were "extra territorial." Historians would come to admit that the thinker was more important than the man of action and that ideas, representing culture, were an emancipating force. When history was better known, individuals could survey every country and choose their own intellectual "ancestors." Instead of accepting the restraints imposed by national traditions, a person could have the "world to choose from for his governing ideas."

Acton's international eclecticism, a result of his own cosmopolitan background, was essentially ahistorical. He explained it to himself by arguing that "the predominance of mind over matter" releases one from "his nation in the Past." Ideas were always subject to a moral structure and the "predominance of moral over intellectual motives." That meant that people were free to govern themselves by selecting the most noble ideas, whatever their provenance. No one was bound by time or place. In 1900, when preparing for the Romanes Lectures, he began with the Cambridge view that history teaches politics, but he extended the definition of history to include "subsequent events, practically" and, even more centrally, "subsequent opinions, theoretically." What emerges from this lesson first of all is "morality . . . a just severity in public life" by which men are judged and lost. Those necessary judgments on both events and ideas were not the job of the historian. Instead, public opinion, an "enlarged morality," expressed through an ethical code of public life, would decide according to those constant higher values which always governed humanity in the past and present alike.[77]

Acton wanted to preserve only those historical ideas that conformed to moral standards. A belief that the past had no coercive power over the present and that the historian could jettison those aspects of which he disapproved, a view promoted by Seeley before Acton, was a peculiar qualification for a Regius Professor of Modern History. But while Seeley and the other English historians emphasized the relationship between individuals and their uniquely national institutions, customs, and habits, Acton placed his emphasis on a "General History" that went beyond states and on the importance of those who defied historical continuities. The "better men drop out of the system" and were "more important for us" because they supplied the "Kritik."[78] But Acton's Cambridge colleagues were committed to teaching the better men history, so that they would know how best to serve their nation by preserving continuity. Acton tried to repudiate narrowly conceived national history for "Culturgeschichte" or "the wide front" where the "triumph of mind over matter" was achieved by "sympathy and detachment."[79] Although Culturgeschichte was central to Acton's study of history, he subordinated it to moral imperatives that exceeded time and place because they were governed essentially by religious requirements. In "great measure," the study of intellectual and cultural history really meant "the study of religion," which demonstrated that a higher progress occurred in history.[80]

Although Acton conceded that people made both ideas and the moral distinctions upon which the success or failure of those ideas depended, he distrusted individuals. His suspicion of individual motives and his skepticism about the historical effect of individual actions left him, as it did contemporary German historians, with a theory of progress rooted in forces larger and more permanent than the brief and inconsequential life of any one human being. Ideas were the most powerful of those forces for Acton, but he gave them a largely wasted life of their own, in which they bided their time until the world was ripe for them. These convictions ran against English faith in great men whose progressive acts were perpetuated within institutions which persisted because they were just. For Acton's English colleagues, institutions, when informed by equitable, legal and customary restraints, had binding authority. But Acton saw authority in the German context as a force that concealed and controlled. Lutheranism and its Prussian state governed by "authority" or force, and not by "opinion" or morality, through their management of the press and schools. But Acton joined the mainstream of English historiography in seeing liberalism as the antiauthoritarian force that curbed political power. Where he differed from his colleagues was in his emphasis upon the selfishness of unchecked individuals. The English historians, including Seeley, saw liberalism as a uniquely English political achievement that sanctioned the individual's pursuit of self-improving and socially desirable ends.[81]

Acton's preference for cultural and intellectual history was reflected in the adoption of a new select subject for examination, the History of Thought, Literature, and Art. But there were no disciples who extended and developed his thought. Even J. N. Figgis, perhaps Acton's most important student at Cambridge, drew his intellectual and historical inspiration from F. W. Maitland's legal history rather than from Acton. Figgis, an Anglican priest who joined the Order of the Resurrection at Mirfield in 1907, developed concepts that Acton would have found antithetical to his own most basic beliefs. Figgis argued that liberal interpretations of Western political society as a confrontation between individuals and the state were wrong and that the state should be understood instead as a "pluralistic" association of groups (families, boroughs, guilds, universities, churches), each with its own special rights and responsibilities, which had to be brought together by an organic ideal. He saw that ideal in a truly "Catholic Church . . . united by Common Worship, and bound by the one universal tie of love, [in which] there are no barriers of sex or race or age or circumstance."[82] It was not until the late 1930s, when the consequences of fascism made a moralistic view of history newly engaging, that the four volumes of Acton's lectures and essays, posthumously published by Figgis and R. Vere Laurence, were revived and read.

*

Acton arrived in the Regius Chair after a lifetime spent in contemplative browsing. His successor in 1902, the classical historian J. B. Bury, made his way from the static subject of philology to the dynamic study of history.[83] Although retaining a largely progressive reading of events, he repudiated both Seeley's attempt to find national purpose in history and Acton's synthetic, moralistic and cosmopolitan reading. His famous inaugural address defined history as a neutral, rationalistic science divorced as much from present politics as from the story of liberty. But he believed, with both Acton and G. M. Trevelyan, his successor in 1927, in the liberty of opinion, scholarship, and thought. But to Bury, freedom was, above all, intellectual, and in his *History of the Freedom of Thought* (1913), "reason pushed its way towards liberty over the fences erected by churches."[84] In this polemic, an exception to his typically narrative and dry historical work, Bury wrote that "nothing should be left undone to impress upon the young that freedom of thought is an axiom of human progress."[85] But even in a deliberately dispassionate history of Greece in 1900, Bury's epithet on the end of Greek civilization was: "The republics of Greece had performed an imperishable work; they had shown mankind many things, and, above all, the most precious thing in the world, fearless freedom of thought."[86]

For the quarter of a century in which he held the Regius Chair, Bury gave the Cambridge Historical Tripos very little guidance.[87] His one serious intervention, in 1909, was to protest the proposed removal of General Ancient History from the first part of the exam. Bury's case for the superior "educational value" of ancient history assumed, first, that the past was unique and should be studied for its own sake and second, that the study of Greece and Rome was a salutary antidote to the excessive "concentration on English History," which gave a "deplorable note of insularity" to the Tripos.[88] Bury neglected the Tripos because he was unwilling "to make the sacrifice of time which administrative duties demand."[89] But he did take on the editorship of both the *Cambridge Medieval History* and the *Cambridge Ancient History*. The medieval project, launched under Bury's control in 1905, proceeded with increasing anachronism for more than 30 years under the limitations he imposed. Bury rejected the thematic approach that Acton had adopted in the *Cambridge Modern History*. Instead, he imposed 30-page narrative chapters based, as T. F. Tout observed critically, on the "old practice of pigeon-holing history by reigns of kings."[90] In addition, Bury prescribed a set of inflexible directives which the two generations of Cambridge historians who edited the *History* from 1904 to the appearance of the last volume in 1936 treated "as Holy Writ." Bury was committed to the importance of research and to a wider historical view than Britain's national history. But for the two decades after 1914, German scholars were ostracized from the *History*, and ill-equipped Englishmen wrote in their stead.[91]

The only controversy in which he was involved, briefly and unwillingly, was when his inaugural appeal for scientific historical practice was challenged by G. M. Trevelyan.[92] When Bury said that it "has not yet become superfluous to insist that history is a science, no less and no more," he meant that historians must deal objectively with the facts by discarding "political and ethical encumbrances."[93] Bury repudiated the conventional "politico-ethical" theory which concentrated on those periods which appeared especially valuable in moral and political lessons. As a Professorial Fellow of King's College after 1902, Bury occasionally attended Politics Society meetings where teachers and students debated how one arrived at judgments about character and national conduct. In 1905, when the Society addressed the question of whether the moralist should influence politics, Bury, unlike his colleagues, took no position for the same reasons that he could admire, but ultimately condemn, Stubbs.[94] Granting that Stubbs's "own scientific work was a model for all students," Bury could not accept his measuring "out the domain of history with the compasses of political or ethical wisdom."[95] That same year, in his *Life of St. Patrick,* Bury condemned an earlier biography which lacked a thorough Germanic criticism of sources, a "methodical *Quellenkritik,*" because of the author's interest in establishing a "particular thesis." The business of the historian, for Bury, was "to ascertain facts. There is something essentially absurd in his wishing that any alleged fact should turn out to be true or should turn out to be false."[96] But Bury could suspend his insistence upon critical methods in the case of historians like E. A. Freeman, whose concept of the unity of history he found congenial.

In common with his colleagues at both Cambridge and Oxford, Bury believed in the increasing importance of history as training for national leadership. He never questioned the indispensability of a study of history "for the man who undertakes to share in the conduct of public affairs" or for the "private citizen who votes, and criticizes, and contributes to the shaping of public opinion."[97] But Bury, who never accepted progress as inevitable, believed that human evolution must be guided by a "scientific" study of history, which meant the "discovery, collection, classification, and interpretation of facts." Later did not necessarily mean better to Bury, and he urged that all periods be studied with the same attention, since the end of higher education was "the training of the mind to look at experience objectively, without immediate relation to one's own time and place."[98]

Bury's commitment to making Cambridge a center of historical inquiry rested on his conviction that continued progress depended upon the wisdom such investigation would discover. He attempted to promote research as President of the Union of Students in Historical Research, founded in 1920 exclusively for women students from Girton and Newnham. When C. R. Fay asked about the possibility of coordinating the group with the Historical Association, a body headed by university historians but with a membership essentially of school teachers, the Union decided to remain independent because, unlike the Association, they were concerned with research. Bury stated their objects as "mainly to bring together Teachers and Students in Historical Research, and enable them to know something about each other's work."[99] Within a few years, the universitywide Cambridge Historical Society was founded and Bury became its first President, and when the *Cambridge Historical Journal* was established in 1923, he was a member of the editorial board as well as a contributor.[100] From July 11, 1921 until the year before his death, Bury served as a Cambridge delegate to the Anglo-American Conference of Historians.

Bury's insistence upon research produced a personal bibliography of 369 entries. But his major work on Rome, Greece, and Byzantium, begun in the 1890s and continued until the 1920s, changed little in its interpretations from the 1890s despite the results of new research by other scholars throughout those two decades. In part that failure was due to chronic illness after 1910 and in part to his own temperament and limitations. When he published the *History of Greece to the Death of Alexander the Great* (1900), Sir Arthur Evans's excavations of Crete had begun. Although the book was reprinted eight times by 1912, it was not until 1913 that Bury rewrote the first chapter to incorporate the new evidence. Only "a few minor changes" were made apart from that and the book was reprinted twelve more times until the Balliol scholar Russell Meiggs revised it in 1951.[101] "Literature and art, philosophy and religion," were "touched upon only when they directly illustrate, or come into specially intimate connexion with, the political history." His "aim" was "to help education," and he intended the book for "a wider circle than those merely who are going through a course of school or university discipline."[102] While preaching the unity of European history, he approached it, consistently, through administration and political institutions. Culture, as a historical concept, he left contemptuously to anthropologists who "love it."[103] And he never appreciated the role of religion in the life of the peoples whose administrative history he studied.

By 1915, Bury's view that contingency was a historical determinant, although not necessarily the dominant one, made it increasingly difficult for him to make generalizations.[104] What he wanted to avoid was a view of history dependent on patterns of cause and effect. History was "not the dossier of an incompetent Providence, but the record of an uphill struggle" in which the human race, "heavily handicapped," has "accomplished wonders."[105] Five years later, when he traced the development of the "idea of progress" from the sixteenth century to his own time, Bury argued that belief in progress was an act of faith, "a dogma," connected with "the growth of modern science, with the growth of rationalism, and with the struggle for political and religious liberty." Although he concluded that all dogmas must escape from "the illusion of finality," which meant that eventually the belief in progress would also be transcended, Bury's own faith rested on the trinity of science, reason, and liberty, which he associated with a belief in progress as an act of dedicated human will.[106]

*

G. M. Trevelyan, at the opposite pole from Bury, was appointed Regius Professor on July 27, 1927 by Stanley Baldwin. Although he reached a greater audience than any historian of his time, he had even less impact on the development of history at Cambridge than his predecessor. The values which his writing continued to champion were taught to him first by Harrow schoolmasters who were Cambridge graduates. Trevelyan translated those values more widely and more effectively than anyone else. In his autobiography in 1949 he confessed that he had always "had a liking for those bits of history that have clear-cut happy endings," partly because such sections "have more artistic unity than history as a whole, which is a shapeless affair; and partly no doubt because they are more cheerful to contemplate." Saddened by World War I, he determined to write English history with a "more realistic and less partisan outlook," but when he published the *History of England* (1926) to the end of Victoria's reign and *England under Queen Anne* (1930–34), they too turned out to be stories with happy endings. Trevelyan remained an unregenerate optimist during a tenure that coincided with developments in economics, politics, and society that made happy endings increasingly improbable.

In the aesthetic and moral pleasure he drew from history, Trevelyan perpetuated the vanishing ethos of the independent gentleman delighting in his freedom and his surroundings. Just as Julian Huxley made his name and career in biology as a result of lying happily concealed in the marshes watching the mating habits of the grebe, Trevelyan became famous as an observer of the historical past. He delighted in walking and cycling over Garibaldi's battlefields or reading "old letters in their original homes, with the descendant as your kind helper and host."[107] When describing the use of history in his inaugural address, Trevelyan said not only that history "can make people wiser," but that it could "give them intellectual pleasure of a very high order indeed."[108]

Trevelyan began a short-lived academic career in 1898 when, after taking a first class honours degree in history and encouraged by Acton, he won a six-year Fellowship, the first ever awarded by Trinity College in History. In 1901, he was appointed a College Assistant Lecturer in History and taught Modern European History until 1903, when he left Cambridge to live in London and write literary history in more "spiritual freedom away from the critical atmosphere of Cambridge scholarship."[109] What appears to have bothered him more than the new scientific or "academic" emphases in history was the characteristically Cambridge tendency to analyze issues as if they were part of a Union debate, where cleverness took precedence over substantive understanding. Trevelyan had been secretary of the Union, where mental agility was often valued more than intellectual and moral principles.

As a young Fellow at Trinity, Trevelyan had "a single aim with two sides: to write history and to work for society."[110] When he went to London, it was for both reasons and he became actively involved in Liberal Party politics and in a variety of working people's clubs and unions.[111] But in 1908, he refused the Directorship of the London School of Economics in order to conserve his energies and devote them entirely to the writing of history. Three years later, he declined the Readership in History at Cambridge for the same reasons. But, unlike Oxford where teaching had won out over provisions for research, the new Readership at Cambridge had as its two statutory functions research and the writing and publication of books which would bring distinction to the University; and, acting as a friend, mentor, and adviser to the best third year men and young B.A.'s, about fifteen a year.[112] He continued to teach on an irregular basis until his appointment as Regius Professor.[113] Trevelyan's independent income permitted him the pleasure of remaining a gentleman historian outside the university, in marked contrast to almost all his university friends who depended on their salaries.

In 1903, he published "The Latest View of History," in the *Independent Review* in reply to Bury's inaugural address. When Trevelyan reprinted the essay in 1913, he cut out all references to Bury "against whom I never had any personal feeling." Trevelyan's antagonist was Seeley, who had told him that Carlyle and Trevelyan's great-uncle, Thomas Babing-ton Macaulay, were charlatans. Unlike Seeley, Trevelyan argued, Bury "was a real scientific historian" who had "a perfect right to say, like the cobbler, that 'there was nothing like leather.' "[114] "Clio," the 1913 version of "The Latest View," and his most thoughtful analysis of the uses and meaning of history, rejected the analogy between history and physical science because the historian should educate the mind of the citizen rather than deduce causal laws or trace social evolution. The "deeds themselves," which could be known with great precision, were, to Tre-velyan, "more interesting than their causes and effects." As an "art of narrative" history was "the tale of the thing done . . . which trains the political judgment by widening the range of sympathy and deepening the approval and disapproval of conscience; that stimulates by example youth to aspire and age to endure." What history trained was "a state of mind," which compelled a reader "to form judgments on a society or political problem without previous bias and with a knowledge of what was done." Trevelyan expected that this exercise would send the reader "back to still unsettled problems of modern politics and society, with larger views, clearer head, and better temper." Trevelyan wanted the study of history to destroy prejudice and to "breed enthusiasm." That was done by presenting ideals and heroes from other ages in a context written and read with an "intellectual passion" that was always associ-ated, for Trevelyan, with moral sensibility.[115]

Trevelyan never denied that history had a "scientific" function in accumulating facts and sifting evidence. But a literary imagination was more crucial in that it allowed the historian to "play" with the gathered facts, selecting, classifying, and making guesses and generalizations until he wrote the results in a form that would "attract and educate our Fel-low-countrymen." While Trevelyan warned the historian to tell a story, without attempting to discover either cause or effect or a direction in historical events, he also believed that the story must be told so that the essential lessons about decency, responsibility, duty, obligation, heroism, and their relation to free institutions, would be plain. Lack of bias was not so much objectivity as that combination of moral values and good sense that he found in his great-uncle's writing. Mommsen and Treitschke, "at whose German shrines we have been instructed to sacri-fice the traditions of English history," were partisans, "blind and bitter," while Macaulay was characterized by a "generosity of mind." The "glow of pride with which he speaks of our country or of European civilization, his indignation with knaves, poltroons and bullies of all parties and creeds, his intense and infectious pleasure in the annals of the past, rendered his history of England an education in patriotism, humanity and statesmanship." Macaulay's history made "men proud of their country, it made them understand her institutions, how they had come into existence and how liberty and order had been won by the wear and tear of contending factions."[116] In Trevelyan's portrait of Macaulay, he drew himself. His Whiggish view of history was never the product of a narrowness of mind or heart but represented warm and expansive affection for people and places. He knew that Macaulay had faults, but he could not admit that they were the errors that Herbert Butterfield had identified in his famous *The Whig Interpretation of History* (London, 1931), a critique of the optimistic English historiography that Trevelyan continued to champion for the rest of his life.

Trevelyan's 1927 inaugural lecture on *The Present Position of History* is striking for the tenacity of his fundamental opinions. He continued to distance himself from Seeley who, Trevelyan thought, had wrongly limited history to politics and who had written as "a publicist." Trevelyan was also a publicist, but of little England's liberal values rather than of an expanding empire, even though he maintained that history could not be "propaganda even in the best of causes." In a retrospective consideration of the development of Cambridge history, he stressed Acton's width of outlook, deep insight into the effect of principles upon action and ideals, and his sense of great issues and their significance. But most of all, Trevelyan admired Acton's "passionate feeling about right and wrong which often flared up from under his dignified and reserved manner of speech." In his immediate predecessor, Trevelyan found a training in the old-fashioned school of classical linguistic scholarship which gave Bury a mind of "unrivalled accuracy in detail." But it was Acton, rather than Bury, who represented the best Cambridge traditions to Trevelyan.[117]

Trevelyan remained a Whiggish historian who believed still in 1938 that the English preference for reform over revolution in the nineteenth century was a "happy choice" due "in part to our national character but also to our national institutions in which the oppressed saw a way of escape."[118] But in the early 1930s, he had also written about the lives, diets, and recreation of ordinary people, as well as about villages, women, education, and the social structure of the city of London.[119] Although his social history was pioneering and perceptive, Trevelyan had little direct effect on the organization, content and teaching of history at Cambridge.

The successful attempt of university historians in the twentieth century to establish control over their discipline meant that eventually they had to reject Trevelyan's view of every man's history-as-literature. Instead, they defended an enterprise learned within universities by methods of critical and comparative analysis which confirmed both the veracity of their work and their membership within the professional community of historians. But if the speech from the throne to both Houses of Parliament is generally an expression of prevailing national sentiment, then it is significant that George V's Silver Jubilee speech in 1935 should, as Asa Briggs points out, be based on a text by G. M. Trevelyan. "It is to me a source of pride and thankfulness," the King told the country, "that the perfect harmony of our Parliamentary system with our Constitutional Monarchy has survived the shocks that have in recent years destroyed other empires and other liberties." What George V saw in the "complex forms and balanced spirit of our Constitution" was "the slow accretion of centuries, the outcome of patience, tradition and experience, constantly finding channels old and new for the impulse towards liberty, justice and social improvement inherent in our people down the years." [120] Trevelyan's view of historical development, widely held by the great majority of Cambridge and Oxford historians before World War I, was increasingly rejected as professional historians became newly reflective about the uses of history. But to a larger educated public who had assimilated English history in the public schools and universities for the preceding half-century, Trevelyan's message, resonant in George V's Silver Jubilee speech, was a source of self-respect and national pride.

Chapter 6

Tutors and Teaching

The organization of history teaching in the Oxford and Cambridge colleges created a division of labor between professors, who gave leisurely public lectures and chose whether or not to pursue research and writing, and tutors, whose time was largely consumed by college work. Some tutors admired the German ideal of scholarship, but their careers as teachers rarely allowed them to pursue it. The subject was growing so rapidly that tutors had great difficulty in keeping up with the new literature.[1] Instead, teachers drew contemporary parallels for students whose empathic capacities were in doubt, and they tried to reach historical conclusions from a connected series of events. Authorities were compared to see whether they agreed rather than to examine their underlying assumptions or unstated intent. Comparative method established what happened, illustrated historical patterns, or demonstrated England's essentially sound development in contrast to that of other countries. For A. L. Smith, the "comparative method has shown that not derivation but development is the law among nations." Charles Boase, the history tutor at Exeter College from 1855 to 1894, began his lecture on "French Constitutional History" by pointing out that France, unlike England, had no constitutional history.[2] Seeley's assumption that the "history of England ought to end with something that might be called a moral . . . to set us thinking about the future and divining the destiny which is reserved for us," was incorporated into the Historical Tripos under the requirement of a paper in political science that compared the political institutions of ancient, medieval, and modern states. In 1917, when the Vice-Chancellor asked Cambridge's History Board to comment on the proposed examinations for Class I of the Civil Service, they replied that they "would regret the absence . . . of the comparative study of institutions at different stages in their development."[3] The past was used to document the values preserved and extended through England's evolution rather than to explain what had really happened in a particular historical time and place.

Oxford tutors, far more than their Cambridge colleagues, felt that their teaching obligations prevented them from either launching a collaborative workshop or keeping abreast of more specialized work. Even those engaged in research were prepared to move towards a more professional discipline only if they could move slowly. The "immense power of accumulated tradition in the Oxford system" was a formidable barrier which few overwhelmed tutors could surmount. The reluctance of examiners to accept new subjects, which they would have to learn as teachers, was an even more serious obstacle to innovation.[4] But the tutors were proud of their personal, collegiate methods, which relied often on long "walks, muddy boots," and "an abundance of discursive talk."[5]

Although more actively engaged in research than their Oxford colleagues, Cambridge tutors also had to learn nearly all the subjects required by the honours examinations. Thomas Thorneley, at Trinity Hall, lectured most on international law, political economy, and political science, but he also taught every other subject that was required: "As lecturers on history and allied subjects were few in number at that time, I was sent about from one subject to another, and was painfully conscious that my knowledge of some of them was far from profound, and that I was only scratching the surface when I ought to be digging." Thorneley retired early because there were few subjects that he could have lectured upon "without gross presumption."[6] As late as the 1920s, the young Charles W. Crawley was asked to examine in ancient history for the Historical Tripos. Crawley demurred because he was unfamiliar with the field. R. Vere Laurence of Trinity College reproved Crawley by observing that anyone hired as a history teacher should be able to teach and examine in any historical subject.[7] At Cambridge, as at Oxford, college tutors continued through the late 1920s to carry the "burden of College teaching and administration"; while the "progress of the higher studies and of original work in history" very largely depended "on the adequate provision of Professors at the head of the main branches of the subject, who can advance knowledge by their own work and by the assistance they give to others."[8]

When the subject of history was introduced as an honours degree course at both universities, few colleges had a historian. By the twentieth century many Oxford colleges had both a medievalist and a modernist who were expected to teach all of English history and the variety of alternatives in the Foreign Period and Special Subject. While Litterae Humaniores Honours students tended to choose the same options of the Roman Republic and fifth-century Athens, candidates for Honours in Modern History were faced with proliferating choices. It was fortuitous when all these subjects were taught competently. As early as 1869, the history tutors recognized that the contents of a rapidly developing discipline could not be mastered by any single college lecturer. Charles Shadwell of Oriel College, Robert Laing of Corpus Christi College, and Mandell Creighton of Merton College agreed to open their lectures to one another's pupils. By 1877, without any official recognition from the university, this voluntary association included all the colleges except Worcester and Hertford, and the Non-Collegiate body of students who were not affiliated with any college. By World War I, there were nearly 100 authorized teachers in modern history, including those in geography, paleography, diplomatic, political science, political economy, Indian history, military history, political theory and institutions, archaeology, epigraphy, papyrology, and anthropology. But there was no single prospectus for those reading history and information on lectures had to be collected and collated from announcements each term by the several Faculty boards. The insistence of Oxford tutors on independence from the university meant that there was no central organization of teaching and no ready way for students to figure out the best means of preparing themselves for the honours examinations. J. N. L. Myres, critical of the tutor's exclusive and jealous control over students, observed dryly, "no one unprovided with a tutor would ever find his way to lectures."[9]

*

When the new Cambridge Historical Tripos was launched in 1873, there were only two teachers of history, the Regius Professor and a lecturer at Trinity College. The following year G. W. Prothero left Eton for King's College and in 1875 Oscar Browning followed him. At its first meeting in November 1876, a year after the first Historical Tripos examination was given, the new Board of Historical Studies established that only those lecturers whom they recognized would be allowed to advertise their lectures. A month later, the Board confirmed its new authority by publishing the approved list of lectures for successive terms in the *Cambridge University Reporter*.[10] Then, in May 1877, when Boards of Studies were given jurisdiction over the competence of those college lecturers who wished to lecture to all members of the university either "freely or on payment of a fee approved by the Board," the Historical Board secured its control over the teaching of History throughout the university.[11] The Board, empowered to admit lecturers to a Conference of Teachers, approved and publicized lectures in meetings held at least annually with professors. They also recognized intercollegiate lecturers and arranged a plan of combined teaching.[12] But it was not until 1885 that the first five university lectureships in history were created.[13] By the following year, both Trinity Hall and St. John's had a history lecturer; F. W. Maitland had left his law practice to become a University Reader in English Law and an occasional teacher and examiner in the Historical Tripos; and Mandell Creighton had emigrated from Oxford to fill the new Dixie Professorship of Ecclesiastical History.

It took a decade for the new tripos to secure university lecturers and a generation for it to find a place in the university. When the degree course in history began, James Bryce approached Henry Sidgwick about launching a historical journal at Cambridge. Sidgwick replied despondently that there was an "extreme barrenness of this land" and that no "single man in Cambridge" was "competent to deal with modern history in an intelligent way." Sidgwick found instead "antiquarians and grubbers of facts" but "no young men interested in history."[14] A dearth of university and college provision for history teaching in Cambridge was both cause and effect of undergraduates' and dons' initial lack of interest in the subject. The subsequent development of the Historical Tripos at Cambridge was marked consistently by complaints about the insufficiency of staff, teaching rooms, and reference books. In 1888, the General Board, despite continuing requests from the History Board, had still not provided a room for the Professor, a reading room, or a location for a library. Even when the colleges were willing to provide some funds for additional teachers in history, a rare circumstance after the 1870s when college revenues were eroded by the agricultural depression, the university was unwilling to make up the necessary difference.[15] There was no permanent home for the historical library until 1913, when it was moved to a bay of the Departmental Library in the University Lecture Rooms, where it shared a floor space of 2,250 feet with the Medieval and Modern Languages Library, the Moral Sciences and Economics Library, and the Bendall Sanskrit Library.[16] Even in 1928, there was only one professor, the Regius Professor of Modern History, "concerned directly with the general historical field that is traversed by all the students."[17]

In the scuffle for university resources, the history faculty tried to compete with their colleagues in the sciences and other new disciplines by demonstrating that they served larger national purposes. In February 1878, the Board of History tried to provide for Indian Civil Service (ICS) candidates by requesting a salary from the University Chest and permanent university provision for either a Professor or Reader in Indian History. Two months later, the Senate granted £100 for the next three years for instruction in Indian History and Geography, and the grant was renewed for three additional years in 1881.[18] But before the grant expired, a separate Board of Indian Civil Service Studies was set up on May 10, 1883 and expanded on March 11, 1897 into a Special Board of Studies to which the Regius Professor of Modern History was added as one of three *ex officio* members, along with the Professors of Arabic and Sanskrit.[19] Although two University Teachers in History participated in training ICS candidates, resources and recognition went to the Special Board of Indian Civil Service Studies and not to the History Board. In contrast, at Oxford until 1930, the History School taught ICS candidates and could prove that it was training national and imperial leaders by pointing proudly to the continuous success of its graduates in Indian Civil Service careers.

Cambridge slighted history because its teachers could not at first attract students to the new Tripos. In part, that was due to the reluctance of the colleges to promote new liberal studies such as history by providing college entrance scholarships in the subject. In 1883 there were 80 history undergraduates, but although nine colleges offered entrance awards in the natural sciences, none were available in history. As scholarship awards in history increased, able men found the new discipline increasingly attractive. By 1888, the number of undergraduates reading history had grown to 115. Five years later, in addition to fourteen entrance prizes for the natural sciences, there were five for history and by the end of the next decade, the thirteen awards available in the sciences were nearly matched by twelve in history.[20]

While the most distinguished Oxford historians went out to colonize the history faculties within the new British, colonial, and North American universities, Cambridge's outstanding young historians tended to remain at their own university. It is ironic that those who left Oxford to teach history in universities all over the English-speaking world took a parochial and limited historical view in their intellectual baggage, while those who never left Cambridge responded to a wider and more cosmopolitan vision of their discipline. But unlike Oxford, history at Cambridge did not become the most popular of the new disciplines until the late 1920s.

Another explanation for the small numbers who read history in the early years lies in the colleges' inability, noticeable even in the twentieth century, to provide history teaching. The transition from the older system of college lectures to the modern practice of personal teaching, called "supervision" in Cambridge and tutorials in Oxford, was very slow. Alfred Marshall, who returned to Cambridge from Oxford in 1885 as the Professor of Political Economy, attempted in 1897 to introduce the "Oxford system of essays which the writers come and read aloud." [21] But even so large and well-endowed a college as Trinity did not supervise its history students when Trevelyan was an undergraduate there in the late 1890s. E. A. Benians arrived at St. John's College in 1899 to find that although the history lecturers provided individual weekly teaching during a student's first term, such teaching was only occasional for the rest of the year. When Z. N. Brooke was elected to a fellowship at Caius College in 1908, he was the first historian on the staff. From 1886 to 1888, the much smaller and poorer college, Corpus Christi, had a history fellow, A. A. Cooper, who had taken a first class honours in the Tripos in 1883 after graduating as nineteenth Wrangler. But after his premature death, there was no history teaching until Geoffrey Butler was appointed in 1910. [22]

Cambridge historians, enthusiastic about their subject, cannot be blamed for history's relative failure in comparison with the glamorous success of the new sciences. Trinity College, where Henry Sidgwick was a Fellow, offered a scholarship in natural science as early as 1867. The following year, the college decided to award at least one fellowship every three years to a graduate of the Natural Sciences Tripos. Clerk Maxwell, a Trinity man, was appointed the first Cavendish Professor of Experimental Physics in 1871. The colleges, which had been asked to contribute to a physics laboratory, had not been particularly forthcoming, and the cost of the chair and of the extravagantly built Cavendish Laboratory was borne by the Chancellor of the University, William Cavendish, seventh Duke of Devonshire and himself a Trinity product. [23] Physiology, founded by another Trinity Fellow, "became firmly established and internationally recognized" after 1880. Gerald Geison has argued that the Emersonian dictum that "an institution is the lengthened shadow of one man" is largely true in the case of Michael Foster's creation of a flourishing school of physiology in Cambridge. [24] Personal energy and the ability to recognize and organize talent were crucial to scientific enterprises where cooperative effort was required for research into previously uninvestigated phenomena. But in history, where efforts were devoted more to transmitting lessons taught by the transparent past than to discovering unanticipated or concealed knowledge, individual personality played a lesser, though not unimportant, role in cultivating and perpetuating the new field. An even more important difference may have been that in the sciences, unlike history, individual sponsors such as Cavendish were willing to lavish money upon costly facilities. While history did not need the expensive construction of a laboratory, its teachers would certainly have welcomed a wealthy donor willing to build a library and to endow scholarships for students, fellowships for teachers and professorships in specialized areas. But it was not financial support, charismatic personality, or novel discoveries that shaped the subject of history. The importance of the history teachers lay more in the consistency of their views and in the ways in which they reflected and extended a national consensus.

*

While Cambridge teachers actively sought greater university endowment of their activities, the Oxford history tutors successfully resisted university intrusion at every level. The greatest benefit of their independence was that they defined and regulated their own teaching and the standard of work required for honours students. Especially through the Modern History Association, established by college teachers to control curriculum, teaching, and examinations without interference from professors or the university, the tutors successfully rebuffed regulation. But that Association did not necessarily make them specialists either in the 1860s when they began intercollegiate teaching or in the early twentieth century when history had become the most popular subject at Oxford. Specialists, as the concept came to be recognized by the turn of the century, earned a scholarly reputation by consulting original materials in a particular field and writing about them, as Firth did on seventeenth-century English history.[25]

As the numbers of honours students grew at Oxford, university lecturers were appointed to supplement the more general teaching of the college tutors. These "specialists" were hardly a threat to the tutors since they were usually recruited from among them. Boase was University Reader in Modern History from 1884 to 1894, but his only scholarly work was a translation of the first volume of Ranke's eight-volume *History of England* (1875). The first Reader in Indian History, from 1864 to 1913, was Sidney Owen. Although he had spent two years as Professor of History at Elphinstone College, Bombay, he had never studied Indian history. Eight years after becoming Reader, he wrote *India on the Eve of the British Conquest* (1872). The book, which described the "moral turpitude of most of the prominent personages that occupy these sheets," was, as he admitted, based entirely on secondary sources.[26]

Cambridge historians were more receptive to the ideal of specialized research for college teachers. But in 1897, when the History Board was empowered to appoint University Teachers to the Special Board of Indian Civil Service Studies, they appointed first Gerald Patrick Moriarty of Pembroke and then C. J. B. Gaskoin of Jesus, although neither was a scholar of Indian History.[27] Only in late 1922, after continuous prodding by Firth, the Oxford Modern History Board accepted that "the methods of teaching and examining in Special Subjects should be improved . . . if the teaching of Special Subjects were, as far as is practicable, entrusted to the Professors, Readers, and University Lecturers, and others who might be invited by the Board to give instruction in each subject."[28] But seven years later, J. C. Masterman at Christ Church wrote to F. F. Urquhart, then Chairman of the Board of Modern History, to protest that it was still the tradition of the Board, in selecting University Lecturers, to appoint "roughly in order of seniority those members of the Faculty whose work in Oxford has been of value to the School" rather than those "whose published work gave evidence of their preeminence in research."[29]

*

The new teachers of history at both universities tried to achieve an accurate knowledge of their subject, but their teaching was directed towards success in examinations, which were devised according to the "testability" of a common level of knowledge. Examinations were governed by the Examiners who, as Goldwin Smith had predicted accurately in 1868, became the "most important officers of the University."[30] The history tutors at Oxford, who were Examiners generally for at least one three-year period during their teaching careers, controlled their subject by setting its examination standards and by nominating its Examiners. Very few agreed with E. A. Freeman's complaint that examinations had "degraded teaching into a trade."[31] On the contrary, the Examiners' annual three-week meeting, lasting at least five hours a day to discuss hundreds of papers, provided a rare opportunity for common reflection upon their subject with outside Examiners from other universities. But, since the outside Examiners were nearly all Oxford graduates, there was considerable unanimity of perception and purpose even though there was often criticism of the methods by which history was taught at Oxford.[32] The examination system in modern history, in spite of continuing objections, persisted in Oxford almost unchanged into the present.

After the mid-nineteenth century, for most tutors in universities and for the students they guided, examinations became a disciplinary force that regulated how both groups spent their time.[33] Examinations disciplined teachers because they had to learn the subject which was being examined so as to teach it. But from the 1860s until the turn of the century, chronic debate raged in the universities and in the educated public about the role of examinations.[34] A general defense was based upon their presumed ability to awaken and encourage latent or unknown interests; and they were considered a test of the "possession of mental power" and of "industry in accumulating knowledge."[35] Another consensus held that examinations were a more democratic, more equitable means of awarding merit than any other system.[36] Accepting these arguments, history teachers believed further that their final honours examinations permitted the Examiners to recognize and reward the best qualities of mind more justly than either a series of tests or an undergraduate research thesis. Honours examinations were devised to judge first-class quality. Those with such quality were expected to pass successfully into influential careers and they did.[37] But in July 1884, when Mandell Creighton left Oxford for Cambridge, he insisted that he did not want "*ever*" to lecture directly on any period offered for examination. Instead, he preferred to take "a subject" within a period "concerned with intellectual history, and show its general bearing on the problems of the time."[38] Creighton found that such lectures were much more acceptable in Cambridge than in Oxford.

Beyond the universities, faith in examinations took hold in the second half of the nineteenth century as a measure of both quality and performance in the developing professions, which came to depend on the new educational system developed for primary and secondary education. The great educational reforms were begun by the Newcastle Commission, appointed in 1858, which recommended the establishment of local boards of education and the construction of elementary schools in every area. Then, in 1862, the Clarendon Commission investigated the nine great endowed public schools where the wealthy sent their children en route to Oxford and Cambridge. A graduate of Eton, Harrow, Rugby, or the other great public schools easily moved into the governing classes in every area of British life until the last two decades of the nineteenth century. But by the late 1870s, a first or second class honours degree from Oxford or Cambridge had become a necessary requirement for entrance into the best public and private careers.

Reforms at the major public schools were not devised to provide greater opportunities for larger numbers of secondary school students. The innovators at every level of education wanted the existing structure of schools to be more efficient. In 1864 the Taunton Commission turned to middle-class and endowed grammar schools and their report led to the Endowed Schools Act of 1869. At every level, from Robert Lowe's "revised code," which instituted a system of payment by results for teachers in elementary schools aided and inspected by the state, to the Oxford and Cambridge Schools' Examination Boards, established in 1857 to set the Local Examinations, the reformers wanted a common instrument for judging the newly national education system. They put their trust in examinations as the most impartial way of measuring educational achievement throughout the country.[39]

Within higher education, for "good or evil," Montagu Burrows pointed out in 1868, "the system of Examinations had taken entire possession of the University" and "woe to the study" not included in honours examinations.[40] Four years later, A. W. Ward predicted accurately that examinations would determine the contents of a degree course. What "the University cannot test," he wrote, "it is contented not to control."[41] Examinations were meant to test moral fiber as well as what was learned. By 1877, Henry Latham, first tutor and then Master at Trinity College, Cambridge, insisted that his twenty years of experience with the examination system revealed it to be "a very valuable piece of mental discipline" which called out the "courage and the resources that there are in a man." Merely to take the test "conscientiously and [to] have done his best, gives a moral elevation to his character, even if he fail in winning any very marked success."[42]

In spite of its advocates, no aspect of the reformed university was denounced as much as the honours examinations. What especially disturbed the critics was the consistent gap between theory and practice. Instead of encouraging character and independent thought, both teachers and their students relied on mindless cramming as the route to a high class of honours. It might be argued that even the brightest and best students always prepare for extensive examinations by cramming. But concentrated study can be compatible with thinking. The opponents of history honours examinations charged that the examinations relied on mere memory rather than on an understanding of information within a wider and often ambiguous context that required students to make reflective discriminations. If the historical past was meant to serve England's future, then examinations might have been early exercises in recognizing that large amounts of information, from recent or distant time, were often ambiguous and incomplete. Instead, the study of history was organized as an unequivocal narrative demonstrating how the well-meaning and well-educated were bound to succeed in any enterprise diligently pursued.

The final two papers in the Cambridge Historical Tripos, Subjects for Essays, were a characteristically Cambridge departure from the Oxford model. In addition to requiring the mastery of a body of information, the Essays tested a quality of mind.[43] In 1898, a discussion of the grounds for awarding classes of honours led the Examiners to adopt a principle which was to remain perhaps the major criterion for success in the Tripos examinations: a candidate's essay made evident the way in which he thought and no amount of historical information could compensate for poor thinking. M. H. Visnam, of St. John's College, received 342 points, normally sufficient for third class honours, but he was only given an Ordinary Degree because the Examiners agreed unanimously that his "essay was quite worthless."[44]

The Oxford Examiners also worried that students learned by rote instead of thinking autonomously. An Oxford undergraduate who came back as an outside Examiner for Oxford was Ramsay Muir, Professor of History at Liverpool. In 1913, Muir concluded his three-year term with an indictment of teaching within the Oxford School that might have been written a generation earlier or a generation later. Muir criticized the tutors for providing the student with a "pemmican" that made it "superfluous for him to read and think for himself." The answers Muir saw "had not passed through the crucible of the student's mind" but were merely "neatly-made up packets of correct opinions, still in the original wrappers in which they were served."[45] Muir's charges were corroborated by the other Examiners whose annual reports complained to the Board of Modern History that the curriculum and examinations were not achieving their ends. A chronic criticism was that students were not reading even their limited assigned pages but were relying instead on cram sheets prepared by their tutors to furnish the principal answers for each possible question.

*

The examination system and fundamental teaching rested on tutors who devoted themselves unstintingly to their students' intellectual and emotional maturation. Those Oxford history tutors to whom students felt the greatest debts from the 1870s until the 1920s were Franck Bright of University College, Arthur Johnson of All Souls College, H. A. L. Fisher of New College and, above all, A. L. Smith of Balliol College. The Cambridge undergraduates who were most interested in history during the same period were generally King's or Trinity College men and they depended on G. W. Prothero, Oscar Browning, and J. H. Clapham, all at King's. Trinity College, too, tried to develop history teaching, and the college's undergraduates gave extraordinary performances in the Historical Tripos and in their eventual professions. But until the 1930s, although the Historical Tripos attracted talented Trinity undergraduates like B. G. Brown, who became Emmanuel and Downing College's Director of Studies in History, George Kitson Clark, G. P. Gooch, and C. P. and G. M. Trevelyan, neither Trinity nor any of the other colleges was as successful as King's in winning students over to a concentration on historical studies.

Nearly every student who became a teacher of history at Oxford from 1877 until 1916, as well as many distinguished statesmen, were pupils of A. L. Smith.[46] In his responsible elitism and his active social conscience, Smith represented the Oxford ideal generally and the Balliol ethos in particular. His entire adult life, first as a teacher and after 1916 as Master, was spent at Balliol teaching that ideal as the essential lesson of national history. There, he drew undergraduates into his family, his vacations, and his enthusiasm for sports. Although recognizing that he was an inspiring teacher and a model for his students, H. A. L. Fisher said that Smith was "too busy pushing young gentlemen over exam fences to be a profound scholar." Fisher believed that Smith lacked learning, but he gave him credit as a teacher who made the "men and women of the past" come alive. Ernest Barker saw him as loving the "whole play of social life, which the scholar, by the very nature of his vocation, must very largely abjure." Smith's lectures on the "Steps to Stubbs," an introduction to Stubbs's *Select Charters*, did not prepare his students to think of him as someone "who 'led you on' to the sources and to research." V. H. Galbraith, a Smith student who became Regius Professor, felt that had "A. L. given to personal research what he gave to young men he could, one felt, have been an outstanding historian."[47]

To dismiss Smith as merely a tutor, no matter how effective, sells him considerably short. His Ford lectures in 1905 on *The Church and State in the Middle Ages* (1913) and two published lectures on *Maitland* (1908) demonstrated "brilliant . . . thinking and writing and original research."[48] But it never occurred to Smith that the historian should strive to control his inclinations, instincts, and passions. On the contrary, he felt deeply that history, essentially a testimony to individual effort, was the best spur to an altruistic career. With first class honours in Greats and second class in Modern History, Smith lost an Open Fellowship at Trinity because of his marriage. That was the best thing that could have

happened to him because it meant that he could accept a lectureship in
Modern History at Balliol in 1887. Balliol and Smith were meant for each
other. Jowett was quick to recognize the fit and came to rely upon him
increasingly to carry out Balliol's educational ideals. In 1907, Smith became coholder of the Jowett Fellowship with J. L. Strachan-Davidson
and, in 1916, he succeeded Strachan-Davidson as Master.

Smith was a political liberal who practiced what he preached. Actively engaged in public service outside Oxford, he was a Poor Law
Guardian and a vigorous supporter of Toynbee Hall, and he taught energetically and consistently in University Extension, the Workers' Educational Association, and the Tutorial Classes Movement. When Helen M.
Madeley, a history teacher in secondary schools and training colleges,
wrote *History as a School for Citizenship* (1920) to prepare the schools for
the "reconstruction" required by the postwar years, she naturally turned
to Smith for the foreword.[49] Extending Jowett's legacy, Smith and Balliol
brought the first working-class students to Oxford. He was also one of
the earliest coaches for women; he served on the Council of Lady Margaret Hall (a women's college at Oxford) for over twenty years; three of
his daughters got scholarships at Girton and first class honours in history
and two of them married Oxford historians.

In common with other Oxford history tutors, Smith coached students for their examinations by providing simple "handouts" summariz-
ing examination answers. But if the tutorial tradition tended generally to
conform to handed-down tradition, there was a more exciting side of
teaching identified with Smith which may explain his considerable undergraduate following. His lectures, often based on his own research,
were subtle and historically imaginative. But the consistent thread in all
the subjects he covered was a view of history as instruction in moral and
social obligations and the meaning of nationalism. Throughout his career, in every lecture and piece of writing, he insisted upon the efficacy
of individual effort and argued "very forcibly against the theory of un-
conscious development." In college and public lectures on politics and
economics, he attempted to prove that the history of Britain's institutions
provided "conclusive evidence of the dominant importance" of "individual minds." As a subject, history was expected to provide its students
and the public with a "general idea of the world of the past on which the
present is built up; some sense, however dim, of the continuity of national life; some consciousness of the great inheritance transmitted from
past generations to be handed down by us unimpaired to the generations
to come, . . . a necessary part . . . of the moral equipment of a civilized
man."[50]

Smith provided not only an optimistic affirmation of historical directions, but specific, current sources of information to enable future leaders to attack problems successfully. Smith saw history as instruction for a life of dedicated leadership, conducted reasonably, imaginatively, and knowledgeably. He deliberately made his teaching provocative so that a student would be roused "to analyze, to criticize, to recombine for himself." Smith was convinced that the skill required to answer historical questions involved the kind of economical thinking that could be transferred to every aspect of life. To Smith, "History consisted in giving the right answers to the right questions."[51] He never doubted that he knew both.

Smith's enormously popular lectures, especially on "Political and Social Questions," were explicit moral lessons but they were also complex and full of ambiguities and qualifications. The "Questions" covered the poor laws, federal and local government, state intervention, population, socialism, the census, statistics, taxation, political ideals, and land tenure. In these topics, as in his more traditional courses on Stubbs, English constitutional history, and the popes in the thirteenth century, he went beyond the limited authorities formally recommended by the Board of Modern History and required his students to read a wide variety of primary sources and the most recent secondary scholarship.[52] Although the "Questions" were not directly related to the honours examinations, Smith taught them to thousands of students because they "interested me and set me reading and thinking"; and they were all matters of "social urgency" that revealed "proper tendencies." But most of all they proved how "surely if slowly" progress rewards the right efforts and "how hopeful and how stimulating is the ultimate outlook . . . because that progress depends on the sum of individual minds and individual conduct."[53] The "Questions," although peripheral to the traditional history curriculum, were characteristic of the Oxford School in their emphasis upon the importance of rationality, social duty, perseverance, methods of analysis, discrimination, and citizenship. Smith, more than any other teacher, made a growing national commitment to the state consistent with individual choice and the exercise of informed and rational will.

The ethics of national history inspired teaching throughout Oxford. In Balliol, in addition to the large collections of notes by A. L. Smith, Richard Lodge's handouts, and odd bits of work prepared for students by H. W. C. Davis when he was tutor from 1902 to 1921, also recited the articles of the History School's faith. In Lodge's handout on "The Tudor Period," a four-page summary of the salient features of 150 years, the final sentence is: "A nation's character is the product of its history."[54] Davis, characteristically, read a paper to the members of the Balliol History club in 1907 on "The Meaning of History." We "resort to history," he said, "for a confirmation of our faith in the value of human effort; we go to it for examples" and learn "the duty of spending ourselves in order that the toils of those who preceded us may not be in vain, and that the ages to come may not reproach us with a careless stewardship of human destinies. . . ."[55] When Davis became the Regius Professor of Modern History in 1925, he made the point that Oxford historians still found the "real stuff and substance of history" in the "Sisyphean" common human intellectual efforts to establish the "fabric of a just, harmonious, and well-ordered state."[56] Charles Boase, at Exeter College, echoed and re-enforced the same themes.[57] When the young Herbert Gladstone was asked in 1876 to lecture twice a week at Keble College on German and Italian history, he thought that in addition to reading the standard books for those lectures, he should also read F. D. Maurice's book on philosophy as preparation for any other history assignment because it dwelled so helpfully "on the connection between ethics and politics and argues that to understand the latter one must study the moral nature of man."[58]

*

While the development of the English state provided tutors with an ideological stability that ignored other, potentially divisive, issues, the college remained the immediately secure center of their life. But the need to teach larger numbers of students a greater variety of subjects meant that college teachers of history began to feel inadequate before their growing responsibilities. One response was to turn to a wider intercollegiate life where teachers from different colleges could discuss and share their obligations. Throughout the nineteenth century university clubs had existed either to explore serious philosophical or contemporary problems or to provide relief from the company and conversation predictable at a college's high table. But the development of new degree subjects created innovative kinds of organizations, more specific in their purposes, that were directed to the development and control of disciplines.

At Oxford, college history teachers were brought together in their own formidable organization with the expansion of the late nineteenth-century History Tutors' Association. In 1891, Arthur Johnson succeeded H. B. George, a military historian from New College and the Association's first Honorary Secretary, and although he shared the post with Arthur Hassall of Christ Church six years later, Johnson remained the dominant figure until the 1920s. With Johnson in charge, the Association decided every substantial issue concerned with the teaching and study of history at Oxford. The only exception was the curriculum which was nominally under the control of the universitywide Modern History Board created in 1883. But in spite of the Statute of 1882, which divided Board seats equally between those elected by the college tutors and those appointed *ex officio* by the university, the Modern History Board, when in session, generally had a majority of three teachers to two *ex officio* members. As a result, the college tutors determined "every question connected with the study of Modern History exactly as they pleased."[59] Perhaps most importantly, the tutors controlled the nomination of Examiners in history. It was no accident that Arthur Johnson examined the greatest number of students.[60] Stubbs was elected chairman of the first Board in February 1883 and for the next decade, a Regius or Chichele Professor chaired the Board but none of them ever led it.

When Arthur Johnson was elected chairman in 1893, the last fiction of professorial influence over teaching was abandoned. The professors continued to provide the basic textbooks that interpreted the meaning of history, while the tutors maintained exclusive control over every other aspect of instruction. Johnson remained a vigorous chairman until 1912, supported by the truest, most aggressive believers in the tutorial ideal, A. L. Smith and Edward Armstrong of Queens. In January 1908, the Association was divided into a larger Modern History Association of professors, readers, tutors, and lecturers, responsible for the lecture list and all ordinary business, and a smaller Tutors' Association, which met to consider matters concerning only college tutors and lecturers. Then, in February 1913, the Modern History Association's functions were transferred to the new Faculty of Modern History, which elected the Board. After the war, the Tutors' Association became a social dining club.

Unlike the Oxford Modern History Association, which existed essentially as a vehicle for the tutors' supervision of historical studies, the Cambridge Junior Historians was formed in 1911 to "give one another practical assistance in such matters as the direction of studies and the recommendation of books."[61] At Oxford, the Tutors' Association acted to protect the independence of the college teacher from encroachment by any centralizing force of the university, including that of the professors. At Cambridge, where the professors held a crucial position in the History Board, which assigned subjects, lecturers, and examination questions, the Junior Historians concentrated instead on their fields of study. The names of the two organizations indicate their different emphases. The members of the Oxford Modern History Association were the college teachers who not only taught modern history for the honours examination, but shared a fundamental conviction that the teaching of history was a preparation for civic and imperial leadership. The Junior Historians shared their Oxford colleagues' identification of history and citizenship, but they felt themselves to be apprentices in a continuous process of learning their craft so that they would become full-fledged historians.

The Junior Historians met first on January 26, 1911, in C. K. Webster's rooms in King's College, where nine history lecturers heard Z. N. Brooke of Gonville and Caius College on "The Teaching of Medieval History." Present as founding members were Geoffrey Butler, F. G. M. Beck, C. A. Elliot, C. R. Fay, J. W. Reynolds, F. R. Salter, G. R. Tatham and H. W. V. Temperley. By the fall of 1912 the Society was limited to sixteen members and a rotating historical book club had been launched. There was an occasional paper on a topic for the Tripos, such as A. A. Seaton's "Toleration under the Stuarts," on October 24, 1912; Seaton was an established scholar, who had recently published a monograph with the same title.[62] But the general practice was to use the meeting for discussion of historical and pedagogic methodology, bibliography, the state of historical fields in England, the U.S., and the continent, and the relation of history to other Tripos subjects such as political science. In the spring of 1913, the list of speakers was extended to Oxford men such as A. J. Carlyle and W. G. S. Adams. From then on the speakers were invited on the basis of their original research and writing. By the beginning of the academic year in 1913, the Society began to suggest to the Board of History and Archaeology that Tripos reforms were needed to encourage students to proceed from a general study of history in Part I of the examinations to a more specialized study in Part II.

On May 20, 1919, the 35th meeting of the Society was held after a hiatus of five years, new members were elected to replace the five who had died during the war, and the decision was made to extend the influence of the group. During the interwar years, the Society requested and received from individual teachers analyses of the lectures those teachers were giving as well as new book lists for the Tripos so that the faculty could keep up with the rapidly developing literature. They sent a steady stream of memorandums to the Board of History with the Society's recommendations on improving history teaching and examining in Cambridge. They also initiated and maintained regular conferences with headmasters to guide both history teaching and examining in the schools for screening students with a capacity for history. The possibility of forming a postgraduate school in history was explored, and they tried generally to make the discipline of history, as taught and examined in

Cambridge, an expert and self-sufficient field of study. When the Society discussed the Political Science requirement in both parts of the Tripos, they listened to those who had done the most to develop the subject, such as Graham Wallas and Harold Laski, as before the war they had heard Adams and Carlyle. As a result of these deliberations, they concluded that the history of political thought was more valuable than Seeley's preference for the inductive study of civic and national constitutions.[63]

Consistently throughout the minute books, the various secretaries recorded that the meetings usually ran well past the scheduled hour. The topics and the lively participation of the members leave an impression of a group who took their subject and their responsibilities as history teachers very seriously. When Previté-Orton read a paper on "Italian History and the Way It Has Been Written," on February 28, 1923, the Secretary noted: "Even the aridity of the minute book must contain a record of the unanimous and emphatic opinion of the few members present that Mr. Previté-Orton's paper was the best thing in their experience of the Society's meetings." This observation was not made to parochial friends who read and approved one another's papers, but to a well-informed and diverse group who heard and challenged the most distinguished, most adventurous scholars of their day such as Firth, Pollard, Pitt-Rivers, Carlyle, Adams, Bury, Tout, A. P. Newton, R. W. Seton-Watson, J. L. Hammond, Eileen Power, E. F. Jacob, J. W. Allen, and even Don Augustine Edwards, the former Chilean Ambassador to England. They continued to consider the requirements of the syllabus; the most recent reading lists, which were discussed and compared critically; the historian's training; the controversies in methodology and interpretation; the supervision of students; and the condition of each field of history and those affecting it such as anthropology and political science. Recognizing, perhaps, that the coming of age for adults within a university cannot be indefinitely prolonged, they decided that anyone over 40 could no longer be a "Junior" historian. In 1927 the membership had grown beyond 25, and the group remained lively and professional. The 117th and last meeting before World War II was on November 22, 1939. In 1946 the society was revived and again inaugurated serious discussions about the profession and the reform of the Tripos.[64]

*

Historians in late nineteenth-century Cambridge recognized that the prestige of the new sciences left little room for competing disciplines without patrons willing to provide the quickening inducement of scholarships, fellowships and prizes that rewarded excellence and conferred standing. But two colleges deliberately attempted to distinguish themselves in the new arts subject of history. King's and Trinity both had intellectual aspirations, and it was no accident that they supplied most of the members of the Apostles, the most intellectually select of the undergraduate societies. The sense of community which each college created was maintained by the large numbers of graduates who chose to remain as fellows of their colleges for the rest of their lives. By 1922, Trinity graduates made up 97 percent of the College's fellows, and in King's the percentage was 85.[65] King's had been intended for the King's Scholars at Eton and ties between the public school and the college were so close that even in the late nineteenth century all the Eton masters had been chosen from the younger fellows at the college. In 1882, a series of statutes transformed King's. Resident members were given a dominant part in college government; fellowships, no longer tied to celibacy and now awarded competitively as a result of a dissertation involving original work, were terminated in six years unless held in conjunction with a College office.[66] These positions acknowledged demonstrated ability and provided an opportunity for research. To promote scholarship further, four professorial fellowships were created.

Trinity was the first college to appoint a history fellow, but the energies and resources there were devoted largely to making Trinity the leading college in the new sciences, and the history appointment lapsed towards the end of the century. In 1892, G. P. Gooch came up to Trinity where he was influenced by the economic historian, William Cunningham, by Seeley, and by the philosopher, J. M. E. M'Taggart. In 1894, Gooch took first class honours in the Historical Tripos. Although he also won both the Lightfoot Scholarship in Ecclesiastical History and the Members' Prize for an English Essay in 1895 and the Thirlwall Prize in 1896, he failed to obtain either of the two available Trinity fellowships in 1896, which went instead to a mathematician and a physiologist. Had there been a third, Gooch was told, he would have received it. He attributed his failure to the lack of weight given to history at Trinity, even though the examiners for the fellowship were Cunningham and the classical historian B. E. Hammond.[67] In 1898 G. M. Trevelyan was appointed a history fellow at Trinity, where both Frederick Pollock and Frederick Maitland were then undergraduates. Lord Acton, after his appointment as Regius Professor, was attached to Trinity. But it was not until 1906 that the College appointed a History Lecturer.[68]

Although none of the Cambridge colleges approximated Balliol in its prevailing ethos of public service, in its emphasis upon history and classics, or in the entry of its students into the principal levels of public office, King's came the closest. In 1873 King's became the first Cambridge college to admit only honours students, and until after World War I, King's turned out the largest numbers of history honours students of any college. King's undergraduates also excelled in classics, in which they received as many first- and second-class honours degrees as any other college, and they easily surpassed all other candidates in the moral sciences from 1889 to 1913. In the postwar years, history became more interesting to Kingsmen than either classics or the moral sciences, and it was a close rival to the natural sciences.

King's was dragged into the modern world by devoted teachers who made their college capable of producing a national elite. Brooke Foss Westcott, Regius Professor of Divinity at Cambridge from 1870, a major historian of religious thought and later Bishop of Durham, was elected to one of the new King's professorial fellowships in 1882. There he enthusiastically joined Austen Leigh, who became Provost of King's and Vice-Chancellor of the University, George Prothero, and Oscar Browning in effectively carrying out the reconstruction of the college. With the subsequent help of Nathanial Wedd and Goldsworthy Lowes Dickinson, they created a closely-knit society of 46 fellows and about 150 undergraduates who "carried the special atmosphere of the place and the influence" of their "teachers with them all their lives."[69]

In 1872 G. W. Prothero received a first in Classics and a temporary assistant mastership at Eton. The following year he had to choose between a mastership at Marlborough College and a lectureship in history at King's. Marlborough offered a secure career, while history at Cambridge was still part of the disappointing Law and History Tripos. Henry Jackson of Trinity advised Prothero to return to Cambridge because a new Historical Tripos was imminent. But he warned Prothero that the "candidates will not be men of great calibre; or . . . the best men who go in will have already graduated in Classics or Mathematics." At the same time, Jackson predicted correctly the abolition of celibacy restrictions and absentee life-tenures. That would mean, he pointed out, that college places would become available for ambitious young men interested in a teaching career at Cambridge.[70]

When the Historical Tripos was established at Cambridge in 1873, Prothero decided that the teaching of history could be developed there to attract the best men. Before returning to Cambridge, he spent a year at the University of Bonn in von Sybel's seminar, an advanced Rankean class for the study of original sources. In October 1874 he returned to

King's, inspired by his German training in research and method. Seeley welcomed him as an ally, advising him to prepare for his history lectures by following his "strongest inclination" to "study recent times."[71] But there were so few history teachers in the first two decades of the Tripos that Prothero, like his Cambridge and Oxford colleagues, was compelled to lecture on every subject set for examination. He was too busy to follow Seeley's advice until after he left university life. Then he concentrated his interest on modern Germany. Prothero exemplified the assumption, in both ancient universities, that a historian could teach, examine, or write on any historical subject or period.[72]

Prothero's greatest service to the Historical Tripos from 1875 was his administration of the Board of Historical Studies. That management was done simultaneously with his appointment in 1876 as the first College Lecturer in History at King's which had a total membership of fewer than 50 undergraduates then and a considerable number of nonresident or idle fellows. After two years of unsuccessful attempts to increase college lecturers by ousting the nonteaching fellows, Prothero and the reformers prevailed. In 1881, Prothero began eleven years as Senior Tutor and by 1885 he was also a University Lecturer in History. The Special Board for History and Archaeology, set up by the Senate in 1873 to administer the new Tripos, tried to make history a subject attractive to bright undergraduates and young dons. But by November 1884, when the Board was expanded to fifteen, including Alfred Marshall, Mandell Creighton, and A. W. Ward, its members had to admit that the new subject was not as compelling as they had expected it to be.

The dons believed that the relative failure of their subject was not due to exaggerated expectations or the quality of teaching, but was explicable rather by the contents of the Tripos. After considerable debate, reforms were adopted in 1885.[73] The new requirements provided a consistent model for subsequent revisions and, even more importantly, they reasserted Seeley's interpretation of history. In an attempt to broaden that interpretation, Prothero, supported in the university by Ward and Sidgwick, drew upon German historical scholarship to advocate more thorough, professional training. Prothero wanted undergraduates to prepare a written dissertation based upon primary sources. He also argued for extending the curriculum to cover comparative politics, political geography, and the general history of Europe and its colonies from the Roman Empire to the present. Seeley, who also greatly admired German historical scholarship and was responsible for Prothero's return to Cambridge, wanted the Tripos to have able lecturers doing original work and encouraging their best students to write dissertations. But the essence of Seeley's position, in contrast to Prothero and those who emphasized original research for undergraduates, was that the Historical Tripos must be organized around the teaching of the laws of politics by which England should be governed.

In the regulations that emerged, the idea of a dissertation disappeared, and the study of general history, as distinct from English history, was abandoned until the Tripos revisions of 1897, when Lord Acton was Regius Professor. In 1885, "political science," the new name for the older course on political philosophy, triumphed by remaining compulsory. The new theoretical papers were optional and students continued to hear Seeley's view that an inductive political science must be a wide comparative study of political institutions from the ancient to the modern world. Discussion on subsequent modifications of the Tripos centered on the best pedagogy for stimulating the intellectual maturation of an elite destined to control the critical areas of British life. From 1885 until the 1930s, the Tripos changed only four times: in 1896, 1909, 1913, and 1929. Prothero's attempt to make history a broader, more professional discipline was not dismissed; it was simply subordinated to Seeley's emphasis upon schooling for statesmen. But under Seeley's successors, Acton and then Bury, Prothero's professional ideal was revived.

Prothero was Secretary of the History Board from 1879, Pro-Proctor of the University in 1877 and 1879 and Senior Proctor in 1888, an active member of University Syndicates, a constant Examiner for the Historical Tripos and for the Victoria University (the forerunner of the University of Manchester), a frequent Examiner in the Oxford and Cambridge Public School Examinations and in the Higher Local and other examinations, and an active member of the Newnham College Council. But these considerable responsibilities did not prevent him from spending a great deal of time with students.[74] Unlike Oscar Browning, who established a permanent open house for students in his college rooms, or A. L. Smith at Balliol, who drew students into his family's life, Prothero always maintained a distance which conformed to his notions of the proper role of a don. When Senior Proctor, he censored student writing in the undergraduate magazine *Granta* and warned one offensive writer that "anyone who persists in doing this sort of thing when his mistake has been pointed out to him is unfit to remain in the society of gentlemen."[75] Prothero always retained views and habits formed as the eldest son of the Canon of Westminster and Chaplain in Ordinary to Queen Victoria. But he extended the definition of a gentleman beyond inherited place and its attendant duties to include, for him, accountability for the organization and transmission of a body of knowledge.

An extensive discussion of Prothero's part in the Tripos and his standing among scholarly historians occurred in the testimonials written in 1894 to support his application for the new history chair at Edinburgh. While testimonials generally praise rather than bury candidates, faint praise, balanced assessments, and even fulsome endorsements are often more revealing than their authors intended. Twenty-eight people, former students or colleagues, spoke for Prothero. They were major figures in Cambridge, Oxford, London, and Owens College, or distinguished French and German historians writing about English history, or eminent leaders of the professions. What their letters have in common is acclaim for Prothero's breadth of learning and literary style and admiration for his importance as a teacher of history, evident in his large and popular following of students.

What they all found most remarkable was his success in organizing historical studies at Cambridge against formidable obstacles.[76] Henry Sidgwick, the Professor of Moral Philosophy who was intimately involved in that development, described Prothero, whose students stood at the top of each honours examinations, as the major figure in historical study in the university.[77] Helen Gladstone, Vice-Principal of Newnham and the daughter of W. E. Gladstone, sent the college's women to lectures at King's and arranged that every history student come under Prothero's teaching "as we consider it one of the most valuable parts of her training."[78] Few history lecturers welcomed women so warmly. Maitland, with his characteristic ability to reach the essential point expeditiously, said that a "very large share of the anxious labour of organizing a new school and developing a new study has fallen upon" Prothero. But, he continued, "when I say that he discharged his duties admirably, I am only repeating what is common knowledge in the University." The History School, should Prothero go to Edinburgh, will "suffer a loss that would be felt for many years."[79]

Prothero went to Edinburgh and tried to persuade his new colleagues to accept the principles of organizing and teaching that he had developed at Cambridge. Without attempting to recreate Cambridge in Edinburgh, he imposed high standards of research, scholarship and teaching and encouraged postgraduate study, which he had been unable to develop at Cambridge, by promoting scholarships and fellowships. Prothero tried to introduce that quality of student life which he had learned and personally fostered at Cambridge because of its effect upon character. When he pressed for the expansion of the hostel system, to reduce the student's financial burden and on moral, intellectual, and especially "social" grounds, he imagined the hostel as a substitute for the Cambridge college. Prothero thought of the university as qualifying undergraduates for a degree by subjecting them to "academic influence," and he tried to furnish that influence first at Cambridge and later at Edinburgh.[80]

*

After Prothero left King's, Oscar Browning remained as an uniquely influential figure. Among the reformers, Browning, more than anyone else, as even those who disliked him were compelled to admit, fashioned a distinctive social setting in King's. Browning persuaded King's to give the first openly competitive college scholarship for history, and he enthusiastically supported Seeley's goal of educating statesmen.[81] At Eton Browning had flamboyantly courted ruin and he was forced to resign as housemaster in 1876 because of alleged improprieties. He was not always serious, but there was nothing frivolous about his commitment to King's as a training ground for national obligations. In King's and in the Historical Tripos, as well as in the subsequent careers of his students, his influence was apparent. The majority of his protegés assumed professions directly serving the national interest and the ideal of citizenship which he so passionately fostered: five became bankers, eleven chose some kind of religious life, eighteen entered the military services, 33 went into the civil and colonial service, and 32 into education and scholarship.[82] These figures do not include those who died in World War I. Browning's correspondence reveals his energetic, usually successful, intervention for his pupils with powerful national leaders, the regard expressed for him by these figures, and the long-standing affection his former pupils felt for him.[83]

Browning was a radical and an imperialist who stood three times unsuccessfully as a Liberal Party candidate. Together with Seeley, Prothero, Bury, and Clapham, he supported the Imperial Federation League and often wrote for its journal and advised council members.[84] He also founded, and for eighteen years was principal of, the Cambridge Teachers Day Training College. He had no direct effect upon either politics or historical scholarship, but he influenced both fields by using his friendships to promote the careers of his students. Besides *The Flight to Varennes and Other Historical Essays* (1892), dismissed by other historians, he produced secondary school manuals.[85] In 1884, when Prothero undertook a translation of the first volume of Ranke's *Universal History,*

Browning wrote to him to ask if they could work together on the project. The publisher, Kegan Paul, vetoed Browning's participation because he doubted "exceedingly" that he was capable of it.[86] But Browning was the first university historian to write for the *Transactions of the Royal Historical Society* (in 1885). He chaired the Society's new Council, and in 1886, induced Acton, William Cunningham, and Mandell Creighton to serve on it. He also actively recruited university historians, mostly from Cambridge, as Fellows of the Society.[87] His two pieces on the Triple Alliance of 1788 and the Anglo-French Commercial Treaty of 1786, which concentrated on international politics and diplomacy, were not only representative of the breadth of the Cambridge Historical Tripos, but they marked a new departure for the *Transactions*, which had, until then, concentrated on narrow antiquarian interests.[88]

What Browning understood as the proper uses of history can be deduced from his assessment in 1899 of R. Geike's thesis explaining the Barrier Treaty of 1709. Browning admired Geike's independent research and the way he had dealt "intelligently and accurately" with new sources of information while presenting his conclusions in "a clear and attractive form." These judgments were corroborated by the external judge from Oxford, A. H. Hassall of Christ Church College. But beyond Hassall, Browning found in Geike that quality "invaluable in a historian, a firm grasp upon the political significance of events." Browning's only reservations were that he was "perhaps less successful in his judgment of character and motives," but he expected that experience would remedy that.[89]

*

When J. H. Clapham succeeded Browning as Assistant Tutor in History and as President of the King's Politics Society in 1908, he tried, not altogether successfully, to move the Society beyond a concentration upon character and politics, but not so far as to recognize the validity of subjects such as intellectual history or as to challenge the Society's traditional concern with moral conduct in history. As an undergraduate in 1893, Clapham had stood against the "politico-international" view as the most important approach to history, but within the next decade he cultivated a set of political and international preferences from which he never swerved. For him, ideals ruled the world. Clapham was convinced that England's economic and imperial development was continuously progressive because it was guided by moral purposes. His support in 1916 for collecting indemnities from Germany and his argument in 1921 that Germany had been responsible for the war rested on moral criteria of judgment. In 1925 the Society considered whether they would prefer to be governed by Mazzini, Lenin, or Mussolini. The only choice for Clapham was the nineteenth-century Italian liberal who had also believed that nations must be moved by moral principles. But unlike Mazzini, who fought for the self-determination of small states, Clapham was an Imperial Federalist who saw the empire as a valid extension of the English nation. In the early 1890s, Clapham spoke in favor of an imperial community dominated by England; prior to World War I he rejected the possibility of a world state; and in 1929, he was convinced that South Africa must remain a white nation.[90]

Clapham's influence in King's rested on his enormous popularity with undergraduates. When King's searched for Oscar Browning's replacement as a history tutor in 1907, the provost, M. R. James, tried to decide between Clapham and H. O. Meredith, a King's classicist. James decided that Meredith might "go farther," but he "would not possess the same sympathy and the same power of attracting and stimulating young students at the beginning of their time here, as Clapham."[91] James's expectations about Clapham's rapport with students were capably fulfilled. When Clapham became the History Tutor in 1914, he complained to Prothero that the larger size of the college by then made it "hard to know the men as one could wish. A hundred and fifty personalities are not easily mastered."[92] But Clapham managed to know and inspire them. Tripos candidates believed that it was possible to get first class honours on Clapham's lectures alone, and they attended those lectures religiously. In 1918, when the War Office asked Cambridge for a list of Teachers of History whose immediate return from war service to the university was necessary to restore normal teaching conditions, the History Board asked only for Clapham who was serving on the Board of Trade.[93]

Clapham grew up as a devout Methodist in the Lancashire town of Broughton, Salford as the son of a jeweler and silversmith. He was an Exhibitioner at King's in history before becoming a fellow in 1898. Four years later, he went to Leeds as Professor of Economics and returned to King's in 1908 as Dean and Assistant Tutor in History. He remained at King's into the 1930s, served as Vice-Provost, and became the first Professor of Economic History in 1929. During all those years Clapham taught economic history as a demonstration of the dependence of British progress upon entrepreneurial individuals. But when the depression led many undergraduates to question the status quo, Clapham continued to argue that a laissez-faire economy was responsible for a consistent rise in the standard of living. He worried in the late-nineteenth and early twentieth centuries that on "every side the State has utterly broken down the fences of the old individualism." And he was opposed not only to socialism but to the "too facile acceptance of any of the more absolute modern theories of the State" in which he included not only Bernard Bosanquet's Hegelian idealism, but also the thought of Henry Sidgwick. Clapham's youthful Methodism, which he later abandoned for Anglicanism, led him to fear the state's power to "persecute."[94]

Clapham was not an unfeeling man, indifferent to the effects of economic hardship. In a lecture on "Irish Immigration," he discussed the period 1770 to 1830 in which Irish immigrants became a permanent part of the laboring population of Great Britain. He was interested especially in their effect upon the standard of living and social life of England and Scotland at a very critical period in the economic history of these countries. Citing parliamentary committees, contemporary writings of the late-eighteenth and early-nineteenth centuries, official inquiries into the Poor Law from 1815 to 1830, and census returns, he concluded that especially in the period 1825 to 1845, conditions of life "were terrible"— most terrible for the Irish. These "immigrants from a poor and over-populated and ill-governed country driven out often by sheer starvation to seek a living in Britain, the historian may not blame." But they brought down the standard of living around them because they lived with "their pigs in the cellars of Manchester as they had lived at home."[95] While compassionate towards the immigrants, Clapham was still able to blame them for remaining Irish with deplorable Irish vices instead of becoming English with admirable English virtues. Clapham saw the historical evidence of economic evils, but his economic history held to the tenet that the standard of living had risen and would continue to rise.

The first volume of his *An Economic History of Modern Britain* (1926–28) opposed Arnold Toynbee's late-nineteenth-century, catastrophic interpretation of the industrial revolution, which had been reenforced from 1911 through the interwar years by the work of J. L. and Barbara Hammond. G. M. Trevelyan, Clapham's undergraduate contemporary at Trinity, said of the book that no "more completely and characteristically Cambridge product was ever published by the University Press."[96] What did Trevelyan mean? In 1909, Clapham read a paper to the Politics Society on "Scientific History" which indicates what Trevelyan meant by "Cambridge product." Clapham dismissed the discussion about history as an art or a science, in which Trevelyan was to remain involved for the next generation. While Clapham echoed Trevelyan by defining good history as "the imaginative, the artistic presentation of facts scientifically established and scientifically correlated," he went much further to identify historical processes with those employed in the natural sciences. In an implicit criticism of Trevelyan and "purists of the accumulative school" who despise "ambitious philosophies of history" he pointed out that "their facts must be held together by some more or less hypothetical claim of causation, their men and women must be made to act. If they have not deliberately cultivated the critical study of cause and effect, they may wallow all their days in a shallow, muddy, sea of *post hoc ergo propter hoc.*"

Clapham readily conceded that every historian had to do a journeyman's apprenticeship in both establishing and "disestablishing" fact, and he found the latter, the "attaching to traditional narratives a high degree of improbability," to be the greater fun because we are "pugnacious creatures. There is all the excitement of the chase in finding a suspicious statement . . . tracing it to the footnote of a 5-volume history, finally running it to . . . earth in a collection of statutes, a blue book, a chronicler, or a volume of MS dispatches." Although Clapham was self-consciously trying to create a new field which would be historically accurate because it studied unexplored manuscript sources, his published work rested on printed materials exclusively. But he was cautious about the construction of a narrative and about tools such as statistics which registered, but did not explain, social change. Although statistical facts, when available, could only be neglected at the historian's peril, they remained only an aspect of his raw material. Avoiding Trevelyan's concentration on great people and Acton's preference for great ideas, Clapham argued that sometimes historians studied individuals and sometimes groups. Seeley seemed excessively narrow to Clapham because he made the state the sole subject of history. Clapham saw instead the various parts of nonpolitical history as "crying aloud to heaven for cultivation by the specialist historians. Where is the adequate history of common beliefs? the history of morals? of class relations? of aesthetic culture?" The work of synthesis lay ahead.

Rejecting an all-embracing social science, Clapham argued that some social sciences might throw light on the "causal connection of successive states of society" and suggested turning to the young science of social psychology, which, he confessed, had not yet helped him. But causal explanations, he warned, "can never be more than probable." What Clapham advocated, and tried to do in his own work, was to set individuals, ideals, economic institutions, and motives in a more complex historical context than was possible by a study of politics alone. Peel's political convictions, for example, were inexplicable without understanding the economic conditions and the larger conditions of his time, just as Gladstone's influence could not be estimated without understanding his religious views.[97]

Even though Clapham did not adjust either his thinking or his subject to the postwar world after 1918, he continued until his retirement to teach almost every student in the Historical Tripos a deliberately commonsense economics, which insisted that a person could not be more honestly employed than in making money for himself and his family.[98] For more than two generations, Clapham was concerned with the virtues of the British Empire, the obligations of patriotism, the demonstration of melioristic social and economic developments, the limitations upon human reason, the diversity of historical subjects and the variety of methods by which they could be studied, and the need for moral judgment in the teaching and writing of history. Where he was close to the inclinations of other twentieth-century Cambridge historians, as in his stand for a wider content and more imaginative methods in the study of history, Clapham spoke with authority. But by the end of the 1920s, he had long ago dismissed new economic and social ideas in which Cambridge students were increasingly interested. His unchanged reading of English history as political, economic, social, moral, and imperial progress became unpopular in the years after World War I not only because of events, but because some of the most clever students moved to a new left.[99] Clapham had no student disciples except for John Saltmarsh.

If Clapham was characteristically "Cambridge," it was because of at least three qualities: a breadth of outlook, dissatisfaction with the historical methods and interpretations of his colleagues and predecessors, and a tendency to be hypercritical of opinions with which he disagreed. If Oxford historians were remarkable for a persistent unanimity about procedures and meaning, Cambridge historians agreed rather to disagree. That may be an important part of the explanation for the fact that the Oxford School so easily recruited students and the Cambridge Tripos did not. It was much easier to prepare for exams where teachers taught a reliable tradition of study which could be mastered than where the accepted wisdom was never accepted for very long. But tutors and teaching, essential to the continuity of a discipline, were only half the story of the making of a national elite. The teachers at both Oxford and Cambridge relied for their immediate justification and their ultimate reputations on the achievements of their students.

Chapter 7

Students and Learning

 B efore Oxford and Cambridge undergraduates took their honours degree examinations, they had learned that a good degree, especially for the upwardly mobile, could satisfy both private ambition and a desire to contribute to public good. A first- or second-class honours degree was a direct avenue to important careers and a rewarding future as well as an outlet for genuinely altruistic impulses. That was especially true of a degree in history. When students read national history as the evolution of harmonious institutions, dependent upon individual capacity and responsibility, they found confirmation of their own select position within society. If high places were reserved for those educated to fulfil the duties of leadership, then an individual could find justification through good works. Other students, who valued intellectual coherence above other ends, also found history satisfying because it systematically explained the past as a reasoned, comprehensible prelude to the present.

Diverse and often idiosyncratic inclinations led students to read history, but what they all had in common was an appreciation of the orderly teaching of digestible facts, demonstrated in compilations of illustrative sources and narrative textbooks, which could be assimilated and applied first to examinations and then to real life.[1] But even more than the introduction of a manageable subject and the reward of an influential life, the discipline of history promised to cultivate the best qualities in those who studied it. For those young people torn between the demands of selfishness and self-sacrifice, the historical record made it clear that the selfish suffered and lost. While the good did not always prevail, the higher val-

ues, for which they gave up more private ends, endured as a result of
their aspirations. Idealism, as their teachers were always pleased to notice, was perhaps the most conspicuous of their students' attributes.

Even the most genuine idealism, in both universities, did not, however, necessarily encourage breadth or depth. At Cambridge the first students of the Historical Tripos were offered a modified version of the
Oxford program, requiring a limited number of authoritative texts covering vast periods of time. But while Oxford continued to concentrate
almost entirely on England's national traditions and institutions, Cambridge teaching offered political thought, international law, a strong emphasis on Europe, and intellectual, cultural, and economic history as the
legacies of the various Regius Professors and prominent tutors. During
the subsequent three generations, Cambridge historians altered the Oxford model by proposing subjects with greater intellectual breadth and
depth. But until the 1920s, although college teachers and professors tried
consistently to introduce an international, thematic curriculum, most
Cambridge honours students, in common with their peers at Oxford,
preferred a narrower, more traditional focus upon the political and constitutional history of England, learned through a body of required reading. Only a few were responsive to a broader curriculum.

Although Cambridge dons were more adventurous in curriculum,
most history teachers in both universities were unwilling to give undergraduates courses in historical methods because such preparation, they
argued, was appropriate only for a professional education. But some responded that methodological training prepared one for life because it
honed powers of discrimination. The critical analysis of manuscripts or
secondary authorities within the historical setting of their time could
create habits of weighing and assessing evidence that were applicable to
all kinds of information in the past and present alike. At Cambridge this
debate was resolved by allowing students to study methodology, if they
chose. But at Oxford few opportunities existed for learning historical
procedures and few tutors recommended that students attempt them.
When H. A. L. Fisher became interested in history in 1889, after taking
first class honours in Greats, F. Y. Powell sent him to France. Fisher
learned paleography at the École des Chartes, geography at the Collège
de France, medieval English chronicles at the École des Hautes Études,
and modern European history at the École Libre des Sciences Politiques.[2]
Neither the technical tools of analysis nor the content of these courses
were available in Oxford until 1908.

When classes were introduced in Oxford in the analytical use of historical materials, students ignored them.[3] A. F. Pollard, who filled great halls in University College, London when he taught about "Sources," was invited to give the same lectures at Oxford in 1911. There he found himself lecturing to a tutor from St. Edmund's Hall and three undergraduates. "Original investigation is not a strong point at Oxford," Pollard explained to his father. Oxford tutors in history "don't in the least realize that some notion of historical evidence and of the materials and sources of history is indispensable to anyone who wants to apply critical judgment to historical matters; even undergraduates should be taught how to test the truth of what they learn."[4] History teachers commonly asserted that the pursuit and grasp of truth was both possible and necessary, but they were consistently indifferent about "how to test the truth."

But from the point of view of the Oxford undergraduate reading history, Fisher's needs, Pollard's lectures, and methods for discriminating truth from error all seemed extraneous. For anyone attempting an honours degree in history, the strength of the Oxford School was exactly its orderly teaching of "facts." These students wanted a "first" or a "second," and Oxford teachers organized history to enable students to achieve their goals. While Fisher was nearly unique as a young Oxford graduate in going abroad to learn historical craft, Cambridge graduates were more exposed to historical work done outside England. Few undergraduates actually studied abroad, but they were taught by teachers with strong ties to Continental historians and their research methods.

*

Most honours students at Oxford had largely an "examining" interest in history; their studies were shaped and limited entirely by the requirements of the final honours examination. Only a rare teacher, such as A. L. Smith, prompted students to extend their curiosity beyond the examination questions. The modern history honours examinations were particularly vulnerable to the charge of cramming, because they relied more upon memory than upon "reflective or logical faculties."[5] In contrast to Oxford, however, history students at Manchester were not given examinations that required a student to read and reproduce selected sections of books and make "obvious generalizations" without understanding what "historical evidence" was by handling "all sorts of sources for himself."[6] T. F. Tout, in his successful Manchester school of history, deliberately rejected the Oxford examination model. Instead, Tout devised examinations that required undergraduates to use original materials and to think about them. At Manchester, Tout was able to shape his new history school because he had control over it and, even more important, because he was not saddled with two generations of traditions in teaching and examining. He had the further advantages of fewer students and a large library which students could readily use.

Students in Oxford, to be sure, were required to read original sources and foreign languages in the Special Subject. But their teachers were disappointed to find that very few of their best students chose those papers in the Special Subject that required either a foreign language or original sources. In the early twentieth century, the Examiners complained to the History Board that "so many candidates seek to obtain a knowledge of their special subjects by other means than a study of the prescribed texts." The Examiners recommended that "instruction in these special subjects should rather take the form of guidance in the methods of using original authorities." The following year they noted further that there "is a distinct falling off in the knowledge of the authorities in the Special Subjects."[7] They also attempted regularly and unsuccessfully to make the language requirement more stringent. Because students were showing insufficient knowledge of foreign languages, which meant that they could not read recommended foreign authors for their special subject, a required paper of unprepared translation was set in 1908. That year, the Examiners found that although the candidates had the option of offering more than one language, the great majority offered French alone and "in some cases the ignorance of the language was so great that the Examiners had to determine the standard which would justify them in accepting the translation as satisfactory."[8] Students were untrained in modern foreign languages and unable to read either the new research done in Germany and France on England or other national histories.[9] When the assigned foreign books were available in English, as many were, the students were allowed to read the translation. Books in foreign languages that were not translated often had extracts selected from them and these set portions, as the students knew, were repeated from one examination to another.

Even in those special subjects which focused on a narrower field or a particular figure, the student did not investigate his topic but instead mastered an existing, already organized body of knowledge in the form of broad surveys and prepared "outlines."[10] Secondary or synthetic studies were carefully selected by tutors for their students, often as limited passages to be memorized for examination. Moreover, in their lectures on the Special Subjects, some tutors discussed the foreign and original sources in such detail, including an analysis of their major points and weaknesses, that a student who was pressed for time might do well in his examinations by simply repeating what he heard in lectures. Most tutors, inundated by the numbers of students they taught, relied upon such historical syntheses as Stubbs's *Constitutional History of England* or the *Annals of England*, which could be taught didactically. As a result, a student was rarely exposed to either primary sources or monographs. While some tutors wanted their students to recognize historical ambiguities, there was little encouragement of such critical thinking either in the prescribed course of study or the examinations. Both the curriculum and the examinations largely excluded contemporary scholarship, historiography, and evaluations of historical method and meaning. Many tutors disapproved of cramming, but felt that they were driven to it. Until 1913, the Oxford requirement that students first take Classical Moderations meant that many undergraduates had only two years in which to complete the entire history syllabus.

As late as 1914, the Oxford Examiners were finding still that in political history, the School's major emphasis, "very few men seem to read any of the principal authorities or to specialize in historical literature." Had they specialized, there "would have been less sameness in the answers sent in. The very excellence of some of the lectures on our present system," the Report observed dryly, "tends to discourage independent study." A decade later, the Examiners were complaining still that the general paper "tends to degenerate into unoriginal work derived from a knowledge of a fairly elaborate text book."[11] Nearly every Examiners' report found that knowledge of English political history remained inadequate. Undergraduates were hard put to master the broad and demanding requirement of continuous English history. When an opportunity to write a thesis was introduced in 1908, few students chose the option. By 1914, the Examiners found in the five theses submitted, a "tendency to substitute mere literary presentment for historical research." And they repeated a complaint which had begun a decade earlier and was to recur through the 1920s that lectures, because they were so comprehensive, were hardly an incentive to independent study.[12]

A. L. Smith encouraged students to make comparisons among authorities, but his handouts for all the papers in the examination indicated unequivocally which authorities were wrong, which were acceptable interpretations, and what judgments were to be drawn.[13] When the Royal Commission on Oxford and Cambridge in 1922 looked at "self-reform and development" since the preceding Royal Commission in 1881, they found that historical studies, "both at Oxford and Cambridge, are in danger of becoming provincialised and cut off from the investigation of all records save those of our own island." That was hardly a new danger, since the overwhelming attention of both schools had concentrated consistently on English constitutional history. But in both universities after World War I, a growing majority of students became increasingly interested in "the modern periods of history" and in "Economics and Economic History."[14] An interest in unorthodox historical periods and fields may have reflected the experience of the war, but it was also a consequence of the greater diversity to be found in the growing numbers drawn to the subject. There was more than a doubling of those reading for history in Oxford since the immediate prewar years; the academic year 1920–21 saw 534 candidates for the final honours examination in History, as compared with 225 in 1913–14. At Cambridge, in 1920–21, about 300 candidates prepared for the two parts of the Historical Tripos.

At Cambridge, unlike Oxford, teaching was separated from examinations and an academic division of labor established essentially a "federal" system of higher education.[15] But at Cambridge, too, the preferred subjects, which were in English history, were not done as thoroughly as the history teachers expected. When the Historical Tripos was altered in 1886 and the new examinations were administered, the "Subjects for Essays in English History" did not turn out, as the reformers had intended, to remedy either superficiality or an ignorance of the continuity of English history. A paper on the "General History of England," framed "so as to elicit a correct general knowledge of the subject rather than a minute knowledge of detail," was substituted in May 1892 and applied in 1894.[16] In the Special Subjects, where a student could emphasize a particular set of events or individuals, the reading also tended to be circumscribed.[17] The history faculty complained that students were ignoring theoretical subjects entirely and instead were habitually memorizing "facts instead of interpreting them . . . at the expense of independent thought."[18]

*

We know what subjects the teachers taught. It is more difficult to find out what students learned. What is available of the undergraduate work of thousands of Oxford history honours students from the 1870s to the 1920s are a few tutorial essays; only one examination script, containing six answers, by an anonymous candidate in 1873 who achieved a second class; and three students' lecture notes, one set from 1870 to 1874, another from 1882 to 1883, and the last in the mid-1920s. While no Cambridge scripts are available, we know what papers were set in examinations and that they changed with time as the Oxford papers did not. J. H. Clapham preserved his undergraduate lecture notes, tutorial essays, and the undergraduate papers which he delivered to the King's Politics Society and the Gwatkin papers contain some of Gwatkin's lecture notes and the English history questions he set for tutorial students at St. John's College.

Among the Oxford historians, A. L. Smith kept occasional student essays that reflected the values he taught. J. P. Younger, writing for Smith about the Special Subject of Englebert, found him to be a man of "swift judgment and a ready wit . . . who preferred deeds to words, he was decisive and self-reliant. His strong sense of justice and the warmth of his heart raised him above vulgar class prejudices, and enabled him to see men and things in their true light and just relations. . . . The great hated him, but he found his satisfaction in the love of the people."[19] The qualities ascribed to Englebert were those Smith wanted his students to learn and act upon. The one remaining script reveals similar processes of thought and judgment. In his answer to question 2, which asked for a discussion of the constitutional difficulties faced by William III and the House of Brunswick in relation to their continental dominions, the candidate compared the liberties and sovereignties of the English under William to the subservience of the Dutch. In England, William "was a limited constitutional sovereign, without control of the public purse from which all other power naturally flows; and besides this he was the nominee of the English people, his claim resting not on hereditary right, but on election by a popular parliament liable therefore to deposition in case of his actions being displeasing to the sovereign people, or by contravention of the terms upon which he was appointed." In the Netherlands, the "people could not get on without him and were therefore obliged to acquiesce in whatever he might do."[20] In England, only the people and their accumulated liberties, represented by the constitution, were sovereign.

In the two sets of lecture notes by M. E. G. Finch-Hatton from 1870 to 1874 and by E. W. Watson in 1882–83, there is a similar reading of the meaning of history. Finch-Hatton was an undergraduate at Balliol who studied English history with A. H. Johnson, the most persistent advocate of the broad tutorial tradition of teaching, and then took first class honours in Modern History. He held the honorific office of High Sheriff in Lincolnshire, entered public service as a member of the Kesteven County Council and became M.P. for South Lincolnshire, and then the twelfth Earl of Winchelsea. To the young Finch-Hatton, English history revealed a linear development of English virtues from Edward I to 1874: "All previous English History converges to, all subsequent diverges from *his reign* in Bravery, patriotism, consummate Statesmanship, domestic values, religion and chivalric feeling, trained in adversity, nursed in War."[21] E. W. Watson, later Regius Professor of Ecclesiastical History at Oxford, in his notes on the lectures of J. Franck Bright on the "Social History of England till the Conquest," describes the early political unity of a national church and state, one of Stubbs's favorite themes. In his notes from A. L. Smith on Stubbs's *Charters*, Watson emphasized the importance of the shire and the prevention of too rapid centralization in English government.[22]

At least one other set of Oxford lecture notes exist, by Marjorie Reeves, who received a first-class honours degree in modern history in 1926 and went on to become a productive, original, and distinguished historian of the Renaissance and of higher education, and a tutor in the very best traditions of Oxford teaching.[23] Reeves's notes are from the postwar period, but when compared to those of Finch-Hatton and Watson, they reveal remarkable continuities in the tone and contents of history teaching at Oxford. All three sets of notes are thorough and workmanlike. Whether they are in any way typical in method or contents, even for those who took first class honours, cannot be established. But there are striking similarities in their reading of historical events and their meaning.

In Reeves's notes on Roman Britain to the Norman Conquest, taken from R. H. Hodgkin's lectures at Queen's College, the last lecture concludes: "*English wanted above all discipline in Church and State—They got it! from Norman barons, bishops, lawyers, civil servants—and above all from Norman monarchy.*" It is remarkable how closely the attributes of Hodgkin's Norman monarchy and barons resembled those of a twentieth-century Oxford-produced elite. When Reeves synthesized her own reading and lectures, the result was far more sophisticated. She had the advantage over Finch-Hatton and Watson of new primary and secondary materials, and of a more precociously acute mind. Her discussion of Edward I leaves him a heroic character whose achievements occur in a larger "age of definition." Whenever lecture notes are used as evidence there is good reason to wonder if students hear what lecturers actually say, but Reeves's reliability is demonstrated by her notes on church and state in the Middle Ages. Taken from A. L. Smith's lectures in 1924, they accurately mirror Smith's own lecture notes. The multiple copies of Smith's notes reveal that, in spite of his wide reading and research, he scarcely changed any of them from his earliest lectures in the 1870s.[24]

Of the papers set for the Cambridge Historical Tripos honours examination, those most representative of the spirit of the Tripos were the Special Essays. The five or six topics offered each year were never repeated in the two decades from 1904 to 1923. Covering a wide spectrum of subjects that required analytical and introspective thought, some represent the major interests of teachers such as Browning, Clapham, and Temperley. Others show a continuous concern with character, patriotism, and moral obligation, and still others reflect the changing fashions in history that attracted Cambridge historians while repelling their Oxford colleagues. The papers set in May 1904 were the most conventional, although far less so than at Oxford. During the subsequent years, the essay subjects became increasingly unorthodox.

Bury, when Regius Professor, could hardly have approved of any of these papers set in 1904: "Criteria of good government; The insoluble problems of history; The persistence of national character; Slavery and servitude; All understanding of history depends on one's understanding of forces that make it, of which religious forces are the most active and the most definite; The state is Prior to the individual." The influence of both Seeley and Acton was clear. But in the 1906 essays, Acton's legacy was dominant in two papers that raised moral issues. The first asked for comment on the proposition: "The first lesson of history is the good of evil," and the second posed: "It is not so hard to have a noble aim; The difficulty lies in working it out by worthy means. That is the great moral lesson which history teaches." There were also less conventional questions about "The relations between the literature and the national history of England," and "The most essential quality of the historian is imagination." The following year candidates considered: "The function of the philosophy of history is not to solve problems but to transform them." The Oxford School did not recognize the philosophy of history as a topic suitable for discussion by mature historians, let alone undergraduates.

In subsequent years all the Regius Professors and the active tutors had their special interests represented. There was at least one question in each examination which involved moral dilemmas, citizenship, and national obligations as well as provocative papers on history as an art or a science, the possibility and desirability of objectivity, and the reality of progress. Broad and undefined topics such as "Ravenna," or "Medieval historians," or "The Writing of History is in some sort a religious act" were also set. By 1912, there were papers on "The influence of biology on politics," "History in the future will be the history of ideas," and "The novels of Dickens as historical documents." The year before the war, students were asked to write about "The problem of form in the fine arts," and, prophetically, "In national history opportunity is as powerful as purpose." In 1915, the essay subjects reflected the new times and their concerns and an interest in recent history by asking for discussion of "German v. English methods of government" and "The Victorian Era." When the war was over, returning students were given "Patriotism is not a natural instinct but an acquired habit," and "It is one of the fallacies of our social system to believe that a ladder should only be used in one direction." From 1921 to 1923, Tripos students confronted subjects such as "Human nature has not been changed by civilization; The myth of progress is our form of apocalyptism; Corporate personality; Men love ritual, and modern life starves their appetite for it; The study of the past is futile unless it helps us to explain the present; The craft of fiction; and Malthus and the Modern World."[25]

Although we do not know how candidates for the Tripos answered these complex and intellectually teasing questions, one undergraduate, J. H. Clapham, kept his lecture notes and tutorial essays. While a student at King's College in the early 1890s, he arrived at an individualist philosophy and a set of progressive views about his country which he retained, unaltered by personal or public experience, for the rest of his life. These views were mediated by his Northern background and his Methodist conscience, but they owed most to his Cambridge training. Clapham was a pupil of Oscar Browning and of Alfred Marshall, and he attended Acton's lectures. In 1894, Clapham wrote essays for Browning on such conventional Tripos examination subjects as Freeman's *Federal Government* and Bagehot's *English Constitution.* But he also wrote about the relation between history and geography, Russia, Communism, the referendum, the historical value of architecture, political morality, and the scope and limits of philanthropy. The topics themselves and the notes Clapham took provide some evidence that Browning was not, as Clapham observed, "altogether a fool." Clapham's notes warned against the "bad habit of collecting mere evidence and calling them essays" and against "overelaboration." Things "about facts," Browning told him, "not facts themselves, should form the main body. Don't begin with sententious platitudes." Browning criticized his essay on Russia "severely" for its inaccuracy and because it was "altogether, too newspaper-foolish." In his six-page essay on the "History of the Map of Europe," he associated climate with national character and speculated about the ways in which successive maps revealed "new national factors and the elimination of old ones," so that the gradual course of political and industrial enterprise could be traced. When he told Browning that Freeman had concluded with a eulogy of federalism as the best means of maintaining peace in history, Browning responded that "circumstances are not uniform."[26]

The papers that Clapham prepared for the Politics Society, while an undergraduate and later as a don, record his consistent support for individual rights and obligations, the imperatives of country and God, and the duties of an imperial citizen. Those were values he put together from listening to Browning, Marshall, and Acton. Although Browning was a radical and Clapham a conservative, Clapham followed Browning in adopting the imperialist preferences represented so forcefully by most of the other Cambridge history professors and tutors until the 1930s. Marshall led him to economic history and Acton reenforced his convictions about the importance of moral judgment in history. In the same way that the remaining student notes in Oxford reveal the consistent character of history teaching there, Clapham's notes reflect the diversity of interests characteristic of his Cambridge teachers.

*

The relation between teachers and their students was only one part of the milieu in which students learned about history. While the formal side of the university, and especially the relationship between teaching and the future conduct of the governing elite, is now receiving long-overdue attention, the informal side, especially the role of student subcultures, has been almost entirely neglected.[27] Outside the curriculum and formal instruction, and parallel to the course of study culminating in the final examinations, the student society developed as one of the most effective new educational traditions. Just as the tutors had found that the requirements of a large and growing school meant that college teaching was not sufficiently complete, some history students, too, decided to form intercollegiate associations. These organized history societies attempted to explore examination subjects more deeply and at the same time to transcend the constraints imposed by the curriculum. Students increasingly demonstrated their capacity for an energetic intellectual life, independent of the formal structure of either college or university, as they overcame the early nineteenth-century fear that excessive mental work damaged young lives.[28]

Groups of students, often from a number of colleges, came together to pursue a variety of interests that were not addressed within the official structure of university life. Some of these were frivolous releases for surplus energies or dining clubs that periodically broke out from the confinement of colleges. But others were intellectually vital societies that went beyond the regular courses of study available in the new disciplines.

Friendships made here, often in heated controversy, became enduring personal alliances that survived party allegiances or socially incompatible backgrounds. Opportunities for fulfilling an ideal of friendship were greater within these clubs than in any subsequent adult encounter. These societies encouraged an original quality of mind that was imaginative and forceful, and their success depended upon the quality of the students who participated in them. At both Oxford and Cambridge, the goal of such students was not simply a high class in the final honours examinations, although many used these groups to supplement and deepen their understanding of the curriculum. Within these societies young men learned the skills of debate, discussion, and reflection which inspired them to emerge as national figures. When Newnham College was established at Cambridge for the higher education of women, Newnham undergraduates formed their own active Politics Society which prepared them for entry into positions within government even though such careers were still restricted to men.[29] In their very existence, these societies for men and women idealized honorable camaraderie based upon inquiry and honesty.

The traditional liberal ideal of university education could be transmitted more effectively than ever through the additional reenforcement provided by the various history societies. These societies, debating controversial issues and then settling their differences by a majority vote, were part of a larger university culture that reflected the increased national importance of parliament in the later nineteenth century.[30] In common with better-known university groups such as the Oxford Union or the Cambridge Apostles, the history societies were forums that, in great part, imitated parliament in its discussion of the major national questions of the time. What was unique about the history societies is that they were organized around the subject matter of a discipline. It was especially in these societies that students learned a consistently high level of self-confidence and assurance. Unlike the Union and the Apostles, these groups were not exclusive, nor did they exist in opposition to formal academic and social institutions as was common in both Germany and France.[31]

The intercollegiate Stubbs Society at Oxford, the History Club and the Brackenbury Society at Balliol, the Politics Society at Kings and the History Societies at Trinity and St. John's in Cambridge, the Historical Society at University College, London, and the Historical Society at Manchester were proving grounds for future leaders and for the founders of new fields of inquiry. In these bodies, students and the dons who joined and encouraged them attempted original scholarship and the criticism of historical materials. They weighed evidence, judged conduct, agreed upon canons of interpretation, and debated conclusions. The result was an intellectual curiosity and élan conspicuously rare in the work done even for the honours degree. At the meetings, inquiry into historical subjects became examinations of human nature, motivation, causality, and accident. Most historians agreed that such abstract problems, to be pursued by those interested in them, were irrelevant to undergraduate teaching and study. The consensus was that undergraduates should learn the content of history rather than its epistemology. But within the student history societies, these complex issues were seen less as questions about knowing and more as necessary insights into the world of affairs. Moreover, young people in transition from dependence, whether on family or college, to independence and its attendant responsibilities were often uncertain about what they wanted to learn. On the one hand, they needed to control and master their studies, especially for performance in the honours examinations, but on the other they yearned for a confrontation with the enigmatic that would stretch them beyond the routine work for their degrees.

Different motives brought students to the history societies. But within them, social attributes of tact and sympathetic discrimination, cultivated as a communal ethic, led undergraduates to believe that if they could trace problems back to their origins and then separate them into their component parts, they could then understand, explain, and finally resolve them. That ethos reenforced personal goodwill and provided for intellectually exciting evenings. It also created an aura of confidence that could be inappropriate within the real world where problems resist clear understanding as well as resolution and men in positions of power do not necessarily act with either benevolence or rationality.

In Balliol, Samuel Brearley, an older American undergraduate who had been in Germany and was driven by reforming zeal, introduced the idea of a "seminary" to undergraduates reading modern history in 1882. His Brearley Improvement Society became first the Oxford Historical Seminar, and then, upon Stubbs's retirement in 1884, the Stubbs Society.[32] That the word "improvement" should have appeared in the society's first title demonstrated that Brearley had succumbed to at least some of the tendencies towards the serious life that swept Oxford in the 1880s. In 1883 E. A. Freeman presided over the Seminar which included Cosmo Lang, subsequently Archbishop of Canterbury; Herbert Hensley Henson, later Bishop of Durham; J. A. R. Marriott, Ryland Adkins, T. E. Ellis, and Charles Oman, who all sat in the House of Commons at some point in their careers; William Holden Hutton, later Dean of Winchester; Sidney Cooper, later Canon-Treasurer of Truro; A. J. Carlyle, a distinguished historian of political thought; and W. J. Ashley.[33] Three years later, when James Tait was elected as the sixteenth or final member, C. H. Firth was in the Chair and F. Y. Powell had become an active participant.[34]

Although the papers delivered to the Stubbs Society generally followed the questions in the final honours examination, they dealt with a greater variety of individuals, events, and historical processes than the curriculum required. The papers included such "recent" movements and events as Socialism, Chartism, and the Industrial Revolution, theoretical questions about the character of history, and discussions about historiographical interpretations.[35] Average attendance from 1884 until World War I ranged between 6 and 10 members, occasionally rising to 16 for a special speaker or to 30 for a commemorative dinner. Few in numbers, the members brought to the society an energetic enthusiasm that in adult life would be translated into the leadership of influential professions. The detailed minutes of each paper and of the ensuing debates reveal a sustained view of history as moral judgment. Throughout the 30 years before World War I, the Stubbs Society consistently praised "national virtues" and condemned "national vices." "Vulgarity and mediocrity" were the personal qualities held in the greatest contempt. To be vulgar meant that an individual had chosen a life dedicated to personal ends instead of to higher public good, and mediocrity was a confession of personal failure to drive oneself towards the highest goals. The unswerving confidence with which these opinions were delivered was due partly to the arrogance of the young and privileged, but even more to the fundamental assumptions characteristic of the School of Modern History at Oxford.

The extensive minutes of the Stubbs Society, from 1884 to 1930, and the papers of the Balliol History Club and the Brackenbury Society reveal the issues that preoccupied two generations of undergraduates who were to become influential leaders in every field. Until World War I the Brackenbury Society debated such propositions as: "That the Decay of Patriotism is Much to be Regretted; That this House Would Approve of the Federation of the British Empire; That this House Would Welcome the Decline of National Sentiment; and That this House Applauds the Influence of the Public School on Character and Conduct in after life." These themes were interrelated and continuous. Patriotism, enlarged by imperial federation and sustained by national sentiment, originated in the public schools which instilled the ideals of those expected to lead. The Stubbs Society discussed these ideals to demonstrate their necessity and coherence. The minutes and remaining essays of all the student societies display a view of historical events consistent with the political and ethical lessons they learned from their teachers and textbooks.[36]

At Cambridge, the counterpart of the Stubbs Society was the King's College Politics Society which Oscar Browning founded in 1876 and directed until his retirement in 1908. When the Bostonian Nathaniel Wedd came to Kings as an undergraduate in October 1883, to remain for most of his life as a teacher of classics and ancient history, he discovered the club. For Wedd, as for so many other Kingsmen and students from other colleges, the Society was the most important part of his undergraduate existence. Wedd saw that Browning's purposes were very explicit. The Society was an extension of the Historical Tripos, which Browning considered the best means for the "training of statesmen," one of the "chief functions of the University."[37] Browning had enormous influence over students reading for the Tripos during its first 25 years. His unconventional open houses on Sunday evenings and his guidance of the Society established a network of friendships that endured long after his students left Cambridge. Browning's successor as president of the Society from 1908 to 1939 was J. H. Clapham. He had been an active member from 1893, except for his six years as Professor at Leeds.

In the Society's meetings, students reviewed original scholarship, historiography, and national issues that were not part of the curriculum. Limited originally to eleven members below the rank of M.A., the Society met on Monday evenings to hear and comment on an original essay read by one of their members. The ordinary members, including the President, were supplemented by 49 honorary members in 1887 and by 70 in 1893. Whenever a current, controversial, topic was offered such as General Booth's scheme for the working classes in 1890 or Sidney Webb's talk on the historical context of socialism in 1899, attendance rose. By the century's end, half the members of the King's Politics Society were from Trinity College, which finally began its own Historical Society in 1897. The King's Society, which also attracted students from Trinity Hall, Peterhouse, Jesus, Christ's, Caius, Corpus, St. John's, and the non-collegiate body, was a unique agency for forming fundamental ideas and attitudes.

Undergraduate members of the Society, including J. Holland Rose, Walter Raleigh, H. Hodgkin, J. R. Tanner, Austen Chamberlain, C. R. Ashbee, G. Lowes Dickinson, C. P. and G. M. Trevelyan, J. M. E. M'Taggart, J. W. Headlam, W. F. Reddaway, J. H. B. Masterman, R. Geike, A. C. Pigou, H. M. V. Temperley, C. R. Fay, C. K. Webster, K. B. Smellie, G. N. Parry, G. P. Gooch, J. M. Keynes, J. H. Clapham, and David Knowles, were introduced to problems they would not have encountered in their preparation for any Tripos. Browning launched the Society to "promote the scientific discussion of political questions." In correct parliamentary form, they divided on the major issue raised by each essay.[38] In 1884, when Paul Fredericq, the Belgian historian, visited Stubbs's newly established Historical Seminar, he was disappointed to hear only an informal evening's summary of a large subject. In contrast, the German historical seminars "scrupulously dissected" documents "one or two at a time, to extract all that each one can furnish." The same year, in the King's College Politics Society, Fredericq found a debating club which made its "members reflect upon questions of history and speculative politics."[39]

Walter Raleigh was one of the most consistent members of the Politics Society, and for some years its Secretary. He became the first Professor of English Language and Literature at Oxford, but as a King's undergraduate he was more interested in acting than in preparing adequately for his Historical Tripos. When Browning wrote to reproach him, Raleigh responded flippantly that he never should have chosen history and had no regrets "in not regarding it as my first business in life." But he was touched by Browning's charge that Raleigh's irresponsible behavior adversely affected "'the standard of duty and seriousness' in the College," which obligated him, Browning pointed out, to do well in the Tripos. It is significant that Raleigh, in spite of his contempt for the Historical Tripos, felt that he had received "great benefit" from the Politics Society and he continued to attend meetings even after he had taken second class honours in history in 1887.[40]

The Minutes of the Society, from their beginnings in 1876 to the late 1920s, reveal consistent themes and purposes, "discussed theoretically and practically."[41] From the earliest essays, a central concern was judgments about character and national conduct. The Society agreed unanimously, on the basis of Seeley's dictum that morality and *Realpolitik* were compatible, that Sardinia was morally right to intervene in the Crimean War, as was Bismarck to unify Germany. When Gladstone's performance as a farseeing statesman was debated in 1912, the definition of moral qualities was stretched further to include political prescience. But when the question of whether the moralist should influence politics was put directly, the only dissenter was the future diplomatic historian C. K. Webster, who subsequently found very little moral influence in the high

diplomacy that he chronicled. The Regius Professor J. B. Bury attended
that meeting but, characteristically, he took no position.[42] It was not until 1918 that the propriety of the historian as a moralist was questioned.
That year, the undergraduate David Knowles first identified himself with
his famous position that the historian must not be a hanging judge.[43]

Although the members accepted common canons of judgment, they
tended to interpret them differently. A paper on Henry George's theories
of land distribution led Austen Chamberlain, Oscar Browning, and
Lowes Dickinson to join in the unanimous rejection of existing views
about private property. Walter Raleigh, then Secretary, ironically entered
into the minutes: "This society proved itself revolutionary by 8 to 0."
Although far from revolutionary, the Society's members were eager to
discuss revolutionary topics. While the discussions were not always profound, serious, or even substantial, they ranged widely. From 1876 the
paper topics concentrated on contemporary political issues such as education, religion, the control of liquor, centralization of government, democracy, sanitary legislation, the colonies, the role of experts, women's
suffrage, compulsory military service, the nature of law, international
morality, a definition of vice, free trade, and the rights of labor. Occasionally there were readings of chapters in various texts set for the Tripos
such as J. S. Mill's *Representative Government* (1861). Beginning in 1880,
more purely historical subjects were introduced, but they always led to
the framing of a contemporary lesson for statesmen that was political or
ethical, or better still, both. Oliver Cromwell was judged by whether he
was "a creator or a creature of history." W. R. Sorley's paper on "Social,
Political and Economic Aspects of Gilds" concluded in the query "Is the
laissez-faire system a satisfactory substitute for gilds?" Niccolo Machiavelli's *Prince* was the occasion for a discussion about whether "the moralist" should "tell the truth."[44]

As early as 1881, a generation before the exchange about the nature
of history between the incoming Regius Professor J. B. Bury and G. M.
Trevelyan, the Society began a continuing discussion about whether history was art or science, as well as the best method for understanding
politics, the role of a priori theory, history as biography, intellectual history, the effect of individuals versus the determinism of circumstances,
the value of economic versus political history, causality, biology and history, religion in history, and the philosophy of history.[45] A recurring debate about the practical purposes of a university course in history raised
questions about the value of academic training for statesmen, the role of
the public schools, and the relation between history and a liberal edu-

cation. Within a Society generally divided in its judgments, the proposition: "That the Historical Sciences are the best basis for a liberal education," was accepted unanimously, but there was no agreement on whether "pure" history should be a major part of the Tripos.[46] In these discussions, Browning tended to set the dominant tone.[47] It was very unusual for him to be in the minority in divisions.[48] When the Society considered the purposes of university education in general and of the Historical Tripos in particular, they tended as late as the 1890s to accept Browning's support of Seeley's dictums that for the student of history generalization was more important than research and that the political concentration of the Tripos should be preserved.[49]

Future statesmen such as Austen Chamberlain and the founders of new disciplines, such as Walter Raleigh, were active in Society deliberations. Austen Chamberlain sided with those who wanted to read political philosophy before Montesquieu, and against those who thought that Marx was a prophet. And together with Walter Raleigh, he took the unusual position of denying that professors should educate statesmen.[50] Chamberlain's other views were equally distinctive: he rejected England's future as an empire, dismissed the idea that a political science was possible, and was enormously enthusiastic for a single chamber legislature.[51] Another future political leader, an undergraduate at Trinity as was Austen Chamberlain, was Stanley Baldwin. There is no record of his attendance at any of the Politics Society meetings and when he took the Historical Tripos in 1888, he was eleventh out of fifty receiving third class honours. It is difficult to know what, if anything, Chamberlain's and Baldwin's political judgments owed to their study of history. But it is interesting that the new honours school in English at Oxford, established by Raleigh, began with a reading of English literature as a revelation of the imperatives of character and conduct.

Within King's, in addition to the Politics Society, students could attend Lowes Dickinson's informal Discussion Society from 1900 to 1918, founded in imitation of Seeley's seminar, to bring together hand-picked undergraduates from every college and every discipline. In addition, Dickinson held an open house on Sunday evenings. One of the few politically liberal tutors in King's, Dickinson was a popular university lecturer in politics, who also lectured at the new London School of Economics and Political Science.[52] A faithful member of the Politics Society from his election in 1884 until he launched his own group, Dickinson occasionally read papers to the Politics Society on such topics as "The Socialism of Plato" (1884) and "Literary History" (1885). In "A Utilitarian View of History" (1896), he maintained that knowledge should not be pursued for its own sake, a characteristically Cambridge stance in contrast to the Oxford view that if knowledge were pursued without any practical motive, implicit lessons would be evident which could then be applied to the world of affairs. Dickinson never cut himself off from the Society and at a joint meeting of the Politics Society and the Trinity Historical Society, during the university year 1912–13, he talked about Chinese civilization.[53]

The only rival in Cambridge to the King's Politics Society was the Trinity Historical Society.[54] Established in 1897, the new historical society marked a turning point in the study of history at Cambridge. It was not a matter of new leaders, because many of the same historians, such as G. M. Trevelyan and F. W. Maitland, formerly active in the King's Politics Society, because Trinity had no history club, now became active in their own college's group. What was different was the purpose. The Trinity society was a more deliberately professional society that tried to present undergraduates as well as dons and research students with new historical research and its implications for historical knowledge. It was Lord Acton's accession to the Regius Professorship and his becoming a Fellow of Trinity that was the occasion for the formation of the group over which he presided. The group never questioned that history was the best training for public life and character or that moral lessons from the past ought to be applied to the present.[55] Appropriately, the Society began with a paper by Acton on the "Study of History," which raised the issue of the "moral standard to be used in judging past ages." But at the same meeting, the Society also discussed "the relative value of historical work based on Manuscript and printed authorities."[56]

From 1897 until 1914, when the Trinity Society stopped meeting, to resume again in 1920, the attendance at meetings was between 11 and 31, an average larger than at the Politics Society, with a more diverse group of visitors from fields other than history, including the philosopher G. E. Moore, the classicist F. M. Cornford, and the physicist J. H. Jeans. Increasingly as the meetings proceeded, less interest was shown in the Whiggish view of history which justified the present by finding its origins in the past. Instead, aspects of a particular historical period were compared within their own setting and the latest discussions of historiography and method were reviewed. Of the 132 papers presented during those seventeen years, only two bore directly upon the present: Acton's "The Problem of 1870," in November 1900 and J. G. Gordon's "The Housing of the Working Classes," in February 1902.[57] But in Trinity, as in King's, the dominant interest of history students continued to be a concern with the meaning of history and the individual's role. When in 1912, the Society's president, R. Vere Laurence, was succeeded by W. F. W. Mortlock, the new president's talk on the "Lessons of History" continued a long-running discussion in which the "influence of personality loomed a leading topic."[58]

After World War I, when the Society resumed activity, the emphasis on historical research was still greater, and each Trinity undergraduate reading history was required to present two papers in each academic year.[59] Until 1921, the new president was T. H. Marshall, and he was succeeded by Charles Crawley, with F. C. Shaw as Secretary. Among the undergraduate members, G. Kitson Clark and W. D. Macpherson were conspicuous, while the honorary members were J. R. M. Butler, R. V. Laurence, G. T. Lapsley, F. A. Simpson, D. A. Winstanley and T. H. Marshall. Within the next decade, nearly every historian then or soon to be important, including many who were not even in Cambridge (such as G. M. Trevelyan, J. C. S. Runciman, J. L. B. Todhunter, G. P. Gooch, C. H. K. Martin, and G. G. Coulton) took a dynamic part in the Society's meetings.

*

Some students joined societies because they were ambitious for distinction. A surer way was to win a university prize. Beginning in the 1860s with A. V. Dicey and James Bryce and continuing into the prewar years with Lewis Namier and Harold Laski, almost every Oxford history prize winner went on to conspicuously successful academic careers. George Curzon, although he read Greats, won the Lothian Prize in 1883 and the Arnold Prize in 1884 and became the only history prize winner to leave the academic world. He became Viceroy of India, but he never severed his ties with Oxford and he returned as a particularly vigorous Chancellor in 1907. In Oxford the prize system was a compromise between the goals of the history professors and those of the tutors. By the 1880s the prize essay encouraged original scholarship among a few students and conferred recognition beyond an honours degree. Students could try for the Chancellor's Prize, the Arnold, the Stanhope, the Lothian, and the Beit. Prize winners were also eligible for college Fellowships.[60]

By contrast, the majority of prize winners at Cambridge went into other careers. There were few practical rewards for young men interested in history until 1885, when the new Prince Consort Prize became available. Until then, only the Thirlwall, awarded in alternate years, existed specifically for those studying history.[61] Only 4 among the 20 Thirlwall winners from 1899 to 1923, and only 7 of the 30 Prince Consort Prize winners between 1888 and 1930, became academics. One, H. J. W. Tillyard, became a don in English. The Seeley Medal, awarded only four times between 1900 and 1930, went to future academics on three occasions. Among the 26 Gladstone Prize winners, only 8 chose careers in higher education.[62]

As late as the interwar decades, contemporaries believed that there were still students who opted for history because they were not bright enough for a good degree in classics. In 1922 the Asquith Commission commented that "The Historical Tripos has carried off from classics the greatest numbers of its old clientele, but not possibly the best men in proportion." Anne Bettencourt, who came to Newnham in 1922 and took the Historical Tripos with first class honours in Part I in 1924 and in Part II the following year, recalled that students then felt that their university could not compare to the Oxford School and especially not to the work of Powicke and Tout at Manchester.[63] Even so, by 1928 there were 649 students reading for the Tripos, 20 research students from outside Cambridge, and additional graduates of the university doing research.[64] At Oxford, by the turn of the century and until the 1920s, there were greater numbers of students studying history than any other Oxford degree course. Was it true that they were possibly not the best graduates in both universities? If it can be established that first- and second-class honours graduates in history were able and effective in the real world, and I believe that it can by looking at their subsequent careers, then how did the discipline of history affect the careers they chose? And, even more problematically, did their understanding of the meaning and direction of history sway their particular judgment and general conduct in the world outside the universities? While these questions cannot be answered unequivocally, there is strong circumstantial evidence that the fundamental values and habits of mind of a significant number of the national elite owed a great deal to their university study of history.

Chapter 8

Life After the University

A funeral sermon on the occasion of Mandell Creighton's death in 1901 suggested a parallel between the former Dixie Professor of Ecclesiastical History at Cambridge and Pope Pius II by quoting Creighton's own description of that Pope: "The study of history was to him the source of instruction in life, the basis for the formation of character. He looked upon events with reference to their results in the future, and his actions were regulated by a strong sense of historic proportion. Similarly, the present was to him always the product of the past, and he shaped his motives by reference to historical antecedents. It was probably the historical point of view which made him engage in so many schemes, because he felt that, when once affairs were in movement, the skilful statesman might be able to reap some permanent advantage."[1] This might be said of the generations of English students of history at both Oxford and Cambridge who preceded and followed Creighton. Consistently, they approached their public responsibilities, whether political, economic, or social, from "the historical point of view." It was an incentive to action, because an understanding of the past uniquely qualified the student of history to anticipate and shape the future. Complex public responsibilities demanded discipline in the widest sense of that word as meaning both rigorous self-control and a special subject of study. The best students, in addition to learning their disciplines, were expected to learn social, political, and aesthetic sensibilities, forensic skills, and develop physical stamina. An honours degree was granted when the graduate performed as a roundly disciplined person. After graduation that person was expected to serve society by imposing order upon private and public inclinations, no matter how irrational and recalcitrant.

This chapter shows that the greatest number of the best graduates in history preferred careers where they could constructively carry out the lofty ideals they had learned at Oxford and Cambridge. When history graduates eventually came to positions of power, they had undergone many experiences that could have modified or altered what they learned as undergraduates. While it is impossible to discover what it was that most affected their adult judgment in the greater world, it is reasonable to assume that as increasingly large numbers of history graduates went from the university into central positions in the English-speaking community, they took with them at least some of the values they had learned. Until the 1930s, whatever evidence remains confirms that their teachers, whether tutors or professors, intended them for the most important places in any profession they might choose, and above all in those serving the public good. The demonstration of those intentions is independent of why students studied history or what they actually did with their lives. Certainly many, and especially those who wound up with a third-class degree or less, may have turned to history because they believed it to be a softer option than other honours degree courses. But if we concentrate on graduates who earned either a first- or second-class degree in history and were probably the brightest or the most interested in success, or both, it seems unlikely that this group turned to history because they were seeking an easy subject. Instead their lives demonstrate that they were driven people who excelled in difficult, demanding careers that fulfilled ideals of public obligation.[2]

Unlike graduates from the 1860s and earlier, those who came out of the universities in the late nineteenth and early twentieth centuries had extraordinary opportunities to enter new careers in the Indian and other colonial services, the civil service, the diplomatic service, the schools and universities, and a large variety of multiplying positions at the national and local level. Those opportunities were seized with alacrity. In 1892 a University Appointments Committee was set up in Oxford, largely to find jobs for school teachers. But by 1912, when the historian K. G. Feiling was its Chairman, the numbers seeking and finding civil and colonial service appointments were becoming larger each year.[3]

We do not have to speculate about the careers history graduates entered. At Oxford after 1901 the Honours School of Modern History produced more graduates than any other degree course and their numbers continued to grow. Between 1873 and 1930 there were 6,575 Modern History graduates in every class of degree.[4] As early as World War I, the School's graduates were conspicuously prominent in the "working life of England" as a "stream of men of sound intellectual training, with a large outlook on life and the high purpose of service to the nation" acting upon "such knowledge as Oxford can supply of the nature of society and of the State."[5] If we compare the numbers of honours degrees in history in every class to the total number of B.A.'s awarded in both universities for the first crucial decade (when history was trying to establish itself as a viable honours degree course at both Oxford and Cambridge), we find that Cambridge, with the greater number of B.A.'s, turned out far fewer history honours graduates. For the years 1878 to 1885, there were 642 honours graduates in history at Oxford and 111 in Cambridge. Oxford consistently had more history graduates than Cambridge until after World War I.[6] By 1900, when new regulations prescribed a two-part Honours Tripos in History in Cambridge, there were 48 candidates for Part I and 26 for the more difficult Part II. By 1906, the total number had almost doubled and the Historical Tripos grew steadily, although not phenomenally, until the 1920s when history came into its own at Cambridge.[7]

Some undergraduates, and especially women excluded from degrees at Oxford until after the First World War and at Cambridge for more than a generation after that, studied history in the Universities of Manchester or London, where they heard the same historical litany as their Oxford and Cambridge counterparts because they, too, were taught by Oxford and Cambridge graduates. In London, the number of graduates in history went from the teens after the Great War to the high twenties by the late 1920s. Tout's school and its teachers were a strong attraction at Manchester, where the number of history students rose from 9 honours students and 46 graduates in 1902, to 40 with honours and 104 altogether in 1912. Ten years later, there were 116 and 231. But the numbers who took history honours degrees in either Manchester or London and their possibilities for entering high-level positions never approached the level of Oxford and Cambridge graduates. For that reason, the best history graduates from Manchester, and occasionally from London, often supplemented their degree by studying history at Oxford or Cambridge.[8] Since neither Manchester nor London, certainly till well after World War II, were able to send more than a few of their history honours graduates into the public offices so easily attained by those from Oxford and Cambridge, there is no point in including those graduates in a comparative analysis of life after the university.[9]

Although there was a great discrepancy among the colleges in teaching and in the performance of their students, it was generally acknowledged that Balliol was the leading Oxford college in history and King's was its Cambridge counterpart. The careers of both colleges' highest-ranking history graduates are worth following for three compelling reasons. First, more first- and second-class honours students read history at Balliol than at any other Oxford college because of a lure no other college could match, the Brackenbury Scholarships, offered through competitive examination.[10] King's was not able to provide such generous support to its students, but those interested in history migrated there because it turned out the greatest number of first- and second-class honours degrees in the Historical Tripos. An extra incentive was the Politics Society, invitingly entrenched there.

Another reason for comparing Balliol and King's is that in the half-century from the mid-1870s to the middle to late 1920s, about the same number of undergraduates in Balliol and King's took first- and second-class honours degrees in history: 304 in Balliol, with 99 in first class and 205 in second to King's 282, divided into 71 and 211. Until 1914, except for the year 1896, Balliol students earned more first- and second-class honours degrees than any other Oxford college in each year's history examinations. King's got off to a slow start and no Kingsmen figured in the Historical Tripos in 1875, 1877, 1879 or 1880, but from 1893 to 1897 the college took nine first class honours in history while all the other men's colleges together took eleven.[11] The College's reputation in history grew steadily and provided serious competition for the sciences, in which Cambridge excelled and upon which its reputation was largely based. In the period from 1916 to 1929, more Kingsmen took the Historical Tripos than any other degree course (see Figure 1).[12]

Finally, Balliol and King's records provide exceptionally complete accounts of the activities of the best students from the two best history colleges. An essentially whole population, instead of a possibly misleading sample from each college, class and generation, allows me to go beyond mere statistical estimates. I have followed the careers of first- and second-class honours graduates, the various public and private positions they filled, the different kinds of obligations to which they devoted their lives, and those aspects of their work that they singled out as most important. As in Balliol and King's, the teaching and study of history in other colleges shared assumptions about the meaning of history and the role of graduates that was encoded in lectures, textbooks, and university-wide honours examinations. Although I do not have comparable evi-

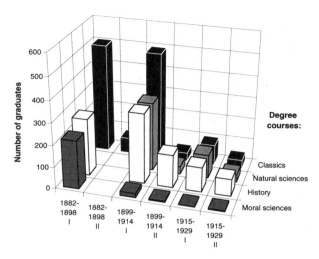

Periods of time and parts of examinations

Figure 1. Degree courses taken by graduates of King's College, Cambridge, 1882–1929. From 1882 to 1898, the Cambridge Historical Tripos was given entirely in one part. In 1899 a two-part examination was introduced and the graph for History, as for the other degree courses, indicates how many students took the simpler Part I and the more difficult Part II. There were no graduates in either part of the History examination for 1915, none for Classics from 1915 through 1919, and none for Moral Sciences in 1914. From 1896 to 1913, the Moral Sciences examination reverted to one part. There were no King's students in the Natural Sciences Tripos until 1905 and none again between 1915 through 1919. (Source information for Figures 1–12 is given in note 12 to this chapter.)

dence from those colleges, Balliol and King's history graduates may reasonably be assumed to represent the kinds of subsequent careers of most first- and second-class history graduates in the two universities.

Similarities among the various colleges were often remarkable, but each had its own defining character. Balliol graduates were sent into the world to run the foreign, diplomatic, civil and imperial services. When Thomas Thorneley, the history don at Trinity Hall, Cambridge, and J. L. Strachan-Davidson, later Master of Balliol, were co-examiners for the Indian Civil Service Exams in the 1880s, they put in nearly double the time expected of them and Strachan-Davidson arranged for their pay to be doubled because, as he told Thorneley, "the Commissioner and all at headquarters are Balliol men." These men were not necessarily graduates in history, but the anecdote makes clear both the reality and the mythology of the Balliol network in public life: if this event had never occurred it would still have made a credible story.[13]

After World War I, Balliol's standing in the study of history declined both absolutely and in relation to the other Oxford colleges, while the best Kingsmen became increasingly interested in the subject. When new students and the large numbers returned from war took their final honours examinations in 1922, there were fewer Balliol students in history than from some other Oxford colleges. That does not mean that the national influence of Balliol began to decline or that Kingsmen or anyone else filled places left vacant by Balliol. Those Balliol graduates who survived the war, by not having to fight or by good luck, remained in the highest public offices through the 1950s. The British delegation to the Peace Conference in Versailles included eleven delegates who had read history at Balliol, a striking example of the college's real presence when crucial decisions were made. The names of those delegates, as of so many other Balliol men, persisted in public life.[14] Kingsmen, too, filled politically powerful positions, but Balliol maintained the tightest hold on national and imperial offices. Kingsmen were in every profession without dominating any of them, although they were especially conspicuous in law and both university and secondary education. But King's was unique in Cambridge as virtually the only college until the late 1920s to teach history systematically, continuously, and successfully. Were it not for World War I, which killed them, eight more top graduates in history from Balliol and fourteen from Kings might have had crucial national and international influence.

The Great War was a turning point in the definition of vocations for some new and returning students and a stimulus to undergraduate interest in the study of history. Those who returned to read for a degree or for the newer short diploma courses, as well as those who had been too young to fight, wanted to understand what the war had been about. This need for explanation helps to explain both the greater popularity of the Historical Tripos in King's and the desertion from Modern History at Balliol.[15] History teachers at King's and in the universitywide History Board had attempted to interest reluctant students in current subjects for two generations. It was not until the postwar years that these topics became attractive. But in Balliol, the traditional contents of history teaching did not address questions about either the war or Britain's future. Students who were curious about such questions tended to turn to the degree course of Philosophy, Politics and Economics (PPE), introduced in 1920, which recognized prevailing, often theoretical, political, social, and economic issues as legitimate subjects for study. Until well after the Second World War, the continuity of history in Oxford as an essentially conservative study of constitutional and institutional development owed a great deal to this degree (known as "Modern Greats"). Many of the keenest Balliol students, and especially those who might have challenged the persistently narrow, hardly modern focus of Modern History, read for PPE. Those like Hugh Gaitskell, who wanted to prepare for civic careers, appreciated the contemporary emphases of the new course. Twenty-six Balliol candidates took the first PPE examinations in 1923 and by 1930 the number had expanded to 102.[16] But even though there were fewer Balliol men studying history after the war, there is no doubt that innovative, first-rate students, such as W. K. Hancock and Dennis Brogan, still found history engaging.[17]

*

On the basis of their own classification of the various positions they held, I have classified the first- and second-class history honours graduates of both colleges into seven career categories: public service; education; writing, editing, and publishing; law; business, finance, commerce and industry; religion; and miscellaneous callings unrelated to their university degrees.[18] Although writing, editing and publishing drew a considerable number of Balliol and King's men, very few were professional men of letters. Most wrote either as an ancillary part of another career, generally in school or university teaching, or public service, or for recreation. Although education was considered a public service not only by Victorian, Edwardian and postwar society and by those working selflessly in universities, secondary schools, and educational administration in Britain and throughout the empire, when graduates were asked to describe their careers, they listed education separately. But there is no doubt that they thought of a career in education as a contribution to the public good.

No matter how many particular jobs an individual may have held in any one category, such as four different positions in the Foreign Service and a stint in the India Office, that category is only counted as one career choice. Occasionally, this kind of accounting conceals the number of actual positions held by any person. F. D. Ackland, for example, worked entirely in the one category of public service, but was a central figure in nine major, entirely disparate government offices. He also chaired six unrelated government committees of inquiry, and assumed miscellaneous civic responsibilities.[19] But there are more graduates who remained within a narrow segment of public service in such agencies as the Foreign Office or the Diplomatic Service, where assignments were mandated by the service rather than chosen by the individual. Although posted to what superficially seem to be different jobs and often moved to new locations, the person usually performed very similar duties. Within the other categories, I have followed the same principle of analysis. For example, G. C. Field taught philosophy first at Balliol and then at the Universities of Birmingham, Manchester, Liverpool and Bristol, where he became Dean of the Faculty of Arts. Field's positions, although they were in different places, were all essentially university teaching and are totaled together as one career. Percentages and numbers used to express how many individuals worked in different careers often exceed 100 percent of the graduates because they count the multiple careers that most graduates had.

Although contemporaries then and historians ever since tended to view World War I as a traumatic break in British history, it is really striking that the war years and their aftermath had so little effect on the working lives of history graduates. From the early 1870s until the late 1920s, there was more continuity than change. That is clear in the persistence of at least five prewar trends throughout the postwar period. First, the great majority of Balliol history graduates had multiple careers, in contrast to Kingsmen (see Figures 2–5). Before the war, 87 percent of Balliol firsts and 68 percent of seconds (75 percent of firsts and seconds together) pursued more than one profession which replaced their initial choices, either temporarily or permanently, or were carried on at the same time. From 1914 through 1927, 67 percent of firsts and 66 percent of seconds (66 percent of combined firsts and seconds) went into various multiple careers. At King's in the prewar period only 47 percent of the firsts and 41 percent of the seconds (43 percent of the firsts and seconds together) followed more than one career. In the years from 1914 the number of firsts who had multiple careers rose dramatically to 76 percent, and the number of seconds rose slightly to 47 percent (51 percent of firsts and seconds together).

Why were there so many more Balliol graduates in multiple careers? (Figure 6). It is difficult to know, in the silence of unstated motives, whether Kingsmen had fewer opportunities, or felt a greater desire for security or a stronger commitment to a particular field, or there was some combination of these factors. It may be that the reasons for either continuing or changing work were not understood even by those who chose as they did. There is no indication that either group was moved by restlessness or an incompetence that pushed them on because they were

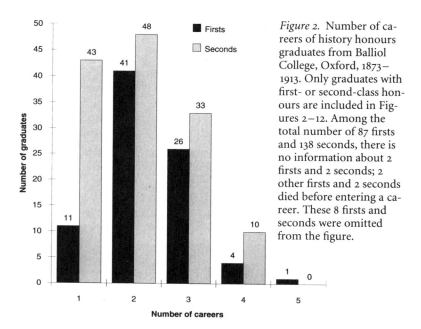

Figure 2. Number of careers of history honours graduates from Balliol College, Oxford, 1873–1913. Only graduates with first- or second-class honours are included in Figures 2–12. Among the total number of 87 firsts and 138 seconds, there is no information about 2 firsts and 2 seconds; 2 other firsts and 2 seconds died before entering a career. These 8 firsts and seconds were omitted from the figure.

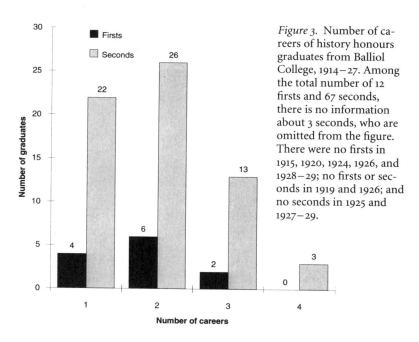

Figure 3. Number of careers of history honours graduates from Balliol College, 1914–27. Among the total number of 12 firsts and 67 seconds, there is no information about 3 seconds, who are omitted from the figure. There were no firsts in 1915, 1920, 1924, 1926, and 1928–29; no firsts or seconds in 1919 and 1926; and no seconds in 1925 and 1927–29.

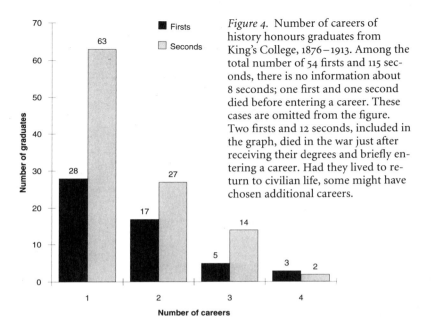

Figure 4. Number of careers of history honours graduates from King's College, 1876–1913. Among the total number of 54 firsts and 115 seconds, there is no information about 8 seconds; one first and one second died before entering a career. These cases are omitted from the figure. Two firsts and 12 seconds, included in the graph, died in the war just after receiving their degrees and briefly entering a career. Had they lived to return to civilian life, some might have chosen additional careers.

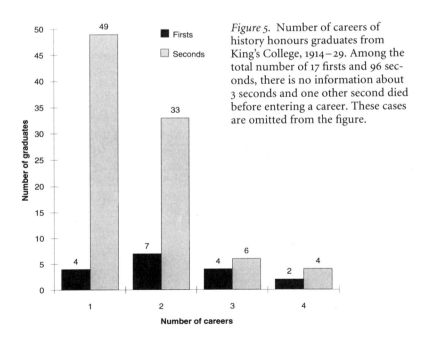

Figure 5. Number of careers of history honours graduates from King's College, 1914–29. Among the total number of 17 firsts and 96 seconds, there is no information about 3 seconds and one other second died before entering a career. These cases are omitted from the figure.

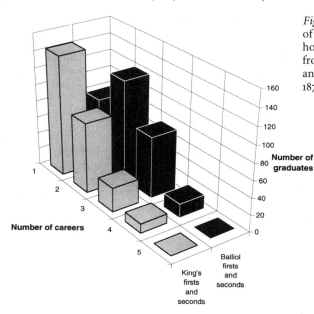

Figure 6. Number of careers of history honours graduates from King's College and Balliol College, 1873–1929.

unable to fill the demands of one position. On the contrary, the nature of the jobs held and the performance within them indicates exceptional ability, supported by both ambition and a sense of propriety that transcended merely personal ends.

Even though prewar Balliol graduates answered more callings than their King's counterparts, both groups had working lives rich in diversity. Their remarkable successes depended on their own efforts and on membership in a small, well-connected elite that led the country and empire in almost every field. The ability of both King's and Balliol men to move from one position to another owed a great deal to the friendships established in college and to the ties between government service and late careers in business. Those who joined boards of directors or became heads of industries towards the end of their working lives often did so as a result of the contacts made while in domestic or imperial government offices. Most graduates fulfilled the obligations of full-time careers and still found time to hold public and charitable positions. Even for those with only one vocation, considerable personal risks were taken, often in foreign service. Almost all of them were in positions that enabled them, if they wished, to exercise decisive authority.

The second continuing pattern from the 1870s to the 1920s was that public service, whether in government or education, drew the greatest numbers of Balliol and King's first- and second-class honours graduates in history (see Figures 7–10). As these newer vocations expanded, religion and law, the goal of the greatest number of graduates during the first three quarters of the nineteenth century, contracted. Among the 304 individuals receiving first- or second-class honours degrees in history at Balliol from 1873 to 1927, more than half devoted part of their lives to public service and education. From 1876 to 1929, of the 282 King's first- and second-class history graduates, slightly less than half the firsts and seconds worked for some time in public service and education.

It was not only in education and the foreign, diplomatic, or imperial services that Balliol and King's men contributed to the public good. One of the first graduates in the new Modern History Honours School in 1873 was C. S. Loch, who, as Secretary to the Council of the Charity Organization Society from 1875 to 1914 and as an indefatigable member of Royal Commissions and other bodies of inquiry, defined private and then public social welfare work in England for more than two generations.[20] Loch's career was especially, but not uniquely, influential; very similar service was carried out by a remarkably large number of Balliol graduates. Among Kingsmen, too, a more detailed scrutiny is revealing. When

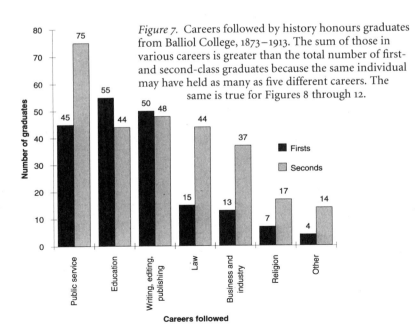

Figure 7. Careers followed by history honours graduates from Balliol College, 1873–1913. The sum of those in various careers is greater than the total number of first- and second-class graduates because the same individual may have held as many as five different careers. The same is true for Figures 8 through 12.

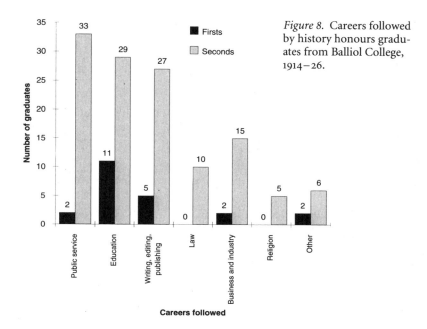

Figure 8. Careers followed by history honours graduates from Balliol College, 1914–26.

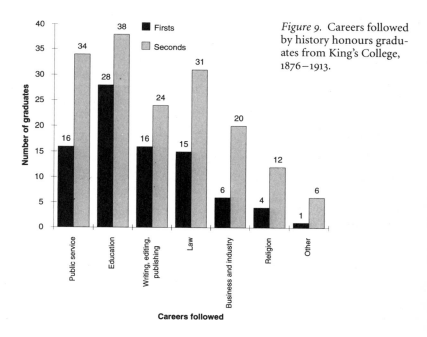

Figure 9. Careers followed by history honours graduates from King's College, 1876–1913.

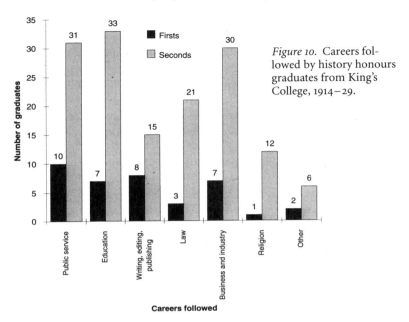

Figure 10. Careers followed by history honours graduates from King's College, 1914–29.

C. R. Ashbee, famous in the arts and crafts movement and a practicing architect, took second class honours in the Historical Tripos in 1886, it was not yet possible to study architecture as a degree course, but architectural papers were often part of the optional or Special Essays part of the Historical Tripos examination. Conventionally, buildings were used to interpret time, place and the trappings of power.[21] But for Ashbee, architecture in particular and the arts in general were repositories of values integral to the well-being of a community. While living in Toynbee Hall he founded the Guild and School of Handicraft to perpetuate both the ideals and skills that had been historically proven. Ashbee found the qualities he believed to be permanent in the work of Ruskin, Morris and the arts and crafts movement and translated them into city planning. Like so many King's and Balliol graduates, he tried to transport and implement the higher qualities of English life abroad.

If we look at the more traditional careers of law and religion, we find that even within these specialized professions, public service went beyond the requirements of particular offices. Many barristers and solicitors undertook public commitments in England as well as becoming judges and colonial administrators throughout the empire. A Balliol ex-

ample and one from King's illustrate a range of activities that lawyers very
often followed. The Balliol graduate, H. L. W. Lawson, later the first Viscount Burnham, chaired the Committee on Teachers' Salaries that established the Burnham scale. Burnham's multiple careers included the
army, the law, the press and higher education as well as membership of
the London County Council, Parliament, Royal Commissions and city
government. Jasper More, from King's, was a barrister, farmer, market
gardener and author of travel books, as well as a member of county and
parliamentary government.[22]

From 1873 to 1924, instead of seeking a parish living as was common
in preceding generations, two-thirds of the firsts and seconds from Balliol who were in religious vocations extended their careers to teaching at
home and abroad. Among them was Cosmo Gorden Lang who, while
still an undergraduate, was Under-Secretary of Toynbee Hall. He, too,
combined teaching with preaching, and in common with those working
in schools or universities, used his pulpit as an educational force. After
obtaining second class honours in Greats in 1885 and a first in history the
following year, Lang read Law and supported himself as a journalist. But
just before he was called to the bar, an intense religious experience led
him to think again about his future. In 1891 he was ordained by the
Bishop of Oxford, William Stubbs, who had taught him history. After
three years as a Fellow and Dean of Divinity at Magdalen College, Oxford, he became an active, peripatetic priest and social reformer until
1908 when Asquith appointed him Archbishop of Canterbury. In King's,
for the same period, one-third of those in religious life also taught and
three more were in other kinds of public service. Among them was Clive
Frederick Parr, who took second class honours in history in 1929 and in
Law the following year. He went to Simla as a schoolmaster, but returned
to England and entered the Church to become a schoolmaster again, a
headmaster, private chaplain to the Archbishop of Canterbury and a
member of the Canterbury City Council. He was also Sheriff and later
Mayor of Canterbury.[23]

*

A third persisting tendency after the war was that students who were
given a chance to supplement their history course with more specialized
or professional studies, either while still an undergraduate or following
graduation, rarely made that choice. Instead, those who pursued additional studies tended to do so in fields that had little utility for their
subsequent working lives. In Balliol, most of those reading history gave
their attention entirely to achieving a high class of honours in the sub-

ject. Conventional wisdom held then, and still holds, that most good Balliol students were examined in a more difficult first degree course such as Greats before turning to history, which was easy enough for them to prepare in one more year. But the figures do not support that contention. Instead, only a total of nine firsts and seconds, from 1873 to 1926, took other fields either before or after completing their history degree. From 1873 to 1914, among the 99 firsts, only four turned to history after winning honours in another subject and only two, H. R. Reichel in 1879 and Lang six years later, earned a first in Litterae Humaniores a year before their first in Modern History.[24] Of the 138 prewar seconds, an even smaller number (three) took another honours examination first. They included A. L. Smith, who took a first in Litterae Humaniores in 1873 (the earliest year the Modern History examination was offered).[25] From 1914, none among the firsts and only five among the seconds supplemented their history honours degrees with newly available diplomas in specialized subjects.[26] In each of these five cases, the diploma was pursued as special training for a particular profession.[27]

A striking difference between Balliol and King's students reading history was that a much more significant proportion of the latter investigated other disciplines and sat a second Tripos examination in addition to history. Although some might have picked a supplementary field applicable to their professional plans, interest in other disciplines rarely turned out to be useful for the professions actually entered and occasionally it was conspicuously irrelevant. There was no clear relation between the additional disciplines studied and the careers eventually pursued and it is equally perplexing to determine whether the study of history was a decisive factor in the choice of other disciplines. No consistent patterns emerge. Since Cambridge teachers, in common with their colleagues in Oxford, denied that university subjects were "professional," many students may simply have explored other fields to satisfy a personal interest. A Tripos in Law or Theology did not necessarily culminate in legal or religious professions and such new subjects as modern languages, while certainly advantageous for foreign service, were not essential. Balliol graduates without such training filled very similar posts. Another of the new subjects, economics, does not seem to have led most of those who studied it into positions in business, industry or finance. Many of the graduates who took other Triposes might have, as readily as their Balliol counterparts, entered the vocation they finally chose without the additional studies pursued.

In the first generation, from 1876 to 1899, when the Historical Tripos was slowly accepted at King's and it was not yet clear to those reading history that their degree would command respect in the greater world or even within the university, seven firsts and ten seconds took another Tripos either before or in the same year that they took history. From 1899, when the two-part Tripos was introduced, to World War I, the prestige of the Historical Tripos grew within and outside Cambridge. The first-class honours students' increased respect for their field may have led to the decline in numbers who took other Triposes. Only seven firsts turned to other fields and the reasons for their choices varied from person to person. A. C. Pigou, who succeeded Marshall as Professor of Political Economy in 1908, may have taken the second part of the Moral Sciences Tripos because no economics course existed yet and the more advanced part of the Moral Sciences examination required more political economy than did history, and it also emphasized the technical and analytical aspects of economics.[28] Two other firsts took the Moral Sciences Tripos; one became a geographer and the other entered the Consular Service. Another took theology, and became a schoolmaster; and the last was examined in classics, but became an economist.[29]

Among 25 King's seconds who took an additional Tripos from 1899 through 1913, there may have been less trust in the sufficiency of their history degree. The greatest number took law additionally and most of them had legal careers exclusively for the rest of their professional lives. Three of the second-class honours graduates took the Economics Tripos, established in 1903: Philip John Baker, an American, became a British representative to international bodies and finally the Cassel Professor of International Relations in the University of London; Malcolm Rowntree became a schoolmaster and then a hotel proprietor; and William Ralph Osborne Moulton died in the war before his career began. Three more supplemented their history with mathematics: Richard F. Bailey became a headmaster, Lancelot Glasson a businessman in Bombay and director of a number of public companies, and Vithal Narayan Chandavarkar returned to his native India as a prominent lawyer and then businessman. Six turned to Classics, including the novelist, E. M. Forster, and they wound up in professions that included school and university teaching, the law, and public office. The one second class honours graduate who also took moral sciences was an artist and a writer, while another took theology and became a university teacher of philosophy and ultimately, a research student.[30] But eight other graduates, two firsts and six seconds, went from both parts of the Historical Tripos to religious vocations without any university study of theology. Two firsts and one second went into both the Anglican Church and education; one second into the Anglican Church, education, and writing; and four seconds were in the Anglican Church exclusively. Two more of these seconds took only Part I of the Historical Tripos: one became a Methodist, with careers in education and writing, and the other devoted himself entirely to the Anglican Church. Hiram Craven and William Hubert Dyson took supplementary degrees in theology; Craven was ordained in the Church of England, and Dyson, who intended to enter the Wesleyan ministry, was killed in the war.

After World War I, 8 firsts and 44 seconds were examined in another discipline which either preceded or supplemented their Historical Tripos. All of the firsts took either both parts of the Historical Tripos or History and another discipline while only seven of the seconds took Part I of History and nothing else. The new Modern Languages Tripos was a practical field for both Roderick Le Mesurier and Paul Mason, who entered the Foreign Service. But another first, W. H. J. Christie, joined the Foreign Service by the older route of classics and history. Two others, I. M. Stephens and A. W. Haslett, also got a first in natural science and both devoted themselves largely to journalism. After a few years in business, Stephens joined the Indian Government's Bureau of Public Information and became editor and member of the board of *The Statesmen* (published in Calcutta and Delhi), as well as a war correspondent and the historian of the Pakistan Army. Haslett became the science correspondent for *The Times* and other publications. S. C. Morland, examined in economics, entered his family business in sheepskin goods and also took an active part in county government. Of the remaining two firsts, George Norman Black studied law and became a barrister in public service while R. E. Balfour, who wound up as a Fellow at King's and a Cambridge University Lecturer in History, was also examined in theology.[31]

The greatest number of seconds took English as a supplementary Tripos and tried a variety of employments. At one extreme, there was John Hill Appleby, a schoolmaster, who was conspicuous among the Cambridge honours graduates in history because his life was so ordinary. But at the other end, there was the far more adventurous Julian Bell, who went to the Chinese University of Hankow as Professor of English. A symbol of the second generation of Bloomsbury, he established himself as a writer of poetry and prose and in 1938 became a martyr for the frustrated idealism of his contemporaries. A year after entering the Spanish civil war on the Republican side, he was killed while driving an ambulance.[32]

The most utilitarian of the additional studies for the King's seconds in history, as in the generation immediately preceding, was law. Six who studied law spent their working lives as lawyers, but three of them also devoted part of their lives to public service.[33] Five, with a Classics Tripos, entered such disparate fields as law, the paper industry, printing and publishing, religion and teaching.[34] Among those studying economics, one went into government, another into medicine, a third chose school-teaching, and the fourth, the Indian Civil Service.[35] Another two studied theology, joined the Anglican Church and migrated to Africa.[36] One more took modern languages and became a schoolmaster. The last two were drawn to the newer, more specialized Triposes of Geography and Agriculture, but these studies had little apparent utility for their subsequent careers.[37]

The majority of Kingsmen with second disciplines studied subjects that were generally irrelevant for the professions in which they worked. Why, then, did more King's than Balliol students supplement their Historical Tripos with other fields of study? Oxford students in every course normally studied for only one honours examination and Balliol graduates may have been particularly certain that history was a preparation for all seasons. But at Cambridge, from the turn of the century, the two-part examination system made it easy for students to move to a second field. An additional explanation for the greater range of disciplines for King's history graduates may lie in the intellectual organization of Cambridge life which brought students from different colleges and different studies together in a variety of societies that were not directed towards preparation for any particular Tripos. Even within those groups concerned with one subject, such as the King's Politics Society, there were students from almost every discipline taught within the university and from many other colleges.[38] The Stubbs Society in Oxford, while also drawing students from a variety of colleges, was made up almost exclusively of those reading history. When Oxford undergraduates mingled with students from other disciplines, it was more likely to be in sports, hobbies, the arts, theater, and most of all in political groups or reformist activities such as settlement or extension work. There were few Oxford societies of broader intellectual inquiry. The experience of Kingsmen in disparate intercollegiate organizations may have accustomed them to the appreciation of intellectual variety.

*

The fourth constant tendency before and after World War I among both Balliol and King's graduates was an idealization of their universities and the education they received there. Opportunities for studying in Europe, which might have been helpful for the international positions these graduates so often filled, were rarely sought before the war and deliberately shunned after. Both Balliol and King's students could have supplemented their study of history by further work in Europe. Before the war, H. A. L. Fisher of New College stands out as one of the very few Oxford teachers to urge history students to go to French and German universities. But only four Balliol firsts and five seconds went abroad to study. One of them was F. F. Urquhart, to be known by several generations of Balliol undergraduates as "Sligger." After receiving his first in 1894, he went to Paris for a year and returned to be a legendary history tutor at Balliol, whose one publication, *The Eastern Question* (1914), was a pamphlet in the Oxford war series. Urquhart's scholarship was negligible in comparison to his college reputation.[39] The five seconds who went abroad included H. J. H. Russell, who received his Modern History degree in 1890 and then went to study at the University of Berlin. After becoming a barrister and joining the Foreign Office, he was Joint Secretary to the Anglo-German Arbitration Tribunal. But he then turned to the study of parasitology and other interests. He wrote *Railway Rates and Charges Orders: The Law of Railway Rates and Charges Orders Confirmation Acts, 1891 and 1892, and the Railway and Canal Traffic Act, 1894* (1907) as well as *Chalkstream and Moorland: Thoughts on Trout Fishing* (1911) and *The Flea* (1913). D. G. Campbell-Johnston, another of these seconds, had a particularly eccentric career, even by the tolerant standards of his time. With a second in 1898, he studied theology first at a Trappist monastery in Palestine and later at the Scots' College in Rome. He became a barrister, but never practiced law. Instead, he settled in Biarritz and privately studied history, comparative religion, and biblical criticism. Then he enlisted in the Foreign Legion, had a distinguished military career, and went on to become British Vice-Consul in Biarritz from 1920 to 1921. The last that was known of him was that he migrated to Canada to become a banker and businessman.[40]

Unlike their Balliol peers, prewar King's students were taught by teachers such as Prothero, Seeley, Acton and Browning with close continental connections and a demonstrated interest in the history of European states. But only three King's history students studied abroad and two of them, in the late 1880s and early 1890s, ventured into Germany and France for utilitarian reasons. Clement Ord studied at Heidelberg from 1885 to 1886, took a job as a schoolteacher at Reichelsheim-in-Odenwald for the next five years, and then returned to lecture in English and German at University College, Bristol. He concluded his career as Head of the German Department at the new University of Bristol from 1908 to 1925. Frederick William Smart, who studied at Paris and Marburg

Universities, was a schoolmaster of modern languages and the author of schoolbooks about Louis XI and Alfred de Musset. But Robert Stewart Leppert's German studies played no part in his subsequent employment. He studied at Leipzig University from 1893 to 1894 before launching a career that began with the teaching of English and history in India and included the editorship of the *Indian Journal of Education* and a Professorship in History and Economics at H. H. the Maha Raja's College, Tranvancore. When he retired in 1911, he acquired a Scientific Research Studentship at the University of London, worked for the Irish Record Office, became a Member of the Advisory Committee on the Ancient Muniments of Northern Ireland, and finally was Governor of the Linenhall Library, Belfast.

Until after 1930, no Balliol student of history and only one from King's (Alfred Thornton Cholerton) went abroad to study. Cholerton, with a double first in 1913 and 1914, was in the War Office for the remainder of the war and then spent the next seven years studying in France before working as a journalist in Russia. But students who returned from the war had seen enough of France from the trenches, while those beginning their studies shared the English-speaking world's repudiation of Germany as a fit place for liberal studies. Instead, both Oxford and Cambridge became centers of learning not only for the British, but also for students from America and the Empire who, with degrees from their own universities, came to England for additional studies for an honours degree. After World War I, Balliol awarded one first class honours degree in history to a student from Canada, and twenty-four second-class degrees to students from abroad. Were it not for these foreign students, there would have been only a total of 11 firsts and 43 seconds in history at Balliol from 1914 to 1927. The foreigners included the humanist scholar Stringfellow Barr, who came as a Rhodes Scholar from the United States, and the cultural historian Gleb Petrovich Struve from Petrograd, who had served with the Russian army during the war, but stayed on in the west as an emigré journalist in Paris. Struve entered academic life as Lecturer in Russian Literature and eventually as Reader in Russian Literature at the University of London.[41] At King's only two undistinguished students with B.A.'s, an Indian and an American, came from abroad to study history after the war. Most of the overseas students at Cambridge came for the sciences, not for history.

*

The last of the five persistent patterns went unnoticed while it was occurring and it has been neglected by historians subsequently. The

Thatcher government and some recent scholars, particularly Martin Wiener in his interesting *English Culture and the Decline of the Industrial Spirit* (1981), argued that British industrial decline was tied to the contempt for business supposedly demonstrated by Oxford and Cambridge graduates. When we look at Balliol and King's history graduates, the records reveal instead that the highest ranking were hardly indifferent to the commercial world. In Oxford generally, during the nine years before World War I, the Appointments Committee was placing between 8 and 14 percent of its clients, from every discipline, in business and industry.[42] Religion, the career that had attracted the greatest number of university graduates before the 1870s, gradually dwindled in its appeal to history honours graduates at both Balliol and King's. Even before 1914 more were drawn to business than to religious occupations (Figures 7 and 9). After 1914, the numbers of Balliol and King's men in business increased conspicuously in comparison to religion as well as to the other traditional occupation of university graduates, law (Figures 8 and 10). Additionally, among Kingsmen business also attracted more high-class history honours graduates than the newer, fashionable careers of writing, editing, and publishing (Figure 10).

King's and Balliol graduates in history entered the commercial and industrial world, as they entered other spheres, with the advantage of college and university connections, which may have been as useful in business as they were in other professions. A. V. Faulkner, a 1908 graduate, went to Shell Oil, a company that later hired three more Kingsmen with history honours degrees in the mid-1920s. It is difficult to know whether this was a coincidence or part of an intentional pattern. What must be remembered when looking for consistent trends is the enormously disruptive effect of World War I. Those who had just graduated or would have graduated in the years 1914 to 1918, even when they returned from the war unharmed, had been swept out of the career paths that ordinarily would have been waiting for them.

Considering Balliol graduates first, with the careers we can trace, the first high-ranking history graduate went into business in 1875 and until 1924, 15 of the 99 firsts and 52 of the 205 seconds found business an attractive vocation at home and abroad. All but one of the firsts and about three-quarters of the seconds found time for multiple careers, including extensive public service. The exception, C. G. Goschen, a first-class honours graduate in 1903, began as a barrister in 1905, turned to stockbroking in 1907, and died in the war. Had he lived, he, too, might have found time for some kind of public service. Among the seconds,

H. A. MacLehose, a graduate in 1908 who went to the University Press, Glasgow, was so severely wounded in the war that his working life ended.

The career of Thomas Brassey, the first Earl Brassey of Bulkeley, Cheshire, indicates the kind of working pattern followed by Balliol men who entered business and enjoyed full multiple careers. In addition to his business duties, he worked in a variety of public offices, any one of which was daunting enough even for the most energetic and ambitious. The heir of a famous iron and steel family, Brassey edited the *Naval Annual* from 1890 to 1902, was Assistant Private Secretary to Lord Spencer, the First Lord of the Admiralty, and Assistant Secretary to the Royal Commission on Opium in 1894. He was also a soldier and the first Civil Governor of Pretoria in 1900. His intimate knowledge of the business community led to his appointment to the Anglican Archbishop's Finance Committee, to the chairmanship of the Central Board of Finance, and to his organization of Balliol's Endowment Fund in 1904. He was also the managing director of lead-smelting and mining businesses in Italy and organized the rail route through Italy to Taranto for the Allied forces in Salonika in 1916. Finally, he was president of the British Federation of Iron and Steel Merchants. When he died in 1919, A. L. Smith gave a moving obituary address for him in the college chapel. Balliol history graduates who became successful businessmen, in common with Balliol graduates in other careers, almost always undertook some kind of public work as well.

For the 41 years from 1888, when the first King's history honours graduate entered business, until 1929, 13 of the 71 firsts at King's and 50 of the 211 seconds went into business.[43] Among the firsts, T. F. Reddaway (1929, 1930) became an insurance broker immediately after receiving his B.A., but by 1935, he had returned to Cambridge as Director of Studies at Clare College, Cambridge. After the war he was Reader in History at University College, London and he wrote about the history of London. Reddaway was the rare King's graduate who entered a business career at the bottom instead of at a high level, but he left business as soon as he could return to university life. Seven of these graduates who intended to enter business, and actually did, devoted considerable time and energy to preparing both parts of a Historical Tripos that had little practical value for them. The first postwar history graduate at King's to supplement a business career with public service was Baden Wilmer Hawke, later the ninth Baron Hawke. He was with the Bombay Co., Ltd. from 1922 to 1937 and after war service with the Ministry of Economic Warfare and the War Office, Chairman of the Conservative Back Bench Peers

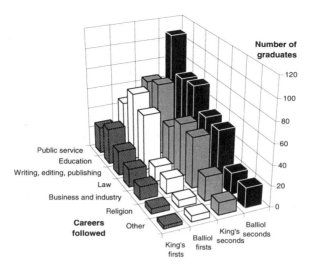

Figure 11. Careers followed by history honours graduates from King's College and Balliol College, 1873–1929. In each of the various careers shown in this figure and Figure 12, the smaller number of King's graduates in comparison to Balliol's results from the higher concentration of Kingsmen in single careers—more than 50 percent higher than in Balliol. Since there were so many more Kingsmen in single careers, there were necessarily fewer in other possible careers. The minor difference between the total number of Balliol and King's graduates has only a negligible effect on the comparisons shown here.

Association and Government whip in the House of Lords. In addition, he supported the Church of England energetically as a member of the Church Assembly, the Board of Governors and Administration Committee of the Church Commissioners, and the Church of England Pensions Board.[44]

Why did so many history graduates choose a business career at some time in their lives even though they had been taught history as a preparatory course for a lifetime of public service? From the mid-1870s at Balliol and the late 1880s at King's to the late 1920s, 15 percent of Balliol firsts and 25 percent of the seconds and 18 percent of the King's firsts and 24 percent of the seconds had business interests (Figure 11). There is no question that such careers provided the majority of these graduates of both Oxford and Cambridge with access to discretionary powers in British and international economic affairs. For the great majority in both colleges who decided upon business, that decision either preceded or was

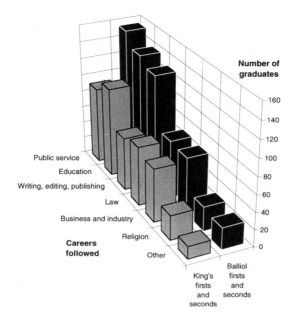

Figure 12. Careers followed by history honours graduates from King's College and Balliol College, 1873–1929. In this figure, the firsts and seconds in each college have been treated together.

accompanied by a commitment to public service. For others, a lifetime in public office, often within the I.C.S. or foreign services, concluded in a high-level administrative position in industry at home or abroad. It would be helpful to know the percentage of graduates from the other liberal subjects—and from economics—who found similar business careers satisfying enough to be at least a significant part of their life's work. The data in the Balliol and King's list do not tell us whether those who prospered conducted their enterprises with greater social goods in mind.

The numbers who turned to business careers at King's can be explained partially by the belief prevalent there that a business calling, especially when carried out at the top and often in the empire, was a genuine contribution to public good. This belief was encouraged by the imposing and persistent presence of J. H. Clapham, whose own personal progress (beginning with a history exhibition that allowed him to attend King's as an undergraduate) and his progressive reading of history supported an understanding of hard work as a necessary civic contribution.

Clapham was also convinced that business, industry, and all forms of commerce were essential to the realization of any practical public goods. It is more difficult to explain the numbers at Oxford. At Balliol, liberal tutors like A. L. Smith propelled their students into Toynbee Hall and then into civic, national, and imperial leadership where they were expected to act in the greater public interest. It never occurred to Smith or to his colleagues to imagine that higher ends could be served equally in business, but many of their students chose careers where business and public service were complementary and compatible.

*

The working lives of both Balliol and King's history graduates testify to their strong sense of political and social obligation (Figure 12). They fulfilled those obligations by occupying prominent positions for which they had no specialized training and very little practical experience. It was expected by teachers and graduates that the particular and essential knowledge necessary for the daily performance of their work would be assimilated when they were in office. Even though some Indian and Colonial civil servants learned enough on their jobs to become scholars in the languages and cultures in which they worked, others remained too ignorant to carry out their responsibilities. As late as 1931, when Sir Philip Cunliffe-Lister became Secretary of State for the Colonies, he was amazed to discover how uninformed his senior and junior staff were about the areas they were supposed to govern. Cunliffe-Lister assembled these officials, who had been there for years, and asked them: "What are the most important products of the Colonial Empire?" Nobody knew.[45]

The lack of knowledge about contemporary history, geography, economics, and languages, pervasive among the governing classes educated in Oxford and Cambridge, did not prevent history graduates from venturing intrepidly into a complex variety of fields both at home and in inhospitable countries abroad. Facing formidable obstacles, normally without any other qualification than an honours degree in history, they rarely recognized inadequacies either in what they understood or were required to do. Their confident idealism was rooted in their understanding of history, their belief in themselves, and their college connections. When they set out to fulfil the ethical and historical imperatives entrusted to them, they were giving purpose to their own lives and to those of their teachers.

The Sin of Omission

W hen Lord Curzon was Chancellor at Oxford in 1909, he tried to strengthen even further the university's part in training a national elite. We "have in our old universities," he wrote, "a mechanism for training the well-to-do to a sense of responsibility, and a capacity for public affairs which it would be the height of folly to throw away."[1] Among those well-to-do, none had benefited more from higher education than the aspiring middle classes. An ethic which associated rights and duties with merit was especially appealing to those whose good university degrees were the means of entry into prominent careers. Even social reformers such as the Balliol teachers Arnold Toynbee and T. H. Green, who wanted to eliminate class barriers and produce a fraternal community of all people, relied upon the continuing leadership of a new "class," the interested, educated elite.[2] It was not only at Balliol but throughout both newly modern, ancient universities that the enjoyment of privileges carried social obligations. This was a different idea from noblesse oblige because its roots lay in a nationalist analysis of history and political power and in a morality that elevated national responsibilities above private interest. University extension lectures and tutorials, similar to those given to Oxford and Cambridge students, were devised to reach a population unable to attend the university. But they rarely touched those with the least opportunities for altering their lives. Instead, social, economic and political reality continued to give power to those individuals who already had privileges and opportunities. The universities created a myth of justified entitlement when they subordinated the claims of birth and property to a higher education that carried with it a subsequent career of public service. The elitist myth was so convincing, especially to university graduates who moved into high positions, that it became a higher reality.

The select structure of higher education persisted well into the twentieth century on the grounds that it was an open meritocracy representing achievement rather than birth or wealth. Merit was decided, the argument ran, on the basis of systematic examinations which initially enabled any clever student to enter the university and eventually resulted in a ranking of those students into comparative classes of achievement.[3] Did this argument accurately describe procedures of selection and final decisions about ability? Did the universities identify and encourage those with demonstrable "merit" or was academic success more a measure of conformity to tradition?

University teachers, who devoted themselves selflessly to the recognition and nurture of ability, recognized merit by the same standards by which they, too, had been selected. But judgments about worth were often narrowly defined on the basis of traditional practices, such as handed-down examinations, which did not necessarily reveal innate intelligence or the capacity for coherent thinking. Dissent, independent or reflective thought, and critical, subversive analysis were not encouraged because greater value was given to a stable, common culture justified by a historical evolution of personal and communal goods. Achievement in the university was measured by honours examinations in disciplines where well-defined contents and standards were transmitted, with minimal change, from one generation to another. It was not simply that these standards had endured or that survival was confused with intrinsic worth. On the contrary, university officers and teachers were convinced that traditions of knowledge should prevail only if they were inherently correct and they believed further that their subjects, when properly studied, were windows to the truth. Academic acceptance and rejection rested upon a self-confidence fostered deliberately within every university community by idealizing discipline in both the narrowest and widest senses. Discipline meant both a particular organization of knowledge and the ability to work productively at an assigned task within existing limitations. Increasingly, though for only a very small fraction of the university-age population, the mastery of both kinds of discipline provided personal social mobility.

University-educated students tended to abandon their social origins and earlier lives to adopt the elitist values by which merit was decided in the universities. Successful graduates accepted a high-ranking degree as a confirmation of qualities of mind and character that they had been taught were appropriate to their education and the future for which they were being prepared. In 1907, when a liberal coalition of William Beveridge, R. H. Tawney, William Temple, Graham Wallas, Charles Gore and others campaigned for the admission of young working-class men and women to Oxford, working-class leaders such as Ramsay MacDonald, who never had the benefit of a university education, understood that the university was "a settled social organism" which would entirely assimilate working-class students.[4] But it was not until after the Second World War that working-class students, in any numbers, had a chance to test their resistance to the seductions of the university. For those middle-class students who preceded them, distinguished university degrees rewarded them with a position, with its attendant responsibilities, duties, and benefits, that was part of the existing social structure. More than for those born to advantage, the success of the newcomers depended essentially upon how well they perpetuated the traditions they learned in the universities.

The generations educated at the universities between the 1850s and the 1920s did not always enter influential offices immediately after leaving the university. On the contrary, for many, full decades intervened between their undergraduate experiences and their accession to positions of relative power. Although it is very difficult, and often impossible, to assess the impact of various influences within the university and later, we do know that the lessons they heard, especially in such new disciplines as history, emphasized their obligation to become rational and effective leaders. We also know that the working lives of most of them were in agencies of public service and education relatively small in size and homogeneous in membership. Those closed and self-perpetuating communities were far more likely to preserve common beliefs and habits than to call them into question. The "organizational intimacy" of the influential ranks of the Civil Service, where so many Oxford and Cambridge graduates spent their lives, was limited, even after the expansion following World War I, to 401 civil servants in 1928 with the rank of assistant secretary or higher. And a "staff generation" within the Civil Service ran from 35 to 40 years. That meant that those who entered the Service in the years before World War I were still in dominant positions after World War II. An additional repercussion was that the more egalitarian reforms introduced by the Royal Commission in 1912 to 1915 and implemented by the Treasury after 1919 could not be fully put into effect until the 1950s.[5]

In England, where democracy was limited by an exclusive system of higher education open only to a small minority of the population, the universities used both traditional and newer forms of knowledge to train those meant to lead the democracy to ends higher than they might have chosen for themselves. In the more egalitarian United States, many of the rapidly proliferating public universities welcomed increasing numbers of students and embraced far less traditional organizations of knowledge, because some university teachers believed that specialized studies would lead to a more accurate control of the real world. Whether the Americans were more shortsighted or more prescient than the English is a question that cannot readily be resolved. What is clear is that the American and English systems of higher education had little in common because national values and the ways in which they were organized were so different. The American views of community, tradition, the role of individuals, the purposes of higher education, and the conflicts between state and federal governments developed in a geographically extended, pluralistic society with many competing cultural and regional demands. While there were many issues separating the English, national culture and society, reflected and endorsed by their universities, were more homogeneous.

The crucial distinctions between the old and the new world resulted in the ready acceptance in the United States and the long rejection in England of the social sciences as disciplines based on criticism and reform of existing institutions and practices. When the staff of the Social Science Research Council in America tried to direct the efforts of their new organization, after it was founded in the mid-1920s, they were bewildered at the amount of power given to them in the form of huge sums of money. They wanted to spend that money wisely and well. To do so, they concentrated on social research that they hoped would culminate in policy, especially because their funding came from private corporations with distinctly expressed needs. But the corporations left major decisions entirely in the hands of the academics who invested in disciplines intended to improve society. They assumed that a properly scientific study of social problems would lead to their solution. In their enthusiasm for a form of knowledge that would be simultaneously rigorous and meliorative, they did not anticipate that the concept of "social science" would come to be challenged as oxymoronic.

English history teachers, professors and tutors alike, at Oxford and Cambridge complained incessantly about the lack of financial support for their discipline. But they rejected money which in any way threatened to compromise their autonomous control of their students and the liberal arts purposes of their subject. When a richly endowed chair in soci- ology was offered to Cambridge in the 1920s by an American donor, the university refused it. In part, this refusal was due to intellectual distaste for the "scientific" assumptions of the social sciences. But another and perhaps more significant reason is that they found the social sciences redundant because they already had a discipline to train students to un- dertake and solve national and imperial problems. If American social scientists thought about promoting public good, the English historians wanted to promote good public servants. It was, in part, a question of the necessary size of the governing groups and the scale of the country. Americans saw in their society large areas of conflict demanding expert social reform, while the English were still betting on the evolution of common political institutions and on the character of these responsible individuals able to govern such institutions with effect. The social sci- ences in which so many American universities invested heavily discov- ered that the direction of events was more opaque and resistant to prediction then they had anticipated. Whether any discipline or any university in England, America, or any other country, could have pre- pared its graduates to control so unpredictable a future remains a moot question.

The graduates of Oxford and Cambridge and of those red-brick uni- versities that imitated them attempted to deal with the world by virtue of a liberal education which they believed gave them knowledge that was both adequate and sufficient. Controversy within the universities about teaching and curriculum in the nineteenth century often centered on the competing values of a "professional" as opposed to a "liberal arts" train- ing. That issue was given a new dimension in the twentieth century by the argument that a dichotomy between the educational purposes of broadly humanistic or more narrowly technical ends was false because the best higher education, whether for the professions or more generally for life, trains individuals to think critically, selectively, rationally, coher- ently, and ethically about the competing claims of different kinds of knowledge and practice.[6] But the university teachers of history, almost unanimously, continued to argue that undergraduates would best learn humane judgment by admiring honorable values and behavior and re- pudiating the dishonorable. They also sought, especially at Cambridge, to reward cleverness and to encourage a quick mind.

What was missing was an emphasis upon critical thinking, skepti- cism, and a salutary sense of irony as preliminary to judgment. The uni- versity study of history emphasized one aspect of the liberal educational ideal at the expense of other interpretations. Historians were attracted more to those attitudes of mind and conduct protected by abiding traditions and institutions than to those encountered in doubt and struggle. The study of history transmitted a package of patriotic and moral sentiments, rather than an ambiguous body of material that compelled discriminating, let alone soul-searching, thought. Most historians assumed that the unequivocally given and objectively true past yielded truth discernible to any interested student. If academics suffered from myopia in the late nineteenth and early twentieth centuries, it was not attributable either to ill will or a denseness of perception. Shortsightedness was directly related to sins of omission rather than to those of commission.

For the great majority of history teachers in the English university, including those who wrote scholarly monographs, there was a single interpretative scheme that was transmitted to students as true, accurate, and reasonable because it explained the historical rectitude of responsible citizenship. Few recognized that their interpretations preceded their evidence. Logically, at least for the purposes of reconstructing the past, interpretation always precedes the evidence to provide a temporary explanatory scheme which allows some facts to be selected and others to be rejected. After World War II, a new generation of historians came to see that if there was no fit between the ideological container and the evidence gathered within it, they must jettison the theory and try another, better fitting analytical device. Until then, historians were not prepared to believe that knowledge could result in impotence or that only equivocal explanations are possible for contingent events. Although they sought ordered patterns in historical processes, they could not ignore the bewildering and complex relationships between motives, conduct, and forces, intentioned and blind, that affect understanding and activity. Their response to the threat of uncertainty was to subsume troubling issues within a larger, more reassuring consensus. They did not realize that conventional wisdom and the search for understanding compete more than they coincide.

Reference Matter

Notes

Introduction

1. Noel Annan, "The Victorian Intelligentsia," in J. H. Plumb, ed., *Studies in Social History: A Tribute to G. M. Trevelyan* (London, 1955); John Roach, "The Victorian Universities and the National Intelligentsia," *Victorian Studies* 2, 2 (1959): 131–50.

2. Sheldon Rothblatt's work is indispensable for a subtle examination of universities. See *The Revolution of the Dons*, with its new preface (Cambridge, 1981), "The Student Sub-Culture and the Examination System in Early 19th Century Oxbridge," in Lawrence Stone, ed., *The University and Society*, vol. 1: *Oxford and Cambridge from the 14th to the Early 19th Century* (Princeton, N.J., 1974), *Tradition and Change in English Liberal Education: An Essay in History and Culture* (London, 1976), "Failure in Early Nineteenth-Century Oxford and Cambridge," *History of Education* 2, 1 (1982), "Historical and Comparative Remarks on the Federal Principle in Higher Education," *History of Education* 16, 3 (1987), and "The Idea of the Idea of a University and Its Antithesis" [published as pamphlet], Seminar on the Sociology of Culture, La Trobe University, Bundoora, Victoria, Australia, 1989.

3. For Cambridge, see C. N. L. Brooke, *A History of Gonville and Caius College* (Woodbridge, 1985), and *A History of the University of Cambridge*, vol. 4: *1870–1990* (Cambridge, 1993); Charles Crawley, *Trinity Hall: The History of a Cambridge College, 1350–1975* (Cambridge, 1976) and "Sir George Prothero and His Circle," Prothero Lecture, July 12, 1969, in *Transactions of the Royal Historical Society*, 5th ser., 20 (1970); T. E. B. Howarth, *Cambridge Between Two Wars* (London, 1978); Thomas Thorneley, *Cambridge Memories* (London, 1936); L. P. Wilkinson, *A Century of King's, 1873–1972* (Cambridge, 1980) and *Kingsmen of a Century, 1873–1972* (Cambridge, 1981); D. A. Winstanley's often idiosyncratic

Later Victorian Cambridge (Cambridge, 1947); and G. M. Trevelyan, *Trinity College: An Historical Sketch* (Cambridge, 1946). See also Ian Anstruther, *Oscar Browning: A Biography* (London, 1983). For Oxford, see E. G. W. Bill, *University Reform in Nineteenth-Century Oxford: A Study of Henry Halford Vaughan, 1811–1885* (Oxford, 1973); J. Buxton and P. Williams, *New College, Oxford, 1379–1979* (Oxford, 1979); John Jones, *Balliol College: A History, 1263–1939* (Oxford, 1988); John Prest, ed., *Balliol Studies* (London, 1982); and E. V. Quinn and John Prest, eds., *Dear Miss Nightingale: A Selection of Benjamin Jowett's Letters, 1860–1893* (Oxford, 1987).

4. These include Christopher Harvie, *The Lights of Liberalism: University Liberals and the Challenge of Democracy, 1860–1886* (London, 1976); C. Hollis, *The Oxford Union* (London, 1965); Alon Kadish, *Apostle Arnold: The Life and Death of Arnold Toynbee 1852–1883* (Durham, N.C., 1986); Standish Meacham, *Toynbee Hall and Social Reform, 1880–1914: The Search for Community* (New Haven, Conn., 1987); and Robert Skidelsky, *John Maynard Keynes*, vol. 1: *Hopes Betrayed, 1883–1920* (London, 1983).

5. Among the general studies of the university, see R. D. Anderson, *Education and Opportunity in Victorian Scotland* (Oxford, 1983); W. H. G. Armytage, *Civic Universities: Aspects of a British Tradition* (London, 1955); Ernest Barker, "Universities in Great Britain," in W. M. Kotsching and E. Prys, eds., *Universities in a Changing World* (Oxford, 1932); Thomas Bender, ed., *The University and the City* (Oxford, 1988). Arthur Engel's "Political Education in Oxford, 1823–1914," *History of Education Quarterly* 20 (Fall 1980) and *From Clergyman to Don: The Rise of the Academic Profession in Nineteenth-Century Oxford* (Oxford, 1983) are important discussions of the development of professional teaching in Oxford and can usefully be read together with K. H. Jarausch, ed., *The Transformation of Higher Learning, 1860–1930: Expansion, Diversification, Social Opening, and Professionalization in England, Germany, Russia, and the United States* (Chicago, 1983), especially the essays by Roy Lowe, "The Expansion of Higher Education in England," Sheldon Rothblatt, "The Diversification of Higher Education in England," Harold Perkin, "The Pattern of Social Transformation in England," and Arthur Engel, "The English Universities and Professional Education." Other comparative analyses occur in Charles F. McClelland, *The German Historians and England* (Cambridge, 1971); Fritz Ringer, *Education and Society in Modern Europe* (Bloomington, Ind., 1979); and D. K. Muller, Fritz Ringer, and Brian Simon, *The Rise of the Modern Educational System* (Cambridge, 1987). See, too, Martha Garland, *Cambridge Before Darwin: The Ideal of a Liberal Education, 1800–1860* (Cambridge, 1980); T. W. Heyck, *The Transformation of Intellectual Life in Victorian England* (New York, 1982) and "The Idea of a University, 1870–1970," *The History of European Ideas* 8, 2 (1987); Michael Sanderson, ed., *The Universities in the Nineteenth Century* (London, 1975). Some of the detailed studies are: John Dunbabin, "Oxford and Cambridge Finances, 1871–1913," *Economic History Review* 28 (1975); A. G. L. Haig, "The Church, the Universities and Learning in Later Victorian England," *The Historical Journal* 29, 1 (1986); Renata

Simpson, *How the Ph.D. Came to Britain: A Century of Struggle for Postgraduate Education* (Guildford, 1983); and volumes 6 and 7 of the *History of Oxford University* (Oxford, forthcoming).

6. See F. Madden, "The Commonwealth, Commonwealth History, and Oxford, 1905–1971," in F. Madden and D. K. Fieldhouse, eds., *Oxford and the Idea of Commonwealth: Essays Presented to Sir Edgar Williams* (London, 1982) and Richard Symond's perceptive *Oxford and the Empire* (London, 1986).

7. Norman Chester's *Economics, Politics, and Social Studies in Oxford, 1900–1985* (London, 1986) and Peter Slee's *Learning and a Liberal Education* (Manchester, 1987) are typical of the first category. In the second category, economic history has been discussed by T. C. Barker, "The Beginnings of the Economic History Society," *Economic History Review*, 2d ser., 30 (1977); D. C. Coleman, *History and the Economic Past: An Account of the Rise and Decline of Economic History in Britain* (London, 1987); Negley Harte, Introduction, "The Making of Economic History," in N. Harte, ed., *The Study of Economic History: Collected Inaugural Lectures, 1893–1970* (London, 1971); Alon Kadish, *The Oxford Economists of the Late Nineteenth Century* (Oxford, 1982) and *Historians, Economists, and Economic History* (London, 1989); G. M. Koot, "English Historical Economics and the Emergence of Economic History in England," *History of Political Economy* 12 (Summer 1980) and *English Historical Economics, 1870–1926: The Rise of Economic History and Neo-Mercantilism* (Cambridge, 1987). The law is the subject of Daniel Duman's *The Judicial Bench in England* (London, 1982), and M. Jeanne Peterson's *The Medical Profession in Mid-Victorian London* (Berkeley, Calif., 1978) is a model of the ways in which professions can be studied. Harold Perkin has treated both the organization of the university teachers' union in *Key Profession: The History of the Association of University Teachers* (New York, 1969) and the larger question of *The Rise of Professional Society: England Since 1880* (London, 1989). See, further, Reba N. Soffer, *Ethics and Society in England: The Revolution in the Social Sciences, 1870–1914* (Berkeley, Calif., 1978) and "Why Do Disciplines Fail? The Strange Case of British Sociology," *English Historical Review* (Oct. 1982).

8. The organization of history as a profession has been treated by Doris S. Goldstein, "The Organizational Development of the British Historical Profession, 1884–1921," *Bulletin of the Institute of Historical Research* 55, 132 (Nov. 1982), "The Professionalization of History in Britain in the Late Nineteenth and Early Twentieth Centuries," *Storia della Storiografia* 1 (1983), and "The Origins and Early Years of the *English Historical Review*," *English Historical Review* 101 (Jan. 1986); by Philippa Levine, *The Amateur and the Professional: Antiquarians, Historians, and Archaeologists in Victorian England, 1838–1886* (Cambridge, 1986); and by Slee, *Learning and a Liberal Education.* Slee uniquely denies that the teaching and writing of history carried any implicit message and argues instead that historians at Oxford, Cambridge, and Manchester were disinterested and objective. Although his book lacks critical analysis, it does provide a useful narrative of the adoption of degree courses in history. Various aspects of the intellectual

history of history are covered in P. B. M. Blaas's thoughtful *Continuity and Anachronism: Parliamentary and Constitutional Development in Whig Historiography and the Anti-Whig Reaction Between 1890 and 1930* (The Hague, 1978). J. W. Burrow is always provocative and interesting; see "The English Tradition of Liberal Education," *Historical Education Quarterly* 20 (1980), *A Liberal Descent: Victorian Historians and the English Past* (Cambridge, 1981), *Whigs and Liberals: Continuity and Change in English Political Thought*, The Carlyle Lectures 1985 (Oxford, 1988), "Victorian Historians and the Royal Historical Society," *Transactions of the Royal Historical Society*, 5th ser., 39 (London, 1989); and Burrow, Stefan Collini, and Donald Winch, *That Noble Science of Politics: A Study in Nineteenth-Century Intellectual History* (Cambridge, 1983). Christopher Parker's *The English Historical Tradition Since 1850* (Edinburgh, 1990) continues and expands Duncan Forbes's *The Liberal Anglican Idea of History* (Cambridge, 1952). See, too, Rosemary Jann, *The Art and Science of Victorian History* (Columbus, Ohio, 1986). And see Reba N. Soffer, *The Cloister and the Hearth: The Emergence of History as a University Profession in England*, Occasional Paper 31 (May 1982), Center for Studies in Higher Education, University of California, Berkeley, "Nation, Duty, Character, and Confidence: History at Oxford, 1850–1914," *Historical Journal* 30 (Mar. 1987), "The Modern University and National Values, 1850–1930," *Historical Research* 60, 142 (June 1987), "The Development of Disciplines in the Modern English University," *Historical Journal* 31, 4 (1988), "The Honours School of Modern History," in Michael Brock and Mark Curthoys, eds., *The History of Oxford University*, vol. 7 (Oxford, forthcoming), "History and Religion: J. R. Seeley and the Burden of the Past," in R. W. Davis and R. Helmstader, eds., *Religion and Irreligion in Victorian Society* (London, 1992), and "Authority in the University: Balliol, Newnham, and the New Mythology," in Roy Porter, ed., *Myths of the English* (Oxford, 1992). The secondary schools are interestingly considered in V. Chancellor, *History for their Masters: Opinion in the English History Textbook, 1800–1914* (New York, 1970), and the role of the classics in those schools is the subject of Gary McCulloch's *Philosophers and Kings: Education for Leadership in Modern England* (Cambridge, 1991). A more complete selection of recent writing for the areas covered in notes 4 through 8 may be found in the Sources, pp. 275–99.

9. See James A. Schmiechen, "The Victorians, the Historians, and the Idea of Modernism," *American Historical Review* 93, 2 (1988), esp. 307, for an interesting discussion of the ways in which Victorian designers used history.

10. As Sheldon Rothblatt concludes in *Tradition and Change*, "what survives from a tradition is most often phrase and form" (206).

Chapter 1

1. See Ray Jones, *The Nineteenth-Century Foreign Office: An Administrative History* (London, 1971), Appendix C, 165–88.

2. On the Colonial Office see Stephen Constantine, *The Making of British Co-*

lonial Development Policy, 1914–1940 (London, 1984), 21, who argues that "few recruits to the Colonial Office [before 1914] had much of the appropriate economic or scientific knowledge." The method of promotion was through office hierarchy and the result was considerable continuity of service in a single department. Most senior posts went normally to men who had made service in the Colonial Office a lifelong career: In 1929, among the nine department heads (called assistant secretaries since 1920), eight had served no less than 18 years and some had served 34 (280–83). Even after 1914, when the war made it clear that experts were needed for policy decisions, there were few professional advisers. It was not until 1930 that the patronage system gave way to a Colonial Service Appointments Board, associated with the Civil Service Commission, and only in 1948 did the Colonial Office begin to recruit experts to handle some tasks. See D. J. Morgan, *The Official History of Colonial Development*, vol. 1: *The Origins of British Aid Policy, 1924–1945* (Atlantic Highland, N.J., 1980), xxiv, xx; and Gerald L. M. Clauson, "Some Uses of Statistics in Colonial Administration," *Transactions of the Manchester Statistical Society* (Jan. 15, 1937).

3. See R. D. Anderson, *Education and Opportunity in Victorian Scotland* (Oxford, 1983).

4. John L. Herkless, "Economic Change and the Idealist Revival in Historiography at the Turn of the Century," *History and Theory* 26, 2 (1987): 178–79.

5. Goronwy Rees, a student at Oxford in the late 1920s, argued half a century later that "it was not . . . a good thing that young men designed and destined to form the executive and governing class of a great country should have received their higher education at institutions which were a combination of a monastery and a nursery." *A Chapter of Accidents* (London, 1972), 96. An outsider, by virtue of his lower-class Welsh family and his state secondary school, Rees was embittered by his university experience, but he was an astute observer.

6. See Reba N. Soffer, "Authority in the University: Balliol, Newnham, and the New Mythology," in Roy Porter, ed., *Myths of the English* (Oxford, 1992).

7. Roy Porter, review of the 5th volume of the *History of the University of Oxford*, *English Historical Review* 102, 404 (July 1987): 680–81.

8. Henry Latham, *On the Action of Examinations Considered as a Means of Selection* (Cambridge, 1877), 6, 458.

9. Stefan Collini, "The Idea of 'Character' in Victorian Political Thought," *Transactions of the Royal Historical Society*, 5th ser., 35 (1985): 48 and *Public Moralists: Political Thought and Intellectual Life in Britain, 1850–1930* (Oxford, 1991).

10. J. A. R. Marriott, *Oxford and its Place in National Life* (Oxford, 1907), 32.

11. Letter to J. P. Forbes, Feb. 20, 1850, in Isaac Todhunter, *William Whewell, D.D., Master of Trinity College, Cambridge: An Account of his Writings* (London, 1876), vol. 2, 355.

12. The Report was signed by Sir Stafford H. Northcote and C. E. Trevelyan, Nov. 23, 1855. Printed in Appendix 2, K. M. Reader, *The Civil Service Commission, 1855–1975* (London, 1981), 85, 90–91, 84.

13. K. M. Reader, *The Civil Service Commission*, 42. See Harold Perkin, *Key*

Profession: The History of the Association of University Teachers (New York, 1969), 49, 170–91; and "The Historical Perspective," in Burton Clark, ed., *Perspectives on Higher Education* (Berkeley, Calif., 1984), 43.

14. F. M. Cornford, *Microcosmographia Academica: Being a guide for the young academic politician* (London, 1908), 4–5, 14.

15. See especially *Oxford University Archives*, Bodleian Library, NEP/subtus, Register of Convocation, 1846–52, Minutes, Dec. 7, 1849; E. G. W. Bill, *University Reform in Nineteenth-Century Oxford: A Study of Henry Halford Vaughan, 1811–1885* (Oxford, 1973), 84; and *Report of Her Majesty's Commissioners to Investigate Cambridge* (1852), 164, 197.

16. Quoted in F. C. Montague, *Arnold Toynbee* (Baltimore, 1889), 14.

17. J. H. Newman, "Knowledge Viewed in Relation to Professional Skill" and "Knowledge Its Own End," in his *The Idea of a University* (New York, 1959), 192, 144–45.

18. During the nine years before World War I, the Cambridge Appointments Association, founded with business backing in 1899, was placing between 8 and 14 percent of its clients in business and industry. The Oxford Appointments Board was begun in 1892, mostly to find jobs for schoolteachers, but by the first decade of the century it had expanded its activities to a wide variety of other fields in which graduates were being placed. See *Annual Reports of Oxford Appointments Committee, 1906–1914*; and F. B. Hunt and C. E. Escritt, *Historical Notes on the Oxford University Appointments Committee (1892–1950)* [Reproduced from typewriting] (Oxford, 1950).

19. Alon Kadish, *Apostle Arnold: The Life and Death of Arnold Toynbee, 1852–1883* (Durham, N.C., 1986), esp. 177, 231–32.

20. Cornford, *Microcosmographia Academica*, 16, 14.

21. See Soffer, "Why Do Disciplines Fail? The Strange Case of British Sociology," *English Historical Review* (Oct. 1982). Sociology was not accepted at either Oxford or Cambridge until after World War II.

22. See G. Kitson Clark, *The Making of Victorian England* (London, 1962), 255–60, for a discussion of the role of education and the professions in the making of gentlemen.

23. *Royal Commission on Oxford and Cambridge Universities: Appendices* (London, 1922), 170.

24. J. R. Green, "Oxford as It Is" (1870), in J. R. Green and K. Norgate, eds., *Oxford Studies* (London, 1901), 260–63. Quotes in preceding paragraph on the "modern reforms" are also from this source.

25. W. H. G. Armytage, *Civic Universities: Aspects of a British Tradition* (London, 1955), 267; and Ernest Barker, "Universities in Great Britain," in W. M. Kotsching and E. Prys, eds., *Universities in a Changing World* (Oxford, 1932), 119.

26. Roy Porter, *Gibbon: Making History* (New York, 1988), 38.

27. See M. Jeanne Peterson's perceptive study, *The Medical Profession in Mid-*

Victorian London (Berkeley, Calif., 1978); Jose and Noel Parry, *The Rise of the Medical Profession: A Study of Collective Social Mobility* (London, 1976); Eliot Friedson, *The Profession of Medicine: A Study of the Sociology of Applied Knowledge* (New York, 1970); and Jeffrey C. Berlant, *Profession and Monopoly: A Study of Medicine in the United States and Great Britain* (Berkeley, Calif., 1975).

28. There were more exceptions in Cambridge than in Oxford. When Charles Oman became an Oxford teacher in Greats and in Modern History in 1883, he had 41 students and gave each a full hour of tuition, which meant seven hours of "criticism and catechizing" six days a week, besides incidental examining and lectures. In 1885 Oman went to New College as full-time lecturer for 25 men, half in Greats and half in Modern History. See his *Memories of Victorian Oxford and of Some Early Years* (London, 1941), 136. Oman's many books were based on secondary sources and he did not publish the first, *Warwick the Kingmaker*, until 1891. In Cambridge, George Prothero, who taught a similarly large number of students, established a reputation as a scholar with a *Life of Simon de Montfort* (1877), an edition of Voltaire's *Siecle de Louis XIV* (1879–1882), a translation of the first volume of Ranke's *Universal History* (1884), the *Life of Henry Bradshaw, University Librarian* (1899), and the *Select Statutes and Other Documents Illustrative of the Reigns of Elizabeth and James I* (1894), beside more than 20 articles for the *Encyclopedia Britannica* and essays for the *English Historical Review* and the *Athenaeum*, all written before 1894 when he left Cambridge for a chair in Edinburgh.

29. See Chapter 8 for a discussion of the subsequent careers of history graduates from Balliol and from King's College, Cambridge.

30. See Soffer, "Authority in the University: Balliol, Newnham, and the New Mythology," for a discussion of Jowett's effect upon Balliol students and their places in the world.

31. David Davies, for Lloyd George, to H. A. L. Fisher, 2/9/16, in H. A. L. Fisher Papers, box 6, 178–81, the New Bodleian Library. There is no list of this kind in the Fisher Papers, but it may have been compiled, sent, and acted upon. "A. S. C." stands for Army Service Corps.

32. G. G. Coulton, *Fourscore Years* (Cambridge, 1943), 101; T. R. Glover, *Cambridge Retrospect* (Cambridge, 1943), 110–11.

33. See Sheldon Rothblatt, "Historical and Comparative Remarks on the Federal Principle in Higher Education," *History of Education* 16, 3 (1987): 169–70 for a persuasive development of this argument.

34. T. F. Tout, "The Future of Victoria University" (1902), reprinted in *The Collected Papers of Thomas Frederick Tout, with a Memoir and Bibliography* (Manchester, 1932), vol. 1, 48–49. Beyond founding the flourishing Manchester School, with its emphasis on administrative history, Tout became one of the leading statesmen among historians with a well-placed hand in appointments to nearly every British university position in history during the first two decades of the twentieth century.

35. Hastings Rashdall, *The Universities of Europe in the Middle Ages*, 3 vols. (Oxford, 1895).

36. Hastings Rashdall, "The Functions of a University in a Commercial Centre," *Economic Review* 12 (Jan. 1902): 76–77.

37. David R. Jones, *The Origins of Civic Universities: Manchester, Leeds and Liverpool* (London, 1988), 66. Jones demonstrates that the new civic universities were not founded primarily to teach science and technology and that "the least community support was given to those institutions with the heaviest technological bias, like Leeds" (18).

38. See Michael Sanderson, ed., *The Universities in the Nineteenth Century* (London, 1975), 4–5.

39. For a subtle discussion of the various elements identified with the ideal of a "liberal education" from the eighteenth through the nineteenth centuries, see Sheldon Rothblatt, *Tradition and Change in English Liberal Education: An Essay in History and Culture* (London, 1976).

Chapter 2

1. Owen Chadwick, *Westcott and the University*, Bishop Westcott Memorial Lecture, 1962 (Cambridge, 1962), 7.

2. William Stubbs, "On the Purposes and Methods of Historical Study" (May 17, 1876) and "Address on the Opening of a Course of Lectures on England under the Stewarts" (1889), in *Seventeen Lectures on the Study of Medieval and Modern History and Kindred Subjects* (Oxford, 1900), 103, 465–68.

3. C. Firth, *A Plea for the Historical Teaching of History* (Oxford, 1904), 8, 11.

4. James Bryce, "John Richard Green" (1903) in his *Studies in Contemporary Biography* (London, 1923), 149, 146, and "On the Writing and Teaching of History," Commencement Address as Chancellor of Union College, Schenectady (1911), in his *University and Historical Addresses* (New York, 1913).

5. See J. B. Bury, "The Science of History," in his *Selected Essays*, ed. by Harold Temperley (Cambridge, 1930); G. M. Trevelyan, "The Latest View of History," *Independent Review* 1 (1903): 395–414; Rosemary Jann, "From Amateur to Professional: The Case of the Oxbridge Historians," *Journal of British Studies* 22, 2 (1983): 122 and *The Art and Science of Victorian History* (Columbus, Ohio, 1986).

6. R. B. Haldane, "The Meaning of Truth in History," Creighton Lecture delivered to the University of London (1914), in his *The Conduct of Life and Other Addresses* (New York, 1915), 60.

7. G. M. Trevelyan, "Autobiography of an Historian," in *An Autobiography and Other Essays* (London, 1949), 11–12; C. H. K. Marten, a graduate of Balliol and eventually Provost of Eton, "The Teaching of History in the Public Schools," in W. A. J. Archbold, ed., *Essays on the Teaching of History* (Cambridge, 1901), 62; and Ian Anstruther, *Oscar Browning: A Biography* (London, 1983), 52.

8. Only J. B. Bury, a man of exceptionally minimal influence in the university,

repudiated both Seeley's attempt to find a utilitarian national purpose and Acton's synthetic unity. See Chapter 4 of this book.

9. V. H. Galbraith, quoted in H. Hartley, "Successors to Jowett," supplement to H. W. C. Davis, *A History of Balliol College* (Oxford, 1963), 242.

10. A. L. Smith, "The Teaching of Modern History," in Christopher Cookson, ed., *Essays on Higher Education* (Oxford, 1898), 180.

11. J. H. Clapham, *An Economic History of Modern Britain: The Early Railway Age, 1820–1850* (Cambridge, 1959), 114, ix.

12. The universities controlled the teaching of history in the schools by controlling school examinations. In 1857 Oxford established a Delegacy to administer uniform secondary school examinations, on a voluntary basis for "middle-class" secondary schools. One year later, a Cambridge Syndicate initiated a similar scheme. In the first examination given by the Oxford Delegacy in 1858, held at eleven separate centers, history was the most popular subject, attracting 357 of the 401 candidates who entered. See John Roach, *Public Examinations in England, 1850–1900* (Cambridge, 1971), 94. Until at least 1914, Valerie Chancellor argues, school children read textbooks in history "designed to educate the rising generations to uphold the tradition of society rather than to reform it. . . . There was a complacency of tone about the condition of society and of the constitution which militated against the pupil being encouraged to consider change in the future." See her *History for Their Masters: Opinion in the English History Textbook, 1800–1914* (New York, 1970), 139–42. Textbooks for schools have always taught what are perceived to be a society's most valued traditions, and probably always will. The lessons presented dogmatically and without dissent in the textbooks were, however, repeated and strengthened in the universities and in almost every other agency of adult educational influence. See John M. MacKenzie, *Propaganda and Empire: The Manipulation of British Public Opinion, 1880–1960* (Manchester, 1984), chap. 7.

13. J. H. Round, one of Stubbs's Balliol students in the mid 1870s, passionately condemned historians who attempted to arrive at synthetic conclusions; Round to T. F. Tout, Jan. 27, 1910, *Tout Papers*, John Rylands Library, Manchester. Round was expressing a general consensus, especially characteristic of Oxford, when he wrote that the function of the historian was the "'minute sifting' of facts and figures," the "only sure method by which we can extend knowledge." *Feudal England* (London, 1895), x.

14. William Whewell, *On the Principles of English University Education* (London and Cambridge, 1837), 50–51, 25–26; Barry Smith, "Stalwarts of the Garrison: Some Irish Academics in Australia" (1988), 5. I am grateful to the author for making this unpublished MS available to me. See also William Stubbs, "On the Present State and Prospects of Historical Study," *Seventeen Lectures*, 34.

15. J. A. R. Marriott, *Memories of Four Score Years* (London, 1946), 116. For a discussion of A. L. Smith's political views, see Chapter 6.

16. For a fuller discussion of the tutors at both universities, see Chapter 6.

222   *Notes to Pages 38–40*

17. Peter Novick, *That Noble Dream: The "Objectivity Question" and the American Historical Profession* (Cambridge, 1988), 85.

18. W. E. Gladstone, "On the Place of Homer in Classical Education and in Historical Inquiry," *Oxford Essays* (London, 1857), 19–45, 23.

19. J. A. Froude, "Suggestions on the Best Means of Teaching English History," *Oxford Essays* (London, 1855), 62, 66.

20. Roy Porter, *Gibbon: Making History* (New York, 1988), 162.

21. G. M. Trevelyan was an exception. See Chapter 5.

22. It is interesting that three of the best and most successful biographers, John Morley in the nineteenth century and Roy Jenkins and John Grigg in the twentieth, were all eminent political figures. Morley's books on Edmund Burke, Diderot, Machiavelli, Richard Cobden, W. E. Gladstone, Oliver Cromwell, Rousseau, Voltaire, and Walpole went through many editions for more than a generation. Roy Jenkins has produced studies of Attlee, Asquith, Baldwin, Charles Dilke, and most recently, Truman, in addition to other political literature. Although John Grigg has written about Nancy Astor, religion, and political affairs, he is admired most for his magisterial three-volume study of Lloyd George: *The Young Lloyd George* (London, 1973), *Lloyd George: The People's Champion, 1902–1911* (London, 1978), and *Lloyd George: From Peace to War, 1912–1916* (London, 1985).

23. See the correspondence from A. Howard Clark, Assistant Secretary to the American Historical Association, to Herbert B. Adams, May 22, 1900, which argued that the Association did not need more members "unless it be historians or those positively interested in it, and who will consider membership an honor and be an honor to the Association." *Historical Scholarship in the United States, 1876–1901: As Revealed in the Correspondence of Herbert B. Adams.* Ed. W. Stull Holt (Baltimore, 1938), 279.

24. When an American Historical Association committee of seven major figures in the profession, all at universities, was set up in the fall of 1900 to consider a cooperative "History of the United States," they identified themselves by their cities. It is not clear if this was because they and their associations with particular universities were widely known, or because affiliation with a university was not yet of defining importance for historians. They were C. F. Adams, Herbert B. Adams, W. A. Dunning, A. B. Hart, J. B. McMaster, Frederick J. Turner, and M. C. Tyler. "Queries as to a Cooperative History of the United States under the Auspices of the American Historical Association," in *Historical Scholarship in the United States, 1876–1901,* 283–86.

25. Fritz Ringer argues that the "common element in all mandarin political theorizing" (and historians were leaders within this movement) was "a characteristically 'idealistic' and 'apolitical' approach." *The Decline of the German Mandarins: The German Academic Community, 1890–1933* (Cambridge, Mass., 1969), 120. See too Charles E. McClelland, *State, Society, and University in Germany, 1700–1914* (Cambridge, 1980), esp. 316–17; 325–26.

26. Martin Doerne, "Problems of the German University," in W. M. Kotsching and Elined Prys, eds., *The University in a Changing World: A Symposium* (1932) (New York, 1969), 64–65.

27. Herbert B. Adams, *Methods of Historical Study* (Baltimore, 1884), esp. 5–23; Thomas L. Haskell, *The Emergence of Professional Social Science: The American Social Science Association and the Nineteenth-Century Crisis of Authority* (Urbana, Ill., 1977); Terry N. Clark, *Prophets and Patrons: The French University and the Emergence of the Social Sciences* (Cambridge, Mass., 1973); William R. Keylor, *Academy and Community: The Foundation of the French Historical Profession* (Cambridge, Mass., 1975); Fritz Ringer, *The Decline of the German Mandarins*; and K. H. Jarausch, *Students, Society, and Politics in Imperial Germany: The Rise of Academic Illiberalism* (Princeton, 1982).

28. Herbert B. Adams, "Special Methods of Historical Study," in G. Stanley Hall, ed., *Methods of Teaching History*, vol. 1, 2nd. ed. (Boston, 1885), 113, 127, 132, 138.

29. David O. Levine, *The American College and the Culture of Aspiration, 1915–1940* (Ithaca, N.Y., 1986), 19. Peter Novick argues that in Germany young American historians of the 1880s found the models that inspired a revolution in higher education in America. There they learned that "a 'proper' university was a community of investigators, concerned with pursuing their researches while training the next generation of *Gelehrten*; rigorous scholarship, rather than religious or philosophical orthodoxy, was the criterion of academic excellence." *That Noble Dream*, 22.

30. Arthur S. Link, "The American Historical Association, 1884–1984: Retrospect and Prospect," Presidential Address to the American Historical Association, *American Historical Review* (1985): 8.

31. See John Higham, in John Higham, Leonard Krieger and Felix Gilbert, *History: The Development of Historical Studies in the United States* (Englewood Cliffs, N.J., 1965), 111.

32. Peter Novick, *That Noble Dream*, 100–106, 107.

33. James Truslow Adams, *The Epic of America* (Garden City, N.Y., 1947), 374–75, 380, 384. Adams, no relation to the famous family to which Herbert B. Adams belonged, won the Pulitzer prize in 1922 for his *The Founding of New England* (Boston, 1921). It is interesting that he spent many years in London as a representative for his publisher, Scribners.

34. Committee on Political Science, Modern History Reports, vol. 2 (Nov. 18, 1914). In Cambridge, during the war years papers in the Historical Tripos, set in general European history, political science, international law, political economy, and the subject for an essay, addressed themselves directly to the origins, morality, and consequences of the war. Similar examinations at the University of Manchester had no question directly bearing on the war, although some of the general essay questions could have been answered in terms of contemporary events.

35. Ernest Barker, H. W. C. Davis, C. R. L. Fletcher, Arthur Hassall, L. G. Wickham Legg, and Frank Morgan, *Why We Are at War* (Oxford, 1914), 121.

36. J. Holland Rose, letter to *The Times* (Sept. 3, 1914).

37. A. F. Pollard to his father (Jan. 17 and Oct. 1, 1916), Pollard Papers, Letters (1915–1919), Paleography Room, Senate House Library, University of London.

38. See the Prothero Papers, The Royal Historical Society, University College, London.

39. Robertson won the Stanhope Prize in 1891 and took first-class honours in Litterae Humaniores in 1892 and in Modern History in 1893. That year he became a fellow at All Souls College and was also a history tutor at Exeter College from 1895 to 1899 and at Magdalen College from 1905 to 1920, when he became principal of Birmingham University and subsequently vice-chancellor from 1927. Before 1914, he had published a textbook, *England under the Hanoverians* (London, 1911) and a collection of *Select Cases, Statutes, and Documents to Illustrate English Constitutional History, 1660–1832* (London, 1904). In 1918, he produced *Bismarck* (London, 1918) and just before World War II wrote *Religion and the Totalitarian State* (London, 1937) and *The Edict of Nantes and Freedom in the World Today* (London, 1939). His postwar historical interests returned to English constitutional studies with *Chatham and the British Empire* (London, 1946) and *Bolingbroke* (London, 1947).

40. *The Times,* Aug. 31 and 26, 1914.

41. See Catherine Ann Cline, "British Historians and the Treaty of Versailles," *Albion* 20, 1 (1988): 57. See, too, J. M. Winter's "Oxford and the First World War" in Brian Harrison, ed., *The History of Oxford University,* vol. 8 (Oxford, forthcoming), and *The Great War and the British People* (London, 1986).

42. Ludwig Bernhard was a theoretician and exponent of German might.

43. James Bryce, *Essays and Addresses in War Time* (New York, 1918) and *Appendix to the Report of the Committee on Alleged German Outrages* (London, 1915); Bryce to Prothero (Oct. 9, 1914), in Prothero Papers.

44. H. H. Henson, *Retrospect of an Unimportant Life,* 5 vols. (Oxford, 1942–50), vol. 1, 187. An Oxford-trained historian, Henson moved by 1900 from Anglo-Catholicism to theological liberalism. Owen Chadwick, *Hensley Henson: A Study in the Friction Between Church and State* (Oxford, 1983).

45. H. A. L. Fisher, *An Unfinished Autobiography* (Oxford, 1941), 91, 97, 119; and Hugh and Christopher Seton-Watson, *The Making of a New Europe: R. W. Seton-Watson and the Last Years of Austria-Hungary* (Washington, 1981), 105–18. In 1916 Seton-Watson pursued his "New Europe" ideal by organizing a group to "provide intelligent and consecutive criticism of foreign policy" in a weekly publication which would be a "focussing centre for all serious writers here and in allied countries, who really want a 'victoire intégrale.'" Letter from Seton-Watson to G. W. Prothero, Oct. 23, 1916, Prothero Papers.

46. Lord Hardinge of Penshurst to Prothero (Nov. 8, 1918; Mar. 14 and Mar. 17,

1919), Prothero to Penshurst (Mar. 16, 1917), Prothero Papers. J. H. Clapham, the economic historian from Cambridge, served at the Board of Trade during the war, but the extent of his influence there is not known.

47. William H. McNeill, *Arnold J. Toynbee: A Life* (Oxford, 1989), 75–80.

48. *Oxford University Gazette* 42, 1370 (June 19, 1912): 958; Board of Modern History, *Minutes* 3 (Nov. 17, 1922): 232. This was Firth's second motion of the day. The first, that in the later paper on English politics, "more attention should be devoted to the History of English Colonies and Dependencies" was defeated by eight votes to five (231).

49. A. J. P. Taylor, *A Personal History* (London, 1983), 83.

50. Board of Modern History, *Minutes*, 4, Oct. 28, 1926, 99.

51. *Royal Commission on Oxford and Cambridge Universities: Appendices* (1922), 35.

52. See the History Board, Minutes, 1918–28: May 20 and Nov. 23, 1919; Mar. 7, 1922.

53. H. M. V. Temperley, *Research and Modern History*, An Inaugural Lecture delivered at Cambridge, Nov. 19, 1930 (London, 1930), 20.

54. Political Science B deleted Bosanquet's *Philosophical Theory of the State* and added, "for reference" rather than "for study," recent works, including Graham Wallas's *The Great Society*, which was not yet published when the prescribed list was released. In Political Economy, the whole list for study, with the exception of the Webbs's *Industrial Democracy* was deleted and W. H. Beveridge's *Unemployment* was added together with Edwin Cannan's *Wealth* and F. W. Taussig's *Principles of Economics*, vols. 1 and 2. Historical Tripos, Part II, 1917, in papers of the History Board.

55. Goronwy Rees, *A Chapter of Accidents* (London, 1972), 95. See Jonathan Rose, *The Edwardian Temperament* (Athens, Ohio, 1986) for a very persuasive discussion of "connection."

Chapter 3

1. H. H. Henson, *Retrospect of an Unimportant Life* (Oxford, 1942), vol. 1, 69.

2. In the Syndicate's amended Report, Mar. 2, 1873, which the Senate confirmed, the definition of the subject and its method of teaching were produced by W. H. Thompson, J. T. Abdy, H. Latham, F. J. A. Hort, E. C. Clarke, H. Sidgwick, A. Marshall, B. F. Hammond, and J. R. Seeley. Eight papers were stipulated for examination: one on English History, three on special subjects in Ancient, Medieval, and Modern History, one on Principles of Political Philosophy and of General Jurisprudence, one on Constitutional Law and Constitutional History, one on Public International Law in connection with selected Treaties, and a final paper called Subjects for Essays. Each year there was a variety of special subjects such as the History of England, 1042–66 or the Foreign Politics

of France, 1789–1815, which required a knowledge of the "chief original sources."

3. Quoted from the evidence of Montagu Burrows and F. Y. Powell to the *Select Committee on Higher Education*, 1867, 13 (July 23, 1867), 410, 414.

4. Between 1870 and 1895, 232 first class clerkships, about ten a year, were filled by competitive examination in the civil service. More opportunities existed in the Indian Civil Service where, to look at random years, there were 38 appointments in 1874, 40 in 1883, and 38 in 1891. John Roach, *Public Examinations in England, 1850–1914* (Cambridge, 1971), 213. But careers newly available in county councils and expanding secondary schools and universities at home and abroad drew larger numbers of graduates.

5. F. M. Powicke, "Historical Study in Oxford" [an inaugural lecture] (1929), in *Modern Historians and the Study of History* (London, 1955), 172.

6. That observation is attributed to the Classical Fellow and Apostle at King's, F. L. Lucas. T. E. B. Howarth, *Cambridge Between Two Wars* (London, 1978), 15. Howarth was High Master of St. Paul's School, and then Senior Tutor of Magdalene College.

7. H. R. Luard, *Suggestions on 1. The Election of the Council 2. The Duties of the Vice-Chancellor 3. The Establishment of a Historical Tripos* (Cambridge, 1866), 14.

8. Ibid., 15.

9. Sidgwick to Bryce, Dec. 28, 1867, Bryce MS, 15: 2–3.

10. From Bury St. Edmund's Grammar School, Ward went as pensioner to Peterhouse College in 1855, where he received a first class honours in the Classical Tripos in 1859. From 1866, he was Professor of History and of English Language and Literature at Owens College where he created the degree courses in the new Victoria University, including the Honours School of History. Although Ward gave up the English Language part of his charge in 1880, he remained responsible for both English Literature and the whole of history until, in 1889, he was appointed Principal of Owens College (which was to become the University of Manchester). Until 1897, when he moved to Kensington, he remained an active Professor of History who gave a course on Roman History each year. And, to absorb his energies fully, he served as Vice-Chancellor of the Victoria University from 1886 to 1890 and again from 1894 to 1896. Ward lived in London from 1897 to 1900, where he was a governor of Royal Holloway College and president of the Royal Historical Society from 1899 to 1901. He used his presidential address to plead for a school of advanced historical training in London. During his London years, he also held the Ford Lectureship in English History at Oxford. He returned to Cambridge in 1900, aged 63, as an active Master of Peterhouse and the following year he became Vice-Chancellor of the University. He energetically guided research students, served vigorously on the Library and Press Syndicates, worked successfully for the separation of economics from the Historical Tripos into its own independent degree course, but failed to persuade the history faculty to adopt the compulsory study of universal history. He even found time to be

Vice-President of the Historical Association, beginning in 1906, and President of the British Academy from 1911 to 1913. When Acton died in 1902, Ward succeeded him as editor-in-chief of the *Cambridge Modern History* and from 1907 to 1916 he was coeditor with Alfred Rayney Waller of the *Cambridge History of English Literature* and from 1922 to 1923, coeditor with G. P. Gooch of the *Cambridge History of British Foreign Policy, 1783–1919*. His best-known historical work was his three-volume political history, *Germany, 1815–90* (Cambridge, 1916–18). The third volume had an epilogue which concluded in 1907.

11. Ward, *Suggestions*, 13–15.

12. Ibid., 9–10.

13. *Notes on the Development of the Historical Tripos 1875–1932*, unsigned and undated typescript, Seeley Library, 4, 5, 2. The *Notes* were all published in the *Cambridge University Reporter*. "Statements of Principles from Reports and Supplementary Regulations" were quoted verbatim in the *Notes*, together with those parts of the "ensuing discussion that seem to throw light upon the feeling of the time." The Syndicate included not only J. R. Seeley, Regius Professor of Modern History from 1868 to 1895, but his close supporters, Alfred Marshall, Professor of Political Economy from 1885, and Henry Sidgwick, Knightbridge Professor of Moral Philosophy from 1883 to his death in 1900.

14. J. P. Whitney, *Prothero*, MS in King's College Library, Cambridge, 12.

15. *Cambridge University Reporter*, Dec. 1872; Feb. 1873.

16. Michael Sanderson, ed., *Universities in the Nineteenth Century* (London, 1975), 7–8.

17. See Gary McCulloch, *Philosophers and Kings: Education for Leadership in Modern England* (Cambridge, 1991).

18. G. W. Prothero, "The Historical Tripos," *Student's Guide* (Cambridge, 1893), 3–6.

19. In the curriculum as a whole the recently modern benefited at the expense of the ancient world. Part I of the Tripos exam wound up with seven papers in which students could choose to study the history of Europe, beginning with the Ancient period, in the same chronological order which prevailed before 1909. Part II, to be taken usually a year later than Part I by more specialized and advanced students, recognized the autonomy of history as a discipline and accepted the recent past as a legitimate area for study and understanding. The seven papers for Part I were: Subjects for an Essay, General European History (Medieval), Select Periods of English History, English Constitutional History to 1485 and from 1485, English Economic History, including some knowledge of elementary economic theory in relation to history, and Political Science A, to include a comparative survey of political institutions and their development, some political theory, and the definition of political terms mainly in relation to the ancient city state and the modern nation state, or General European History (Ancient). Part II examined: Subjects for an Essay, General European History (Modern), and Special Historical Subjects together with one or two of either Political Science B

(the nature and end of the state, the grounds for political obligation, and the structure and functions of government, especially in the modern state), Political Economy, or International Law. *Report to the Board of History and Archaeology* (1909) Papers, 48, Seeley Library, Cambridge. Subjects for Essays covered first cultural, scientific, intellectual, and literary general history, and second, English history, excluding constitutional and economic issues.

20. William Stubbs, "On the Purposes and Methods of Historical Study," (May 17, 1876), in *Seventeen Lectures on the Study of Medieval and Modern History and Kindred Subjects* (Oxford, 1900), 86.

21. T. W. Hutchison, *On Revolutions and Progress in Economic Knowledge* (Cambridge, 1978), 54–55; D. C. Coleman, "Rebels, Outsiders, and Economic Historians," in *History and the Economic Past: An Account of the Rise and Decline of Economic History in Britain* (Oxford, 1987), 37.

22. Alon Kadish, *Historians, Economics, and Economic History* (London, 1989), 34, 61. This book is the most comprehensive study of institutions, individuals, and the nature of thought and practice in the relationship between economics and economic history. The development of economic history has been treated extensively by the books already cited and by Alon Kadish, *The Oxford Economists of the Late Nineteenth Century* (Oxford, 1982); Negley Harte's Introduction, "The Making of Economic History," in *The Study of Economic History: Collected Inaugural Lectures, 1893–1970* (London, 1971); T. C. Barker, "The Beginnings of the Economic History Society," *Economic History Review*, 2nd ser., 30 (1977), and G. M. Koot, "English Historical Economics and the Emergence of Economic History in England," *History of Political Economy* 12 (Summer 1980).

23. W. J. Ashley, *The Faculty of Commerce in the University of Birmingham: Its Purposes and Programme* (Birmingham, n.d. [1906]), 1,2,9; *The Calendar of the University of Birmingham* 1902–3, 285.

24. W. J. Ashley, *Surveys, Historic, and Economic* (New York, 1966), 429–30.

25. Stubbs, "On the Purposes and Methods of Historical Study," 111.

26. H. O. Wakeman and A. Hassall, eds., Preface, *Essays Introductory to the Study of Constitutional History* by Resident Members of the University (Oxford) (London, 1901). The three volumes of Stubbs's *Constitutional History* were: *From the Roman Era to the Death of Richard II, From the Accession of the House of Lancaster to Charles I,* and, *From the Commonwealth to the Death of Queen Anne.*

27. W. J. Ashley, "The Study of History at Oxford," *The Nation* 60, 1554 (1895): 275. When H. O. Wakeman suggested to the Modern History Board that a book of documents on all English constitutional history be substituted for the *Select Charters,* he was defeated by six votes to five. May 2, 1898, Board of the Faculty of Arts (Modern History) Minute Books, vol. 2, 67, Bodleian Library. The suggestion was never introduced again in the prewar years.

28. Charles Oman, *Memories of Victorian Oxford and of Some Early Years* (London, 1941), 105.

29. Ashley, "The Study of History at Oxford," 275. Medley, also a Modern

History graduate, went from Oxford, where he was a tutor at Keble College, to the University of Glasgow where he transformed the Scottish teaching of history into conformity with the Oxford model. See Michael Sanderson, *Universities in the Nineteenth Century*. Medley's *Manual* was reprinted in six editions until 1925.

30. D. J. Medley worried that in bringing "together new work," his attempt might be "premature" and he made no attempt "except very indirectly, to decide upon" the "respective merits" of such contemporary historians as Maitland, Dicey, and Sir W. Anson. *A Student's Manual of Constitutional History* (Oxford, 1894), vii, viii.

31. L. L. Price became a fellow of Oriel College in 1888. As a result of his persistence, Oxford created a Diploma in Economics in 1903. Although not the Honours School that Price really wanted, it did increase the demand for economics teaching, and it emphasized practical, inductive, and historical work. An Honours School in Philosophy, Politics, and Economics was not created until the 1920s. Price thought of himself more as an "economist devoted to economic history" than as an economic historian. Ashley died in 1927 after serving for a year as the first President of the Economic History Society. During the 1890s he tried to foster economic history as a separate discipline. From his various posts, he did more than anyone else to keep English readers aware of German historical economic scholarship. When he returned to England he became increasingly skeptical of the social utility of economic history, but he still believed that it was essential for understanding the direction of social evolution and to reveal the relativistic and hypothetical character of economic theory. G. M. Koot, *English Historical Economics, 1870–1926: The Rise of Economic History and Neo-Mercantilism* (Cambridge, 1987), 101 and chap. 5. See too Alon Kadish, *The Oxford Economists in the Late Nineteenth Century* and *Historians, Economists, and Economic History*, esp. 89–95 and 229–33. The first Lectureship in Economic History went to Lillian Tomm (later Knowles) at the London School of Economics (LSE) in 1904, followed in Manchester by H. O. Meredith in 1905, Price in 1907, George Unwin at Edinburgh in 1908, and R. L. Jones at Belfast in 1910. Unwin received the first chair in economic history at Manchester in 1910 and Lillian Knowles the second, at LSE in 1921.

32. Kadish, *Historians, Economics, and Economic History*, 142. Cunningham, who was chaplain at Trinity College, became a lecturer there in 1888 and a fellow in 1891, when he left his university lectureship.

33. See J. H. Clapham, "Of Empty Economic Boxes," *Economic Journal* 17 (Sept. 1907).

34. Economic history did not become a central study at either Oxford or Cambridge, but it did at Manchester under George Unwin, and at the London School of Economics, inspired by its first director, W. A. S. Hewins, with a staff that included from 1897 Sidney Webb, E. C. K. Gonner, Ellen A. Macarthur, H. LLewellyn Smith, A. L. Bowley, C. P. Sanger, F. W. Lawrence, Lillian Knowles, and Eileen Power.

35. W. J. Ashley, letter to his future wife, in Anne Ashley: *William James Ashley:*

A Life with a Chapter by J. H. Muirhead and a Foreword by Stanley Baldwin (London, 1932), 33.

36. Frederick Pollock, Corpus Christi Professor of Jurisprudence from 1883 to 1903, in his *An Introduction to the History of the Science of Politics* (London, 1890), 119. Pollock was specifically criticizing E. A. Freeman, but the same criticism might have been extended to most of the Oxford teachers of history.

37. Report to the Board of History and Archaeology (1909), 40–41.

38. J. R. Tanner, *English Constitutional Conflicts of the Seventeenth Century, 1603–1689* (Cambridge, 1961), 265. Published originally in 1928 and reprinted seven times until 1961, these essays were delivered as lectures in Cambridge when Tanner acted as Deputy for the Regius Professor in 1926–27.

39. William Hunt, *The History of England from the Accession of George II to the Close of Pitt's First Administration (1760–1801)* (London, 1924), esp. 328–29; and George D. Brodrick (completed and revised by J. K. Frotheringham), *The History of England from Addington's Administration to the Close of William IV's Reign (1801–1837)* (London, 1906), 307, 342.

40. MSS material A-E, Col. 9, Gwatkin Papers, Lecture Notes & Sermons, Easter Term, 1894, 396, Emmanuel College Library. I am grateful to Peter Slee for telling me about this collection.

41. For a discussion of conservatism as a "frame of mind" see Arthur Mejia's introduction to J. A. Thompson and Arthur Mejia, eds., *Edwardian Conservatism: Five Studies in Adaptation* (London, 1988), 1–10. The arguments in Hugh Cecil's *Conservatism* (London, 1912) are compatible with a Whig interpretation of history.

42. Bruce Coleman, *Conservatism and the Conservative Party in Nineteenth-Century Britain* (London, 1988), 200.

43. Bruce Coleman, *Conservatism and the Conservative Party in Nineteenth-Century Britain*, 202–3. Coleman contends further that in the late nineteenth and early twentieth centuries, leaders of the Conservative Party tended to be pragmatists or "unremarkable conservatives quite prepared to leave contentious interests alone and even to flavor their resistance to radical change with a pinch of progressivism" (205).

44. Charles Oman, *Memories of Victorian Oxford*, 104.

45. R. L. Poole, "The Teaching of Paleography and Diplomatic," in W. A. J. Archbold, ed., *Essays on the Teaching of History* (Cambridge, 1901); and V. H. Galbraith, "Diplomatic," *Oxford Magazine* 49 (1930): 238.

46. Montagu Burrows, *Inaugural Lecture* (on the foundation of the Chichele Professorship of Modern History) (Oxford, 1868), 16. Burrows had taken first class honours in both Litterae Humaniores and Law.

47. Stubbs, "Address on the Opening of a Course of Lectures on England under the Stewarts" (1889), in *Seventeen Lectures*, 465–68.

48. J. H. Round, *Peerage and Pedigree*, 2 vols. (Baltimore, 1910), vol. 1, ix. See also P. B. M. Blaas, *Continuity and Anachronism: Parliamentary and Constitutional Development in Whig Historiography and the Anti-Whig Reaction Between*

1890 and 1930 (The Hague, 1978), 260–62; A. V. Dicey, Mar. 23, 1911, to James Bryce in Bryce MS 3:87, the Bodleian Library, Oxford.

49. F. M. Powicke described Maitland as "one of the immortals" who "transcends all boundaries" and whose "greatness may have put every other influence in the shade and created a fresh tradition." Although he assumed that Maitland "must have affected the interests" of his successors such as Gaillard Lapsley, W. J. Corbett, Z. N. Brooke, and C. W. Previté-Orton, he found that the historical tradition in Cambridge derived rather from Seeley, Acton, Ward, Bury, Cunningham, Creighton, Gwatkin, and Whitney, which was "on the whole more in line with the general course of Cambridge interests than the work of Maitland." "Three Cambridge Scholars: C. W. Previté-Orton, Z. N. Brooke and G. G. Coulton," *The Cambridge Historical Journal* 9 (1944–46): 107, 108.

50. F. W. Maitland, "Materials for English Legal History" (1889), in *Collected Papers of Frederick W. Maitland,* ed. by H. A. L. Fisher (Cambridge, 1910), vol. 2, 7.

51. Letter to A. V. Dicey (probably July, Aug., or Sept. 1896), quoted in C. H. S. Fifoot, *Frederick William Maitland: A Life* (Cambridge, Mass., 1971), 294, n. 52.

52. F. W. Maitland, "The Gild Merchant" (1891), in *Collected Papers,* vol. 2, 230.

53. F. W. Maitland, "History of English Law" (1902) and "English Law, 1307–1600," in *Selected Historical Essays of F. W. Maitland* (Boston, 1962).

54. Pollock was coauthor with Maitland of the *History of English Law Before Edward I* (Cambridge, 1895), but he wrote only about one-tenth of the book.

55. Maitland, "The Body Politic" (c. 1899) in *Collected Papers,* vol. 3, ed. by H. A. L. Fisher, 286. For an interesting response to the question, "How great a historian was Maitland?" see Geoffrey Elton, *F. W. Maitland* (New Haven, Conn., 1985).

56. E. L. Woodward, *Short Journey [An Autobiography]* (London, 1942), 36, 41; H. W. C. Davis to T. F. Tout, Sept. 27, 1914, Tout Papers, John Rylands Library, Oxford Road, Manchester.

57. Frank Turner, *The Greek Heritage in Victorian Britain* (New Haven, Conn., 1981), esp. 263, which demonstrates how the "problems and anxieties of British citizenship had passed and merged into the being of the Greeks." In the Homeric Greeks, W. E. Gladstone found the origins of Christian, Victorian values. See his "On the Place of Homer in Classical Education and Historical Inquiry," in *Oxford Essays* (London, 1857), *Studies on Homer and the Homeric Age,* 3 vols. (Oxford, 1858), *Juventus Mundi: The Gods and Men of the Heroic Age* (London, 1869), and "Universities Hominium; or the Unity of History," *North American Review* 145 (1887).

58. Benjamin Jowett, *The Dialogues of Plato: Translated into English with Analyses and Introductions,* 4 vols. (Oxford, 1871).

59. Ernest Barker, *Political Thought of Plato and Aristotle* (London, 1906) and *Greek Political Theory: Plato and his Predecessors* (London, 1918).

60. William Stubbs, "Inaugural" (1867), in *Seventeen Lectures,* 15; James Bryce,

"The Historical Aspects of Democracy," *Essays on Reform* (London, 1867), esp. 263, and Bryce to E. A. Freeman, Bryce MS 9:107, Jan. 27, 1867, Bodleian Library, Oxford; T. E. May, *Democracy in Europe: A History* (London, 1877), vol. 1, 127–28; J. R. Seeley, *Introduction to Political Science: Two Series of Lectures* (London, 1908), 79–82, 313–14.

61. Stubbs, "Inaugural" (1867) in *Seventeen Lectures*, 15.

62. Stubbs, "Inaugural," 16, 15.

63. Bryce to E. A. Freeman, Bryce MS 9:107, Jan. 27, 1867 and "The Historical Aspects of Democracy" in *Essays on Reform*, 167.

64. W. J. Ashley, "The Study of History at Oxford" (1895), 294.

65. T. F. Tout, "The Manchester School of History," University Supplement to the *Manchester Guardian* (1920), in *The Collected Papers*, vol. 1, 85.

66. *Notes on the Development of the Historical Tripos, 1895–1932*, 35–36.

67. Report to the Board of History and Archaeology (1909), 37.

68. J. R. Seeley was a Moral Sciences graduate. Until 1881 those Cambridge graduates who were to distinguish themselves subsequently as historians, including F. W. Maitland, William Cunningham, J. N. Keynes, T. E. Scrutton, and H. M. Gwatkin, took first class honours degrees in the Moral Sciences, just as many of the new historians at Oxford had taken their degrees in Litterae Humaniores. But in the 1880s and 1890s the Historical Tripos produced a generation of historians who would remain dominant, especially at Cambridge, for the rest of their lives: J. P. Whitney, 1881; J. R. Tanner, 1884; Neville Figgis, 1889; G. P. Gooch and W. F. Reddaway, 1894; J. H. Clapham, 1895; G. M. Trevelyan, 1896; R. V. Laurence, 1898; D. A. Winstanley, 1899 and 1900; and H. W. V. Temperley, 1900 and 1901. Winstanley and Temperley took advantage of the new Tripos rules to be examined in both Parts I and II of the examination.

69. F. M. Powicke, "After Fifty Years" (1944), *Modern Historians and the Study of History*, 226.

70. Powicke, "Historical Study in Oxford," ibid., 177.

71. W. J. Ashley, "The Study of History at Oxford," 275. C. H. K. Marten, a Balliol student of A. L. Smith, became Assistant Master and subsequently Provost at Eton. Writing on "The Teaching of History in the Schools—Practice," Marten said: "It may and should provoke patriotism and enthusiasm; it should help to train the Citizen or the Statesman; its study should lead to right feeling and to right thinking." W. A. J. Archbold, ed., *Essays on the Teaching of History*, 91.

72. T. R. Glover, "Obituary of Gwatkin," in *The Eagle*, St. John's College Magazine, Dec. 1917, 115.

73. The scheme of 1899 omitted the paper on General English History, the "Outlines" paper, and retained the Special History Subjects as compulsory. Part I, to be taken at the end of two years, had papers in Medieval General European History, English Constitutional History to 1485, Comparative Politics or Ancient General European History, English Economic History or Political Economy, and two on Special Subjects. Part II continued chronologically the second two papers in Part I by examining Modern General European History

and Constitutional History from 1485. The student could choose no less than two or more than four of the following papers: two on Special Subjects, two on Political Economy, and one each on Comparative Politics, Analytical and Deductive Politics, International Law, and the History of Thought, Literature, or Art. When the Moral Philosophy Tripos was abolished, economic history and political economy were left in the Historical Tripos as two separate papers set by the History Board.

74. Maitland, "The Body Politic," 294, 295, 297, 300, 303.

75. Political Economy also remained an optional paper until 1930.

76. *Notes on the Development of the Historical Tripos,* 27–28.

77. A. J. P. Taylor, *A Personal History* (London, 1983), 83.

78. John Burrow has argued, interestingly, that it was the Whig historian's function to "celebrate and defend" the benefits of a "fruitful historically given variety" in S. Collini, D. Winch, and J. W. Burrow, *That Noble Science of Politics* (Cambridge, 1983), 205.

79. The joint efforts of the Hammonds appeared as *The Village Labourer* (London, 1911), *The Town Labourer, 1760–1832* (London, 1917 [finished in 1914]), *The Skilled Labourer, 1760–1832* (London, 1919), *Lord Shaftesbury* (London, 1923), *The Rise of Modern Industry* (London, 1925), *The Age of the Chartists, 1832–1854: A Study of Discontent* (London, 1930), *James Stansfeld: A Champion of Sex Equality* (London, 1932), and *The Bleak Age* (London, 1934). Alone, J. L. Hammond wrote *Charles James Fox* (London, 1903), *C. P. Scott* (London, 1934), and *Gladstone and the Irish Nation* (London, 1938).

80. Linda Colley suggests that Balliol "produced in him an almost uncritical admiration for the country's ruling class, and strengthened his belief that a highly gifted and homogeneous oligarchy was the political ideal." *Lewis Namier* (New York, 1989), 10.

81. Ward's education in Saxony was the result of his father's position as Minister-Resident to the Hanse Towns. When Lord Bryce could not attend, Ward acted as President of the first British meeting of the International Historical Congress in London in Apr. 1913, an occasion that must have meant a great deal to a man who had all his life tried to persuade his countrymen to be less insular. See T. F. Tout, "Sir A. W. Ward," *Proceedings of the British Academy,* vol. 11 (1924) in *Collected Papers,* vol. 1.

82. Temperley visited Serbia in 1905 and Slovakia in 1907.

83. John D. Fair, "The Peacemaking Exploits of Harold Temperley in the Balkans, 1918–1921," *Seer* 67, 1 (Jan. 1989): 70.

84. F. M. Powicke, "Three Cambridge Scholars: C. W. Previté-Orton, Z. N. Brooke, and G. G. Coulton" (1944) in *Modern Historians and the Study of History* (London, 1955), 127, 132, 134. Powicke believed that Z. N. Brooke's work stimulated a new kind of scholarship (135). Brooke, a pupil of Gwatkin's, was the first "professional" teacher of history in Caius College when he arrived there in 1908 from St. John's College. His preparation included Part I of the Classics Tripos and Part II of History. At the beginning of his career he taught Ancient History at

Bedford College, London, but it was as a medievalist that he distinguished himself. He was especially interested in the issues surrounding the investiture contest and Gregory VI. Brooke studied in Rome from 1911 to 1912, while in his early twenties. He died in the autumn of 1946 at the age of 63.

85. Richard W. Southern, *The Shape and Substance of Academic History* (Oxford, 1961), 5. Of the eight or nine subjects required for success in the new examinations for the Home, Indian, and Ceylon Civil Services which came into effect in 1892, anyone who took Classical Moderations, and then the Final Honours School in History, would be completely prepared. It was not until after the war that the new Class 1 Examination for the Civil Service required that anyone admitted to an influential position in government understand historical methods and sources, the relationship between geography and history, and some European history. *Report of the Royal Commission on the Civil Service* (1917), 22–23.

86. A. L. Smith, "The Teaching of Modern History" in Christopher Cookson, ed., *Essays on Secondary Education* (Oxford, 1898), 150.

87. For a discussion of Marshall's part in founding the Economics Tripos, see Reba N. Soffer, *Ethics and Society in England: The Revolution in the Social Sciences, 1870–1914* (Berkeley, Calif., 1978), chaps. 3–5. Marshall's insistence upon economic history did not protect him from his colleague William Cunningham's attacks on his neoclassical economic theory for its lack of historical context. See Cunningham's 2nd edition of his *The Growth of English Industry and Commerce*, 2 vols. (Cambridge, 1890–92), and "The Perversion of Economic History," *Economic Journal* 2 (1892).

88. Coulton to Tout, Tout Papers, Letters, Aug. 3, 1906.

89. G. G. Coulton, *Fourscore Years* (Cambridge, 1943), 350. Coulton, elected to a research fellowship at St. John's College in 1919, attracted students of history, English literature, and other subjects, who came to Cambridge because of his reputation. The volumes he edited for the series on "English Studies in Medieval Life and Thought" included Margaret Deanesly's *The Lollard Bible and Other Medieval Biblical Versions* (Cambridge, 1920); Eileen Power's *Medieval English Nunneries, c. 1275 to 1535* (Cambridge, 1922); G. R. Owst's *Preaching in Medieval England: An Introduction to Sermon Manuscripts of the Period c. 1350–1450* (Cambridge, 1926) and *Literature and Pulpit in Medieval England: A Neglected Chapter in the History of English Letters and of the English People* (Cambridge, 1933); H. S. Bennett's *Life on the English Manor: A Study of Peasant Conditions, 1150–1400* (Cambridge, 1937); K. L. Wood-Legh's *Studies in Church Life in England Under Edward III* (Cambridge, 1934); and Coulton's own *Five Centuries of Religion*, 4 vols. (Cambridge, 1923–50). See F. M. Powicke, "Three Cambridge Scholars," 140.

Chapter 4

1. J. A. Stewart, *Oxford After the War and a Liberal Education* (Oxford, 1919), 5–6.

2. When the advanced degrees of D. Phil. and Ph.D. were introduced respectively, in the early 1920s, at Oxford and Cambridge, students had an opportunity for more specialized professional training. Although adopted to attract graduates from the United States and the Dominions, the effect of the new postgraduate degrees was rather to draw British students. Of the 538 D. Phil.'s awarded in Oxford, 279 (more than half) went to British students, 85 to students from the United States, and 113 to students from the Dominions. At Cambridge, out of 1,104 Ph.D.'s, 757 (about two-thirds) went to British students, 60 to Americans, and 204 to students from the Dominions. See Renata Simpson, *How the Ph.D. Came to Britain: A Century of Struggle for Postgraduate Education* (Guildford, 1983), 162.

3. William Stubbs, "On the Present State and Prospects of Historical Study," (May 17, 1876), in *Seventeen Lectures on the Study of Medieval and Modern History and Kindred Subjects* (Oxford, 1900), 35–36; W. H. Hutton, ed., *Letters of William Stubbs, Bishop of Oxford 1825–1901* (London, 1904), 81; Herbert Paul, *The Life of Froude* (New York, 1905), 384. See C. Firth, *A Historic Controversy, 1904–1905* (Oxford, 1905) for a statement of the professorial and tutorial views. F. W. Maitland's history lectures from 1885 to 1906 were attended by only a few students, and he was never able to attract research students who were willing to follow in his steps.

4. Tout's school at Manchester was not established until after World War I. In 1906 he condemned English historians for being far behind the continent and America in that "we have still in our midst no school of history" See "Schools of History" [Lecture at Newnham College, Cambridge] (Jan. 26, 1906), in *Collected Papers*, vol. 1, 96. At London, A. F. Pollard succeeded in dominating the teaching of history at University College, but he was unable to establish a research institute, in spite of heroic efforts, until the late 1920s. Pollard Papers, box 4, Paleography Room Senate House Library, University of London.

5. By Oct. 25, 1882, the Board agreed to have a chair and a secretary appointed annually. After 1882, the substantial business of the Board was conducted during the first meeting, including discussions of curriculum, appointments and nominations to various Board offices, such as Examiners, adjudicators on Prize Committees, and members of the Library Committee. Seeley was not only chair but the Board's representative on the General Board of Studies from 1882 to 1895. In the second meeting of each term, a list of Lecturers for the following term was created, a conference was set with those Lecturers, and special subjects for both the Tripos and Special Examinations were announced. The first conflict over the History Board's right to choose its own staff according to its own estimate of need did not occur until the fall of 1911, when the General Board appointed a University Lecturer to the vacant Lectureship in Ancient History. The History Board, refusing to confirm that appointment, told the Senate that they preferred to use the money to put a Readership in Modern History, then established for ten years, on a more permanent basis. The General Board complied by appointing the History Board's candidate, J. Holland Rose, as Reader in Modern History until 1921. History Board, Minute Book, II, Nov. 15, 1911, 120a; Nov. 21, 22, and

28, 1911, 121; and, Mar. 5, 1912, 123. In early 1924 the Romanian government offered to provide a three-year salary for a University Lecturer in the History of Romania and the Near East. But despite the urging of the General Board, the History Board turned it down and reiterated their historic entitlement to be consulted on "general policy relating to the endowment and development of historical teaching within the University." The Lectureship was rejected. Minute Book, 1918–28, Jan. 29 and Feb. 5, 1924.

6. G. W. Prothero, "Memoir" in J. R. Seeley, *The Growth of British Policy: An Historical Essay*, 2nd ed., 1897 (Frankfurt, 1962) vol. 1, xii. This work was unfinished when Seeley died in 1895; it was edited and published by Prothero in 1897.

7. Quoted from the *Returns from the University of Oxford and Cambridge Commissioners* (1886), 51, 550, 558. The information on the number and content of classes held and on attendance was given in 1886 in response to inquiries by the University of Oxford and Cambridge Commissioners about the duties of the various university teachers of history. These returns reveal not only the statutory requirements for the different kinds of teaching, but the subjects taught, the kind of teaching, whether there was personal supervision, lectures, or conversation classes, and the numbers of students involved.

8. George I had created the Regius Professorships at both universities to teach modern languages and history to an aristocracy whose King also governed Hanover.

9. Thomas Arnold, "Inaugural" (1841) in *Introductory Lectures on Modern History* (New York, 1884), 436.

10. Sidney Lee, "Goldwin Smith," *Twentieth Century Dictionary of National Biography, 1901–1960* (Oxford, 1975), 2891–92.

11. Goldwin Smith's *Lectures on Modern History, Delivered in Oxford, 1859–61* (Oxford, 1861; Freeport, N.Y., 1972) were "An Inaugural Lecture," "On the Study of History," "On Some Supposed Consequences of the Doctrine of Historical Progress," and "On the Foundation of the American Colonies." See, too, *Three English Statesmen: A Course of Lectures on the Political History of England* (New York and London, 1867). The book contains an appendix on "Ancient Freeholders of England." Smith, a fellow and tutor at University College, allied himself with the university reformers Benjamin Jowett and Charles Lake in 1850 to urge a Royal Commission of Inquiry into the university. Lord John Russell appointed the Commission on Aug. 31, 1850, and Smith became joint secretary, together with Arthur Penrhyn Stanley. When the Executive Commission was appointed to carry out the Oxford University Act of 1854, Smith was made a member, and in 1858 he was appointed to the Newcastle Commission on national education. He wrote for the Peelite *Morning Chronicle*, the *Saturday Review*, and the *Daily News* and lectured and wrote on Ireland, America, and political and university reform. In 1868, he left Oxford to become the first Professor of English and Constitutional History at Cornell.

12. Goldwin Smith, "On the Study of History" (1859), in *Lectures on Modern*

History, 55, *An Inaugural Lecture as Regius Professor of Modern History, November, 1859* (Oxford, 1859), 27 and "On Some Supposed Consequences of the Doctrine of Historical Progress" (1860), in *Lectures on Modern History,* 1–9.

13. Smith, *Inaugural,* 16.

14. See Dorothy Owen, "The Chichele Professorship of Modern History, 1862," *The Bulletin of the Institute of Historical Research* 35, 90 (Nov. 1961): 217–20. The electors were the Archbishop of Canterbury, J. B. Sumner; Lord John Russell; Lord Chancellor Bethell; Judge of the Admiralty Court, Dr. Lushington; and the Warden of All Souls, Dr. Leighton.

15. M. Burrows, *Autobiography,* ed. by Stephen Montagu Burrows (London, 1908), 216.

16. Burrows, *Antiquarianism and History: A Lecture Delivered before the University of Oxford, May 26, 1884* (Oxford, 1885), 7–8.

17. J. R. Green, "Professor Stubbs's Inaugural Lecture," *Saturday Review* 22 (Mar. 2, 1867), in *Oxford Studies* (London, 1901), 279. Stubbs's prefaces and notes to the *Rolls Series, Charters and Documents Illustrative of English History* (Oxford, 1870–1901), *Registrum-Sacrum Anglicum* (Oxford, 1858), *Councils and Ecclesiastical Documents Relating to Great Britain and Ireland,* ed. with A. W. Hadden (Oxford, 1869–78), and the *Itinerarium Regis Ricardi* (London, 1864–65), were characterized by meticulous comparative research. See also Stubbs's "On the Purposes and Methods of Historical Study," *Seventeen Lectures,* 3.

18. Memorandum from the Earl of Carnarvon to the Derby-Disraeli Cabinet and letter from H. L. Mansell to Carnarvon, July 15, 1866, quoted in N. J. Williams, "Stubbs's Appointment as Regius Professor, 1866," *Bulletin of the Institute of Historical Research* 33, 87 (May 1960): 123.

19. Stubbs, "A Last Statutory Public Lecture" (May 8, 1884), in *Seventeen Lectures,* 442–43.

20. Stubbs, "On the Present State and Prospects of Historical Study," 35–37.

21. Stubbs to Freeman, in *Letters of William Stubbs,* 264.

22. Stubbs, Preface in 1900 to *Seventeen Lectures.*

23. Paul Fredericq, *The Study of History in England and Scotland* (Baltimore, 1887), 44.

24. Stubbs, "On the Present State and Prospects of Historical Study," *Seventeen Lectures,* 53–54. See also J. R. Green, "Professor Stubbs's Inaugural," 268.

25. Stubbs, "Inaugural," *Seventeen Lectures,* 16. See also, "Address on the Opening of a Course of Lectures on England under the Stewarts," *Seventeen Lectures,* 465–68.

26. Stubbs, "Address on Church History to the Oxford Diocesan Church History Society" (Jan. 10, 1890), *Seventeen Lectures,* 452.

27. See Robert Brentano, "The Sound of Stubbs," *Journal of British Studies* 6, 2 (May 1967): 1–14.

28. Stubbs, *The Constitutional History of England,* vol. 1, 4th ed. (Oxford, 1883), 266.

29. Stubbs, "Inaugural," *Seventeen Lectures*, 27.

30. Stubbs, "Address on Church History to the Oxford Diocesan Church History Society," *Seventeen Lectures*, 452.

31. Stubbs, "A Last Statutory Public Lecture," *Seventeen Lectures*, 442–43.

32. Quoted in J. A. R. Marriott, *Memories of Four Score Years* (London, 1946), 60.

33. Stubbs, "A Last Statutory Public Lecture," *Seventeen Lectures*, 442–43.

34. Stubbs, "On the Present State and Prospects of Historical Study," *Seventeen Lectures*, 34.

35. F. W. Maitland, "William Stubbs, Bishop of Oxford," *English Historical Review* 16 (1901), 503.

36. Stubbs, "On the Purposes and Methods of Historical Study," *Seventeen Lectures*, 130 and "Address on the Opening of a Course of Lectures on England under the Stewarts," *Seventeen Lectures*, 471.

37. Stubbs, "On the Purposes and Methods of Historical Study," *Seventeen Lectures*, 3–4.

38. Stubbs, "Inaugural," *Seventeen Lectures*, 20.

39. See Chapter 3 for a discussion of Ashley and the field of economic history to which he turned.

40. J. R. Seeley, "Liberal Education in the Universities" (1867), *Lectures and Essays* (London, 1870), 214.

41. The Commission was set up by Gladstone in 1872 to inquire into the revenues and property of both ancient universities. Mark Pattison was in the chair for the meeting on Nov. 16, 1872, which Henry Sidgwick attended. Renata Simpson, *How the Ph.D. Came to Britain*, 38–39.

42. J. R. Seeley, "The Teaching of Politics," *Lectures and Essays*, 298–99.

43. For an analysis of the relation between Seeley's views of history and religion, see Soffer, "History and Religion: J. R. Seeley and the Burden of the Past," in Richard Davis and Richard Helmstadter, eds., *Religion and Irreligion in Victorian Society* (London, 1992); and for a perceptive discussion of Seeley's "priesthood of the historian," Richard Shannon, "John Richard Seeley and the Idea of a National Church," in R. Robson, ed., *Ideas and Institutions of Victorian Britain* (New York, 1967), 248.

44. J. R. Seeley, *Life and Times of Stein, or Germany and Prussia in the Napoleonic Age* (New York, 1968), vol. 1, 406; vol. 2, 435.

45. Only in 1887, when Seeley delivered his *A Midland University: An Address* (Birmingham, 1887), did he argue instead that the purpose of a university was the acquisition of knowledge.

46. Seeley, "The Teaching of Politics," *Lectures and Essays*, 296–99.

47. Ibid., 296.

48. Shannon, "John Richard Seeley and the Idea of a National Church," *Ideas and Institutions of Victorian Britain*, 241.

49. J. R. Seeley, "The Teaching of Politics," *Lectures and Essays*, 298, 296.

50. Ibid., 315.

51. J. R. Seeley, "History and Politics," *The Expansion of England* (London, 1894), 169.

52. J. R. Seeley, "Schism in Greater Britain," *Expansion of England*, 142, 144.

53. J. R. Seeley, "The Teaching of Politics," *Lectures and Essays*, 316.

54. J. R. Seeley, "History and Politics," *Expansion of England*, 25–26, and *An Introduction to Political Science* (London, 1923), 25–26. *An Introduction* was edited and published posthumously by Henry Sidgwick in 1896. Between 1896 and 1923, there were seven printings.

55. Ibid., 386.

56. G. W. Prothero, "Memoir," xix. See J. R. Seeley, "The Teaching of History," in G. Stanley Hall, ed., *Methods of Teaching History*, vol. 1, 2nd. ed. (Boston, 1885), 196, 199, 249.

57. J. R. Seeley, "The English Revolution of the 19th Century I," and "The English Revolution of the 19th Century II," *Macmillan's Magazine* (Aug. 1870), 243; (Sept. 1870): 348–50.

58. Seeley, "The English Revolution of the 19th Century III," *Macmillan's Magazine* (Oct. 1870): 442, 450.

59. J. R. Seeley, "The Teaching of Politics," *Lectures and Essays*, 315–16.

60. J. R. Seeley, *Life and Times of Stein*, vol. 1, 18, 33, 66; vol. 3, 558; vol. 2, 96.

61. Richard Shannon argues interestingly that Seeley's reinterpretation of English history as power politics provided the necessary basis for a revised agenda for national debate, upon which "the general pattern of intellectual responses to the politics of England from the 1870s to the First World War is most properly to be considered." "John Robert Seeley and the Idea of a National Church," *Ideas and Institutions of Victorian Britain*, 266.

62. J. R. Seeley, *The Growth of British Policy: An Historical Essay*, 1897 (Frankfurt, 1962), vol. 2, 384.

63. J. R. Seeley, "Phases of Expansion," *Expansion of England*, 119–40.

64. J. R. Seeley, "Tendency in English History," *Expansion of England*, 3, 16.

65. J. R. Seeley, "History and Politics," *Expansion of England*, 174–75.

66. Ibid., 196.

67. J. R. Seeley, "How We Govern India," *Expansion of England*, 228.

68. J. R. Seeley, "Recapitulation," ibid., 301.

69. Ronald Robinson, "Oxford in Imperial Historiography," in A. F. Madden and D. K. Fieldhouse, eds., *Oxford and the Idea of Commonwealth* (London, 1982), 33.

70. A. P. Newton, *An Introduction to the Study of Colonial History*, Helps for Students of History, no. 16 (London, 1919), 6. This series was published by the S.P.C.K. (Society for the Promotion of Christian Knowledge), the educational arm of the Anglican Church.

71. Cambridge produced distinguished Commonwealth scholars such as Nicholas Mansergh, Ronald Robinson, and John Gallagher. For Oxford, see

Richard Symonds, *Oxford and Empire: The Last Lost Cause?* (London, 1986) and his chapter in Michael Brock and Mark Curthoys, eds., *History of Oxford University*, vol. 7 (Oxford, forthcoming).

72. See Soffer, "History and Religion: J. R. Seeley and the Burden of the Past," *Religion and Irreligion in Victorian Society.*

73. Charles Firth thought Froude's appointment "simply an enormity and the greatest possible discouragement to the study of history here" and R. L. Poole confided to Tout that many "of us were keen upon a public protest." Firth to Tout, Apr. 10 and Poole to Tout, Apr. 30, 1892, Tout Papers.

74. Charles F. McClelland, *The German Historians and England* (Cambridge, 1971), 236. In the spring of 1900, Albert Bushnell Hart of Harvard called upon President McKinley and presented the plans of a committee of historians "organized to obtain and publish the facts relative to the Philippine problem." Quoted from *The Washington Post* in W. Stull Holt, ed., *Historical Scholarship in the United States, 1876–1901, As Revealed in the Correspondence of Herbert B. Adams* (Baltimore, 1938), 280, n. 1.

Chapter 5

1. E. A. Freeman, "The Office of the Historical Professor," in *The Methods of Historical Study: Eight Lectures Read in the University of Oxford in Michaelmas Term, 1884* (London, 1886), 36. See Freeman to Bryce, Bryce MS 7:120, Feb. 3, 1884; Bryce, "E. A. Freeman," in his *Studies in Contemporary Biography* (London, 1923), 281; H. A. L. Fisher, "Modern Historians and their Methods," *Fortnightly Review* 62 (Dec. 1894): 805–6; and Horace Round's *Feudal England: Historical Studies on the Eleventh and Twelfth Centuries* (1895) (London, 1964), esp. 251.

2. E. A. Freeman, *Comparative Politics* (London, 1873). See S. Collini, D. Winch, and J. W. Burrow, *That Noble Science of Politics: A Study in Nineteenth-Century Intellectual History* (Cambridge, 1983), 219–23.

3. Freeman, "Historical Study at Oxford," *Bentley's Quarterly Review* 1 (1859): 295 and "The Office of the Historical Professor," *Methods of Historical Study*, 8. See, too, J. W. Burrow, *A Liberal Descent: Victorian Historians and the English Past* (Cambridge, 1981), 165; and P. B. M. Blaas, *Continuity and Anachronism: Parliamentary and Constitutional Development in Whig Historiography and the Anti-Whig Reaction between 1890 and 1930* (The Hague, 1978), 188.

4. H. A. L. Fisher, "Modern Historians and their Methods," *Fortnightly Review* 62 (Dec. 1894): 805.

5. Freeman to Bryce, Bryce MS 7:119, Feb. 3, 1884.

6. T. F. Tout, "Edward A. Freeman," *Manchester Guardian*, Mar. 18, 1892, in *Collected Papers*, vol. 1, 130.

7. Tait, Notebooks and Diaries, May 1886, in Tait Papers, the John Rylands University Library of Manchester, Oxford Road.

8. Freeman to Bryce, Bryce MS 6:31, Apr. 20, 1873; Dicey to Bryce, Bryce MS

2:133, Mar. 23, 1892; and Bryce, "E. A. Freeman," *Studies in Contemporary Biography*, 263–64, 288.

9. Freeman, preface to *The Methods of Historical Study*, v.

10. Ibid., iii. The lectures were the Inaugural, "The Office of the Historical Professor"; 1. "History and its Kindred Subjects"; 2. "The Difficulties of Historical Study"; 3. "The Nature of Historical Evidence"; 4. "Original Authorities"; 5. "Classical and Medieval Writers"; 6. "Subsidiary Authorities"; 7. "Modern Writers"; 8. "Geography and Travel." Freeman told the story of the clergyman's daughter to Charles Oman, who retells it in "History at Oxford," in his *On the Writing of History* (New York, 1939), 237.

11. See Chapter 4.

12. Herbert Paul, *The Life of Froude* (London, 1905), 412; and W. H. Dunn, *James Anthony Froude: A Biography, 1818–1856* (Oxford, 1961), chaps. 13 and 15. Froude regretted taking orders in 1842 to qualify for a Fellowship at Exeter College. After the publication of the *Nemesis* and the reaction against it in Oxford and in the press, he resigned his Fellowship.

13. C. H. Firth to T. F. Tout, Apr. 10, 1892, and R. L. Poole to Tout, Apr. 30, 1892, Tout Papers.

14. J. A. Froude, *The Science of History: A Lecture Delivered at the Royal Institution* (1864) (London, 1886), 28, 21–22.

15. J. A. Froude, *The Science of History*, 35.

16. J. A. Froude, "Inaugural Lecture," *Longman's Magazine* 21, 158 (Dec. 1892).

17. See esp. J. A. Froude, *Oceana, or England and her Colonies* (London, 1886), 10.

18. H. A. L. Fisher, "Modern Historians and their Methods," 804.

19. J. A. Froude, *The Science of History* (1864), 21–22.

20. J. A. Froude, "Suggestions on the Best Means of Teaching English History," in *Oxford Essays, Contributed by Members of the University* (London, 1855), 62, 66, 74; and *The Science of History*, 7.

21. J. A. Froude, "Inaugural Lecture," *Longman's Magazine*, 144–58.

22. "Obituary," *Oxford Magazine*, May 18, 1904.

23. H. A. L. Fisher, *An Unfinished Autobiography* (Oxford, 1940), 57.

24. F. Y. Powell, "The École des Chartes and English Records" (1897), *Proceedings of the Royal Historical Society* 11 (1897), 31–40. See, too, *The Study of History in Universities: An Address* (Bangor, 1902).

25. C. H. Firth to Tout, Tout Papers, Nov. 25, 1894.

26. F. Y. Powell, "Inaugural Lecture," *Oxford Chronicle* (May 1, 1895), reprinted in a condensed version in *The Academy* 1201 (May 11, 1895): 401–2.

27. Oliver Elton, *Frederick York Powell: A Life and A Selection from Letters and Occasional Writings*, vol. 1: *Memoirs and Letters* (Oxford, 1906), 195; Oman, *Memories of Victorian Oxford and of Some Early Years* (London, 1941), 26; Firth to Tout, Nov. 25, 1894, and Powell to Tout, 1894, Tout Papers.

28. For some of Firth's failures on the Modern History Board see *The Minority*

Report for Oxford Curriculum Reform (Oxford, 1892) written by Firth and Tout, Firth's letters to Tout, and the papers of the Modern History Board.

29. Firth to Tout, Mar. 13, 17, 1892, Tout Papers.

30. A. L. Smith, "Political and Social Questions," A. L. Smith Papers, Box 1, n.d., Balliol College Library.

31. Firth wrote nine major books on history and on history and literature, apart from his writings on the university, including *Cromwell's Army: A History of the English Soldier during the Civil Wars, the Commonwealth, and the Protectorate* [The Ford Lectures delivered at Oxford, 1900–1901] (London, 1902), *The Last Years of the Protectorate, 1656–58*, 2 vols. (London, 1909), *The House of Lords during the Civil War* (London, 1910), and his famous *Commentary on Macaulay's History of England* (London, 1938). He also wrote a schoolbook on *Oliver Cromwell and the Role of the Puritans in England* (London, 1900), thirteen important articles and essays, and edited or introduced 23 collections of documents, memoirs, and other primary sources.

32. Firth's *The Last Years of the Protectorate* continued the *History of the Commonwealth and the Protectorate*, left unfinished by S. R. Gardiner's death.

33. C. H. Firth, "Burnet as an Historian," Introduction to T. E. S. Clarke and H. C. Foxcroft, *A Life of Gilbert Burnet* (1907) in Godfrey Davies, ed., *Essays Historical and Literary* (Oxford, 1938), 195–96. Davies was Firth's most important disciple.

34. C. H. Firth, "Macaulay's Conception of History," *Commentary on Macaulay's History*, 27–30.

35. C. H. Firth, "Macaulay's Third Chapter," ibid., 117, 119, 123.

36. C. H. Firth, "Macaulay's Conception of History," ibid., 140.

37. C. H. Firth, *A Plea for the Historical Teaching of History* (Oxford, 1904), 21–22, 30.

38. C. H. Firth, Preface to *Plea*, 5, Firth to R. H. Hodgkin, A. L. Smith Papers, Box 4, Miscellaneous (Nov. 14, 1904). Hodgkin, Smith's son-in-law, gave Smith this letter.

39. *A Letter to the Regius Professor on the Teaching and Study of History at Oxford* (Oxford, 1905), 4–8. The *Plea*, the tutor's *Letter*, and Firth's *Reply* are collected in *An Historic Controversy, 1904–5* (Oxford, 1905).

40. For the sake of his mother, he turned down the Indian Civil Service and an educational appointment in India and eventually returned to Oxford. See J. A. R. Marriott, *Memories of Fourscore Years* (London, 1946), 61–62, 51.

41. For Aydelotte (1880–1956), this was the beginning of a distinguished career as a literary scholar who taught English at M.I.T. in 1915–21, became an innovative president of Swarthmore College from 1921 to 1940 and Director of the Institute for Advanced Study at Princeton.

42. *A Letter to the Regius Professor*, 7, 9–10, 11. Aydelotte's copy was very kindly lent to me by his son, the historian William Aydelotte. For Aydelotte's admiration for Oxford, see *The Oxford Stamp and Other Essays: Articles from the Educational Creed of an American Oxonian* (1917) (Freeport, 1967).

43. R. L. Poole, "The Teaching of Paleography and Diplomatic," in W. A. J. Archbold, ed., *Essays on the Teaching of History* (Cambridge, 1981). Poole had written *Illustrations of the History of Medieval Thought in the Departments of Theology and Ecclesiastical Politics* (London, 1884) after resigning his post in the manuscript section of the British Museum in 1873 to devote himself to medieval studies.

44. V. H. Galbraith, "Diplomatic," *Oxford Magazine* 49 (1930): 238.

45. C. H. Firth, *Modern History in Oxford, 1841–1918* (Oxford, 1920), 43.

46. Firth, *Memorandum on the Organization of Advanced Historical Teaching in Oxford* (June 12, 1908).

47. Charles Oman, *Memories of Victorian Oxford*, 241.

48. Charles Oman, "Inaugural Lecture on the Study of History," in *Lectures on the Study of History* (Oxford, 1906), 15.

49. Oman, "Inaugural," ibid., 23–24.

50. Oman, *Memories*, 160–61.

51. Oman, "History at Oxford," in *On the Writing of History*, 254–55.

52. Oman, *Memories*, 163.

53. Ibid., 148.

54. Ibid., 268, and Oman, "Some Notes on Professor Burrows and All Souls College," in M. Burrows, *Autobiography*, ed. by Stephen Montagu Burrows (London, 1908), esp. 254.

55. Round to Tout, Tout Papers, Jan. 17, 1910. Oman wrote histories of Greece, England, the Byzantine Empire, Europe, the sixteenth century, Anglo-Saxon England, the Middle Ages, the nineteenth century; military history about the Middle Ages, the sixteenth century, Wellington, Napoleon, and the Peninsular war; special studies of Warwick, Roman statesmen of the later Republic, the outbreak of the Great War, the reign of George VI, English castles, English coinage; and books of essays and memoirs. Almost all went into many editions.

56. After *A History of Balliol College* (London, 1899), a schoolbook on *Charlemagne* (New York, 1899), and articles on medieval history for the *English Historical Review*, W. H. C. Davis's most original work, *England under the Normans and Angevins* (London, 1905) was reprinted in ten editions by 1930. It was followed by a Home University volume on *Medieval Europe* (London, 1911), and he undertook a revision of Stubbs's *Select Charters* (Oxford, 1913) and began a calendar of royal charters in 1913.

57. H. W. C. Davis, *The Study of History* [an inaugural lecture delivered before the University of Oxford on Nov. 4, 1925] (Oxford, 1925), 5.

58. H. W. C. Davis, *The Age of Grey and Peel* [Ford Lectures, 1926] (New York, 1964), 48. The lectures were published posthumously under the supervision of G. M. Trevelyan, whose uncritical treatment of Grey in *Lord Grey of the Reform Bill* (London, 1920) is criticized by Davis for idealizing and magnifying his subject. See 196.

59. H. W. C. Davis, *The Study of History*, 5, 7, 9–10, 18, 20.

60. F. M. Powicke wrote extensively, beginning with *The Loss of Normandy*

(1189–1204): Studies in the History of the Angevin Empire (Manchester, 1913), followed by a war piece, *Bismarck and the Origin of the German Empire* (London, 1914); *Christian Life in the Middle Ages and Other Essays* (Oxford, 1935); *The Thirteenth Century, 1216–1307* (Oxford, 1935) for the Oxford History of England, which he edited together with G. N. Clark and C. R. Cruttwell; the Riddell Memorial Lecture: *History, Freedom, and Religion* (Oxford, 1938); *The Reformation in England* (London, 1941); and *King Henry II and the Lord Edward*, 2 vols. (Oxford, 1947). He also edited five volumes, translated another, and wrote for journals and the *Cambridge Modern History*.

61. F. M. Powicke, "The School of Modern History," *Oxford Magazine* 48 (1930): 528.

62. Richard Southern, *The Shape and Substance of Academic History* (Oxford, 1961), 4.

63. P. L. Lee and John Wilkes, "History at the Universities: The Consumer's View," 1: Oxford History, *History* 55 (Oct. 1970): 332–33. In 1970 Lee, who read Modern History at Oxford from 1961 to 1964, was teaching at the University of London's Institute of Education.

64. F. M. Powicke, *Historical Study in Oxford* [an inaugural lecture] (Oxford, 1929), 172, 173, 175, 177–79.

65. F. M. Powicke, "Three Cambridge Scholars: C. W. Previté-Orton, Z. N. Brooke, and G. G. Coulton," in *Modern Historians and the Study of History* (London, 1955), 108–9.

66. Arthur Sidgwick to James Bryce, Jan. 25, 1895, Bryce MS 15: 93–4.

67. F. W. Maitland, "Lord Acton" (1902), *Collected Papers*, vol. 3, 513, 514.

68. In 1896, the young Cambridge graduate G. P. Gooch first met Acton in the Athenaeum Club. G. P. Gooch to Acton, Jan. 31, 1896, quoted in Frank Eyck, *G. P. Gooch: A Study in History and Politics* (London, 1982), 33–34. When A. V. Dicey met Acton in 1887, he said that he would have liked to see more of him, but was "afraid of boring him." Dicey "never knew anyone whose knowledge seemed to me more extraordinary. Its mass oppresses one with a sense of own's own ignorance." Dicey to Bryce, May 6, 1887, Bryce MS 2:104.

69. On Feb. 6 and 8, 1895, Acton described to Bryce what the Regius Professorship would require of him, and he told Bryce in a P.S. on Feb. 8 that "I am consulting nobody else." Bryce MS 1:86, 88.

70. James Bryce, "Lord Acton," *Studies in Contemporary Biography*, 397. Owen Chadwick has argued that Acton was a profoundly thoughtful and erudite man who only wrote for three people: his old teacher, Dollinger, Mary Gladstone, and his own daughter Mamy, who, when she grew up, became his most intimate correspondent. But most of all, Chadwick points out, he wrote for himself. *Acton and Gladstone* [Creighton Lecture, 1975] (London, 1976).

71. Oscar Browning, *Memories of Sixty Years* (London, 1910), 17.

72. Thomas Thorneley, *Cambridge Memories* (London, 1936), 117–18; and

Charles Crawley, *Trinity Hall: The History of a Cambridge College, 1350–1975* (Cambridge, 1976), 144.

73. Gwatkin, the Dixie Professor of Ecclesiastical History, was elected Chairman in Acton's stead. Letter of Oct. 31, 1900 in Historical Board, Minutes, Nov. 10, 1900, 61d.

74. O. Chadwick, *Acton and Gladstone*, 28 and his Butterfield Memorial Lecture, "Acton and Butterfield," *Journal of Ecclesiastical History* 38, 3 (July 1987): 386–405.

75. Charles Oman, "Inaugural," in *Lectures on Study of History*, 27.

76. See Acton Papers, Add. 4929, 9–10, 47.

77. Notes for Romanes Lecture, 1900. Acton Papers, Add. 4981 F, 77, 33, 23, 6, 21, 73.

78. Acton Papers, Add. 4981 F, 63, 97.

79. Acton Papers, Add. 4931 F, Nov. 24 (no year given), 102, 188.

80. Acton Papers, Add. 4931 F, Nov. 24 (no year given), 53, 196; 4891 F, 94.

81. Acton Papers, Add. 4977 F, 189; Add. 4929 F, 66–79; Add. 4991 F, 198.

82. Quoted in Jonathan Rose, *The Edwardian Temperament, 1895–1919* (Athens, Ohio, 1986), 60–61. Figgis died after his ship was torpedoed during the war. R. Vere Laurence was Acton's other student.

83. In 1893, Bury became the Erasmus Smith Professor of Modern History at Trinity College, Dublin, where he had received his classical training, and five years later, he was also appointed Regius Professor of Greek there. After Acton's death, when F. W. Maitland turned down the Regius Professorship of Modern History at Cambridge, Bury was offered the position.

84. Owen Chadwick, *Freedom and the Historian: An Inaugural Lecture* (Cambridge, 1969), 27–28.

85. J. B. Bury, *History of the Freedom of Thought* (London, 1913), 251. The titles of the chapters describe the themes: 1. Freedom of Thought and the Forces Against It; 2. Reason Free (Greece and Rome); 3. Reason in Prison (The Middle Ages); 4. Prospect of Deliverance (The Renaissance and the Reformation); 5. Religious Toleration; 6. The Growth of Rationalism (Seventeenth and Eighteenth Centuries); 7. The Progress of Rationalism (Nineteenth Century); and 8. The Justification of Liberty of Thought.

86. J. B. Bury, *A History of Greece to the Death of Alexander the Great* (London, 1955), 836.

87. Norman Baynes said that Bury "had no admiration for the Historical Tripos and he refused to adapt his lecturing to meet the needs of students working for the Tripos . . . (his) lectures appealed to few . . . the undergraduate saw little of Bury and Bury never sought the intimacy of undergraduates." But he was interested in promoting research among postgraduate students. Norman H. Baynes, *A Bibliography of the Works of J. B. Bury: Compiled with a Memoir by Norman H. Baynes* (Cambridge, 1929), 49–50.

88. Report to the Board of History and Archaeology (1909), Papers, 37.

89. Baynes, *A Bibliography of the Works of J. B. Bury*, 51.

90. T. F. Tout, in his review of vol. 5 of the *Cambridge Medieval History*, in *English Historical Review* 42 (1927): 112–13.

91. The story has been well told by Peter Lineham, "The Making of the Cambridge Medieval History," *Speculum* 57, 3 (1982). Robert Laffan, at Queen's College, was given the chapter on the German Empire of the Fifteenth Century, even though he readily admitted a lack of proficiency in German. Laffan to Tanner, Oct. 12, 1922, Cambridge Medieval History Papers, Box I, The Library of St. John's College, Cambridge. The prewar editors were J. P. Whitney, Professor of Ecclesiastical History at King's College, London from 1908 and Dixie Professor of Ecclesiastical History at Cambridge from 1919 to 1939, and H. M. Gwatkin, his predecessor as Dixie Professor from 1891 to 1916. In June, 1918, J. R. Tanner, History Tutor at St. John's College, Cambridge, whose interests were in modern rather than medieval history, replaced Gwatkin, who had died in 1916, as editor. Tanner inherited and continued Bury's original scheme for each chapter.

92. In G. M. Trevelyan, "The Latest View of History," *The Independent Review* (Dec. 1903).

93. J. B. Bury, "The Science of History" (1903) in *Selected Essays of J. B. Bury*, ed. by H. W. V. Temperley (Cambridge, 1930), 4.

94. King's College Politics Society, Minute Books, 4, Mar. 7, 1905, in King's College Library. The only one who argued against applying moral tests to politics was the future diplomatic historian C. K. Webster.

95. J. B. Bury, "The Science of History," *Selected Essays*, 10, 11.

96. J. B. Bury, *The Life of St. Patrick and His Place in History* (New York, 1971), vi, vii.

97. J. B. Bury, *The Ancient Greek Historians* ([the Lane Lectures, Harvard, 1908] London, 1909), 249.

98. J. B. Bury, "The Science of History," 13, 16.

99. MS Notebook, Seeley Library, Cambridge, contains only the account of the organizing meeting of the Union of Students in Historical Research held in Professor J. P. Whitney's rooms at Emmanuel College. Bury, the two other professors, the four dons, and the four students present agreed that women interested in research were to be taken seriously and not treated as if they were just passing through Cambridge on their way to teaching positions in the schools. It is not surprising that G. G. Coulton, notorious for his public rudeness to any women who attended his lectures, sent his apologies for not attending. What is more interesting is that neither Catherine B. Firth nor Eileen Power attended, although they were invited.

100. The first article in the first number is by Bury. See "A Lost Caesarea," *Cambridge Historical Journal* 1 (1923): 1.

101. See "Preface to the Third Edition," by Russell Meiggs in J. B. Bury, *A History of Greece* (London, 1955), v.

102. J. B. Bury, "Preface to the First Edition," *A History of Greece*, vii.

103. J. B. Bury to J. R. Tanner, Aug. 27, 1921, Cambridge Medieval History Papers, Box II.

104. J. B. Bury, "Cleopatra's Nose," *R.P.A. Annual and Ethical Review for 1916*. Doris Goldstein argues, suggestively, that Bury "sought not to make a priori judgements about the role of chance in history but to suggest that historians examine more carefully the nature and dynamics of accidental causes within specific historical contexts." See "J. B. Bury's Philosophy of History: A Reappraisal," *American Historical Review* 82 (1977): 903.

105. J. B. Bury, "Theism," *R.P.A. Annual and Ethical Review for 1920*, 13.

106. J. B. Bury, *The Idea of Progress: An Inquiry into Its Growth and Origin* (New York, 1955), 346, 348, 351–52.

107. G. M. Trevelyan, "An Autobiography," in *An Autobiography and Other Essays* (London, 1949), 34, 47.

108. G. M. Trevelyan, *The Present Position of History* (Cambridge, 1927), 20.

109. G. M. Trevelyan, "An Autobiography," in *An Autobiography*, 21.

110. Owen Chadwick, *Freedom and the Historian*, 19.

111. As early as Oct. 1899, before his appointment as a college lecturer, Trevelyan taught for the Working Men's College in London. The founder, F. D. Maurice, and his friends were mainly Cambridge men and chiefly from Trinity College. In addition to teaching there himself, Trevelyan enlisted Francis Cornford, G. P. Gooch, and Hilton Young from Trinity. Together with Cornford, Trevelyan raised money for a College Building Fund and built a facility for the WMC to come to Cambridge annually for a summer term, and he formed a Literary and Historical Society for the WMC students in London. Mary Moorman, *George Macaulay Trevelyan: A Memoir by His Daughter* (London, 1980), 70–72.

112. Trevelyan wrote to H. A. L. Fisher on July 5, 1911, to urge him to accept the new Readership because it would allow him time to write as it was "next door to a sinecure, as the Reader is not to lecture unless he wishes, and can lecture on any thing he likes, or on nothing." H. A. L. Fisher Papers, 4, 18.

113. From 1909 to 1912, after lecturing at Oxford for University Extension classes, Trevelyan accepted employment at Trinity College, Cambridge to give a course of lectures on English History, 1660–1714. From 1909 to 1912, in Michaelmas Term, he came twice a week from London to lecture to a filled Hall at Trinity. In 1915, he lectured in the U.S. and went to Harvard in the spring of 1924 to give the Lowell Lectures on English History, which became his one-volume *History of England* in 1926. A year earlier, he gave the Sidney Ball lecture at Oxford on the "Historical Causes of the Present State of Affairs in Italy," and in 1926, he returned to Oxford to give the Romanes Lecture on "The Two-Party System in English Political History." When he accepted the Regius Professorship at Cambridge, he was reelected to a Trinity Fellowship. He became Master of his college in 1940 and retired eleven years later to the largely honorific office of Chancellor at Durham University.

114. G. M. Trevelyan, *Autobiography*, 30.

115. G. M. Trevelyan, "Clio," in *Clio, a Muse and Other Essays Literary and Pedestrian* (London, 1913), 19, 20, 22, 23.

116. Ibid., 30.

117. G. M. Trevelyan, *The Present Position of History*, 9, 4, 5, 11.

118. Trevelyan, *The English Revolution, 1688–1689* (1938) (London, 1956), 243.

119. Trevelyan, *England Under Queen Anne*, 3 vols. (London, 1930–34).

120. Quoted in Asa Briggs, "G. M. Trevelyan: The Uses of Social History," *The Collected Essays of Asa Briggs*, vol. 2: *Images, Problems, Standpoints, Forecasts* (Brighton, 1985), 241.

Chapter 6

1. A. L. Smith to F. W. Maitland, Nov. 17, 1905, Smith Papers, Balliol College Library.

2. A. L. Smith, "Feudalism," in 1. Historical and Scholarly Papers (a) Historical Papers, Box: "English Constitutional History," Smith Papers. Boase went on to say of the French that in "default of reform they had revolution." College History, Box 5. Boase Papers, vol. 102, 6, 1, dated between 1890 and 1894, Exeter College Library. For another view of the "comparative method" used by nineteenth-century historians and political scientists see S. Collini, D. Winch, and J. Burrow, *That Noble Science of Politics: A Study in Nineteenth-Century Intellectual History* (Cambridge, 1983), chap. 7.

3. J. R. Seeley, *The Expansion of England* (London, 1894), 1; G. W. Prothero, "The Historical Tripos" in *A Student's Guide to the University of Cambridge*, 5th ed. (Cambridge, 1892), 3; *Memorandum of the Special Board for History and Archaeology*, Nov. 8, 1917.

4. R. L. Poole to Tout, May 21, 1906, Tout Papers. H. W. C. Davis, then a tutor at Balliol, approved of Firth's plan in 1906 to introduce a history thesis in lieu of a special subject, but he worried that "most potential examiners" would "shriek aloud at the prospect of examining a hundred men annually in theses on variable special subjects." Davis to Tout, June 12, 1906, Tout Papers, John Rylands Library, Oxford Road, Manchester.

5. Richard Southern, *The Shape and Substance of Academic History* (Oxford, 1961), 17–18.

6. Thomas Thorneley, *Cambridge Memories* (London, 1936), 78–79.

7. Personal interview with Charles W. Crawley, July 1981.

8. Report to the General Board of the Faculties from the Faculty Board of History on the need for new Professorships in History, Jan. 31, 1928, typescript in Seeley Library, 3.

9. J. N. L. Myres, *The Provision of Historical Studies at Oxford Surveyed in a Letter to the President of the American Historical Association on the Occasion of its Meeting in California, 1915* (Oxford, 1915), 6.

10. The original members of the first Board of Historical Studies in Oct. 1876

were the Regius Professor of Modern History, the Regius Professor of Civil Law, the Professor of Political Economy, the Whewell Professor of International Law, and J. Westlake, V. H. Stanton, and B. E. Hammond of Trinity College, J. B. Mayor of St. John's College, F. J. A. Hort, and the Hulsean lecturer in divinity, G. W. Prothero of King's College, and after November, Henry Sidgwick, of Trinity. Until 1882, there were the four Professors and between eight and eleven college representatives. The Regius Professor of Modern History was Chairman throughout his tenure; Hammond was Secretary until Mar. 25, 1879, when Prothero took over. In Oct. 1882, the Board of Historical Studies became the Board of History and Archaeology under the new statutes. It included, by statute, the Regius Professor of Modern History, the Disney Professor of Archaeology, the Slade Professor of Fine Arts, and the Dixie Professor of Ecclesiastical History; and, by a Grace of the Senate, the Professor of Political Economy, the Whewell Professor of International Law, and twelve college teachers. A quorum of four members was established and meetings were set for twice each term. Board of Historical and Archaeological Studies, Minutes, 1876–82.

11. This reform was the result of a Syndicate appointed on May 27, 1875 to consider the requirements of the university in different departments of study.

12. Cambridge University, Printed Report of the Syndicate meeting at Clare College Lodge, Apr. 17, 1877. Beginning in the fall of 1883, the routine work of the History Board was made more formal and control was extended further over intercollegiate lectures and the students who were supposed to attend them. A subcommittee was appointed to revise annually the Lists of Books recommended to the students in the four major areas of examination: political philosophy and jurisprudence, general English and constitutional history, political economy and economic history, and international law and treaties. To insure that students attended intercollegiate lectures, a record of attendance was kept and notice of non-attendance was sent to college tutors. A committee was also appointed to draw up a report urging the General Board to separate History and Archaeology, but the Board retained its dual title until the 1920s. History Board, Minutes 1, 63 (Oct. 23, 1883), 65 (Nov. 28, 1883), 70 (Feb. 9, and May 8, 1884).

13. On May 5, 1884, the General Board, following the History Board's nominations appointed Browning, Hammond, Prothero, William Cunningham, and Thomas Thorneley as the first University Lecturers in History. History Board, Minutes, 1, 72.

14. Sidgwick to Bryce (Apr. 19, 1872), Bryce MS 15:10–12.

15. When Trinity College proposed a Professorship in History in memory of Connop Thirlwell who had died in 1875, the Statutory Commissioners at Cambridge responded that the £500 annual stipend should be contributed entirely by Trinity. The result was that the project to found the Chair was abandoned by November 1880. D. A. Winstanley, *Later Victorian Cambridge* (Cambridge, 1947), 301, 354. While Winstanley's judgments were not consistently reliable, he usually got the narrative sequence straight.

16. In the spring of 1890 the Library had moved to King's College where the

Board rented a room for £10 a year. History Board, Minutes, 1, 130 (Mar. 11, 1899). As late as the spring of 1893, the History Board was still unable to persuade the Senate to give them permanent facilities, but as a result of the Senate's acceptance in April of the Report of the Law and History Rooms Syndicate, the Vice-Chancellor was authorized to assign a room in the Literary Schools occasionally to the History Board for a period of two years. *The Cambridge University Reporter* (1893), 783. Oscar Browning was Librarian until Nov. 1888, when he resigned and was succeeded by H. M. Gwatkin, and in 1913, by H. W. V. Temperley. *The Student's Handbook to the University and Colleges of Cambridge*, 12th ed., revised to June 30, 1913 (Cambridge, 1913), 238, 264–65.

17. On Jan. 31, 1928, the Faculty Board of History sent the General Board of the Faculties a Report pointing out that for the preceding twenty years, the History Board had been asking, in vain, for additional professors in history. Typescript of Report, signed by Z. N. Brooke, Chairman of the Faculty Board of History, Seeley Library. Although there were four other professors attached to the Faculty of History, three—the Professors of Naval History, Ecclesiastical History, and Ancient History—were concerned with the work of other faculties and therefore were of limited use to students reading for the Tripos. The fourth, the Professor of Political Science, was newly installed in 1928. The History Board asked for professors in economic, modern, and medieval history.

18. Feb. 8, and Apr. 4, 1878, History Board, Minutes, 1, 12, 42, 43.

19. In 1892 the Secretary of State for India began to pay £500 per annum towards the expenses of the I.C.S. courses from Indian revenues. *Cambridge University Reporter* (1890–91), 949.

20. *Cambridge University Reporter* (1882–83), 179–80, 380–1; (1892–93), 571; (1903–4), 758.

21. A. Marshall to J. N. Keynes, Sept. 30, 1897, Keynes Papers, I (112), the Marshall Library, Cambridge.

22. I am very grateful to John Roach for the material contained in this paragraph. See too, Edward Miller, *Portrait of a College: A History of the College of St. John the Evangelist, Cambridge* (Cambridge, 1961), 104; and C. N. L. Brooke, *A History of Gonville and Caius College* (Woodbridge, 1985), 245.

23. Romualdas Sviedrys, "The Rise of Physics Laboratories in Britain," *Historical Studies in the Physical Sciences* 7 (1976).

24. Gerald L. Geison, *Michael Foster and the Cambridge School of Physiology: The Scientific Enterprise in Late Victorian Society* (Princeton, N.J., 1978), 363, xiii.

25. The fellowship which Firth was awarded at All Souls in 1901 was the same kind of research award as that given to S. R. Gardiner, and it involved, as Firth wrote to T. F. Tout, the "obligation to write a certain period of English history." Mar. 16, 1901, Tout Papers.

26. Quoted in Richard Symonds, *Oxford and the Empire: The Last Lost Cause?* (London, 1986), 113. In 1877, after Owen had been Reader in Indian History for thirteen years, he was lecturing not only on some British administrators in India, but on Anglo-Scottish History from the accession of Elizabeth and the Anglo-

French Wars. *Oxford University Gazette* June 5, 1877, 7 (1876–77). As late as 1896, Bury complained to Prothero that the process of arranging for his series of books on Foreign Statesmen "is revealing to me how surprisingly few people there are who are competent to write on foreign history." Dec. 3, 1896, Prothero Papers.

27. G. P. Moriarty served from 1895 to 1923 when he was succeeded by C. J. B. Gaskoin.

28. Board of Modern History, Minutes 3 (Dec. 1, 1922) 235.

29. June 8, 1929, typescript, in Modern History: Reports & etc., 1, 6. Masterman pointed out that none of the previous appointments made by the Board had been in the School later than 1913. In his answer, Urquhart denied that appointments were based upon seniority and said that the Board had no rules or regulations to govern its system of appointments and relied instead upon the discretion of a Standing Committee, subject to the Board's authority. Ibid., Nov. 15, 1929.

30. Goldwin Smith, *The Reorganization of the University of Oxford* (Oxford, 1868), 3, 7.

31. E. A. Freeman, "Oxford after Forty Years," *Contemporary Review* 51 (1887): 618–20.

32. Between the 1850s and 1900, all the outside examiners were Oxford graduates. All the data about honours graduates, collected in *The Historical Register of the University of Oxford, being a Supplement to the Oxford University Calendar with an Alphabetical Record of University Honours and Distinctions Completed to the End of the Trinity Term, 1900* (Oxford, 1900) and *Supplement to the Historical Register of 1900 Including an Alphabetical Record of University Honours and Distinctions for the Years 1901–1930* (Oxford, 1934), were entered into a statistical analysis program. The computer study documents the numerical dominance of history in Oxford by 1901, and it reveals 23 other pieces of information about honours graduates, such as their class of degree, college, prizes, fellowships, which tutors did the most examining, who won historical prizes and whether they then became tutors or officers within colleges or the university, the steady advance of the numbers of history honours students in comparison to Litterae Humaniores and other fields year by year, and those colleges, and the tutors within them, which produced the greatest number of first- and second-class degrees.

33. For the first half of the nineteenth century, see Sheldon Rothblatt, "The Student Sub-Culture and the Examination System in Early 19th Century Oxbridge," in Lawrence Stone, ed., *The University and Society 1: Oxford and Cambridge from the 14th to the Early 19th Century* (Princeton, N.J., 1974), 302–3.

34. See M. Burrows, *Inaugural Lecture* [on the foundation of the Chichele Professorship of Modern History in 1868] (Oxford, 1868), 4; A Don [pseudonym], "University Organization," *Fraser's Magazine* 77 (Feb. 1868): 148–49; "Protest Against Examinations" [signed by 424 academics and intellectuals, including seventeen university tutors and professors of history], *Nineteenth Century* 24 (Nov. 1888): 617–37; Auberon Herbert, ed., *The Sacrifice of Education to*

Examinations: Letters from all Sorts and Conditions of Men (London, 1888), see esp. James Bryce, 21, H. A. L. Fisher, 57–59, S. R. Gardiner, 77, and Frederick Harrison, 172; Mark Pattison, *Suggestions for Academical Reform* (Edinburgh, 1868), 293–94; T. Fowler, "On Examinations," *Fortnightly Review* 111 (Mar. 1876): 428; Henry Latham, *On the Actions of Examinations, Considered as a Means of Selection* (Cambridge, 1877), 35–36, 338, 358; J. Thorold Rogers, "Oxford Professors and Oxford Tutors," *Contemporary Review* 56 (Dec. 1889): 934; W. L. Courtney, "Oxford Tutors and their Professorial Critic," [Thorold Rogers] *Fortnightly Review* 53, n.s. (Feb. 1890): 295; "Oxford Professors and Oxford Tutors: Reply of the Examiners in the School of Modern History," *Contemporary Review* 57 (Feb. 1890): 183; and A. L. Smith, "The Teaching of Modern History," in Christopher Cookson, ed., *Essays on Secondary Education* (Oxford, 1898), 182–83, 191.

35. S. R. Gardiner, Letter, in Auberon Herbert, ed., *The Sacrifice of Education to Examinations,* 77.

36. See letter by H. A. L. Fisher in ibid., 55.

37. A. L. Smith, "The Teaching of Modern History," in Cookson, ed., *Essays on Secondary Education,* 1, 282, 191.

38. Mandell Creighton to H. M. Gwatkin, July 1884, copy in Prothero Papers.

39. See John Roach, *Public Examinations in England, 1850–1900* (Cambridge, 1971), *A History of Secondary Education in England, 1800–1870* (London, 1986), and *Secondary Education in England, 1870–1902: Public Activity and Private Enterprise* (London, 1991); Gillian Sutherland, *Ability, Merit and Measurement: Mental Testing and English Education, 1880–1940* (Oxford, 1984); and J. M. Prest, ed., "Jowett's Correspondence on Education with Earl Russell in 1867," in Supplement to the *Balliol College Record* (Oxford, 1965).

40. M. Burrows, *Inaugural,* 4–5.

41. A. W. Ward, *Suggestions towards the Establishment of a History Tripos* (Cambridge, 1872), 4.

42. Henry Latham, *On the Action of Examinations,* 35–36.

43. In 1888, when Mandell Creighton was Chairman and two of the other Examiners were F. W. Maitland and George Prothero, the guiding principle they adopted for setting the papers in the Special Subject followed lines suggested by A. W. Ward in 1872: one paper dealt with a historical period as a whole and the other with the texts of books specified for study and with subjects arising from them. Thirty-seven men and five women took the Tripos in 1888; only J. Neville Figgis got first class honours, even though his 736 points were inferior to E. A. Marshall's marks of 745. But Marshall was a woman at Girton College, and the Cambridge examiners, including Prothero, who was a champion of women's higher education, were not apparently inclined to award her first class honours. Women could attend lectures and take the examinations, but they could not receive a degree. History Tripos Examiners' Book (1889–1910), Nov. 14, 1888, Seeley Library, Cambridge.

44. The examiners were B. E. Hammond, W. J. Corbett, J. N. Figgis, and

E. C. K. Gonner, from Oxford, History Tripos Examiners' Book (1889–1910), June 22, 1898. Because of the increase in candidates by 1905 to over 100, the Examiners asked for additional help and the History Board responded by nominating six. Letter from Examiners for Tripos of 1905 to History Board and the Board's response, Oct. 30, 1905, in History Board, Minutes 2, 83.

45. R. Muir, *The School of Modern History: A Letter upon the Working of the School* (Oxford, 1914), 8–15.

46. From 1877 to 1914, Smith taught 81 percent of those receiving a first class honours degree in Modern History at Balliol and 72 percent of those receiving a second, as well as women and many students from other colleges. *The Balliol College Register 1833–1933*, 2nd ed.; *1916–67*, 4th ed. His students included three future Regius Professors at Oxford: Maurice Powicke, H. W. C. Davis, and V. H. Galbraith; a future Regius Professor at Cambridge, G. N. Clark; the prominent historians A. G. Little, Ernest Barker, Richard Lodge, Lewis Namier, Ramsay Muir, F. D. Ackland, R. C. K. Ensor, R. H. Tawney, G. D. H. Cole, C. H. K. Marten of Eton, and John O'Regan of Marlborough. Such great statesmen as Elgin and Herbert Samuel were also his pupils. See M. F. Smith, *Arthur Lionel Smith, Master of Balliol, 1916–24: A Biography and Some Reminiscences, by his Wife* (London, 1928); and Rowy Mitchison, "An Oxford Family," privately printed, in A. L. Smith Papers.

47. H. A. L. Fisher, *Unfinished Autobiography* (Oxford, 1940), 85; Ernest Barker, *Age and Youth* (Oxford, 1953), 328–29; V. H. Galbraith and F. M. Powicke, quoted in Hartley, "Successors to Jowett" in H. W. C. Davis, *A History of Balliol College* (London, 1899), 242, 240. For an opposing view, see C. H. K. Marten, *On the Teaching of History* (Oxford, 1938), 34.

48. V. H. Galbraith, quoted in Hartley, "Successors to Jowett," 240.

49. The "History teacher who achieves . . . civic orientation will share more certainly perhaps than any other member of the community in the work of reconstruction." Helen M. Madeley, *History as a School for Citizenship* (Oxford, 1920), 10. Madeley had been the organizing history mistress at Leeds Girl's High School, lecturer in history at Bingley Training College, Warden of the Birmingham Women's Settlement, and Director of Practical Work for the Social Study Course of Birmingham University.

50. A. L. Smith, "Historical Fatalism" [address to the eleventh Annual Meeting of the Historical Association] (Jan. 12, 1917), 2–3, and "The Teaching of Modern History," in Cookson, ed., *Essays on Secondary Education*, 180.

51. A. L. Smith, "The Teaching of Modern History," 178, 192.

52. To prepare the "Social and Political Questions," Smith read newspapers, journals, local Government Reports, Parish Council figures, Census reports, Parliamentary returns, and Poor Relief statistics; he compared them locally, regionally, and nationally and then put them in the context of the most recent monographs in French, English, and German. Box 1, Lectures on "Social and Political Questions," A. L. Smith Papers.

53. Box 1 (1913), A. L. Smith Papers.

54. The undergraduate Oliver Wardrop labeled these printed handouts to students on the Tudor and Stuart periods "Lodge's Lectures." Balliol College Library Uncatalogued manuscript; Wardrop, J. O.: English constitutional history— outline of lectures delivered at Oxford by A. L. Smith of Balliol College and other members of the university, 1889–90, "The Tudor Period, 1485–1603," 4. For a discussion of Wardrop's later career, see Chapter 8.

55. H. W. C. Davis, "The Meaning of History," 20, typescript in box: *Papers of the Balliol History Club, 1907–1909,* Balliol College Library.

56. H. W. C. Davis, *The Study of History* [an inaugural lecture], Nov. 4, 1925 (Oxford, 1925), 78.

57. Charles Boase's papers are in the Exeter College Library.

58. Herbert Gladstone to his father, W. E. Gladstone, on what he needed to do to be a history tutor, in Glynne-Gladstone MSS, Hawarden. I am indebted to Colin Matthew for this reference.

59. C. H. Firth, *The Faculties and Their Powers: A Contribution to the History of University Organization* (Oxford, 1909), 12.

60. The only Oxford professor to serve as an examiner between the 1850s and 1900 was Stubbs, who examined a total of 506 students during the years 1865, 1866, 1871, 1872, 1873, 1874, 1877, 1878, 1882, and 1883. But Arthur Johnson was the examiner with the greatest total number of students, 1,076, in 1878, 1879, 1887, 1888, 1889, 1890, 1898, 1899, and 1900. Richard Lodge came next with a total of 750 students. *Historical Register of 1900.*

61. All citations from the Junior Historians' meetings are from CU6, the Seeley Library, Junior Historians' Minutes, IX.52.

62. A. A. Seaton, *The Theory of Toleration under the Later Stuarts* (Cambridge, 1911). The book was reissued by Octagon Books (New York, 1972).

63. The Secretary, C. R. Fay, reported that Lowes Dickinson had provided a "full analysis of the lectures upon Political Science B (political theory) which he intended to give during the next academic year," in compliance with Fay's request, including a list of recently published books, which Fay was going to duplicate and circulate among the members. On Feb. 11, 1921, Graham Wallas, and in Nov. 1922, Harold Laski spoke on "The Teaching of Political Science." Junior Historians, Minutes, Seeley Library. For a discussion of Graham Wallas and the development of political science in England see Soffer, *Ethics and Society in England: The Revolution in the Social Sciences, 1870–1914* (Berkeley, Calif., 1978); and Martin J. Weiner, *Between Two Worlds: The Political Thought of Graham Wallas* (Oxford, 1971).

64. On Nov. 30, 1938, Kitson Clark, seconded by Christopher Morris, proposed that women teaching in the women's colleges be eligible for membership, but women were finally admitted only after World War II. The members in the interwar years included: John Saltmarsh, C. A. Eliot, J. R. M. Butler, E. J. Passant, R. Vere Laurence, Kenneth Pickthorn, Paul Vellacott, T. H. Marshall, Bernard Manning, C. W. Previté-Orton, H. W. V. Temperley, E. A. Benians, C. R. Fay,

Robin Laffan, Geoffrey Butler, Frank Birch, E. Welbourne, G. N. Clarke, Charles
W. Crawley, Herbert Butterfield, G. Kitson Clark, Anthony Steele, F. E. Adcock,
F. Mc. D. C. Turner, G. B. Perret, H. O. Evenett, M. J. Oakeshott, F. H. H. Clarke,
Charles Smyth, R. E. Balfour, G. C. Morris, E. E. Rich, J. Dennis Ward, Hugh
Gatty, J. P. T. Bury, J. C. Walker, M. M. Postan, H. S. Offler, Phillip Grierson, G.
Barraclough, J. Sikes, R. F. Bennett, H. J. Habbakuk, A. Hope-Jones, J. M. K.
Vyvyan, and R. J. White. Among those nominated for election from 1911 to 1939,
only one person was blackballed, and he was eventually elected five years later.
Junior Historians, Minutes.

65. *Royal Commission on Oxford and Cambridge Universities: Appendices*
(London, 1922), 170.

66. C. R. Fay, *King's College, Cambridge* (London, 1907), 85.

67. Frank Eyck, *G. P. Gooch: A Study in History and Politics* (London, 1982),
14–17. Although Gooch never knew it, he was opposed by Archdeacon Cunningham, who said that his dissertation showed no signs of original thought and was
merely a compilation. John Pollock, *Time's Chariot* (London, 1950), 137–38.

68. William Cunningham to T. F. Tout, Tout Papers, Letters, Jan. 16, 1906.

69. Robert Skidelsky, *John Maynard Keynes,* vol. 1: *Hopes Betrayed, 1883–1920,*
(London, 1983), 107–9.

70. Henry Jackson to Prothero, Feb. 5, 1873, Prothero Papers.

71. J. R. Seeley to Prothero, Prothero Papers, Dec. 6, 1873. In need of money,
Prothero also lectured for university extension at Nottingham and Leicester, and
examined in the schools.

72. At Cambridge, Prothero produced a *Life of Simon de Montfort* (London,
1877), an edition of Voltaire's *Siècle de Louis XIV* (Cambridge, 1879–82), a translation of the first volume of Ranke's *Universal History: The Oldest Historical
Group of Nations and the Greeks* (London, 1884), a *Life of Henry Bradshaw, University Librarian* (London, 1888), and *Select Statutes and other Documents Illustrative of the Reigns of Elizabeth and James I* (Oxford, 1894), besides more than
twenty articles for *Encyclopedia Britannica* and essays for the *English Historical
Review* and the *Athenaeum.* See Charles W. Crawley, "Sir George Prothero and
His Circle" [The Prothero Lecture, July 12, 1969] in *Transactions of the Royal
Historical Society,* 5th ser., 20 (1970).

73. Nov. 27, 1884, Oct. 27, 1885, History Board, Minutes, vol. 1, 78, 91.

74. J. P. Whitney, "Sir George Walter Prothero as a Historian" [Address at a
Special Meeting of the Royal Historical Society] (Nov. 23, 1922). Typescript in
King's College Library, 1–6. Whitney was sent to King's in 1877 by A. W. Ward,
whose student he had been at Owens College, and he remained there as an undergraduate, with Prothero as his History Tutor, until 1882.

75. Prothero Papers, 1889.

76. The testimonial writers were Walter Raleigh, a pupil of Prothero's for four
years at King's; L. J. Maxse, editor of the *National Review*; Alfred Lyttelton, a
former Trinity man who attended Prothero's lectures consistently and became a

lawyer and a member of the Cabinet in 1903; Jane Harrison, the distinguished classicist whose reputation has survived far better than her teacher's; Helen Gladstone, who became Vice-Principal of Newnham College; John Willis Clark, the Registrary of the University of Cambridge, a Fellow of Trinity, an architectural historian, and a biographer; Thomas Hodgkin, a historian who wrote on Italy, Theodoric, and Theodosius; R. C. Jebb, M.P. for Cambridge, Regius Professor of Greek, and an eminent classical scholar; Henry Sidgwick; the Rev. Dr. Westcott, Bishop of Durham and a major historian of religious thought; Austen Leigh, Provost of King's and Vice-Chancellor of the University; English historians, including Firth, Seeley, Ward, S. R. Gardiner, James Gairdner, Mandell Creighton, Hubert Hall, William Cunningham, J. Franck Bright, Maitland, and Stubbs; and the continental historians Rudolf von Gneist, Felix Liebermann, and Charles Bémont.

77. Henry Sidgwick, Testimonial (May 4, 1894), in Prothero Papers.

78. In 1880 Prothero was elected to the Newnham College Council and in 1892 he wrote to Eleanor Sidgwick on behalf of the college to offer her the post of Principal. The Prothero Papers show how active he was in the work of the Council in securing consensus and expediting planning. Helen Gladstone, Testimonial for Prothero, Prothero Papers (Apr. 23, 1894).

79. F. W. Maitland, Testimonial, Prothero Papers (May 9, 1894). William Cunningham wrote that the "progress and present prosperity" of the Historical School at Cambridge are "almost entirely due to his constant care and attention to details." Ibid., Apr. 30, 1894.

80. Prothero to Dr. Wallace in response to Wallace's letter asking Prothero how to improve the Scottish universities, n.d., Prothero Papers (1900). See too "A Liberal Education and the Function of a University" [an address before the University of Edinburgh at the graduation ceremony, 11th Apr., 1896], in *Scottish Review* (Oct. 1896).

81. Skidelsky, *John Maynard Keynes*, vol. 1, 107–9. Skidelsky is entirely correct to point out that Browning's "genius was to make young men feel he was on their more interesting side against authority and convention" (109), but he does him an injustice to overlook his seriousness and consistency of purpose.

82. *Report on the Correspondence and Papers of Oscar Browning (1837–1923), Historian and Educational Reformer 1853–1913 at King's College, Cambridge.* Listed by the Royal Commission on Historical Manuscripts (London, 1978).

83. His correspondents include William St. John Brodrick Midleton Montague, a Conservative statesman in the India Office in the early twentieth century, Edward Frederick Bulmer, a joint founder of the cider manufacturing company H. P. Bulmer, Ltd., James Bryce, who, when at the Foreign Office, sought Browning's advice about launching a historical journal, Henry Campbell-Bannerman, when Prime Minister, Arthur Temple Lyttelton, the author of *The Influence of National History on National Literature* (1883) and the first Master of Selwyn Col-

lege, Cambridge, and Edwin Samuel Montague, the Liberal Secretary of State for India.

84. See Oscar Browning, Correspondence and Papers, King's College Library, Cambridge.

85. These were *Napoleon: The First Phase* (1904) and after his retirement in 1908, a two-volume *History of the Modern World, 1815–1910* (1912), *A General History of the World* (1913), and *A Short History of Italy, 375-1915* (1917).

86. Browning to Prothero (July 15, 1884), Kegan Paul to Prothero (July 23, 1884) in the Prothero Papers. As Browning got older, and especially after he left Cambridge in 1908 to retire in Rome, his letters to Prothero reveal a man increasingly occupied with trivial issues.

87. J. W. Burrow, "Victorian Historians and the Royal Historical Society," *Transactions of the Royal Historical Society*, 5th ser., 39 (London, 1989): 136.

88. *Transactions*, n.s., 2 (1885): 77–96 and 349–64. Burrow's "Victorian Historians and the Royal Historical Society" makes the point that "Browning's papers would have looked more in place in the new *English Historical Review*, with its emphasis on politics and the state" (128–29). Browning took part in the coup that converted the Royal Historical Society into a more "professional" body (130).

89. Browning Papers, n.d.; Arthur Hassall's comments in Browning Papers (Jan. 14, 1899).

90. Politics Society Minute Books, 3 (Dec. 4, 1893), 7 (Nov. 6, Dec. 4, 1916; Oct. 17, 1921; Feb. 26, Nov. 12, 1917), 3 (Jan. 20, Dec. 4, 1893), 4 (1908), 6 (1912–13), 7 (Oct. 24, 1921), 8 (Nov. 2, 1925; Feb. 11, 1929).

91. M. R. James to T. F. Tout, Tout Papers (Dec. 8, 1907).

92. J. H. Clapham to George Prothero, Prothero Papers (Jan. 9, 1914).

93. History Board, Minutes, Nov. 26, 1918 (1918–28).

94. J. H. Clapham, "Persecuting and Professor Sidgwick," n.d., King's College Library, Cambridge.

95. J. H. Clapham, "Irish Immigration," n.d., King's College Library, Cambridge.

96. Quoted in T. E. B. Howarth, *Cambridge Between Two Wars*, 109.

97. J. H. Clapham, "Scientific History," MSS (1909), 3, 4, 10. King's College Library.

98. Charles Crawley told me in June 1981 that this is what he heard first as a student and then as a young don from the early 1920s.

99. See the Politics Society, Minute Books, 3 (Oct. 16, 1893) to 8 (1930.)

Chapter 7

1. James Bryce, "On the Teaching of History in Schools," Historical Association Leaflet No. 4 (London, 1907): 3. D. J. Medley's *A Student's Manual of Consti-*

tutional History (Oxford, 1894), reprinted in six editions until 1925, is a good example of an easily digested compilation of historical facts.

2. H. A. L. Fisher, *Unfinished Autobiography* (Oxford, 1940), 63.

3. C. H. Firth, "The Study of Modern History in Great Britain," *Proceedings of the British Academy* 6 (1913): 142.

4. A. F. Pollard to his father (Jan. 22 and 29, 1911) in Pollard Papers, Letters (1911–14).

5. J. Thorold Rogers, *Education in Oxford: its Methods, its Aids and its Rewards* (London, 1861), 45.

6. T. F. Tout, "Schools of History" [Lecture at Newnham College, Cambridge] (Jan. 26, 1906), in *Collected Papers of Thomas Frederick Tout, with a Memoir and a Bibliography* (Manchester, 1932–39), vol. 1, 101.

7. Signed by C. R. L. Fletcher, J. A. R. Marriott, A. G. Little, A. F. Pollard, and Ernest Barker in Report of Examiners (1905), Reports of Examiners in the School of Modern History (1905–12), Modern History Reports, vol. 1, 38, the Bodleian Library, Oxford; and Report of Examiners (1906) in ibid., 46. Before the turn of the century, two reports by the Examiners appear in the Modern History Board Papers (see the report of July 10, 1889, in Modern History Reports, vol. 1, 142), but it was not until 1903 that the Board decided to print Reports.

8. Report of the Examiners (1908), signed by W. H. Hutton, Arthur Hassall, Richard Laing, H. W. C. Davis, and G. Baskerville. Modern History Reports, vol. 1, 57.

9. Paul Fredericq, *The Study of History in England and Scotland* (Baltimore, 1887), 21, n.1. Fredericq, the Belgian historian and colleague of Henri Pirenne at Ghent, visited Oxford in 1884 as part of a comparative inquiry into the state of historical studies in various countries. While Fredericq's impressions were sometimes mistaken, his observations about foreign language deficiency were still being repeated in the early twentieth century by the history honours Examiners.

10. See Ramsay Muir, *The Study of Modern History*, 8–15.

11. Signed by C. R. L. Fletcher, F. Morgan, F. F. Urquhart, R. H. Hodgkin, and H. W. V. Temperley, Reports of the Examiners (1914), vol. 2, 42; and Reports of the Examiners (1923), signed by L. G. Wickham Legg, L. Stampa, A. L. Poole, F. M. Powicke, and C. R. M. F. Cruttwell, vol. 4, 39.

12. Reports of the Examiners (1914), vol. 2, 41, 42.

13. A. L. Smith's lectures and handouts on the Special Subjects, as well as on English and constitutional history, were detailed and comprehensive enough to provide students with complete examination answers. He gave handouts, often printed, on every topic required for examination by the Examination Statutes. Smith Papers I. Historical and Scholarly (a) History Papers, Box 9, Stuarts 1, n.d., contains a typescript of 24 topics and the way to answer them, in outline, including the appropriate pages in the recommended authorities. See too his lectures on the "Papacy," Box 7; Miscellaneous Papers, Box 2; "Cromwell," Box 6; "Feudalism," "People," and, "the Barons," Box: "English Constitutional History."

While the lectures are rarely dated, some in the constitutional history box may belong to 1890, the date of other papers in that box. There are other copies, written apparently over different periods of time, but the contents are the same. See, too, Charles Boase's lecture notes, especially on "Constitutional History" and on "French Constitutional History." Boase Papers, 2, CII, 6, 1880 and 1890–94.

14. *Royal Commission on Oxford and Cambridge, Report* (London, 1922), 30, 35.

15. The federal principle, the separation of functions, "was Cambridge's gift to higher education generally and to wherever the British model was exported." Sheldon Rothblatt, "Historical and Comparative Remarks on the Federal Principle in Higher Education," *History of Education* 16, 3 (1987): 156.

16. *Notes on the Development of the Historical Tripos, 1875–1932* [unsigned and undated typescript], Seeley Library, 7, 8.

17. At Cambridge, the popular Special Subject "The History of the Netherlands" was based entirely upon J. L. Motley's *Rise of the Dutch Republic* (London, 1869). Another, "James II and the Revolution," was studied only in the appropriate volumes of T. B. Macaulay's *History of England* (London, 1849–61), vols. 1–3, chaps. 4–14. Faculty Board of History and Archaeology, Minutes, vol. 1, 35 (May 19, 1880), 47c (Mar. 11, 1898), Seeley Library. When three books were prescribed in 1914, the Examiner's Reports pointed out that "few of the candidates had read more than one." Ibid., vol. 2, 134a (Dec. 17, 1914).

18. *Notes on the Development of the Historical Tripos*, 30. To remedy this evasion by students taking Part I, the reformers proposed to make Comparative Politics (defined to include theory) compulsory and to include an elementary knowledge of economic theory in the paper on Political Science and Economic History.

19. J. P. Younger, "Englebert" and an essay by Katherine M. Thomas in Box 1 and essays by J. H. Burrows and E. Whitman in Box 2 of the A. L. Smith Papers, n.d., Balliol College Library.

20. Peter Slee has included this script in his "History as a Discipline at the Universities of Oxford and Cambridge, 1848–1914," Cambridge Ph.D., 1983, Appendix 2, together with the Constitutional and Political Paper, Michaelmas Term, 1873, that the script answered. He examines parts of it in *Learning and a Liberal Education: The Study of Modern History in the Universities of Oxford, Cambridge and Manchester, 1800–1914* (Manchester, 1986), 111–13, including question 2, but he does not look critically at what the answers actually said.

21. M. E. G. Finch-Hatton, Modern History Lectures Notes, Reading Lists and Notes, and Essays, 1870–74, six vols., 1, 135. Once part of the library of Herbert John Gladstone, this MS collection came to the Bodley in 1980. Finch-Hatton attended J. Franck Bright's lectures on Europe 1600–1815, and he read the French Revolution, his Special Subject, and English History 1600–88 and 1760–91, with his tutor, Arthur H. Johnson.

22. E. W. Watson, undergraduate lecture and reading notes, MS. Top Oxon.e.378, Bodleian Library.

23. Dr. Reeves intends to deposit her notes in the Bodley. I am most grateful to her for making them available to me and for valuable conversations about the School of Modern History.

24. In Dr. Reeves's notes on Political History, Trinity Term 1924, "From Roman Britain to Norman Conquest," she responds to the question "Why did Wessex achieve what Northumbria and Mercia failed to achieve?" with: "Personal Character of Kings" and "Relative solidarity," but the first is noted as "More important." Lecture 4 (May 9, 1924).

25. Historical Tripos Honours Examinations, May 31, 1904; May 28, 1906; May 27, 1907; June 4, 1908; May 31, 1909; May 26, 1910; May 30, 1911; May 27, 1912; May 27, 1913; June 3, 1915; May 27, 1919; June 2, 1920; May 31, 1921; May 30, 1922; May 29, 1923.

26. J. H. Clapham, "Many Inventions," Clapham Papers, King's College Library, Cambridge (May to Nov. 1894).

27. Sheldon Rothblatt is unique in concentrating upon students in "The Student Subculture and the Examination System in Early Nineteenth-Century Oxbridge," in Lawrence Stone, ed., *The University and Society 1: Oxford and Cambridge from the 18th to the Early 19th Century* (Princeton, N.J., 1974), and "Failure in Early Nineteenth-Century Oxford and Cambridge," *History of Education* 2, 1 (1982). The only full-length study of British students, Eric Ashby's and Mary Anderson's *The Rise of the Student Estate in Britain* (Cambridge, Mass., 1970), examines a "student view" and student representation in university government. Students in the history societies at Oxford, Cambridge, Manchester, and London were interested less in governing their university than in governing their country and its empire.

28. Rothblatt, "Failure in Early Nineteenth-Century Oxford and Cambridge," 10.

29. Soffer, "Authority in the University: Balliol and the New Mythology," in Roy Porter, ed., *Myths of the English* (Oxford, 1992).

30. For a penetrating discussion of the importance of extra-Parliamentary debating societies, see H. C. G. Matthew, "Rhetoric and Politics in Great Britain, 1860–1950," in P. J. Waller, ed., *Politics and Social Change in Modern Britain: Essays Presented to A. F. Thompson* (Brighton, 1987), 34–58.

31. See George Weisz, *The Emergence of Modern Universities in France, 1863–1914* (Princeton, N.J., 1983), 303–8; and K. H. Jarausch, *Students, Society, and Politics in Imperial Germany: The Rise of Academic Illiberalism* (Princeton, N.J., 1982).

32. There were two classes of members: sixteen chosen from those reading in the Honours School of Modern History, and ten elected from those who had taken an honours degree in the School. Three regular meetings were held each term at which one paper would generally be read and discussed. "The Oxford Historical Seminar (Rules)" (Oxford, 1882).

33. Charles Oman, *Memories of Victorian Oxford and of Some Early Years* (London, 1941), 105–6.

34. Tait Papers, Notebooks and Diaries (May 31, 1886).

35. Stubbs Society, Minute Books 2 (1894–98), Mar. 6, 1896, 28–29; May 7, 1897, 56. I found the Minute Books in the Magdalen College rooms of the student president of the Society. The box had passed, unopened, from president to president for at least a decade. They are now in the Bodleian Library.

36. The Stubbs Society Minutes have summaries of papers delivered by undergraduates, graduates, and fellows. Within the colleges, Balliol had its own History Club in the 1880s, and in 1907, it existed again under the leadership of F. F. Urquhart and H. W. C. Davis. Papers of the Balliol History Club, 1907–9, Balliol College Library. The Minute Books of the Brackenbury Society, which included history tutors, students, and future statesmen, are available from 1890 to 1940. F. F. Urquhart was an active member, as were K. N. Bell, T. A. Spring-Rice, B. H. Sumner, and J. R. Balfour. Minute Books, 1890–97, 1902–12, 1913–40. Christ Church College had a historical society, too. There were also the Society for the Study of Social Ethics (renamed the Social Science Club in 1897); the Oxford University Branch of the Christian Social Union; the Cabinet Club; the Edward Lhuyd Society, a Welsh history group; and the Oxford Economic Society. Miscellaneous Papers, 1889–1914, Bodleian Library.

37. Nathaniel Wedd, "Memoirs of the University" (1883?) 68, King's College Library.

38. Rules of the Political Society in the Minute Books 1, 1876–82, MS in Kings College Library.

39. Paul Fredericq, *The Study of History in England and Scotland*, 52, 31.

40. Walter Raleigh to Browning, Feb. 15, 1886, Browning Correspondence. Raleigh was head of the Second Class Honours list in the Tripos.

41. Politics Society Minute Books 2 (Feb. 18, 1884).

42. Politics Society Minute Books 3 (Mar. 5, 1900); 5 (Feb. 10, 1908); 4 (Mar. 7, 1905).

43. Politics Society Minute Books 7 (Mar. 12, 1918). See David Knowles's inaugural lecture in 1954 as Regius Professor of Modern History, *The Historian and Character* (Cambridge, 1955).

44. Politics Society Minute Books 1 (Oct. 25, Nov. 1, 1880; Feb. 13, 1881).

45. Among the other topics addressed between the 1870s and 1930 were the theory of communism; Locke's *Treatises on Civil Government* (London, 1698); the contrast between cabinet and presidential government; the teaching of history in the schools; the merits of literary history, biography, political economy and political science; and increasingly, those questions that appeared in some part of the Tripos examinations, such as the Revolution of 1688, the responsibility of James I for the events of 1640 to 1642, Napoleon, international law, the comparative study of constitutions, world religions, American history, the respective merits of democracy and socialism, tariffs, the future of the Liberal Party, central and eastern Europe, the moral and intellectual condition of the working classes,

the role of art in history, the colonies, the dissolution of the monasteries, St. Francis, classical economics, the Reformation, and Henry Sidgwick's *Elements of Politics* (London, 1891).

46. Politics Society Minute Books 3 (Nov. 22, 1897; Oct. 20, 1902; Oct. 22, Nov. 19, 1906).

47. Politics Society Minute Books 1 (Feb. 7, May 2, Nov. 7, 1881); 2 (Nov. 12, 1883; Oct. 25, 1886; Nov. 23, 1891; Feb. 1, 8, 22, and 29, 1892); 3 (Nov. 13, 1893; Feb. 4, 26, 1894; Feb. 10, Mar. 2, 1896; Nov. 21, 1898; Jan. 30, 1899; Oct. 28, 1901; Jan. 19, Nov. 2, 1903; Feb. 20, 1906).

48. One of the few times Browning's views did not prevail was in 1887. He found himself opposed when he argued that it would have been better if the English Reformation had never taken place. But two weeks later, the same question was put again and this time the vote was equally divided 4 to 4. And, in the debate over the value of studying the Philosophy of History, he voted with the 4 nays against the 5 ayes. Politics Society Minute Books 2 (Feb. 21 and Mar. 1, 1887); 3 (Feb. 1, 1891).

49. Politics Society Minute Books 3 (Oct. 16, 1893; Jan. 25, 1897). But while the economist A. C. Pigou had supported the continuity of a politically oriented Tripos in 1897, as did the future economic historian Clapham, two years later Pigou discussed "education vs. the Historical Tripos" in which he was the sole dissenter to the question of whether the Tripos was an efficient form of education. Minute Books 3 (Oct. 23, 1899).

50. Politics Society Minute Books 2 (Jan. 29, Feb. 26, Mar. 23, Nov. 26, 1883; Feb. 25, Mar. 3, 1884).

51. Politics Society Minute Books 2 (Feb. 18, 1884; Mar. 9, 1885; Nov. 17, 1884).

52. N. Wedd, "Memoirs," 8; L. P. Wilkinson, *A Century of King's, 1875–1972* (Cambridge, 1980), 52.

53. Politics Society Minute Books 2 (Mar. 3, 1884; Feb. 2, 1885); 3 (Mar. 9, 1896); 6 (1912–13).

54. The character of Trinity College, apart from its distinction in science, is revealed by the number of its men who belonged to the most select and most intellectual of all Cambridge societies, the Apostles. The early twentieth-century Trinity Apostles included John Maynard Keynes, Lytton Strachey, Leonard Woolf, Bertrand Russell, R. C. and G. M. Trevelyan, G. E. Moore, and Desmond MacCarthy. Lowes Dickinson and Oscar Browning were also members. Among the Trinity undergraduates were the future George VI, then Prince Albert, from 1919 to 1920, and his younger brother Prince Henry, later Duke of Gloucester. In the 1920s, the Trinity history teachers were the Reverend F. A. Simpson, whose first two volumes of a projected trilogy on Louis Napoleon appeared in 1909 and 1923, D. A. Winstanley, remembered as one of the "outstanding college tutors" of his time; and a young George Kitson Clark. See T. E. B. Howarth, *Cambridge Between Two Wars* (London, 1978), 110–11.

55. See Trinity Historical Society Minute Books 1 (Oct. 22, 1897), 8, in Trinity

College Library, for a paper by the economic historian, the Rev. Dr. William Cunningham, later Archdeacon of Ely, on "The Edict of Diocletian," a "treatment of Capital and Capitalists in the later Roman Empire and drawing a moral with reference to the present day." Both Cunningham and F. W. Maitland took a first in the Moral Sciences Tripos at Trinity in 1872, the year before the Historical Tripos was introduced.

56. R. Vere Laurence, the first Secretary and an important figure in the Society, Trinity Historical Society Minute Books 1 (Jan. 29, 1897), 2.

57. Trinity Historical Society Minute Books 1, 43, 55.

58. W. B. Copeland (the Secretary) in Trinity Historical Society Minute Books 1 (Dec. 4, 1912), 125.

59. Trinity Historical Society, "Rules for the Trinity Historical Society," Minute Books 2 (Oct., 1920).

60. The Chancellor's Prize, founded in 1772, was sometimes awarded for a historical subject. The Arnold Prize, founded in 1850, was awarded alternately to graduates for work in Ancient and Modern History. The Stanhope Prize in Modern History, founded in 1855, was restricted to undergraduates. The Lothian Prize, founded in 1869, was for postgraduate work in foreign history and the Beit Prize, founded in 1908, was for Commonwealth History. When the Lothian was established, the Hebdomadal Council, Oxford University's governing body, did not appoint the Regius Professor as a judge because the University had no power to enforce "any fresh duties on him." Hebdomadal Council Minutes 1 (Nov. 1, 1869), 160. By the 1880s, the Regius Professor was sitting on the Lothian Committee. At All Souls, by the Ordinances of 1858, Fellowships existed for those who had either a first class, a university prize, or a Scholarship in History. In 1883, the Chancellor's Prize went to Hastings Rashdall for his "The Universities of the Middle Ages," published as *The Universities of Europe in the Middle Ages*, 3 vols. (Oxford, 1895). The Arnold Prize winners were A. V. Dicey for *The Privy Council*, 1860 (London, 1887); James Bryce for *The Holy Roman Empire*, 1863 (London, 1864); R. L. Nettleship for "The Normans in Italy and Sicily, A.D. 1070–1270" (date unknown); G. N. Curzon for "Thomas More," 1884; A. F. Pollard for "Somerset the Protector," 1898, published as *England under Protector Somerset* (London, 1900); and J. N. L. Myres for "The Place of the Greek Islands in the Early History of Greek Civilization," 1899. The Stanhope went to Richard Lodge for "Cardinal Beaufort," 1875; C. H. Firth for "The Marquis Wellesley," 1877; Hastings Rashdall for "John Hus," 1879; and W. H. Hutton for "The Political Disturbances which Accompanied the Early Period of the Reformation in Germany," 1881. The Lothian Prize winners were Thomas Raleigh for "The History of the University of Paris from its Foundations to the Council of Constance," 1873; A. L. Smith for *Erasmus*, 1874 (Oxford, 1874); Richard Lodge for "The Causes of Failure of Parliamentary Institutions in Spain and France as Compared with their Success in England," 1876; R. L. Poole for "The Emigration Consequent on the Revocation of the Edict of Nantes," 1879, published as *A History of*

the Huguenots of the Dispersion at the Recall of the Edict of Nantes (London, 1880); A. H. Hardinge for "Queen Christina of Sweden," 1880; W. J. Ashley for *James and Philip Von Artevelde,* 1882 (London, 1883); G. N. Curzon for "Justinian," 1883; Charles Oman for "The Art of War in the Middle Ages to the Close of the 15th Century," 1884, published as *A History of the War: The Middle Ages from the Fourth to the Fourteenth Century* (London, 1898); Edwin Cannan for "The Duke of St. Simon," 1885; A. F. Pollard for *The Jesuits in Poland,* 1892 (Oxford, 1892); H. W. C. Davis for "Benedict XIV," 1897; and C. T. Atkinson for "L'Hôpital," 1899. The Beit Prize was awarded before World War I to Lewis Namier, A. L. Burt, and Harold Laski.

61. The Thirlwall Prize was awarded in alternate years from 1848 for a subject that required original research. In 1883, the Prince Consort Prize was set up for "dissertations involving original research" to be awarded in alternate years beginning in 1885 and open to all graduates of the university under 27 who had not already obtained the Thirlwall. The Seeley Medal was established in 1897 for the winners of the Thirlwall or Prince Consort Prizes writing about international policy. After 1901, there was the Gladstone Memorial Prize, awarded before 1919 on the basis of an undergraduate's performance in the Historical Tripos and after 1919 in connection with the Prince Consort and Thirlwall Prizes. Historians could also compete for the Cobden Prize from 1879 until 1913, when it expired, the Political Economy Prize, given by Alfred Marshall from 1879 until 1891, and the Adam Smith Prize, from 1891. No historian won the Cobden Prize; one, S. M. Leathes, a fellow at Trinity, took the Political Economy Prize in 1887, and another, E. A. Benians, of St. John's, won the Adam Smith Prize in 1906. The only new prizes established by 1930, both by women who could not take a degree until a generation later, were the Ellen McArthur Prize, awarded annually in economic history and the Sara Norton Prize for the best annual essay on the political history of the U.S.

62. Cambridge Prize winners were listed annually in *The Historical Register of the University of Cambridge,* published by Cambridge University Press.

63. Interview with Richard Gutterridge, then librarian at Selwyn College, Cambridge, June 1981; Royal Commission on Oxford and Cambridge, *Report* (1922) 2, 35; interview with Anne Bettencourt, June 1981.

64. Z. N. Brooke, Report to the Faculty Board of History (Jan. 31, 1928).

Chapter 8

1. Mandell Creighton, *History of the Papacy during the Reformation,* vol. 2: *The Council of Basle* (London, 1882), 489; H. H. Henson, *Retrospect of an Unimportant Life,* 5 vols. (Oxford, 1942–50), vol. 1, 56.

2. It might be assumed that first class honours graduates had their pick of the best positions and those with second class honours took the leavings. While true in some instances, it was hardly a general rule. There were so many high-level

jobs to be filled and so relatively few firsts, that it is hardly surprising that second class honours history graduates are also very conspicuous at the top. Some seconds were elevated over firsts for particular kinds of jobs because of college, family, and personal connections, as well as matters of personality and style suited to some positions but not to others. When it seems appropriate, I separate firsts and seconds for analysis, but when looking for trends, continuities, and changes in career patterns over time, it is often revealing to group both classes of honours graduates together.

3. After 1911 those already selected for the Egyptian or Sudan Civil Service stayed at Oxford after graduation for a short course administered by the Appointments Committee. F. B. Hunt and C. E. Escritt, *Historical Notes on the Oxford University Appointments Committee (1892–1950),* 5–6.

4. University of Oxford, *The Historical Register of the University of Oxford, being a Supplement to the Oxford University Calendar with an Alphabetical Record of University Honours and Distinctions Completed to the End of Trinity Term, 1900* (Oxford, 1900).

5. Spenser Wilkinson, the first Chichele Professor of Military History, in his inaugural, *The University and the Study of War* (Oxford, 1909), 25–26.

6. In figures that follow, the first after the year is the total number of B.A.'s, and the second is the number of honours degrees in history. The third figure is the percentage of B.A.'s that were honours degrees in history. At Oxford, 1878, 445, 69, 15; 1879, 522, 68, 13; 1880, 438, 78, 18; 1881, 512, 88, 17; 1882, 513, 99, 19; 1883, 577, 98, 17; 1884, 590, 74, 13; 1885, 522, 68, 13. The comparable Cambridge figures are 1878, 484, 12, 3; 1879, 544, 18, 3; 1880, 569, 5, 1; 1881, 584, 11, 2; 1882, 550, 5, 1; 1883, 634, 10, 2; 1884, ?, 25, ?; 1885, 653, 25, 4. See *Returns from the University of Oxford and Cambridge Commissioners* 51 (1886), 586.

7. "Proposed Instructions for the [History] Board's Representative on the General Board," (1902) and "Tripos Examiners. Proposed New Ordinances" [Draft by Committee. For the Historical Board only] (1909), Board of History and Archaeology, Papers, Seeley Library.

8. University College, London, *Annual Reports*; T. F. Tout, notes, in "The Manchester School of History," University Supplement to the *Manchester Guardian* (1920), *Collected Papers,* vol. 1, 61.

9. There are no figures for the careers of the few London history graduates before 1930, but by 1927 77 Manchester history graduates were teaching in secondary schools, twelve in colleges, three in elementary schools, and eight in universities. Thirty were either training as teachers or had already received their teaching diploma. Four were studying for the Ph.D. and three for the M.A. in history; and one was studying for another profession altogether. Two were in the Indian Civil Service, one in the diplomatic service, and three in social service. Three were in politics, two in religious vocations, two in business, and one each in law, library work, publishing, and private teaching. See F. M. Powicke, "Information about Some of the Honours Graduates, 1920–1927," Powicke Papers,

UAP\2\1; UAP\1\9; UAP\1\10, John Rylands University Library, University of Manchester.

10. The Brackenbury Scholars included the historians T. F. Tout, W. J. Ashley, R. Lodge, Sidney Low, C. H. Firth, F. C. Montague, R. L. Poole, C. R. Beazley, Ramsay Muir, F. M. Powicke, R. G. D. Laffan, K. N. Bell, G. N. Clark, V. H. Galbraith, and the author Hilaire Belloc. F. S. Pulling, later history professor at Leeds, and Arnold Toynbee were included in the honorably mentioned.

11. During the same period, Girton and Newnham Colleges, whose students were not awarded degrees, earned eight firsts.

12. The data represented in Figures 1 to 12 and the discussion of the careers of graduates are derived from the following materials: I. Elliott, ed., *The Balliol College Register, Second Edition, 1833–1933* (Oxford, 1934); E. Lemon, ed., *The Balliol College Register, Fourth Edition, 1916–1967* (Oxford, 1969); King's College, Cambridge, *Annual Report,* 1882–1909, vol. 1 and vol. 2, 1910–on; and Tripos Lists in the *Historical Register of the University of Cambridge to the Year 1910* and the two *Supplements,* 1911–20 and 1921 on. Beginning in 1914, King's *Annual Report* listed only those who passed. In addition, I have supplemented these sources by consulting the British Library Catalogue, obituaries in *The Times,* college and university newspapers, and journals, memoirs, autobiographies, letters, biographies and other manuscript and printed materials contemporary to the time. For a complete listing, see the Sources.

13. Quoted in Thomas Thornely, *Cambridge Memories* (London, 1936), 175.

14. The Balliol delegates were J. H. Morgan, E. Wright, G. D. Knox, T. A. Spring-Rice, F. B. Bourdillon, H. G. Nicolson (who read Modern History, but never took a degree), J. L. Palmer, I. F. Clarke, M. Sadleir, W. H. Shepardson, and H. W. C. Davis. A Kingsman, Charles Seymour, was also at Versailles as an American delegate. He went on to serve on various international commissions, while simultaneously holding the position of Stirling Professor at Yale.

15. From 1914 until 1927, the last year in the 1920s in which top Balliol students figured in the Modern History Honours Examination, 10 Balliol candidates took first class honours and 62 took second class, compared to 15 firsts and 85 seconds from King's in the Historical Tripos Examination from 1914 to 1929. More of these Kingsmen than other candidates reading for honours in different subjects went on to Part II, the more difficult, more demanding examination. Although many students took both Parts I and II, I am counting them only once and assigning them the class they received in Part II since that was considered the more difficult part. I have credited the candidate with whatever he received in history if he took only one part in history and another part in another tripos. Generally, candidates went up to a first class in Part II when they had received only a second class in Part I. Fewer went down a class and some remained consistent. Only one, in 1904, Illytd Hedley, who became manager of an iron works, went from a third in Part I to a first in Part II.

16. Hugh Gaitskell took a first in PPE in 1927. In 1923, five candidates received

firsts, and eighteen obtained seconds; in 1924, 43 Balliol men sat for honours in PPE; 61 in 1925; 66 in 1926; 60 in 1927; 72 in 1928; and 82 in 1929. For a discussion of the origins of PPE, see Norman Chester, *Economics, Politics, and Social Studies in Oxford, 1900–85* (London, 1986).

17. Hancock and Brogan received first class honours in history in 1923 and 1925, respectively. There were no firsts from 1926 through 1929.

18. The categories were compiled from the following career entries: 1. *Public Service*: Civil Service, Indian Civil Service, other Colonial Services, the Diplomatic Service, the Foreign Office, the Cabinet, Parliament, the Privy Council, Prime Ministers, Royal Commissions, City Councils, County Councils, J.P.'s, politics, other public offices not already included, the military, philanthropy, and social reform. If a career is indicated as "military," it was a peacetime occupation since I have omitted wartime service in both World Wars. 2. *Education*: university teachers, educational administrators, schoolmasters, librarians, independent scholars and history coaches. 3. *Writing, editing, and publishing*: journalists, publishers, editors, printers, and writers (including historians, novelists, poets, popular authors, dramatists, biographers, autobiographers, essayists, economists, and epigraphers). 4. *Law*: barristers, solicitors, judges, and American lawyers who studied in Balliol or King's. 5. *Business, finance, commerce and industry*: businessmen, bankers, merchants, directors of companies, and factory owners. 6. *Religion*: Church of England, other denominations, and missionaries. 7. *Miscellaneous*: landowners, architects, farmers, theater directors, conductors, scientists, and medical researchers. I am omitting noncollegiate women and those from women's colleges because they did not receive degrees during most of the years studied.

19. F. D. Ackland took a second in 1897 and began his professional life as an Examiner in the Education Department. Then, from 1905 through the 1930s, he was Assistant Director for Secondary Education in Yorkshire, Cornwall, and Devon. During the same period he moved from Parliamentary Private Secretary to R. B. Haldane to Financial Secretary to the War Office, then to Under-Secretary for Foreign Affairs, Financial Secretary to the Treasury, and Parliamentary Secretary to the Board of Agriculture. The Government Committees he chaired were on accidents in factories, the purchase of timber, forage, and wheat, luxury taxes, dentistry, forestry reconstruction, and public accounts. He was also Chairman of the Dental Board of the United Kingdom, the President of the National Allotments Society, and finally, Chairman of the Education and Housing Committees of the Devon County Council.

20. In 1888, Loch had studied and reported on German Working Men's Colonies; he was a force on the Mansion House Conference on Distress in London in 1893; he sat on the Royal Commission on the Aged Poor from 1893 to 1895, in 1896, and again in 1902; on the Royal Commission on the Care of the Feeble-Minded in 1908; and on the Royal Commission on the Poor Law in 1909. He was also Donkin Lecturer at Manchester College, Oxford, and from 1904 to 1908,

Tooke Professor of Political Economy, King's College, London. In addition, he was Vice-President of the Institut de Sociologie in 1909. His writings include: *An Examination of "General" Booth's Social Scheme* (London, 1890), *Charity Organization* (London, 1890), *Old Age Pensions* (London, 1903), and *Charity and Social Life* (London, 1910).

21. Until after World War I, the Board of History's full title was the Board of History and Archaeology.

22. With a first in modern history in 1884, Burnham entered the army briefly before becoming a barrister. He represented first St. Pancras and then Whitechapel in the London County Council and was a Unionist M.P. for St. Pancras from 1889 to 1892 and then for a variety of other constituencies between 1893 and 1916. He was also president of the Institute of Journalists, Master of the Spectaclemakers' Company, Vice-Chairman of the Labour Resettlement Committee, president of the International Labour Conference in Geneva in 1921, and a member of the Indian Statutory Commission and of the Joint Select Committee on the Government of India. He also sat on the Royal Commission on Civil Establishments, was Mayor of Stepney, the managing proprietor of the Daily Telegraph and president of Birkbeck College, University of London. Jasper More, with a first in Part I in 1928, and a second in Part II in 1929, became a barrister in 1930 and from 1939 to 1943 was in the Ministry of Economic Warfare, the Ministry of Aircraft Production, and was the Legal Officer for the Allied Commission in Italy. In 1955 he became Deputy-Lieutenant for Shropshire, in 1958, a County Councillor for Shropshire, and in 1960, the Conservative M.P. for Ludlow.

23. For a discussion of the clergy, see A. G. L. Haig in "The Church, the Universities and Learning in Later Victorian England," *The Historical Journal* 29, 1 (1986), and *The Victorian Clergy* (London, c. 1984). See, too, John Jones, *Balliol College: A History, 1263–1939* (Oxford, 1988.)

24. Reichel went on to a career in higher education and public service that began with Fellowships at All Souls and Jesus Colleges. He was also the first Principal of the University College of North Wales, and then Vice-Chancellor of the University of Wales, a member of the Mosley Educational Commission to the United States and of the Consultative Committee of the Board of Education. In 1925, he chaired the Royal Commission on University Education in New Zealand and returned to Britain as chairman of the British Universities Bureau. One of the other two who began with another discipline was E. H. Pelham, with a first in mathematics in 1898 and in modern history in 1899, who entered the Board of Education as Private Secretary to W. R. Anson, the Parliamentary Secretary and a Balliol graduate of 1862. Although a Trustee of the Balliol Endowment Fund and a member of the Council of Lady Margaret Hall, he remained with the Board to become Permanent Secretary in 1931. The last of those who began in another discipline was F. H. Underhill, a Canadian, who took a first in English and in modern history in 1914, and eventually became Professor of History at the Universities of Saskatchewan and Toronto.

25. J. C. Chute was another. With a first in mathematics in 1903 and a second in modern history in 1904, he entered the Church of England and followed a career as Assistant Master and Chaplain at Eton. The third was F. B. Bourdillon, with a first in modern languages (French) in 1907, who taught German at University College, Reading, while simultaneously acting as Warden of Wantage Hall, Reading, as Secretary to the Reading Guild of Help, and as Lecturer in Modern Languages at Balliol. After the war, he was part of the British delegation to the Peace Conference at Versailles, served on the Upper Silesian Plebescite Commission, and was secretary to the Irish Boundary Commission and then Secretary of the Institute of International Affairs, University of London.

26. There was a first class in history in 1926 and a second in 1929, but no Balliol man won either a first or second in 1928 and 1929.

27. L. G. E. Jones's supplementary study in education led him to the offices of lecturer and tutor in Oxford University's Department for the Training of Teachers and, from 1937 to 1950, to that of Deputy Director of Education. He also conducted an inquiry into American "Negro Education" in 1927 and wrote about teacher training in England and Wales and about segregated black schools in the American South. The other education diploma for the history class of 1921 went to G. S. Browne in 1922 and took him through a university career in Hawaii, California, British Columbia, and Australia, which culminated at the University of Melbourne, where he was Professor of Education for 22 years and Dean of the Faculty of Education. After retiring in 1956, he became a radio and television commentator on current affairs. The third second-class history graduate in 1921, S. Landreth, took a diploma in theology and served in the Church of England. The fourth that year, G. E. Lavin, was a South African, whose diploma in economics in 1920 may have served him well in his business career with the Aircraft Operating Company (Africa) in Johannesburg, on the Stock Exchange, and as Managing Director of a timber company. The last of the seconds, A. G. A. Stephens in 1924, went to London University for a diploma in education. In 1934, after teaching in several secondary schools, he emigrated to Canada as Headmaster of Upper Canada College, Toronto, and was appointed in 1957 to the Council and Executive Committee of the Canadian Institute of International Affairs. Upon retirement from the college in 1966, he was made Special Adviser to the Upper Canada College Foundation.

28. Geoffrey E. Toulmin, with a first in Part I of history in 1909, received another first in Part II of the Economics Tripos in 1911 and became the manager of an engineering firm.

29. J. McFarlane, who came to King's after winning first class honours at Edinburgh, took a first in Part I and a second in Part II of history before taking a second in Part II of moral sciences. After beginning as lecturer in history in St. David's College, Lampeter, in Wales, he became Lecturer in Geography at Manchester and from 1919 Lecturer and later Reader in Geography at Aberdeen. In 1920, he was elected a President of Section E of the British Association for the

Advancement of Science. The other first, C. C. Michaelides in 1903, also took a second in Part II of moral sciences in 1905 and entered the Consular Service the succeeding year to become, from 1923, Consul-General at Valparaiso. In 1901, G. B. Smith took a first in Part I of history and in 1902, a second in Part II of theology to follow a secular career from schoolmaster to Headmaster of Sedbergh in 1927. A first in the Classics Tripos in 1899 and a first in Part II of history in 1901 took H. O. Meredith to a Professorship in Economics at the Queen's University, Belfast from 1911.

30. Percival Powell, who had taken a second in classics, worked as a schoolmaster and then died in the war. Alfred Ravenscroft Kennedy passed the bar and spent an eminent life in law, which included the office of legal adviser to the Foreign Office. He also represented Preston in Parliament. Those examined in classics were Richard S. Dunford, a master at Eton who died in the war; John Henry Mozley, a lecturer first in Trinity College in the University of Toronto and from 1920, a lecturer in classics at the East London Technical College of the University of London; and Arthur Roscoe, who taught school for one year before meeting his death in the war. Edward J. G. Alford, examined in the Moral Sciences Tripos, became an artist and writer. F. D. Coope took theology, went to Mansfield College and then the University of Chicago, before joining St. Stephen's College (later Bard College), outside New York City, as an assistant professor of philosophy. In 1928, he went to Yale as a research student.

31. Roderick LeMesurier served for 23 years as consul-general in London for the Principality of Monaco, and during that time was also Assistant Secretary for Military Affairs in the War Cabinet. Additionally, he headed a military mission to Brazzaville and practiced as an international lawyer. Paul Mason took a second in modern languages in 1925 a year before his first in history and entered the Foreign Service to be posted to Brussels, Prague, Ottawa, and Lisbon. In 1934, he returned to the Foreign Office as Assistant Private Secretary to the Secretary of State and two years later was Private Secretary to the Parliamentary Under-Secretary of State. Then he was Acting Counselor, Minister at Sofia, Assistant Under-Secretary of State, and Ambassador to the Netherlands, among other offices. He was awarded numerous honours, including the K.C.M.G. and the K.C.V.O. W. H. J. Christie went into the Indian Civil Service in Bengal and Delhi, to become, in turn, Joint Private Secretary to the Viceroy, an adviser in India to the Central Commercial Committee, a well-placed director of British companies in India such as the Commonwealth Development Financial Co., Ltd., and an O.B.E. Ian Melville Stephens returned to England from India in the 1960s where he continued to write and do broadcasts as well as serving on the council of New Hall, Cambridge. Arthur Woods Haslett also worked for the British Medical Association, and finished his professional life as technical adviser to the Nuclear Investment Co., Ltd. Stephen Colby Morland became Deputy Director of Clark, Son and Morland, Ltd., and served on the Somerset County Council from 1931 for at least 33 years. George Norman Black, with a first in history Part I in 1927,

also took a first in Part II of the Law Tripos and was attached to the Post Office and the northeastern Circuit, as well as becoming Recorder of Pontefract. R. E. Balfour died in World War II.

32. W. D. W. Greenham, with a history degree in 1922, and S. H. H. Johnson, with one in 1926, both took seconds in the English Tripos in 1923 and 1926; both went to Cuddesdon Theological College and followed careers in the Anglican Church. (Johnson, after 27 years, converted to Roman Catholicism.) Basil Norman Reckitt with seconds in Part I of both history and English, ran his family firm, Reckitt and Sons, Ltd., and wrote its history and a study of Charles I. He was also Governor of Hymers College, Hull and Deputy Lieutenant for Kingston-upon-Thames and for the East Riding of York. John Francis Swift, with seconds in history, Part I in 1926 and English in 1927, became a businessman in Calcutta, a publisher in London, a hotel proprietor, a philanthropist, and finally, a schoolteacher. B. H. U. L. Townshend, with a second in history in 1926 and a third in English in 1927, became the Assistant Keeper of Printed Books in the British Museum.

33. W. T. Elverston and V. J. U. Hunt became barristers, and Henry Chandler Lewis, J. B. R. Davies, George Corbyn Barrow, and William Moncur Mitchell, solicitors. Davies also became a civil servant who earned an O.B.E., Barrow an Alderman in Birmingham, and Mitchell a bank director. One other, A. M. S. Mackenzie, became a barrister, but until 1939, he was in the theater. After serving in the war, he entered the Foreign Office in 1947.

34. The five were a solicitor, Roger Chitty, who became the chief solicitor of the British Transport Commission; Patrick Kennedy Webster, a paper merchant and then insurance executive who organized the Claims Commission in the Middle East and won an O.B.E.; Edward Birchall, a director of his family's printing and publishing firm and editor of the *Journal of Commerce and Shipping Telegraph*; and two schoolmasters, the Rev. A. D. Reeve and Charles Arthur Lillingston.

35. They were J. B. G. Bullock, the Southern Counties representative to the League of Nations Union; A. E. Tudor-Hart, a medical doctor in the military from 1931 to 1945 and then in private life; Robert Denis Roper, a schoolmaster at Harrow and then at Michaelhouse; and Ranjit Gupta, who went into the Indian Civil Service to advance to the Chief Secretaryship of the West Bengal Government.

36. Philip Paget went to Ely Theological College and ultimately became a rector in Zululand. Cyril John Potter went to Cuddesdon Theological College and became an Anglican priest. He was also tutor and librarian at Chichester College, Vice-Principal of Westcott House, and finally the Senior Lecturer in History, University College, Ibadan, Nigeria.

37. Malcolm Auld Graham took modern languages and became a schoolmaster who was seconded to the War Office during World War II. J. E. H. White took Geography and was Superintendent of Education for the Southern Provinces of

Nigeria; and D. J. B. Joel, later a casualty of World War II, studied agriculture and became a diamond merchant and then Conservative Member for Dudley in Parliament.

38. The King's Politics Society, the Trinity History Society, and the Stubbs Society are discussed in Chapter 7.

39. Another first who studied abroad was J. O. Wardrop. Educated in Germany and France before coming to Balliol, he took the Taylorian Exhibition in Spanish (1888), French (1899), and Italian (1890) before achieving his first in modern history in 1891. After service in the army as an interpreter of Russian, he became Private Secretary to the British Ambassador in Russia, then Vice-Consul first in Kertch and later in Sebastopol, Acting Consul-General in Poland, Rumania, Tunisia, and Haiti, Consul in St. Petersburg and Rumania, Consul-General at Bergen and then Moscow and Strasbourg, as well as representing Britain in the Republic of Georgia. In addition to his career in the foreign and diplomatic service, he was also the Educational Adviser to the City of London College, a scholar in Georgian history and ethnography, and the cataloguer of Georgian manuscripts in the British Museum. One more first class honours graduate who went abroad was G. Collier in 1901, who studied education in Germany and England and after traveling around the world in 1903, taught modern history as an acting professor at Sydney University, Australia, and returned to England as a Worker's Education Association lecturer and as a tutor at Birmingham. D. C. Rusk, the fourth of the firsts to study abroad, went on to the University of Jena, entered the Presbyterian church, was Acting Professor of History at Madras Christian College, India, and returned to Oxford as Chaplain to Presbyterian members of the university.

40. The third second, J. H. Morgan, came to Balliol from the University of Berlin and passed from A. L. Smith's guidance in 1900 to University Extension lecturing and Toynbee Hall, while on the literary staff of the *Daily Chronicle*. Then he became a leader writer for the *Manchester Guardian* before choosing an academic life as Professor of Constitutional Law and Legal History at University College, London, where he became Rhodes Lecturer in 1913 and a professor the following year. In 1915 he became a barrister, served in the war as an officer, and in 1918 was the Vice-President of the Inquiry into German War Atrocities. With the rank of Brigadier-General, he attended the Peace Conference at Versailles, and sat on the Prisoners of War Commission. In 1926, he returned to civilian life as the Reader in Constitutional History at the Inns of Court. Throughout his working life, he published widely on social policy, the House of Lords, constitutionalism, the new Irish constitution, and political biography, and wrote his memoirs of military life. The fourth, T. K. H. Rae, received his degree in 1911, became an assistant master at Marlborough College, studied in Germany for one year, and was killed in the war. The fifth, M. C. W. Waidyakorn, Prince Varnvaidya, son of the Prince of Siam, prepared for the Siamese Diplomatic Service by attending Marlborough College and then earning a laureate at the École des Sciences Poli-

tiques before taking his history honours degree at Balliol in 1914. After earning international recognition for his leadership in the League of Nations and the World Court, he resigned from his diplomatic activities in the 1930s and became the Head of the English Department at Chulongkorn University in Bangkok.

41. Stringfellow Barr, best known for *The Will of Zeus: A History of Greece from the Origins of Greek Culture to the Death of Alexander* (Philadelphia, 1961) and *The Mask of Jove: A History of Graeco-Roman Civilization from the Death of Alexander to the Death of Constantine* (Philadelphia, 1966), also wrote *Mazzini: Portrait of an Exile* (New York, 1935), *The Pilgrimage of Western Man* (New York, 1949), and *The Three Worlds of Man* (Columbia, Mo., 1963), and some wonderful academic novels, including *Purely Academic* (New York, 1958). Gleb Petrovich Struve was on the staff of *La Russie* and the assistant editor of *Le Monde Slave* in Paris and lectured at the University of California in Berkeley and at Harvard. He wrote *Twenty-five Years of Russian Literature 1918–34* (London, 1944). In addition to Barr and Struve, there were nine seconds from Australia, six from Canada, three from India, one more from the United States, and one each from New Zealand, Capetown, and the Transvaal.

42. *Annual Reports of the Oxford Appointments Committee, 1906–1914.*

43. Among the ten solely in business, nine kept the same job for their peacetime working lives. (In what follows, the first number in parenthesis is the date of Part I of the history honours examination and the second is the date of Part II.) Paul Brewis Redmayne (1920, 1921) worked for Cadbury Brothers, and Douglas Powell (1921, 1922) was a ship broker. Roger Hutchinson (1922, 1923) was director and chairman of his family's flour mills, while Edward Birchall worked in his family's firm, Charles Birchall and Sons, Ltd., printers, publishers, and proprietors of *The Journal of Commerce and Shipping Telegraph*, which he edited and directed. P. A. P. Rathbone (1924, 1925) described his career simply as "business." M. V. W. Goodbody (1925, 1926) was a joint managing director of a firm of metal merchants, and Robert Lindsay Corry (1925, 1926) was with a London shipowning company. R. I. L. Bentley (1926), the third of the nine to join a family business, was managing director and chairman of Isaac Bentley and Co. Ltd., a firm involved in the lubricating oil and grease industry. P. H. B. Learoyd (1926) worked for Burmah-Shell Oil. The last of these seconds, Frank Joseph Ward (1924, 1925), served in the First World War and worked for a Sheffield firm of shipmantlers before entering King's. After receiving his degree, he established shops in London and Brighton to sell books and pictures.

44. Other examples of King's graduates who combined business and public service include Ralph Mirrielees Cazalet (1923, 1924) who joined the Shell Oil Co. in Egypt and Sudan in 1925 and remained with them for the next twenty years until he entered the Board of Trade in 1945 and the Foreign Office seven years later. He was also part of the United Kingdom delegation to the Organization for European Economic Cooperation. Patrick Kennedy Webster (1924, 1925) worked as a paper merchant and as a partner in an insurance firm, as well as organizing

the Claims Commission in the Middle East during World War II. D. J. B. Joel (Part I, History, 1924; Agriculture, 1926) was a diamond merchant who became Conservative M. P. for Dudley and was killed during the war. I. H. D. Rolleston (Part I, Modern Languages, 1923; Part II, History, 1924) was in business for two years before entering the Crown Colonies Colonial Service. He was killed in Zanzibar in 1936 while attempting to quell an Arab riot. Michael Macaulay Bruce (Part I, Economics, 1926; Part II, History, 1927) worked for Unilever, but he was also Secretary of the London Council of Social Service, a regional training officer for London's civil defense, in the Ministry of Education, and the Administrative officer for the National Coal Board in the Yorkshire division.

45. Gerald L. M. Clauson, "Some Uses of Statistics in Colonial Administration," *Transactions of the Manchester Statistical Society*, Jan. 15, 1937. In 1935, a separate Economic Department of the Colonial Office was finally established. Even more important, perhaps, the General Department of the Colonial Office included for the first time "finance" and "economic questions" among the subjects in its entrance examinations. D. J. Morgan, *The Official History of Colonial Development*, vol. 1: *The Origins of British Aid Policy, 1924–1945* (London, 1980), 2.

Epilogue

1. Lord Curzon of Kedleston, *Principles and Methods of University Reform* (Oxford, 1909), 46.

2. See Standish Meacham, *Toynbee Hall and Social Reform, 1880–1914: The Search for Community* (New Haven, Conn., 1987), 17.

3. Gillian Sutherland argues, with persuasive evidence, that from the late nineteenth to at least the mid-twentieth century, the funding and selection for secondary education were determined by the patronage of local elite groups acting upon cultural and social, rather than intellectual, concepts of merit. It is Sutherland's conclusion that because the English educational establishment, with its various levels, was already in control, they had no need for standardized tests to classify children. When mental measurement was used, it was in support of existing elite structures and methods of selection. See her *Ability, Merit and Measurement: Mental Testing and English Education, 1880–1940* (Oxford, 1984).

4. J. R. MacDonald, "Oxford and Democracy," *Labour Leader* 27 (Nov. 1906): 757. See the discussion in Meacham, *Toynbee Hall and Social Reform, 1880–1914*, 185.

5. J. M. Lee, "The British Civil Service and the War Economy: Bureaucratic Conceptions of 'The Lessons in History' in 1918 and 1945," *Transactions of the Royal Historical Society* (London, 1980), 191, 189.

6. See, for example, *Report of the University Grants Committee* (Feb. 3, 1921), 10, discussed in Sheldon Rothblatt, *Tradition and Change in English Liberal Education: An Essay in History and Culture* (London, 1976), 190–93.

Sources

Archival Materials

OXFORD UNIVERSITY

Bodleian Library. University and faculty papers, the minutes and memoranda issued by tutors, professors, faculties, governing bodies, colleges, and students, including boards of faculty minutes of meetings; records of examination questions; written examiners' reports; correspondence about grading, standards, curriculum, teaching, and examinations; and minutes of discussions about the awarding of degrees to particular candidates are in the University of Oxford, Board of the Faculty of Arts (Modern History), Minute Books and other papers; the Modern History Association, Miscellaneous Papers, 1889–1914; Reports of Examiners in the School of Modern History, 1905–12. The *Oxford University Gazette*, printed annually, contains some of these papers. See also the Hebdomadal Council Minutes.

Worcester College. The History Tutors' Association, Minute Books, 1877–1929, are in the possession of the current secretary of the History Faculty. (They were in the care of Harry Pitt at Worcester College, when I saw them in 1982.)

Historical Registers. The Historical Register of the University of Oxford, being a Supplement to the Oxford University Calendar with an Alphabetical Record of University Honours and Distinctions Completed to the End of Trinity Term, 1900 (Oxford, 1900) and *Supplement to The Historical Register of the University of Oxford 1900 Including an Alphabetical Record of University Honours and Distinctions for the Years 1901–1930* (Oxford, 1934) give a complete list of professors, readers, and lecturers. I. Elliott, ed., *The Balliol College Register, Second Edition, 1833–1933* (Oxford, 1934) and E. Lemon, ed., *The Balliol College Register, Fourth Edition, 1916–67* (Oxford, 1969).

Bibliography. E. H. Cordeaux and D. H. Merry, *A Bibliography of Printed Works Relating to the University of Oxford* (Oxford, 1958). (This should be supplemented by the bibliographical listings in the various volumes of *The History of Oxford University* [Oxford] as they appear.)

CAMBRIDGE UNIVERSITY

Seeley Library. The Faculty Board of History Minutes, the History Tripos Examiners' Book, 1889–1910, Printed Reports of various Syndicates, and the Economic History Society Minute Books, beginning with vol. 1, 1926–37.

Cambridge University Library. J. A. Venn, *Alumni Cantabrigienses. A Bibliographical List of All Known Students, Graduates, and Holders of Office at the University of Cambridge from the Earliest Times to 1900*, 6 vols. (Cambridge, 1922–54) can be useful, but it is incomplete and often unreliable. The *Historical Register of the University of Cambridge to the Year 1910* and the two *Supplements*, covering 1911–20 and 1921 on, are far more complete. A list of Tripos candidates and the class they achieved in the honours examination, as well as reading lists and set topics for the Tripos examinations, are given in *The Cambridge University Reporter*. The *Reporter* and *The Student's Handbook to the University and Colleges of Cambridge* were printed annually.

King's College. Annual Report 1 (1882–1909) and 2 (1910 on) contain detailed and thorough accounts of graduates' subsequent careers.

THE HISTORICAL ASSOCIATION

The Historical Association was formed in 1906 to bring together university and secondary school teachers of history throughout the country and to print tracts, bibliographies, and proceedings of annual meetings in which both tutors and professors participated. See *Historical Association Leaflets*, nos. 1–49. The Association's papers are located in its London offices.

REPORTS OF GOVERNMENT INQUIRIES

These contain relevant testimony and reveal national expectations. See especially *Report of Her Majesty's Commissioners to Investigate Cambridge* (London, 1852); *Select Committee on Higher Education* (London, 1867); Henry Bradshaw, ed., *Statutes for the University of Cambridge and for the Colleges within it, Made, Published, and Approved (1878–1882) under the Universities of Oxford and Cambridge Act, 1877* (Cambridge, 1883); *Returns from the University of Oxford and Cambridge Commissioners* (London, 1886); *Royal Commission on Secondary Education* (The Bryce Commission), 9 vols. (London, 1895); *Report of the Royal Commission on the Civil Service* (London, 1917); *Report of the Royal Commission on Oxford and Cambridge Universities and the Appendices* (London, 1922). See also the resulting *Universities of Oxford and Cambridge Act* (London, 1923).

Unpublished Papers

OXFORD AND CAMBRIDGE HISTORIANS

Cambridge. Oscar Browning Papers and J. P. Whitney's manuscripts in King's College; H. W. Gwatkin Papers, Emmanuel College; the Lord Acton MSS., including the Acton and Creighton Correspondence, the University Library; the *Cambridge Medieval History* papers and the J. R. Tanner Notebooks and lecture notes in St. John's College; and the Robert Calverley Trevelyan Papers in Trinity College.

Oxford. Charles Boase Papers, in Exeter College; the papers of James Bryce, M. E. G. Finch-Hatton, C. H. Firth, the Oxford Historical Society, William Stubbs, and A. W. Watson, all in the Bodleian Library; H. A. L. Fisher's papers in the New Bodleian Library; A. L. Smith's papers, and some of Richard Lodge's and H. W. C. Davis's papers in Balliol College.

London. J. R. Green's papers and the Acton and W. E. Gladstone letters in the British Library; A. F. Pollard's papers and letters, 1894–1930 and the J. R. Seeley papers in the Paleography Room of the University of London Senate House Library; and the G. W. Prothero Papers in the Royal Historical Society in University College.

Manchester. F. M. Powicke's letters and papers in the John Rylands University Library, the University of Manchester; James Tait's and T. F. Tout's Papers in the John Rylands Library, Oxford Road.

Reading. The Longmans' Papers in the University of Reading.

Newcastle. Sir George Otto Trevelyan Papers in the University of Newcastle-upon-Tyne.

STUDENT SOCIETY PAPERS

Oxford. In the Bodleian Library, the Stubbs Society Minutes; Minutes of the Society for the Study of Social Ethics (renamed the Social Science Club in 1897); of the Oxford University Branch of the Christian Social Union; of the Cabinet Club; of the Social and Political Studies Association; of the Edward Lhuyd Society; and Miscellaneous Papers, 1889–1914, of the Oxford Economic Society. Papers of the Balliol History Club, 1907–9; and the Minute Books of the Brackenbury Society, 1890–1940, in the Balliol College Library.

Cambridge. The King's Politics Society Minute Books in King's College Library; the Trinity History Society Minute Books in Trinity College Library.

MISCELLANEOUS PAPERS ABOUT OXFORD AND CAMBRIDGE

Oxford (unless otherwise noted, the papers are in the Bodleian Library)
Barker, Ernest, "On the Need for the Redistribution of the Work Prescribed for the School of Modern History" (c. 1908).

Firth, C. H., "Honours in History" [Observations on the Standards of the Modern History School, 1893–1902] (1903), "Memorandum on the Proper State of the Study of Modern History and on University Reform in General" (1907), "On the Desirability of Diminishing the Work Set for the Modern History School, and in Particular the Amount of Early Constitutional History" (1908), "The Principle of the M.A. Statute" (1909), "Memorandum for the Electors of the Beit Professorship of Colonial History" (1914), "Advanced Studies." Modern History (1919).

Freeman, E. A., "The Proposed Degrees of Doctor in Letters and in Natural Sciences" (1887).

Holland, T. E., et al., "Ford's Professorship of English History" (1893).

Jenkinson, A. J., and six others, "The Statute as to the Previous Examination in Modern History" [Arguments against the statute] (1913).

Johnson, A., "Faculty of Arts. Honour School of Modern History" [historical account] (1900).

"The Oxford Historical Seminar (Rules)" (1882).

Penson, T. H., "A Plea for Greater Recognition of Economics in Oxford" (1920).

Price, L. L., "The Present Position of Economic Study in Oxford: A Letter to the Vice-Chancellor of the University" (1902).

"Proposed Scheme for a First Public Examination in History" (1885).

"Reply to Professor Vaughan's Strictures on the Third Report of the Oxford Tutors' Association, by One of the Committee" (1854).

"Report of the Committee [of the Hebdomadal Council on the Proposed Degree in Economics]" (1915).

Reports of the Oxford Tutors' Association: 1. "Recommendations Responding to the Extension of the University, Adopted by the Tutors' Association" (1853); 2. "Recommendations Respecting the Constitution of the University of Oxford" (1853).

Robertson, C. Grant, H. W. C. Davis, and E. Barker, "We venture to address" [Considerations in favour of the amended statute for a previous examination in modern history] (1913).

Cambridge (unless otherwise noted, the papers are in the Seeley Library)

Association for the Consideration of University Questions, Memorandum 1. *Coordination of the Teaching of the University and the Colleges* (1904).

"Notes on the Development of the Historical Tripos 1875–1932" [unsigned and undated typescript].

Reddaway, W. F., *Cambridge in 1891* (1943).

Report of the Syndicate Appointed May 27, 1875 by the University of Cambridge, to Consider the Requirements of the University in Different Departments of Study, with Appendices (1876).

Report to the Board of History and Archaeology. Cambridge University Reform (1909).

Wedd, Nathaniel, "Memoirs of the University" [typescript] (King's College Library) (1883?).

Whitney, J. P., *Sir George Walter Prothero as a Historian* (King's College Library) (1922).

Published Works

THE REGIUS PROFESSORS AT OXFORD

Arnold, Thomas, "Inaugural" (1841) in *Introductory Lectures on Modern History* (New York, 1884).

Davis, H. W. C., *A History of Balliol College* (London, 1899), a schoolbook on *Charlemagne* (London, 1899), *England under the Normans and Angevins* (London, 1905), reprinted in ten editions by 1930, a Home University Library volume on *Medieval Europe* (London, 1911), and a revision of Stubbs's *Select Charters* (Oxford, 1913). During World War I he produced, with other Oxford teachers, *Why We Are at War: Great Britain's Case . . . with an Appendix of Original Documents, Including the Authorized English Translation of the White Book* (Oxford, 1914) and wrote, on his own, *The Political Thought of Heinrich von Treitschke* (London, 1914), *The Retreat from Mons* (Oxford, 1914), *What Europe Owes to Belgium* (Oxford, 1914), *The Battle of the Marne and Aisne* (Oxford, 1914), and *The Battle of Ypres-Armentiers* (Oxford, 1915). After the war he emerged as a modern historian and gave the Ford Lectures in 1926 on *The Age of Grey and Peel* (New York, 1964). *The Study of History* [an inaugural lecture delivered before the University of Oxford on Nov. 4, 1925] (Oxford, 1925) was reprinted in *Henry William Carliss Davis, 1874–1928, a Memoir . . . and a Selection of His Historical Papers*, ed. by J. R. H. Weaver and A. L. Poole (London, 1933).

Firth, C. H., *Cromwell's Army: A History of the English Soldier during the Civil Wars, the Commonwealth, and the Protectorate* [the Ford Lectures delivered at Oxford, 1900–1901] (London, 1902), *The Last Years of the Protectorate, 1656–58* 2 vols. (London, 1909), *A Plea for the Historical Teaching of History* (Oxford, 1904) [The *Plea*, the tutor's *Letter*, and Firth's *Reply* are collected in *An Historic Controversy, 1904–5* (Oxford, 1905)], "Burnet as an Historian," Introduction to T. E. S. Clarke and H. C. Foxcroft, *A Life of Gilbert Burnet* (Cambridge, 1907), in Godfrey Davies, ed., *Essays Historical and Literary* (Oxford, 1938), *Memorandum on the Organization of Advanced Historical Training in Oxford* (Oxford, 1908), *The Faculties and Their Powers: A Contribution to the History of University Organization* (Oxford, 1909), *The House of Lords during the Civil War* (London, 1910), "The Study of Modern History in Great Britain," *Proceedings of the British Academy* 6 (1913), *Modern History in Oxford, 1841–1918* (Oxford, 1920), his famous *Commentary on Macaulay's History of England* (London, 1938), and a schoolbook on *Oliver Cromwell and the Role of the Puritans in England* (London, 1900).

Freeman, E. A., "Historical Study at Oxford," *Bentley's Quarterly Review* 1 (1859), "Froude's *Reign of Elizabeth*," *The Saturday Review* (Jan. 16, 1864): 17, *Comparative Politics* (London, 1873), *History of the Norman Conquest: Its Causes and Results* (Oxford, 1867–79), "The Office of the Historical Professor," in *The Methods of Historical Study: Eight Lectures Read in the University of Oxford in Michaelmas Term, 1884* (London, 1886), "Oxford after Forty Years," *Contemporary Review* 51 (1887), *William the Conqueror* (London, 1888); and R. W. Stephens, *Life and Letters of Edward A. Freeman,* 2 vols. (London, 1895).

Froude, J. A., *The Nemesis of Faith* (London, 1849), "Suggestions on the Best Means of Teaching English History," in *Oxford Essays: Contributed by Members of the University* (1855) (London, 1855–58), *History of England from the Fall of Wolsey to the Death of Elizabeth* (London, 1858–1870), *The Science of History: A Lecture Delivered at the Royal Institution* (1864) (London, 1886), *Worthies* (London, 1874), "Inaugural Lecture," *Longman's Magazine* 2 (Dec. 1892): 158, *Oceana, or England and her Colonies* (London, 1886), *History of the Brocas Family* (London, 1886), *The Cinque Ports* (London, 1888), *Erasmus* (London, 1894), *English Seamen* (London, 1895), and *The Council of Trent* (London, 1896).

Powell, F. Y., *The Corpus Poeticum Boreale* (London, 1881), "Inaugural Lecture," *Oxford Chronicle* (May 1, 1895), reprinted in a condensed version in *The Academy* 1201 (May 11, 1895), "The Ecole des Chartes and English Records," *Proceedings of the Royal Historical Society* 11 (London, 1897), *The Study of History in Universities: An Address* (Bangor, 1902), *Origines Islandicae* (London, 1905); Powell's obituary, *Oxford Magazine* (May 18, 1904); and O. Elton, *Frederick York Powell: A Life and A Selection from Letters and Occasional Writings,* 2 vols. (Oxford, 1906).

Powicke, F. M., *The Loss of Normandy (1189–1204): Studies in the History of the Angevin Empire* (Manchester, 1913), *Bismarck and the Origin of the German Empire* (London, 1914), *Stephen Langton* [the Ford Lectures for 1927] (Oxford, 1928), *Christian Life in the Middle Ages and Other Essays* (Oxford, 1935), *History, Freedom, and Religion* [the Riddell Memorial Lecture] (Oxford, 1938), *The Reformation in England* (London, 1941), *King Henry II and the Lord Edward,* 2 vols. (Oxford, 1947), *The Thirteenth Century, 1216–1307* (Oxford, 1935) for the Oxford History of England, which he edited together with G. N. Clark and C. R. Cruttwell, "The School of Modern History," *Oxford Magazine* 48, 52 (1930), *Historical Study in Oxford* [an inaugural lecture, 1929] (Oxford, 1929), "Three Cambridge Scholars: C. W. Previté-Orton, Z. N. Brooke, and G. G. Coulton," and "After Fifty Years" (1944) in *Modern Historians and the Study of History,* ed. by F. M. Powicke (London, 1955).

Smith, Goldwin, *The Reorganization of the University of Oxford* (Oxford, 1868), *Lectures on Modern History Delivered in Oxford, 1859–61* (London, 1861), *Three English Statesmen; a Course of Lectures on the Political History of England* (New York and London, 1867), and *Reminiscences,* ed. by A. Haultrain (New York, 1910).

Stubbs, William, *Registrum Sacrum Anglicanum* (Oxford, 1858), *Itinerarium Regis Ricardi* (London, 1864–65), *Prefaces and notes to the Rolls Series: Charters and Documents Illustrative of English History* (Oxford, 1870–1901), *Councils and Ecclesiastical Documents Relating to Great Britain and Ireland,* ed. with W. Hadden (Oxford, 1869–78), *Select Charters and other Illustrations of English Constitutional History from the Earliest Times to the Reign of Edward I* (Oxford, 1870), *The Constitutional History of England* (Oxford, 1874–78), *The Early Plantagenets* (London, 1886), *Seventeen Lectures on the Study of Medieval and Modern History and Kindred Subjects* (Oxford, 1900), *Historical Introduction to the Rolls Series,* ed. A. Hassall (London, 1902); *Letters of William Stubbs, Bishop of Oxford, 1825–1901,* ed. by W. H. Hutton (London, 1904), and *Germany in the Later Middle Ages,* ed. by A. Hassall (London, 1908).

THE CHICHELE PROFESSORS OF HISTORY AT OXFORD

Burrows, Montagu, *Pass and Class* (Oxford, 1860), *Inaugural Lecture* [on the foundation of the Chichele Professorship of Modern History] (Oxford, 1868), *Antiquarianism and History: A Lecture Delivered before the University of Oxford, May 26, 1884* (Oxford, 1885), and *Autobiography,* ed. by Stephen Montagu Burrows (London, 1908).

Oman, C., *Warwick the Kingmaker* (London, 1891), "Inaugural Lecture on the Study of History," in *Lectures on the Study of History* (Oxford, 1906), "History at Oxford," in *On the Writing of History* (New York, 1939), and *Memories of Victorian Oxford and of Some Early Years* (London, 1941).

OTHER OXFORD HISTORIANS TEACHING AND WRITING HISTORY

Ashley, W. J., "Modern History," in A. M. M. Stedman, ed., *Oxford, Its Life and Schools* (London, 1887), "The Study of History at Oxford," *The Nation* 60, 1554 (1895), *Surveys, Historic, and Economic* (New York, 1966), *The Faculty of Commerce in the University of Birmingham: Its Purposes and Programme* (Birmingham, n.d. [1906]), *The Calendar of the University of Birmingham,* (1902–3), and the essays by Ashley, C. H. K. Marten, R. L. Poole, and W. H. Woodward in W. A. J. Archbold, ed., *Essays on the Teaching of History* (Cambridge, 1901).

Barker, Ernest, H. W. C. Davis, C. R. L. Fletcher, Arthur Hassall, L. G. Wickham Legg, and Frank Morgan, *Why We Are at War* (Oxford, 1914), and *Age and Youth* (Oxford, 1953).

Boase, Charles, *A History of England Principally in the Seventeenth Century* (Oxford, 1875), translation of vol. 1 of Leopold von Ranke, *Geschichte von England,* 8 vols.

Bosanquet, B., and 75 others, *Presented to the Oxford University Commission, December 6, 1880 [Memorial concerning the Commission's proposals for the future regulation of the professoriate]* (Oxford, 1880).

Brodrick, George D. (completed and revised by J. K. Frotheringham), *The History of England from Addington's Administration to the Close of William IV's Reign (1801–1837)* (London, 1906).

Bryce, James, "The Historical Aspects of Democracy," *Essays on Reform* (London, 1867), "A Few Words on the Oxford University Bill," *Fortnightly Review* 25 (1876), *Studies in History and Jurisprudence* (Oxford, 1901), *The Relations of the Advanced and the Backward Races of Mankind* [Romanes Lecture, 1902] (Oxford, 1902), "E. A. Freeman," and "John Richard Green," in his *Studies in Contemporary Biography* (London, 1923), "On the Teaching of History in Schools," Historical Association Leaflet No. 4 (London, 1907), *The Hindrances to Good Citizenship* (New Haven, Conn., 1909), "On the Writing and Teaching of History," Commencement Address as Chancellor of Union College, Schenectady (1911), in his *University and Historical Addresses* (New York, 1913), *Presidential Address* [to the International Congress of Historical Sciences, London, 1913] (London, 1913), *Race Sentiment as a Factor in History* [Creighton Memorial Lecture, 1914–15] (London, 1915), Appendix to *Report of the Committee on Alleged German Outrages* (London, 1915), and *Essays and Addresses in War Time* (New York, 1918).

Cruttwell, C. R. M. F., *A History of the Great War, 1914–1918* (Oxford, 1934).

Egerton, H. E., *A Short History of British Colonial Policy, 1606–1909* (London, 1897).

Fisher, H. A. L., *Methods of Historical Study* (Oxford, 1892), "Modern Historians and Their Methods," *Fortnightly Review* 62 (1894), "Lord Acton's Lectures," *Independent Review* 11 (1906), ed., *The Collected Papers of F. W. Maitland* (Cambridge, 1911), *The Place of the Universities in National Life* (Oxford, 1919), *Studies in History and Politics* (Oxford, 1920), *James Bryce* (New York, 1927), *Our Universities* [Centenary Oration] (London, 1927), *Pages from the Past* (New York, 1939), and *An Unfinished Autobiography* (Oxford, 1940).

Fletcher, C. R. L., with Rudyard Kipling, *A School History of England* (Oxford, 1911) and *The Great War, 1914–1918: A Brief Sketch* (London, 1920).

Galbraith, V. H., "Diplomatic," *Oxford Magazine* 49 (1930).

Green, J. R., "Professor Stubbs's Inaugural Lecture," *Saturday Review* 22 (March 2, 1867): 592, "Oxford as It Is," (1870), in his *Oxford Studies* (London, 1901).

Hammond, B., *William Lovett* (London, 1922).

Hammond, J. L., *Charles James Fox* (London, 1903), *C. P. Scott* (London, 1934), and *Gladstone and the Irish Nation* (London, 1938). In collaboration with M. R. D. Foot, Hammond also wrote *Gladstone and Liberalism* (London, 1952), and with L. T. Hobhouse, *Lord Hobhouse: A Memoir* (London, 1905).

Hammond, J. L., and B. Hammond, *The Village Labourer* (London, 1911), *The Town Labourer, 1760–1832* (London, 1917), *The Skilled Labourer, 1760–1832* (London, 1919), *Lord Shaftesbury*, 2nd ed. (London, 1923), *The Rise of Modern Industry* (London, 1925), *The Age of the Chartists, 1832–1854: A Study of Discontent* (London, 1930), *James Stansfeld: A Champion of Sex Equality* (London, 1932), and *The Bleak Age* (London, 1934).

Henson, H. H., *Wartime Sermons* (London, 1915) and *Retrospect of an Unimportant Life*, 5 vols. (Oxford, 1942–50).

Hunt, William, *The History of England from the Accession of George II to the Close of Pitt's First Administration (1760–1801)* (London, 1924).

Lee, Sidney, "Goldwin Smith," *Twentieth Century Dictionary of National Biography* (Oxford, 1975).

Marriott, J. A. R., *Oxford and its Place in National History* (Oxford, 1907), *Second Chambers* (Oxford, 1910), and *Memories of Fourscore Years* (London, 1946).

Marten, C. H. K., *On the Teaching of History* (Oxford, 1938).

Medley, D. J., *A Student's Manual of English Constitutional History* (Oxford, 1894) and *The Educational Value of a Study of History: An Inaugural Lecture* (Glasgow, 1899).

Muir, R., *The School of Modern History: A Letter upon the Working of the School* (Oxford, 1914).

Myres, J. L. N., *The Provision of Historical Studies at Oxford Surveyed in a Letter to the President of the American Historical Association on the Occasion of its Meeting in California, 1915* (Oxford, 1915).

"The New History School," [signed Teacher] *Oxford Magazine* 4 (1886): 12.

"Oxford Professors and Oxford Tutors: Reply of the Examiners in the School of Modern History," [to J. Thorold Rogers's "Oxford Professors and Oxford Tutors"] *Contemporary Review* 57 (1890).

"The Oxford School of Historians," *The Church Quarterly Review* 59 (Oct. 1904).

Owen, S. J., *India on the Eve of the British Conquest: An Historical Sketch* (London, 1872).

Palmer, R., *Suggestions with Regard to Certain Proposed Alterations in Oxford* (Oxford, 1854).

Poole, R. L., "The Teaching of Paleography and Diplomatic," in W. A. J. Archbold, ed., *Essays on the Teaching of History* (Cambridge, 1901) and *Illustrations of the History of Medieval Thought in the Department of Theology and Ecclesiastical Politics* (London, 1881).

Rait, R. S., ed., *Memorials of Albert Venn Dicey* [letters and diaries] (London, 1925).

Rashdall, Hastings, *The Universities of Europe in the Middle Ages*, 3 vols. (Oxford, 1895) and "The Functions of a University in a Commercial Centre," *The Economic Review* 12 (Jan. 1902).

Robertson, C. G., *Select Cases, Statutes, and Documents to Illustrate English Constitutional History, 1660–1832* (London, 1904), *England under the Hanoverians* (London, 1911), *Bismarck* (London, 1918), *History and Citizenship*, [Creighton Lecture, Nov. 24, 1927] (Oxford, 1928), *Religion and the Totalitarian State* (London, 1937), *Chatham and the British Empire* (London, 1946), and *Bolingbroke* (London, 1947).

Round, J. H., *Feudal England: Historical Studies on the Eleventh and Twelfth Centuries* (1895) (London, 1964), *Peerage and Pedigree*, 2 vols. (Baltimore, 1910), and *Family Origins and Other Studies*, ed. and with a Memoir and Bibliography by William Page (London, 1947).

Smith, A. L., "The New History School," *Oxford Magazine* 4 (1886), "The Teaching of Modern History," in Christopher Cookson, ed., *Essays on Secondary Education* (Oxford, 1898), *Frederick William Maitland: Two Lectures and a Bibliography* (Oxford, 1908), "Historical Fatalism" [address to the 11th Annual Meeting of the Historical Association] (Jan. 12, 1917), and *Notes on Stubbs's Select Charters and Other Illustrations of English Constitutional History to 1307*, ed. by L. G. E. Jones (Oxford, 1925).

Southern, Richard, *The Shape and Substance of Academic History* (Oxford, 1961).

Taylor, A. J. P., *A Personal History* (London, 1983).

Tout, T. F., "The Future of Victoria University" (1902), "Schools of History" (1906), "The Manchester School of History," University Supplement to the *Manchester Guardian* (1920), review of vol. 5 of the *Cambridge Medieval History*, in the *English Historical Review* 42 (1927), "Sir A. W. Ward," *Proceedings of the British Academy* 11 (1924), in *Collected Papers of Thomas Frederick Tout, with a Memoir and Bibliography*, vol. 1 (Manchester, 1932–34).

Wakeman, H. O., and A. Hassall, eds., *Essays Introductory to the Study of Constitutional History by Resident Members of the University* (Oxford) (London, 1891, reprinted 1901).

Wilkinson, Spenser, *The University and the Study of War* (Oxford, 1909).

Woodward, E. L., *Short Journey (An Autobiography)* (London, 1942).

THE REGIUS PROFESSORS AT CAMBRIDGE

Acton, (Lord), *Letters of Lord Acton to Mary, Daughter of the Right Hon. W. E. Gladstone, with an Introductory Memoir by Herbert Paul* (London, 1904), *Lectures on Modern History* (London, 1906), *Historical Essays and Studies* (London, 1907), *The History of Freedom and Other Essays* (London, 1909), *Lectures on the French Revolution*, ed. J. Figgis and R. Vere Laurence (London, 1920), *Essays on Freedom and Power* (Boston, 1948), *Essays on Church and State*, ed. D. Woodruff (London, 1952), *Essays in the Liberal Interpretation of History*, ed. by W. H. McNeill (Chicago, 1967), and *The Correspondence of Lord Acton and Richard Simpson*, ed. J. Altholz and D. McElrath (Cambridge, 1971–1975).

Bury, J. B., "Anima Naturaliter Pagana: A Quest of the Imagination," *Fortnightly Review*, new ser., 41 (1891), *A History of Greece to the Death of Alexander the Great* (London, 1900), "The Science of History" (1903), in *Selected Essays of J. B. Bury*, ed. by H. W. V. Temperley (Cambridge, 1930), *The Ancient Greek Historians* [the Lane Lectures at Harvard, 1908] (New York, 1958), *History of the Freedom of Thought* (London, 1913), "Cleopatra's Nose," *R.P.A. Annual and Ethical Review for 1916*, "Theism," *R.P.A. Annual and Ethical Review for 1920*, "A Lost Caesarea," *Cambridge Historical Journal* 1 (1923), *The Idea of Progress: An Inquiry into its Growth and Origin* (New York, 1955), and *The Life of St. Patrick and His Place in History* (New York, 1971).

Seeley, J. R., *Ecce Homo* (London, 1865), *Lectures and Essays* (London, 1870), *Life and Times of Stein, or Germany and Prussia in the Napoleonic Age*, 3 vols. (New

Sources

285

York, 1968), "The Teaching of History," in G. Stanley Hall, ed., *Methods of Teaching History*, vol. 1, 2d. ed. (Boston, 1885), "The English Revolution of the 19th Century," 1, 2, 3, *Macmillan's Magazine* (Aug., Sept., Oct., 1870), *A Midland University: An Address* (Birmingham, 1877), *The Expansion of England* (London, 1894), *An Introduction to Political Science: Two Series of Lectures* (London, 1908), and *The Growth of British Policy: An Historical Essay*, 2 vols., 2d. ed. 1897 (Frankfurt, 1962).

Trevelyan, G. M., "The Latest View of History," *Independent Review* (Dec., 1903), *Clio, a Muse and Other Essays Literary and Pedestrian* (London, 1913), *A History of England* (London, 1926), *The Present Position of History* (Cambridge, 1927), *England under Queen Anne*, 3 vols. (London, 1930–34), *Sir George Otto Trevelyan: A Memoir* (London, 1932), *The English Revolution, 1688–1689* (Oxford, 1938), *Trinity College: An Historical Sketch* (Cambridge, 1946), and *An Autobiography and Other Essays* (London, 1949).

PROFESSOR OF MODERN HISTORY

Temperley, H. W. V., the first Professor of Modern History at Cambridge, began his tenure in 1930. See his *Life of Canning* (London, 1905), *Senates and Upper Chambers: Their Use and Function in the Modern State, with a Chapter on the Reform of the House of Lords* (London, 1910), "Introductory Essay on the Earlier History of Hungary," in H. Marczali, *Hungary in the Eighteenth Century* (Cambridge, 1910), "The Relations of England with Spanish America, 1720–1744," in American Historical Association, *Annual Report* (1911) (Washington, 1913), *Frederic the Great and Kaiser Joseph: An Episode of War and Diplomacy in the Eighteenth Century* (London, 1915), *History of Serbia* (London, 1917), *The German Treaty* (London, 1919), ed., *A History of the Peace Conference of Paris* (London, 1920–24), *The Second Year of the League: A Study of the Second Assembly of the League of Nations* (London, 1922), *The Foreign Policy of Canning, 1822–1827: England, the Neo-Holy Alliance and the New World* (London, 1925), *The Unpublished Diary and Political Sketches of Princess Lieven, Together with Some of Her Letters*, ed. with elucidations by H. W. V. Temperley (London, 1925), ed. with G. P. Gooch, *British Documents on the Origins of the War, 1898–1914* (London, 1926–38), *The Victorian Age in Politics, War and Diplomacy* (Cambridge, 1928), *Foreign Historical Novels* (London, 1929), *Selected Essays* (London, 1930), *Research and Modern History* [inaugural lecture in 1930] (London, 1930), with Lillian M. Penson, *Short Bibliography of Modern European History, (1789–1935)* (London, 1936), *England and the Near East: The Crimea* (London, 1936), and with Lillian M. Penson, *A Century of Diplomatic Blue Books, 1814–1914* (Cambridge, 1938).

OTHER CAMBRIDGE HISTORIANS TEACHING AND WRITING HISTORY

Balfour, R. E., "History," in H. Wright, ed., *Cambridge University Studies, 1933* (London, 1933).

Browning, Oscar, *A Short History of Education,* a reprint of the article "Education," from the ninth edition of the *Encyclopedia Britannica* (New York, 1881), *An Introduction to the History of Educational Theories* (New York, 1882), *The Citizen: His Rights and Responsibilities* (London, 1893?), "The Flight of Louis XVI to Varennes: A Criticism of Carlyle," *Transactions of the Royal Historical Society* 3 (1886), *Napoleon: The First Phase* (London, 1905), *History of the Modern World, 1815–1910,* 2 vols. (London, 1912), *A General History of the World* (London, 1913), *A Short History of Italy, 375–1915* (London, 1917), *Memories of Sixty Years* (London, 1910), and *Memories of Later Years* (London, 1923).

Butterfield, Herbert, *The Whig Interpretation of History* (London, 1931), and "Delays and Paradoxes in the Development of Historiography," in K. Bourne and D. C. Watt, eds., *Studies in International History* (London, 1967).

Clapham, J. H., *The Causes of the War of 1792* (Cambridge, 1899), *The Woolen and Worsted Industries* (London, 1907), "Of Empty Economics Boxes," *Economic Journal* 17 (Sept. 1907), *An Economic History of Modern Britain* (Cambridge, 1926–38), *The Bank of England* (Cambridge, 1945), and *Report of the Committee on the Provision for Social and Economic Research* (London, 1946).

Clark, G. Kitson, "The Origin of the Cambridge Modern History," *The Cambridge Historical Journal* 8, 2 (1945).

Coulton, G. G., *Fourscore Years* (Cambridge, 1943), and "Obituary of Gwatkin," *The Eagle* [St. John's College magazine] (Dec. 1917).

Crawley, Charles, *Trinity Hall: The History of a Cambridge College, 1350–1975* (Cambridge, 1976).

Creighton, Mandell, *History of the Papacy during the Reformation,* vol. 2: *The Council of Basle* (London, 1882), *Historical Essays and Reviews* (London, 1902), and *Historical Lectures and Addresses,* ed. by Louise Creighton, 2 vols. (London, 1902 and 1903).

Glover, T. R., *Cambridge Retrospect* (Cambridge, 1943).

Hammond, B. E., "The Historical Tripos," *A Student's Guide to the University of Cambridge* (Cambridge, 1877).

Knowles, David, *The Historian and Character* [inaugural address, 1954, as Professor of Medieval History] (Cambridge, 1955).

Maitland, F. W., *Why the History of English Law Is Not Written: Inaugural Lecture,* Oct. 13, 1888 (London, 1888), "Materials for English Legal History" (1889), and "The Gild Merchant" (1891), in *Collected Papers of Frederick W. Maitland,* vol. 2, "The Body Politic" (c. 1899) and "Lord Acton" (1902) in vol. 3, ed. by H. A. L. Fisher (Cambridge, 1911), *Domesday Book and Beyond: Three Essays in the Early History of England* (Cambridge, 1897), *Township and Borough* (Cambridge, 1898), "History of English Law" (1902) and "English Law, 1307–1600," in *Selected Historical Essays of F. W. Maitland* (Boston, 1962), *Roman Canon Law in the Churches of England* (London, 1898), (together with F. Pollock) *History of English Law before Edward I* (Cambridge, 1895), "William Stubbs, Bishop of Oxford," *English Historical Review* 16 (1901), et al., *Essays on the Teaching of History* (Cambridge, 1901), *The Constitutional History of England:*

A Course of Lectures (Cambridge, 1908), and *The Letters of F. W. Maitland,* ed. by C. H. S. Fifoot (Cambridge, Mass., 1965).

Prothero, G. W., *Life of Simon de Montfort* (London, 1877), an edition of Voltaire's *Siècle de Louis XIV* (Cambridge, 1879–82), a translation of the first volume of Leopold von Ranke's *Universal History: The Oldest Historical Group of Nations and the Greeks* (London, 1884), "The Historical Tripos," *A Student's Guide to the University of Cambridge,* 5th. ed. (Cambridge, 1892), the *Life of Henry Bradshaw, University Librarian* (London, 1888), *Select Statutes and Other Documents Illustrative of the Reigns of Elizabeth and James I* (Oxford, 1894), *Why Should We Learn History?* [an inaugural address delivered at Edinburgh, Oct. 16, 1894] (Edinburgh, 1894), "A Liberal Education: The Function of a University" [an address before the University of Edinburgh at the graduation ceremony, Apr. 11, 1896], in *Scottish Review* (Oct. 1896), "Mandell Creighton," *Quarterly Review* (April 1901), *Historical Societies in Great Britain* (Washington, 1911), and *The American Historical Association,* The Historical Association Leaflet 27 (Jan. 1912).

Raleigh, Walter, *The Meaning of a University. An Inaugural Address . . . Aberystwith October 20, 1911* (Oxford, 1911).

Seaton, A. A., *The Theory of Toleration under the Later Stuarts* (Cambridge, 1911).

Simpson, F. A., *The Rise of Louis Napoleon* (London, 1909), and *Louis Napoleon and the Recovery of France* (London, 1951).

Tanner, J. R., *English Constitutional Conflicts of the Seventeenth Century, 1603–1689* (1928) (Cambridge, 1961).

Thorneley, Thomas, *Cambridge Memories* (London, 1936).

Ward, A. W., *Suggestions towards the Establishment of a History Tripos* (Cambridge, 1872), and *Germany, 1815–1890,* 3 vols. (Cambridge, 1916–18).

OTHER WRITING ON HISTORY AND THE BRITISH UNIVERSITIES
BEFORE 1930

Amery, L. S., *My Political Life,* vol. 1: *England Before the Storm, 1896–1914* (London, 1953).

Aydelotte, Frank, *The Oxford Stamp and other Essays: Articles from the Educational Creed of an American Oxonian* (1917) (Freeport, 1967).

Barker, Ernest, *Political Thought of Plato and Aristotle* (London, 1906), *Greek Political Theory: Plato and his Predecessors* (London, 1918), and his inaugural address as the first Professor of Political Science at Cambridge, *The Study of Political Science and its Relation to Cognate Studies* (Cambridge, 1928).

Biggar, H. P., "On the Establishment of a Graduate School at Oxford," *The University Review* (May 1906).

Board of Education, *Handbook of Suggestions for the Consideration of Teachers and Others Concerned in the Work of Public Elementary Schools* (London, 1929).

Bruce, W. N., *Circular on the Teaching of History in the Secondary Schools* no. 599 (1908), reprinted as Appendix 4 to the Board of Education, *Report on the Teaching of History* (London, 1923).

Buckle, H. T., *History of Civilization in England* (London, 1858–61).

The Cambridge Modern History, an Account of Its Origin, Authorship and Production (Cambridge, 1907).

Cambridge University Association, *Report of the Meeting Held at Devonshire House . . . January 31, 1899 to Inaugurate the Association* (Cambridge, 1899), and *Statement of the Needs of the University* (Cambridge, 1899–1902).

Cornford, F. M., *Microcosmographia Academica: Being a Guide for the Young Academic Politician* (London, 1908).

Courtney, W. L., "Oxford Tutors and their Professorial Critic" [Thorold Rogers], *Fortnightly Review* 53, n.s. (Feb. 1890).

Curzon of Kedleston, *Principles and Methods of University Reform* (Oxford, 1909).

A Don [pseudonym], "University Organization," *Fraser's Magazine* 77 (Feb. 1868).

Fay, C. R., *King's College, Cambridge* (London, 1907).

Fowler, T., "On Examinations," *Fortnightly Review* 111, n.s. (March 1876).

Fredericq, Paul, *The Study of History in England and Scotland* (Baltimore, 1887).

Gladstone, W. E., "On the Place of Homer in Classical Education and in Historical Inquiry," *Oxford Essays* (London, 1857), *Studies on Homer and the Homeric Age*, 3 vols. (Oxford, 1858), *Juventus Mundi: The Gods and Men of the Heroic Age* (London, 1869), and "Universities Hominium; or the Unity of History," *North American Review* 145 (1887).

Haldane, R. B., "The Meaning of Truth in History" [Creighton Lecture delivered to the University of London, 1914], in *The Conduct of Life and Other Addresses* (New York, 1915).

Herbert, Aubernon, ed., *The Sacrifice of Education to Examinations: Letters from All Sorts and Conditions of Men* (London, 1888).

Latham, Henry, *On the Action of Examinations Considered as a Means of Selection* (Cambridge, 1877).

Lewis, George Cornewall, *An Essay on the Influence of Authority in Matters of Opinion* (London, 1849).

Luard, H. R., *Suggestions on: 1. The Election of the Council, 2. The Duties of the Vice-Chancellor, 3. The Establishment of a Historical Tripos* (Cambridge, 1866).

Lyttelton, Arthur Temple, *The Influence of National History on National Literature* (London, 1883).

MacDonald, J. R., "Oxford and Democracy," *Labour Leader* 27 (Nov. 1906).

Madeley, Helen M., *History as a School for Citizenship* (Oxford, 1920).

Mallet, C. E., *A History of the University of Oxford*, 3 vols. (London, 1924–27).

Miller, Edward, *Portrait of a College: A History of the College of St. John the Evangelist, Cambridge* (Cambridge, 1961).

Newman, J. H., *The Idea of a University* (New York, 1959).

Oxford and the Nation [by some Oxford tutors]. Reprinted from the *Times* (London, 1907).

Sources   289

"Oxford Professors and Oxford Tutors: Reply of the Examiners in the School of
   Modern History," *Contemporary Review* 57 (Feb. 1890).
Pattison, Mark, *Suggestions for Academical Reform* (Edinburgh, 1868), and *Mem-
   oirs* (Brighton, 1969).
Pollock, Frederick, *An Introduction to the History of the Science of Politics* (London, 1890), and "Oxford Scholars and Historians," *Cornhill Magazine* 74 (Jan.
   1933).
Pollock, John, *Time's Chariot* (London, 1950).
"Protest Against Examinations," [signed by 424 academics and intellectuals, including seventeen university tutors and professors of history] *Nineteenth Century* 24 (Nov. 1888).
Reports Adopted by the Oxford Tutors' Association: 3. *Recommendations Respecting the Relation of the Professorial and Tutorial Systems, 1853* (Oxford, 1853)
   and 4. *Recommendations Respecting College Statutes and the Alterations Required in Colleges, March 1854* (London, 1854).
Rogers, J. Thorold, *Education in Oxford: Its Methods, Its Aids and Its Rewards*
   (London, 1861), "Oxford Professors and Oxford Tutors," *Contemporary Review* 56 (Dec. 1889), "The Four Oxford History Lectures [A Reply]," *Contemporary Review* 57 (1890).
Somervell, R., *"Modern History": Teaching and Organisation with Special Reference to Secondary Schools: A Manual of Practice*, ed. by P. A. Barnett (London, 1897).
Stewart, J. A., *Oxford after the War and a Liberal Education* (Oxford, 1919).
N. T. [pseudonym], "Teaching at Oxford. 1. The Universities and the Colleges.
   2. The School of Litterae Humaniores," *Oxford Magazine* 1 (May 16 and June 6,
   1883).
"University Reform. 5. What Are We to Do with Our Professors?," *Oxford Magazine* 27 (June 10, 1909).
Vaughan, H. H., *Oxford Reform and the Oxford Professors: A Reply to Certain
   Objections Urged against the Report of the Queen's Commissioners [With post-
   script]* (London, 1854).
Vinogradoff, Paul, "Teaching and Learning in Oxford," *The Morning Post*
   (May 26, 1909).
Whewell, William, *On the Principles of English University Education* (London,
   1837), and *Of a Liberal Education in General; and with Particular Reference to
   the Leading Studies of the University of Cambridge* (London, 1845).
Zimmern, A. E., *The Greek Commonwealth* (Oxford, 1911).

BIOGRAPHIES AND BIOGRAPHICAL ESSAYS

Anstruther, Ian, *Oscar Browning: A Biography* (London, 1983).
Ashley, Anne, *William James Ashley; a Life with a Chapter by J. H. Muirhead and
   a Foreword by Stanley Baldwin* (London, 1932).

Baynes, Norman H., *A Bibliography of the Works of J. B. Bury, Compiled with a Memoir by Norman H. Baynes* (Cambridge, 1929).

Brentano, Robert, "The Sound of Stubbs," The *Journal of British Studies* 6, 2 (May 1967).

Briggs, Asa, "G. M. Trevelyan: The Uses of Social History," in *The Collected Essays of Asa Briggs*, vol. 2: *Images, Problems, Standpoints, Forecasts* (Brighton, 1985).

Chadwick, Owen, *Westcott and the University* [The Bishop Westcott Memorial Lecture, 1962] (Cambridge, 1962), *Freedom and the Historian* (*Inaugural Lecture*) (Cambridge, 1969), *Acton and Gladstone* [Creighton Lecture, 1975] (London, 1976), *Hensley Henson: A Study in the Friction between Church and State* (Oxford, 1983), and "Acton and Butterfield" [Butterfield Memorial Lecture], *Journal of Ecclesiastical History* 38, 3 (July 1987).

Colley, Linda, *Lewis Namier* (New York, 1989).

Crawley, Charles W. "Sir George Prothero and His Circle" [Prothero Lecture, July 12, 1969], in *Transactions of the Royal Historical Society* 5th ser., 20 (1970).

Creighton, L., *Life and Letters of Mandell Creighton, D. D.*, 2 vols. (London, 1906).

Dunn, W. H., *James Anthony Froude: A Biography*, 2 vols. (Oxford, 1961).

Elton, Geoffrey, *F. W. Maitland* (London, 1985).

Elton, O., *Frederick York Powell: A Life and a Selection from Letters and Occasional Writings*, 2 vols. (Oxford, 1906).

Eyck, Frank, *G. P. Gooch: A Study in History and Politics* (London, 1982).

Fair, John D., "The Peacemaking Exploits of Harold Temperley in the Balkans, 1918–1921," *Seer* 67, 1 (Jan. 1989).

Fifoot, C. H. S., *Frederick William Maitland, A Life* (Cambridge, Mass., 1971).

Geison, Gerald L., *Michael Foster and the Cambridge School of Physiology: The Scientific Enterprise in Late Victorian Society* (Princeton, N.J., 1978).

Hartley, H., "Successors to Jowett," supplement to H. W. C. Davis, *A History of Balliol College* (Oxford, 1963).

Himmelfarb, Gertrude, *Lord Acton: A Study in Conscience and Politics* (Chicago, 1952).

Kadish, Alon, *Apostle Arnold: The Life and Death of Arnold Toynbee, 1852–1883* (Durham, N.C., 1986).

Matthew, David, *Acton: The Formative Years* (London, 1946).

McNeill, William H., *Arnold J. Toynbee: A Life* (Oxford, 1989).

Montague, F. C., *Arnold Toynbee* (Baltimore, 1889).

Moorman, Mary, *George Macaulay Trevelyan: A Memoir by His Daughter* (London, 1980).

Namier, Julia, *Lewis Namier: A Biography* (London, 1971).

Paul, Herbert, *The Life of Froude* (London, 1905).

Porter, Roy, *Gibbon: Making History* (New York, 1988).

Report on the Correspondence and Papers of Oscar Browning (1837–1923), Historian and Educational Reformer, 1853–1913, at King's College, Cambridge. Listed by Royal Commission on Historical Manuscripts (London, 1978).

Seton-Watson, Hugh and Christopher, *The Making of a New Europe: R. W. Seton-Watson and the Last Years of Austria-Hungary* (Washington, 1981).

Shannon, Richard, "John Richard Seeley and the Idea of a National Church," in R. Robson, ed., *Ideas and Institutions of Victorian Britain* (New York, 1967).

Skidelsky, Robert, *John Maynard Keynes,* vol. 1: *Hopes Betrayed, 1883–1920* (London, 1983).

Smith, M. F., *Arthur Lionel Smith, Master of Balliol, 1916–24; a Biography and Some Reminiscences, by his Wife* (London, 1928).

Sparrow, J., *Mark Pattison and the Idea of a University* [The Clark Lectures, 1965] (Cambridge, 1965).

Stephen, Leslie, *Letters of John Richard Green* (London, 1901).

Terrill, R., *R. H. Tawney and His Times* (Cambridge, Mass., 1973).

Todhunter, Isaac, *William Whewell, D.D., Master of Trinity College, Cambridge: An Account of his Writings,* 2 vols. (London, 1876).

Weaver, J. R. H., and A. L. Poole, ed., *Henry William Carless Davis, 1874–1928, a Memoir and A Selection of His Historical Papers* (London, 1933).

Withers, H. L., *The Teaching of History and Other Papers,* ed., with Biographical Introduction and a Selection from his Letters, by J. H. Fowler (Manchester, 1904).

Wormell, Deborah, *Sir John Seeley and the Uses of History* (Cambridge, 1980).

Wortham, H. E., *Victorian Eton and Cambridge: Being the Life and Times of Oscar Browning* (London, 1956).

RECENT WRITING ON THE RELATIONSHIP BETWEEN THE DEVELOPMENT OF UNIVERSITIES AND INTELLECTUAL LIFE IN NINETEENTH- AND EARLY TWENTIETH-CENTURY BRITAIN

Anderson, R. D., *Education and Opportunity in Victorian Scotland* (Oxford, 1983).

Annan, Noel, "The Victorian Intelligentsia," in J. H. Plumb, ed., *Studies in Social History: A Tribute to G. M. Trevelyan* (London, 1955), *Leslie Stephen: the Godless Victorian* (London, 1984), and *Our Age: English Intellectuals between the World Wars—A Group Portrait* (New York, 1990).

Ashby, Erich, and Mary Anderson, *The Rise of the Student Estate in Britain* (Cambridge, Mass., 1970).

Armytage, W. H. G., *Civic Universities: Aspects of a British Tradition* (London, 1955).

Barker, Ernest, "Universities in Great Britain," in Kotsching, W. M., and E. Prys, eds., *Universities in a Changing World* (Oxford, 1932).

Bender, Thomas, ed., *The University and the City* (Oxford, 1988).

Bill, E. G. W., *University Reform in Nineteenth-Century Oxford: A Study of Henry Halford Vaughan, 1811–1885* (Oxford, 1973).

Brooke, C. N. L., *A History of Gonville and Caius College* (Woodbridge, 1985), and *A History of the University of Cambridge,* vol. 4: *1870–1990* (Cambridge, 1993).

Buxton, J., and P. Williams, *New College, Oxford, 1379–1979* (Oxford, 1979).

Cecil, Hugh, *Conservatism* (London, 1912).

Chester, Norman, *Economics, Politics, and Social Studies in Oxford, 1900–1985* (London, 1986).

Clark, G. Kitson, *The Making of Victorian England* (London, 1962).

Clauson, Gerald L. M., "Some Uses of Statistics in Colonial Administration," *Transactions of the Manchester Statistical Society* (Jan. 15, 1937).

Collini, Stefan, "The Idea of 'Character' in Victorian Political Thought," *Transactions of the Royal Historical Society* 35, ser. 5, (1985), and *Public Moralists: Political Thought and Intellectual Life in Britain, 1850–1930* (Oxford, 1991).

Constantine, Stephen, *The Making of British Colonial Development Policy, 1914–1940* (London, 1984).

Dale, P. A., *The Victorian Critic and the Idea of History: Carlyle, Arnold, and Pater* (Cambridge, Mass., 1977).

Dunbabin, John, "Oxford and Cambridge Finances, 1871–1913," *Economic History Review* 28 (1975).

Engel, Arthur, "Political Education in Oxford, 1823–1914," *History of Education Quarterly* 20 (Fall 1980), "The English Universities and Professional Education" in K. H. Jarausch, *The Transformation of Higher Learning, 1860–1930: Expansion, Diversification, Social Opening, and Professionalization in England, Germany, Russia, and the United States* (Chicago, 1983), and *From Clergyman to Don: The Rise of the Academic Profession in Nineteenth-Century Oxford* (Oxford, 1983).

Garland, Martha, *Cambridge before Darwin: The Ideal of a Liberal Education, 1800–1860* (Cambridge, 1980).

Grainger, J. H., *Patriotisms: Britain, 1900–1939* (London, 1986).

Guttsman, W. L., *The British Political Elite* (London, 1963).

Haig, A. G. L., *The Victorian Clergy* (London, c. 1984), and "The Church, the Universities and Learning in Later Victorian England," *The Historical Journal* 29, 1 (1986).

Harte, Negley, *The University of London, 1836–1986* (London, 1986).

Harvie, Christopher, *The Lights of Liberalism: University Liberals and the Challenge of Democracy, 1860–1886* (London, 1976).

Heyck, T. W., *The Transformation of Intellectual Life in Victorian England* (New York, 1982), and "The Idea of a University, 1870–1970," *The History of European Ideas* 8, 2 (1987).

Hollis, C., *The Oxford Union* (London, 1965).

Howarth, T. E. B., *Cambridge Between Two Wars* (London, 1978).

Huelin, G., *King's College, London, 1828–1978* (London, 1978).

Jones, John, *Balliol College: A History, 1263–1939* (Oxford, 1988).

Jones, Raymond A., *The Nineteenth-Century Foreign Office: An Administrative History* (London, 1971), and *The British Diplomatic Service, 1815–1914* (Waterloo, Ont., 1983).

Lowe, Roy, "The Expansion of Higher Education in England," in Jarausch, K. H., ed., *The Transformation of Higher Learning, 1860–1930: Expansion, Diversifi-*

cation, Social Opening, and Professionalization in England, Germany, Russia, and the United States (Chicago, 1983).

MacKenzie, John M., Propaganda and Empire: The Manipulation of British Public Opinion, 1880–1960 (Manchester, 1984).

Matthew, H. C. G., "Rhetoric and Politics in Great Britain, 1860–1950," in P. J. Waller, ed., Politics and Social Change in Modern Britain: Essays Presented to A. F. Thompson (Brighton, 1987).

McCulloch, Gary, Philosophers and Kings: Education for Leadership in Modern England (Cambridge, 1991).

Meacham, Standish, Toynbee Hall and Social Reform, 1880–1914: The Search for Community (New Haven, Conn., 1987).

Mejia, Arthur, and J. A. Thompson, eds., Edwardian Conservatism: Five Studies in Adaptation (London, 1988).

Miller, Edward, Portrait of a College: A History of the College of St. John the Evangelist, Cambridge (Cambridge, 1961).

Morgan, D. J., The Official History of Colonial Development, vol. 1: The Origins of British Aid Policy, 1924–1945 (London, 1980).

Newsome, David, Godliness and Good Learning: Four Studies on a Victorian Ideal (London, 1961).

O'Gorman, F., British Conservatism: Conservative Thought from Burke to Thatcher (London, 1986).

Pellew, Jill, The Home Office, 1848–1914: From Clerks to Bureaucrats (Rutherford, N.J., 1982).

Prest, John, ed., "Jowett's Correspondence on Education with Earl Russell in 1867," in Supplement to the Balliol College Record (Oxford, 1965), Balliol Studies (London, 1982), and with E. V. Quinn, Dear Miss Nightingale: A Selection of Benjamin Jowett's Letters, 1860–1893 (Oxford, 1987).

Reader, K. M., The Civil Service Commission, 1855–1975 (London, 1981).

Roach, John, "Victorian Universities and the National Intelligentsia," Victorian Studies 2, 2 (1959), Public Examinations in England, 1850–1914 (Cambridge, 1971), A History of Secondary Education in England, 1800–1870 (London, 1986), and Secondary Education in England, 1870–1902: Public Activity and Private Enterprise (London, 1991).

Rose, Jonathan, The Edwardian Temperament, 1895–1919 (Athens, Ohio, 1986).

Rothblatt, Sheldon, The Revolution of the Dons [with a new preface] (Cambridge, 1981), "The Student Sub-Culture and the Examination System in Early 19th Century Oxbridge," in Lawrence Stone, ed., The University and Society 1: Oxford and Cambridge from the 14th to the Early 19th Century (Princeton, N.J., 1974), Tradition and Change in Liberal Education: An Essay in History and Culture (London, 1976), "Failure in Early Nineteenth-Century Oxford and Cambridge," History of Education 2, 1 (1982), "The Diversification of Higher Education in England," in Jarausch, K. H., ed., The Transformation of Higher Learning, 1860–1930: Expansion, Diversification, Social Opening, and Profession-

alization in England, Germany, Russia, and the United States (Chicago, 1983), "Historical and Comparative Remarks on the Federal Principle in Higher Education," *History of Education* 16, 3 (1987), and "The Idea of the Idea of a University and Its Antithesis," Seminar on the Sociology of Culture, La Trobe University, Bundoora, Victoria, Australia, 1989.

Sanderson, Michael, ed., *Universities in the Nineteenth Century* (London, 1975).

Simpson, Renata, *How the Ph.D. Came to Britain: A Century of Struggle for Postgraduate Education* (Guilford, 1983).

"Some Memories: Interview with Professor Philip Gierson, Who Retired in 1978," *The Caian*, The Annual Record of Gonville and Caius College, Cambridge (Nov. 1978).

Sutherland, Gillian, *Ability, Merit and Measurement: Mental Testing and English Education, 1880–1940* (Oxford, 1984).

Sviedrys, Romualdas, "The Rise of Physics Laboratories in Britain," *Historical Studies in the Physical Sciences* 7 (1976).

Symonds, Richard, *Oxford and Empire: The Last Lost Cause?* (London, 1986).

Taylor, A. J., "History at Leeds, 1877–1974: The Evolution of a Discipline," *Northern History* 10 (1975).

Wilkinson, L. P., *A Century of King's, 1873–1972* (Cambridge, 1980), and *Kingsmen of a Century, 1873–1972* (Cambridge, 1981).

Wilkinson, R., *Gentlemanly Power: British Leadership and the Public School Tradition: A Comparative Study in the Making of Rulers* (Oxford, 1964).

Winstanley, D. A., *Later Victorian Cambridge* (Cambridge, 1947).

Winter, J. M., *The Great War and the British People* (London, 1986), and "Oxford and the First World War" in Harrison, Brian, ed., *The History of Oxford University*, vol. 8, (Oxford, forthcoming).

RECENT WRITINGS ON HISTORIANS AND THE STUDY OF HISTORY

Blaas, P. B. M., *Continuity and Anachronism: Parliamentary and Constitutional Development in Whig Historiography and the Anti-Whig Reaction between 1890 and 1930* (The Hague, 1978).

Burrow, J. W., "The English Tradition of Liberal Education," *Historical Education Quarterly* 20 (1980), *A Liberal Descent: Victorian Historians and the English Past* (Cambridge, 1981), *Whigs and Liberals: Continuity and Change in English Political Thought* [The Carlyle Lectures, 1985] (Oxford, 1988), "Victorian Historians and the Royal Historical Society," *Transactions of the Royal Historical Society*, 5th ser., 39 (London, 1989), and with Stefan Collini and Donald Winch, *That Noble Science of Politics: A Study in Nineteenth-Century Intellectual History* (Cambridge, 1983).

Chancellor, Valerie, *History for Their Masters: Opinion in the English History Textbook, 1800–1914* (New York, 1970).

Cline, Catherine Ann, "British Historians and the Treaty of Versailles," *Albion* 20, 1 (1988).

Cox, C. B., and A. E. Dyson, eds., *The Twentieth Century Mind: History, Ideas, and Literature in Britain*, vol. 1: *1900–1918* (Oxford, 1972).

Forbes, Duncan, *The Liberal Anglican Idea of History* (Cambridge, 1952).

Goldstein, Doris S., "J. B. Bury's Philosophy of History: A Reappraisal," *American Historical Review* 82 (1977), "The Organizational Development of the British Historical Profession, 1884–1921," *Bulletin of the Institute of Historical Research* 55, 132 (Nov. 1982), "The Professionalization of History in Britain in the Late Nineteenth and Early Twentieth Centuries," *Storia della Storiografia* 1 (1983), and "The Origins and Early Years of the *English Historical Review*," *The English Historical Review* 101 (Jan. 1986).

Humphries, R. A., *The Royal Historical Society, 1868–1968* (London, 1969).

Hunt, F. B., and C. E. Escritt, *Historical Notes on the Oxford University Appointments Committee (1892–1950)* (Oxford, 1950).

Jann, Rosemary, "From Amateur to Professional: The Case of the Oxbridge Historians," *Journal of British Studies* 22, 2 (1983), and *The Art and Science of Victorian History* (Columbus, Ohio, 1986).

Kenyon, John, *The History Men* (London, 1983).

Lee, J. M., "The British Civil Service and the War Economy: Bureaucratic Conceptions of 'The Lessons in History' in 1918 and 1945," *Transactions of the Royal Historical Society* (London, 1980).

Lee, P. L., and John Wilkes, "History at the Universities: the Consumer's View, 1: Oxford History," *History* 55 (Oct., 1970).

Levine, Philippa, *The Amateur and the Professional: Antiquarians, Historians, and Archaeologists in Victorian England, 1838–1886* (Cambridge, 1986).

Lineham, Peter, "The Making of the Cambridge Medieval History," *Speculum* 57, 3 (1982).

Madden, F., "The Commonwealth, Commonwealth History, and Oxford, 1905–1971," in F. Madden and D. K. Fieldhouse, eds., *Oxford and the Idea of Commonwealth: Essays Presented to Sir Edgar Williams* (London, 1982).

McLachlan, Jean, "The Origins and Early Development of the Cambridge Historical Tripos," *The Cambridge Historical Journal* 9 (1947).

Milne, A. T., *Centenary Guide to the Publications of the Royal Historical Society, 1868–1968 and of the Former Camden Society, 1838–1897* (London, 1968).

Owen, Dorothy, "The Chichele Professorship of Modern History, 1862" *Bulletin of the Institute of Historical Research* 34, 90 (Nov. 1961).

Parker, Christopher, *The English Historical Tradition since 1850* (Edinburgh, 1990).

Rees, Goronwy, *A Chapter of Accidents* (London, 1972).

Schlatter, R., ed., *Recent Views on British History: Essays on Historical Writing since 1966* (New Brunswick, N.J., 1984).

Slee, Peter, *Learning and a Liberal Education: The Study of Modern History in the Universities of Oxford, Cambridge and Manchester, 1800–1914* (Manchester, 1986).

Soffer, Reba N., *Ethics and Society in England: The Revolution in the Social Sciences, 1870–1914* (Berkeley, Calif., 1978), "Why Do Disciplines Fail? The Strange Case of British Sociology," *English Historical Review* 97 (Oct. 1982), *The Cloister and the Hearth: The Emergence of History as a University Profession in England,* Occasional Paper No. 31 (May 1982), Center for Studies in Higher Education, University of California, Berkeley, Calif., "Nation, Duty, Character, and Confidence: History at Oxford, 1850–1914," *Historical Journal* 30 (Mar. 1987), "The Modern University and National Values, 1850–1930," *Historical Research* 60 (June 1987), "The Development of Disciplines in the Modern English University," *Historical Journal* 31 (1988), "The Honours School of Modern History," in Michael Brock and Mark Curthoys, eds., *History of Oxford University,* vol. 7 (Oxford, forthcoming), "History and Religion: J. R. Seeley and the Burden of the Past," in R. W. Davis and R. Helmstader, eds., *Religion and Irreligion in Victorian Society* (London, 1992), and "Authority in the University: Balliol, Newnham, and the New Mythology," in Roy Porter, ed., *Myths of the English* (Oxford, 1992).

Steig, Margaret, *The Origin and Development of Scholarly Historical Periodicals* (Tuscaloosa, Al., 1986).

Turner, Frank, *The Greek Heritage in Victorian Britain* (New Haven, 1978).

Williams, N. J., "Stubbs's Appointment as Regius Professor, 1866," *Bulletin of the Institute of Historical Research* 33, 87 (May 1960).

STUDIES OF HISTORY, EDUCATION, AND UNIVERSITIES OUTSIDE BRITAIN

Germany

Doerne, Martin, "Problems of the German University," in Walter M. Kotsching and Elined Prys, eds., *The University in a Changing World: A Symposium* (1932) (New York, 1969).

Haines, George, *Essays on German Influence upon English Education and Science, 1850–1919* (Hamden, Conn., 1969).

Herkless, John L., "Economic Change and the Idealist Revival in Historiography at the Turn of the Century," *History and Theory* 26, 2 (1987).

Jarausch, K. H., *Students, Society, and Politics in Imperial Germany: The Rise of Academic Illiberalism* (Princeton, N.J., 1982).

McClelland, Charles F., *The German Historians and England* (Cambridge, 1971), and *State, Society, and University in Germany, 1700–1914* (Cambridge, 1980).

Ringer, Fritz, *The Decline of the German Mandarins: The German Academic Community, 1890–1933* (Cambridge, Mass., 1969).

The United States

Adams, Herbert B., *Methods of Historical Study* (Baltimore, 1884), "Special Methods of Historical Study," in G. Stanley Hall, ed., *Methods of Teaching History,* vol. 1, 2nd ed. (Boston, 1885), and *The Study of History in American Colleges and Universities* (Washington, D. C., 1887).

Adams, James Truslow, *The Founding of New England* (Boston, 1921), and *The Epic of America* (1931) (Garden City, 1947).

"The American Historical Review," *The Nation* 60, 1554 (Apr. 11, 1895).

Haskell, Thomas L., *The Emergence of Professional Social Science: The American Social Science Association and the Nineteenth-Century Crisis of Authority* (Urbana, Ill., 1977).

Higham, John, Leonard Krieger, and Felix Gilbert, *History: The Development of Historical Studies in the United States* (Englewood Cliffs, N.J., 1965).

Holt, W. Stull, ed., *Historical Scholarship in the United States, 1876–1901, As Revealed in the Correspondence of Herbert B. Adams* (Baltimore, 1938).

Jameson, J. Franklin, "The American Historical Association, 1884–1909," *The American Historical Review* 15, 1 (Oct. 1909).

Levine, David O., *The American College and the Culture of Aspiration, 1915–40* (Ithaca, N.Y., 1986).

Link, Arthur S., "The American Historical Association, 1884–1984: Retrospect and Prospect," Presidential Address to the American Historical Association, *American Historical Review* (1985).

McLaughlin, A. C., et al., *The Study of History in Schools: Report to the American Historical Association, by the Committee of Seven* (New York, 1899).

Novick, Peter, *That Noble Dream: The "Objectivity Question" and the American Historical Profession* (Cambridge, 1988).

Robinson, James Harvey, *The New History: Essays Illustrating the Modern Historical Outlook* (New York, 1912).

France

Clark, Terry N., *Prophets and Patrons: The French University and the Emergence of the Social Sciences* (Cambridge, Mass., 1973).

Keylor, William R., *Academy and Community: The Foundation of the French Historical Profession* (Cambridge, Mass., 1975).

Weisz, George, *The Emergence of Modern Universities in France, 1863–1914* (Princeton, N.J., 1983).

Europe

Muller, D. K., Fritz Ringer, and Brian Simon, *The Rise of the Modern Educational System* (Cambridge, 1987).

Ringer, Fritz, *Education and Society in Modern Europe* (Bloomington, Ind., 1979).

ECONOMIC HISTORY

Barker, T. C., "The Beginnings of the Economic History Society," *Economic History Review* 2nd ser., 30 (1977).

Coleman, D. C., *History and the Economic Past: An Account of the Rise and Decline of Economic History in Britain* (London, 1987).

Cunningham, William, *The Growth of English Industry and Commerce*, 2nd ed., 2 vols. (Cambridge, 1890–92), and "The Perversion of Economic History," *Economic Journal* 2 (1892).

"Economic Curricula at Oxford and Cambridge," *Economic Journal* 31 (1921).

Hancock, W. K., *Economic History at Oxford: An Inaugural Lecture, February 1946* (Oxford, 1946).

Harte, Negley, "The Making of Economic History," Introduction in Negley Harte, ed., *The Study of Economic History: Collected Inaugural Lectures, 1893–1970* (London, 1971).

Hutchison, T. W., *On Revolutions and Progress in Economic Knowledge* (Cambridge, 1978).

Kadish, Alon, *The Oxford Economists of the Late Nineteenth Century* (Oxford, 1982), and *Historians, Economists, and Economic History* (London, 1989).

Koot, G. M., "English Historical Economics and the Emergence of Economic History in England," *History of Political Economy* 12 (Summer 1980), and *English Historical Economics, 1870–1926: The Rise of Economic History and Neo-Mercantilism* (Cambridge, 1987).

Rogers, J. E. Thorold, *The Economic Interpretation of History: Lectures Delivered in Worcester College Hall, Oxford, 1887–88* (London, 1909).

HISTORY OF THE PROFESSIONS

Abbott, A., "Status and Strain in the Professions," *American Journal of Sociology* 86 (1981).

Berlant, Jeffrey C., *Profession and Monopoly: A Study of Medicine in the United States and Great Britain* (Berkeley, Calif., 1975).

Carr-Saunders, A. M., and P. A. Wilson, *The Professions* (London, 1964).

Elliott, P., *The Sociology of the Professions* (New York, 1972).

Friedson, Eliot, *The Profession of Medicine: A Study of the Sociology of Applied Knowledge* (New York, 1970).

Halsey, A. H., and M. Trow, *The British Academics* (Cambridge, Mass., 1971).

Millerson, G., *The Qualifying Professions* (London, 1964).

Parry, Jose, and Noel Parry, *The Rise of the Medical Profession: A Study of Collective Social Mobility* (London, 1976).

Perkin, Harold, *Key Profession: The History of the Association of University Teachers* (New York, 1969), "The Pattern of Social Transformation in England," in K. H. Jarausch, ed., *The Transformation of Higher Learning, 1860–1930: Expansion, Diversification, Social Opening, and Professionalization in England, Germany, Russia, and the United States* (Chicago, 1983), "The Historical Perspective," in Burton Clark, ed., *Perspectives on Higher Education* (Berkeley, Calif., 1984), and *The Rise of Professional Society: England Since 1880* (London, 1989).

Peterson, Jeanne M., *The Medical Profession in Mid-Victorian London* (Berkeley, Calif., 1978).

Sharlin, Allan, "On the Universality of Occupational Prestige," *Journal of Interdisciplinary History* 11 (Summer 1980).

Silver, Harold, *Education as History: Interpreting Nineteenth and Twentieth Century Education* (London, 1983).

Thompson, Henry Byerly, *The Choice of a Profession: A Concise Account and Comparative Review of the English Professions* (London, 1857).

Index

In this index "f" after a number indicates a separate reference on the next page, and "ff" indicates separate references on the next two pages. A continuous discussion over two or more pages is indicated by a span of numbers. *Passim* is used for a cluster of references in close but not consecutive sequence.

Ackland, F. D., 184, 267n19
Acton, Lord, 116, 120, 126, 152, 165ff, 175, 244n70; as Regius Professor of Modern History, Cambridge, 7, 73, 79, 99, 115, 146, 149; concept of history, 58, 75, 117f, 155, 197, 221n8
Adams, Herbert Baxter, 42
Adams, James Truslow, 43
Adams, W. S., 144f
Adkins, Ryland, 169
Alford, Edward J. G., 270n30
Allen J. W., 145
Amateurism in public service, 10–11, 217n2
American Historical Association, 42f, 222nn23, 24
American Historical Review, 42f
Ancient history, 120, 129
Anglican Church, *see* Church of England
Annan, Noel, 2
Apostles (Cambridge), 146, 168, 262n54
Appleby, J. H., 195

Armstrong, Edward, 105, 143
Arnold, Thomas (Regius Professor of Modern History, Oxford), 83
Ashbee, C. R., 171, 191
Ashley, W. J., 57–61 *passim*, 87, 90, 170, 229n31
Asquith Commission: 1918, 28; 1922, 177
Authority of professions, 12, 25–26
Autonomy, 12f, 20, 40
Aydelotte, Frank, 108f, 242n41

Bailey, Richard F., 194
Baker, Philip John, 194
Baldwin, Stanley, 174
Balfour, R. E., 195, 271n31
Balliol College (Oxford), 23, 67, 75, 138, 140, 169; history graduates' careers, 8, 68, 163, 181–92, 196–98, 201f; ethos of, 34, 139, 141–42, 146, 193, 205; Regius Professors, 87, 104, 112, 199–203; Brackenbury scholarships, 87, 181
Barker, Ernest, 46, 67, 139
Barr, Stringfellow, 198, 273n41

Barrow, George Corbyn, 271n33
Beard, Charles, 43
Beazley, C. R., 57
Beck, F. G. M., 144
Becker, Carl, 43
Bell, Julian, 195
Benians, E. A., 63, 133
Bentley, R. I. L., 273n43
Birchall, Edward, 271n34, 273n43
Black, George Norman, 195, 270n31
B. Litt. degree (Oxford), 109
Board of Historical Studies (Cambridge), 53, 130–32, 135, 144, 148, 248–49n10
Boase, Charles, 128, 134, 142
Booth, General, 171
Bourdillon, F. B., 269n25
Bowley, A. L., 229n34
Brassey, Thomas (Earl Brassey), 200
Brearley, Samuel, 169
Briggs, Asa, 127
Bright, J. Franck, 138, 164
Brogan, D. W., 184
Brooke, Z. N., 49, 76, 79, 133, 144, 233–34n84
Brown, B. G., 139
Browne, G. S., 269n27
Browning, Oscar, 37, 116, 130, 139, 147, 165, 173f, 197, 257n88; influence on students, 149, 151–52, 166–67, 171
Bruce, Michael Macaulay, 274n44
Bryce, James, 6, 32, 48f, 55, 85, 101, 115–16, 131, 176
Buckle, H. T., 92
Bullock, J. B. G., 271n35
Burnet, Gilbert, 106
Burnham, Viscount, 192, 233n78
Burrow, John, 233n78
Burrows, Montagu, 84, 137
Butler, Geoffrey, 133, 144
Butler, J. R. M., 176
Butterfield, Herbert, 126
Bury, J. B., 79, 124–25, 126, 145, 149, 151, 165, 173, 220–21n8; Regius Professor of Modern History, Cambridge, 7, 58, 70, 99

Cambridge Historical Society, 122

Campbell-Johnston, D. G., 197
Carlyle, A. J., 144f, 170
Cazalet, Ralph Mirrielees, 273n44
Chadwick, Owen, 117, 142, 244n70
Chamberlain, Austen 171, 173f
Chandavarkar, Vithal Narayan, 194
Character, development of, 14, 28, 34, 69, 71, 151, 172, 174; by historical study, 7, 9, 54, 175; by liberal arts education, 14, 67; university role in, 24f, 29
Chichele Professor of Modern History (Oxford), 7, 65, 84, 110, 114
Chitty, Roger, 271n34
Cholerton, Alfred Thornton, 198
Christie, W. H. J., 195, 270n31
Church of England (Anglican Church), 45, 82, 87, 194–95, 201
Chute, J. C., 269n25
Citizenship, 165, 210, 232n71, 253n79; historical study as preparation for, 33, 37, 56, 76, 89, 125
Civil Service Commissioners, 16
Clapham, J. H., 34, 79, 139, 163–67 *passim*, 171f, 202–3; politics, 37, 151; and economic history, 61–62, 96, 152–56
Clark, George Kitson, 139, 176
Classics, 18, 54, 67–71 *passim*
Cleveland Commission, 19, 91f
Coleman, D. C., 58, 230n43
Colleges (Cambridge and Oxford): relation to university, 8, 28, 53
Collier, G., 272n39
Collingwood, R. A., 32, 115
Collini, Stefan, 14
Colonialism, 95f
Colonial Office, 217n2
Conduct, personal, 7, 14, 25, 27, 51, 54, 152, 172, 174
Constantine, Stephen, 216n2
Constitution, British, 34, 69, 71, 75f, 106, 127, 163; constitutional history, 62f, 87, 97, 128, 141, 162
Coope, F. D., 270n39
Cooper, A. A., 133
Cooper, Sidney, 170
Cornford, F. M., 16
Corry, Robert Lindsay, 273n43
Coulton, G. G., 28, 75ff, 176

Cramming, 161
Craven, Hiram, 195
Crawley, Charles, 129, 176, 257n98
Creighton, Mandell, 81, 130f, 136, 148, 152, 178
Cunliffe-Lister, Sir Philip, 203
Cunningham, William, 61, 146, 152, 234n87
Curriculum, history, 50f, 57–58, 76, 109, 161, 227n19
Curzon, Geoffrey, 176, 205

Davies, J. B. R., 271n33
Davis, H. W. C., 7, 46, 57, 67, 99, 112f, 141
Dicey, A. V., 101, 176
Disciplines, academic, 12, 21, 26, 57, 178, 206
Dissenters, 19, 30, 45
Dixie Professor of Ecclesiastical History, 63, 72, 81, 131
Doctoral degrees, 110, 235n2
Dons, 23
D. Phil. degree (Oxford), 110
Dunford, Richard S., 270n30
Duty, 24, 84, 172
Dyson, William Hubert, 195

Ecclesiastical history, *see* Dixie Professor of Ecclesiastical history
Economic history, 34, 58–60, 96, 153, 162, 167, 228n22, 233n73, 234n87; development at Oxford, 61; development at Cambridge, 61–62; at London School of Economics, 229nn31, 34; at University of Belfast, 229n31; at University of Edinburgh, 229n31
Economics, 58; Tripos (Cambridge), 20, 74
Edwards, Don Augustine, 145
Eggleston, Edward, 43
Eliot, Samuel, 45
Elites and elitism, 5, 10, 18, 64, 139, 177, 189, 205f
Elliot, C. A., 144
Ellis, T. E., 169
Elton, Oliver, 104
Elverston, W. T., 271n33
English Historical Review, 57, 110

European history, 122
Evolutionary science, impact on historians, 82
Examinations, 73, 135–38 *passim*, 159, 161, 206, 227n19, 232n73, 234n85; role of in university and society, 8, 10; civil service, 15f, 129; Honours School of History (Oxford), 159; Historical Tripos (Cambridge), 165–66, 225n2; school, 221n12; University of Manchester, 223n34

Faculties, 28, 53
Fair, John, 75
Fay, C. R., 122, 144, 172
Fellows (in Cambridge and Oxford colleges), 12, 19, 23
Field, G. C., 185
Figgis, J. N., 119
Finch-Hatton, M. E. G., 163
Firth, C. H., 41, 87, 100, 112, 134f, 145, 170, 240n73; as Regius Professor of Modern History, Oxford, 7, 32, 99, 104–10
Fisher, H. A. L., 27, 49, 103f, 111, 138, 158, 197
Fletcher, C. R. L., 46, 105, 111
Foreign Office, 47, 50
Forster, E. M., 194
France: history studies in universities, 8
Fredericq, Paul, 172, 258n9
Freeman, E. A., 84ff, 121, 135, 166–67, 169; as Regius Professor of Modern History, Oxford, 7, 99, 100–102
Froude, J. A., 30, 84ff, 88, 98f, 240n73; as Regius Professor of Modern History, Oxford, 7, 102–3

Gaitskell, Hugh, 184
Galbraith, V. H., 67, 139
Gardiner, S. R., 104f
Gascoin, C. J. B., 135
Geike, R., 152, 172
Gentleman, 18, 70, 123
German historians, 40–41, 75–76, 97, 120, 125, 148, 222n25
Germany: study of history in universities, 8

George, Henry, 173
George, Hereford, 64
George, Lloyd, 27, 49f
Gibbon, Edward, 39
Gladstone, Helen, 150
Gladstone, Herbert, 142
Gladstone, W. E., 38–39, 70
Glasson, Lancelot, 194
Glover, R. G., 70
Glover, T. R., 28
Gonner, E. C. K., 229n34
Gooch, G. P., 139, 146, 172, 176
Goodbody, M. V. W., 273n43
Gordon, J. G., 175
Gore, Charles, 207
Goschen, C. G., 199
Graduates in history, 179–89, 185–92, 199–203, 264n2, 268–74nn24–44
Graham, Malcolm Auld, 271n37
Great War (World War I), and role of English historians, 46–50
Green, J. R., 23, 111
Green, T. H., 205
Greenham, W. D. W., 271n32
Grigg, John, 39, 222n22
Gupta, Ranjit, 271n35
Gwatkin, H. M., 63, 72f, 163

Haldane, R. B., 32
Hammond, B. E., 146
Hammond, Barbara, 74, 154
Hammond, J. L., 74, 145, 154
Hancock, W. K., 184
Haslett, A. W., 195, 270n31
Hassall, A. H., 46, 142, 152
Hawke, Baden Wilmer (Baron Hawke), 200
Headlam, J. W., 172
Henson, H. H., 48f, 169
Higher education: English compared with American, 207–8
Historians: American, 38–43 passim, 98; English compared with American, 42–43; English and Great War, 46–50; political preferences of, 111, 121, 140; Cambridge and Oxford compared, 156, 158
Historical Association, 57, 122

Historical Honours Tripos (Cambridge) 54, 58, 63, 76, 130f, 147f, 171; other subjects in, 7, 34, 56, 149, 191; student numbers, 51, 162, 177; Maitland's influence, 66; examinations, 74, 138, 165–66, 194, 223n34, 227n19; international orientation, 75; Seeley's influence, 90
History, as a discipline, 2, 31–32, 37, 58, 102, 154, 165, 173; definition, 7, 38f, 80f, 93, 117ff, 165; as science, 31–32, 73, 121, 125, 154, 165, 173; authorities, 60–61, 71ff, 160; legalistic methods, 63; as literature, 127; Cambridge and Oxford compared, 132; philosophy of, 165, 173
History, study of: for character development, 6f; as leadership training, 8; as preparation for public service, 15; postgraduate, 109f
History Board: Cambridge, 51, 73, 129, 249n12; Oxford, 107
History Tutors' Association (Oxford), 142
Hodgkin, R. H., 107, 164, 171
Honours degree, 22; history, 6–7, 129–30
Honours School of History, Oxford, 50, 54, 57, 59, 63–68 passim, 75, 80f, 107–14 passim, 159
Hunt, V. J. U., 271n33
Hutchinson, Roger, 273n43
Hutchinson, T. W., 58
Hutton, William Holden, 170

Imperialism, 94–97 passim
Indian Civil Service (ICS), 29, 68, 132, 202
Indian history, 132–35 passim
Intellectual history, 173
International Relations, special subject, Oxford, 50

Jackson, Henry, 147
Jacob, E. F., 145
James, M. R., 153
Jenkins, Roy, 39, 222n22
Joel, D. J. B., 272n37, 274n44
Johnson, Arthur H., 114, 138, 142f, 163

Johnston, S. H. H., 271n32
Jones, L. G. E., 269n27
Jones, R. L., 229n31
Jowett, Benjamin, 27, 67, 139
Junior Historians (Cambridge), 143f

Kadish, Alon, 59
Kennedy, Alfred Ravenscroft, 270n30
Keynes, J. M., 172
King's College (Cambridge), 56, 121, 130,
    138–39, 146, 151, 153, 166, 193f; Fellows,
    146, 148; dominance in history stud-
    ies, 147, 183–84; Discussion Society,
    174; graduates' degree courses, 181–82;
    history graduates; careers, 185–92,
    199–203; history students' study
    abroad, 196–98
Kingsley, Charles, 88, 91
Knowles, David, 172f
Knowles, Lilian (née Tomm), 229nn31,
    34

Laing, Robert, 130
Landreth, S., 269n27
Lang, Cosmo Gordon, 169, 192f
Lapsley, G. T., 175
Laski, H. J., 145, 176
Latham, Henry, 14, 187
Lavin, G. E., 269n27
Laurence, R. Vere, 119, 129, 176
Law, study of, 54, 64–67
Lawrence, F. W., 229n34
Lawson, H. L. W., *see* Burnham,
    Viscount
Leaders and leadership: university as
    preparation for, 1, 17, 20, 205; histori-
    cal studies as preparation for, 8, 76,
    91, 121, 141, 144, 157, 207; national and
    imperial, 11, 72; classics as preparation
    for, 57; of professions, 170
League of Nations, 49, 51
Learoyd, P. H. B., 273n43
Leathes, Sir Stanley, 16
Leathes Committee on Civil Service, 16
Leigh, Austen, 147
Le Mesurier, Roderick, 195, 270n31
Leppert, Robert Stewart, 197
Levine, David, 42

Lewis, Henry Chandler, 271n33
Liberal arts disciplines, 3, 14, 22, 29, 37,
    56f, 208–9
Liberal education, 3, 5f, 18f, 24, 30, 79f,
    107
Lillingston, Charles Arthur, 271n34
Link, Arthur S., 42
Litterae Humaniores (classics) at Ox-
    ford, 71
Little, A. G., 57
Loch, C. S., 189, 267n20
Lodge, Richard, 87, 141
Lowes Dickinson, Goldsworthy, 147, 171,
    173ff
Laurd, Henry Richard, 54ff

Macarthur, Ellen A., 229n34
Macaulay, Thomas Babington, 39, 106,
    125f
McCulloch, Gary, 57
MacDonald, Ramsay, 207
McFarlane, J., 269n29
Mackenzie, A. M. S., 271n33
MacLehose, H. A., 200
Macpherson, W. D., 176
M'Taggart, J. M. E., 146, 171
Madeley, Helen M., 140, 253n49
Maitland, F. W., 63–66 *passim*, 89,
    100, 119, 131, 146, 150, 175; definition
    of history, 70–75 *passim*, 115,
    231n49
Manchester School of Administrative
    History, 57
Marriott, J. A. R., 14, 37, 47, 108, 169
Marshall, Alfred, 61, 74, 76, 133, 148,
    166–67, 234n87
Marshall, T. H., 176
Marten, C. H. K., 57, 176, 232n71
Mason, Paul, 195, 270n31
Masterman, J. C., 135
Masterman, J. H. B., 172
Maurice, F. D., 142
Medieval History, 76
Medley, D. J., 61, 228n29, 229n30
Meiggs, Russell, 122
Meredith, H. O., 153, 229n31, 270n29
Meritocracy, 5, 206
Michaelides, C. C., 270n29

Modern history, *see* Chichele Professor of Modern History; Regius Professors of Modern History
Modern History Association, 143
Modern History Board (Oxford), 143
Morality, 142, 152, 156, 165; history studies as training for, 8, 34, 88, 232n71; national, 11, 47–48, 65, 95, 118f, 172, 205; classics as training for, 70; progress of, 77, 87, 102; lessons of history, 38, 97f, 140, 167, 170, 175, 210
Moral philosophy, 55
Moral Sciences Tripos (Cambridge), 55, 71
More, Jasper, 192, 268n22
Morgan, Frank, 46
Morgan, J. H., 272n40
Moriarty, Gerald Patrick, 135
Morland, S. C., 195, 270n31
Morley, John, 39, 222n22
Mortlock, W. F. W., 176
Moulton, William Ralph Osborne, 194
Mozley, John Henry, 270n30
Muir, Ramsay, 57, 138
Müller, Max, 96
Myres, J. N. L., 130

Namier, L. B., 74–75, 176
Nationalism, 43, 140
National values, 56
Newman, John Henry, 18
Newton, A. P., 96, 145
Non-Collegiate students (Oxford), 130
Non-Placet Society (Oxford), 110
Northcote, Sir Stafford H., 217n12
Northcote-Trevelyan Report, 15, 217n12
Novick, Peter, 38, 43

Obligations, moral/social, 54, 57, 89, 179, 181; university training for, 22, 25, 151; history as lessons on, 83, 140, 207; examination questions, 165
Oman, Charles, 7, 60, 64, 104, 110–12, 117, 170, 219n28
Ord, Clement, 197
O'Regan, John, 57
Owen, Sidney, 104, 134
Oxford Economic Society, 59
Oxford Union, 2, 168

Oxford University: role in national life, 1; history honours degree, 6–7

Paget, Philip, 271n36
Parliamentary Commissioners, on higher education, 1
Parr, Frederick, 192
Parry, G. N., 172
Patriotism, 33–34, 156, 170–71, 210
Peel, Robert, 70
Phillips, W. Allison, 49
Philosophy, politics, and economics (PPE, "Modern Greats"), Oxford, 74, 183–84
Pigou, A. C., 194
Political science, 73, 92, 145, 149, 254n63
Politics Society (King's College, Cambridge), 152, 171–74, 261n45
Pollard, A. F., 35, 47, 57, 65, 79, 145
Pollock, Sir Frederick, 66, 146
Poole, R. L., 87, 110, 240n73
Porter, Roy, 13
Potter, Cyril John, 271n36
Postgraduate training in history, 109f
Powell, Douglas, 273n43
Powell, F. Y. (Regius Professor of Modern History, Oxford), 7, 99, 103–4, 158, 170
Powell, Percival, 270n30
Power, Eileen, 145, 229n34
Powicke, F. M. (Regius Professor of Modern History, Oxford), 7, 57, 72, 99, 113, 115, 177, 231n49
Previté-Orton, C. W., 76, 79, 145
Price, L. L., 61, 229n31
Prizes for history, 176–77, 263n60, 264n61
Professionalism, 5f, 11, 75; in training of historians, 78, 109, 127, 209
Professions, 8, 136
Professors of history (Cambridge and Oxford), 19, 54, 80; conflict with tutors, 15, 79–80, 83, 99, 195, 107ff, 111, 235n3
Progress, 34, 77, 84, 91, 118–23 *passim*, 165
Prothero, G. W., 37, 56, 58, 96, 130, 139, 147, 219n28; competence in German history, 47f, 50, 197; on professional historical studies, 75, 79

Public good, 13, 51, 83, 209; graduates'
    role in promoting, 19, 157, 179, 184,
    189, 202–3
Public service, 14, 57, 68, 146, 202–3, 207
Pusey, Edward, 14

Rae, K. H., 272n40
Rait, R. S., 57
Raleigh, Walter, 109, 171–74 *passim*
Rashdall, Hastings, 29
Rathbone, P. A. P., 273n43
Reckitt, Basil Norman, 271n32
Reddaway, T. F., 200
Reddaway, W. F., 172
Redmayne, Paul Brewis, 273n43
Rees, Goronwy, 51, 217n5
Reeve, A. D., 271n34
Reeves, Marjorie, 164
Reform: of universities, 18, 161; social, 205
Regius Professors of Modern History
    (Cambridge and Oxford): listed, 7, 33;
    origin, 7, 236n8
Reichel, H. R., 193, 268n24
Religion, in history, and historians, 25,
    82, 87f, 94, 173, 238n43
Reynolds, J. W., 144
Ringer, Fritz, 222n25
Roach, John, 2
Robertson, C. Grant, 47, 224n39
Robinson, James Harvey, 43
Rolleston, I. H. D., 274n44
Roper, Robert Denis, 271n35
Roscoe, Arthur, 270n30
Rose, J. Holland, 47, 49, 171
Rothblatt, Sheldon, 2, 216n10
Round, J. H., 35, 65f, 87, 112, 221n13
Rowntree, Malcolm, 194
Royal Commission on Cambridge
    (1852), 19
Royal Commission on Oxford and
    Cambridge (1922), 161
Runciman, J. S., 176
Rusk, D. C., 272n39
Russell, H. J. H., 197

Salter, F. R., 144
Sanger, C. P., 229n34
Schlesinger, Arthur, 43
Schmoller, Gustav, 60

Seaton, A. A., 144
Seeley, J. R., 68, 118, 120, 145f, 151, 165,
    174, 197; as Regius Professor of Mod-
    ern History, Cambridge, 7, 90–97;
    history's political lessons for today, 56,
    73, 149, 221n8; admiration for German
    historians, 75, 148f; on professional
    training of historians, 79; religious
    views, 80ff; Travelyan's views on,
    124–25, 126; history's moral lessons,
    128, 170
Seton-Watson, R. W., 49, 145, 224n45
Shadwell, Charles, 130
Shannon, Richard, 92
Shaw, F. C., 176
Sidgwick, Henry, 55, 90, 115, 131, 133, 148,
    150, 154
Simpson, F. A., 175
Skidelsky, Robert, 256n81
Slee, Peter, 215n8
Smart, Frederick William, 197
Smellie, K. B., 172
Smith, A. L., 60, 90, 114, 138ff, 143, 159,
    161, 163f, 193; definition of history, 34,
    76, 141; politics, 37, 64, 111, 203; stu-
    dents of, 105, 149, 253n46; favoring
    comparative method, 128
Smith, G. B., 270n29
Smith, Goldwin, 36, 84, 86, 236n11
Smith, H. Llewellyn, 229n34
Social history, 106, 113, 126
Social sciences, 208f
Sociology, 21
Sonnenschein, Edward, 28
Sorley, W. R., 173
Southern, Richard, 114
Stein, Karl, 94
Stephen, Sir James, 91
Stephens, A. G. A., 269n27
Stephens, I. M., 195, 270n30
Strachan-Davidson, J. L., 140, 182
Struve, Gleb Petrovitch, 198, 273n41
Stubbs, William, 35, 68, 81–85 *passim*,
    102, 121, 143, 164, 192; Regius Profes-
    sor, Oxford, 7, 86–90; on constitu-
    tional history, 58, 60, 69, 96f
Stubbs Society, 169–71
Students of history, 162, 163–64, 182, 193,
    196–98. *See also* Graduates in history

Student societies, 8, 122, 146, 167–76, 254n64, 261n36
Sutherland, Gillian, 274n3
Swift, John Francis, 271n32

Tait, James, 35, 57, 101, 170
Tanner, J. R., 62, 96, 116, 171
Tatham, G. R., 144
Tawney, R. H., 74, 207
Taylor, A. J. P., 50, 74
Temperley, H. W. V., 49, 51, 75, 96, 144, 165, 172, 233n82
Temple, William, 207
Thorneley, Thomas, 116, 129, 182
Thorold Rogers, J. E., 59, 84
Tillyard, H. J. W., 176
Todhunter, J. L. B., 176
Toulmin, Geoffrey E., 269n28
Tout, T. F., 35, 66, 80, 87, 101, 104, 177; Manchester school of administrative history, 29, 159, 219n34; on limitations of examinations, 57; criticism of legalistic approach, 65; on duty, 69
Townshend, B. H. U. L., 271n32
Toynbee, Arnold, 17, 50, 59f, 154, 205
Trevelyan, C. E., 217n12
Trevelyan, C. P., 139, 171
Trevelyan, G. P., 41, 49, 92, 133, 146, 175f, 222n21, 247n113; Regius Professor of Modern History, Cambridge, 7, 99, 123–27; politics, 37; history as an art, 58, 121; definition of history, 120, 154f, 173; as undergraduate, 139, 171; and Working Men's College, 247n11
Trinity College (Cambridge), 23, 116, 124, 129, 133, 137, 146, 262n54
Trinity College Historical Society, 171, 175–76
Tudor-Hart, A. E., 271n35
Turner, Frederick Jackson, 43
Tutors (in Cambridge and Oxford colleges), 8, 23, 26–27; 72, 79; conflict with professors, 15, 83, 99, 105–11 *passim*, 235n3; relation to university, 134, 160; women, 254n64
Tutors' Association (Oxford), 143

United States: history studies in universities, 8
Universities: civic, 5, 29–30, 220n37; Scottish, 11; autonomy of, 12f, 20, 40; reform of, 15, 18, British, American, German compared, 23; American, 44
University teachers, 22, 31; Association of, 16
Unwin, George, 57, 229n31
Urquhart, F. F., 135, 197

Victorianism, 2f, 6, 14
Vinogradoff, Paul, 109f

Waidyakorn, M. C. W., 272n40
Wallas, Graham, 44, 145, 207
Ward, A. W., 54–56, 75, 137, 148, 226n10, 233n81
Ward, Frank Joseph, 273n43
Wardrop, O., 272n39
Watson, E. W., 163f
Webb, Sidney, 171, 229n34
Webster, C. K., 144, 172
Webster, Patrick Kennedy, 271n34, 273n44
Wedd, Nathaniel, 147, 171
Westcott, Brooke Foss, 147
Whewell, William, 15, 35
Whig interpretation of history, 46, 74, 126, 175, 233n78; Pollock's criticism, 62; Maitland's rejection, 66, 73; Stubbs's acceptance, 87; Firth's approval of Macaulay, 106
White, J. E. H., 271n37
Whitney, J. P., 56
Wickham Legg, L. G., 46
Wiener, Martin, 199
Williams, Basil, 49
Winstanley, D. A., 176
Women students, 37, 150, 252n43
Women tutors, 254n64
Working-class students, 207
World War I, *see* Great War

Younger, J. P., 163

Zimmern, A. E., 49, 67

Library of Congress Cataloging-in-Publication Data

Soffer, Reba N.
    Discipline and power : the university, history, and the making of
an English elite, 1870–1930 / Reba N. Soffer.
        p.   cm.
Includes bibliographical references and index.
ISBN 0-8047-2383-4 (alk. paper) :
    1. Great Britain—Intellectual life—20th century.   2. History—
Study and teaching (Higher)—Great Britain—History.   3. Great
Britain—Politics and government—1901–1936.   4. Great Britain—
Politics and government—1837–1901.   5. Universities and colleges—
Great Britain—History.   6. Elite (Social sciences)—Great Britain—
History.   7. Great Britain—Intellectual life—19th century.
8. Education, Higher—Great Britain—History.   9. Historiography—
Great Britain—History.   10. Power (Social sciences) I. Title.
DA566.4.S573   1994
378'.01'0941—dc20
94-9217   CIP

⊗ This book is printed on acid-free paper.